Communications in Computer and Information Science   826

Commenced Publication in 2007
Founding and Former Series Editors:
Alfredo Cuzzocrea, Xiaoyong Du, Orhun Kara, Ting Liu, Dominik Ślęzak,
and Xiaokang Yang

W0079125

More information about this series at http://www.springer.com/series/7899

Nick Bassiliades · Vadim Ermolayev
Hans-Georg Fill · Vitaliy Yakovyna
Heinrich C. Mayr · Mykola Nikitchenko
Grygoriy Zholtkevych · Aleksander Spivakovsky (Eds.)

Information and Communication Technologies in Education, Research, and Industrial Applications

13th International Conference, ICTERI 2017
Kyiv, Ukraine, May 15–18, 2017
Revised Selected Papers

 Springer

Editors
Nick Bassiliades ⓘ
Aristotle University of Thessaloniki
Thessaloniki
Greece

Vadim Ermolayev ⓘ
Zaporizhzhia National University
Zaporizhzhia
Ukraine

Hans-Georg Fill
University of Bamberg
Bamberg
Germany

Vitaliy Yakovyna ⓘ
Lviv Polytechnic National University
Lviv
Ukraine

Heinrich C. Mayr ⓘ
University of Klagenfurt
Klagenfurt
Austria

Mykola Nikitchenko ⓘ
Taras Shevchenko National University
  of Kyiv
Kyiv
Ukraine

Grygoriy Zholtkevych ⓘ
V. N. Karazin Kharkiv National University
Kharkiv
Ukraine

Aleksander Spivakovsky ⓘ
Kherson State University
Kherson
Ukraine

ISSN 1865-0929   ISSN 1865-0937   (electronic)
Communications in Computer and Information Science
ISBN 978-3-319-76167-1   ISBN 978-3-319-76168-8   (eBook)
https://doi.org/10.1007/978-3-319-76168-8

Library of Congress Control Number: 2017957679

Printed on acid-free paper

Check for updates

This Springer imprint is published by the registered company Springer International Publishing AG part of Springer Nature
The registered company address is: Gewerbestrasse 11, 6330 Cham, Switzerland

Preface

This volume contains a number of selected refined and extended contributions to ICTERI 2017, the 13th International Conference on Information and Communication Technologies (ICT) in Education, Research, and Industrial Applications. The conference was held in Kiev, Ukraine, during May 15–18, 2017, with a focus on research advances in ICT, business or academic applications of ICT, and design and deployment of ICT infrastructures.

ICTERI 2017 continued the tradition of hosting co-located events this year by offering three workshops and a PhD Symposium. The workshops addressed:

(1) New and emerging technologies in education, learning environments and methods that aimed at satisfying the life-long learning needs of a person and were based on the use of a person-oriented approach
(2) The problems of developing the theoretical aspects of reliability and safety, based on Markov models, applied to the assessment and creation of dependable and resilient embedded and distributed systems in modern industrial engineering settings
(3) The development and application of formal methods for: software specification, verification, and optimization; software analysis and testing; software re-engineering

The PhD Symposium provided the opportunity for PhD candidates and their mentors to present, listen to, and discuss their research. The symposium also included the PhD Mentors Panel, which gave young researchers the chance to be informed about and inspired by the offers of promising research topics by several internationally renowned experts.

The proceedings of ICTERI 2017 were published by CEUR-WS as two volumes: 1844 for the main ICTERI conference and workshops (http://ceur-ws.org/Vol-1844/) and 1851 for the PhD Symposium (http://ceur-ws.org/Vol-1851/). These two volumes contain 72 papers selected from a total of 151 submissions. Of these, the 25 best papers were nominated by the program and workshop chairs to be invited for submission, in substantially extended and revised versions, for the present proceedings volume. Out of these, 23 extended and refined submissions were received and reviewed by at least three experts. Finally, the Proceedings Review Panel selected the 11 most mature and interesting papers for publication, after further revision. The acceptance rate thus was 7.3% for the overall number of ICTERI 2017 submissions.

The papers in this volume are grouped into three topical parts.

Part I is focused on presenting models and theoretical frameworks related to the design and development of ICT. These contributions elaborate on novel important aspects that increase the expressive power of the corresponding models and theories. Oleksandr Mulyak et al. propose a refined model aimed at enhancing the software reliability of instrumentation and control systems at a nuclear power plant that used

K-phase Erlang distribution. Grygoriy Zholtkevych and Hassan El Zein investigate the problems caused by the non-linearity of logical time in distributed cyber-physical systems. They propose two approaches to modelling such systems with an account of logical time: operational and denotational. In the operational approach, they propose a set of constraints on the possible sets of schedules. In the denotational approach, they used the language of category theory to clarify the concepts used in the operational models. Finally, Mykola Nikitchenko et al. present an inference system for extended Floyd–Hoare logic over relational nominative data and propose an approach for its formalization in Mizar proof assistant. Further, the authors argue that their inference system may be used for formal software verification.

Part II collects the contributions that further elaborate on effective and efficient use of ICT in teaching, learning, and education management. Aleksandra Mreła and Oleksandr Sokolov present their approach on using fuzzification to refine the structure of the ranking of student assessments. In their case study, the authors use the results of final secondary school examination test in mathematics in Poland. Nataliia Morze et al. report on the theoretical and methodic aspects as well as their practical experience in implementing the master program in "E-learning management" for pedagogy students. They showcase how their master program formed professional competence in the use of innovative methods and developed soft skills. Finally, Juan Pablo Martínez Bastida et al. present a methodology and its software implementation, based on a probabilistic model, for generating pedagogical interventions in a self-regulated environment. Their model was encoded in a novel Bayesian network topology that increased fidelity assessment by independently diagnosing the relevant knowledge components and allowing a straightforward interpretation of the knowledge involved in a student task.

Part III deals with the experimental evaluation of ICT and also their application and use. Kosa et al. investigate which software tool for automated term extraction from texts best fits for discovering terminologically saturated sub-collections of professional documents describing a domain. Yuriy Kondratenko et al. argue that using the Internet of Things infrastructure for developing and deploying embedded monitoring and automated control systems in complex industrial settings brought significant benefits. They prove, by referring to their prototype implementations, that using this approach led to a significant increase in energy and economic efficiency of complex technical objects like gas turbine engines. Olena Liashenko et al. reviewed the fitness of several software packages for financial time series modeling and analysis, in particular volatility as an aspect pointing to the potential risks of different financial instruments. This review was conducted based on the use of Polish stock index WIG time series data and GARCH family of econometric models. Jan Rabcan and Miroslav Kvassay report on their refinement of electroencephalogram data transformation pipelines by the introduction of a fuzzification step. They compare the influence of the two types of fuzzification and two types of fuzzy decision trees on the accuracy of the classification of persons suffering from epilepsy, based on electroencephalogram signal data. Finally, Vitaliy Kobets and Alexander Weissblut present their market simulation approach, which used an agent-based model of a microeconomic system implemented in a software application. In their model, a simulated system may have equilibrium and disequilibrium states. The application allowed the authors to study market transitions from stability to dynamic chaos by varying the number of business entities, their types, and beliefs about the market as the environment.

This volume would not have been realized without the support of many people. First, we are very grateful to all the authors for their continuous commitment and intensive work. Second, we would like to thank the Program Committee members and additional reviewers for providing timely and thorough assessments. Furthermore, we would like to thank all the people who contributed to the organization of ICTERI 2017. Without their efforts, there would have been no material for this volume.

December 2017

Nick Bassiliades
Vadim Ermolayev
Hans-Georg Fill
Vitaliy Yakovyna
Heinrich C. Mayr
Mykola Nikitchenko
Grygoriy Zholtkevych
Aleksander Spivakovsky

Conference Organization

General Chair

Aleksander Spivakovsky   Verkhovna Rada of Ukraine, Kherson State University, Ukraine

Steering Committee

Vadim Ermolayev   Zaporizhzhia National University, Ukraine
Heinrich C. Mayr   Alpen-Adria-Universität Klagenfurt, Austria
Mykola Nikitchenko   Taras Shevchenko National University of Kyiv, Ukraine
Aleksander Spivakovsky   Verkhovna Rada of Ukraine, Kherson State University, Ukraine
Mikhail Zavileysky   DataArt, Russian Federation
Grygoriy Zholtkevych   V. N. Karazin Kharkiv National University, Ukraine

Program Chairs

Nick Bassiliades   Aristotle University of Thessaloniki, Greece
Vadim Ermolayev   Zaporizhzhia National University, Ukraine

Presentations Chair

Heinrich C. Mayr   Alpen-Adria-Universität Klagenfurt, Austria

Workshops Chair

Vyacheslav Kharchenko   National Aerospace University Kharkiv Aviation Institute, Ukraine

PhD Symposium Chairs

Frédéric Mallet   Université Cote d'Azur, CNRS, Inria, I3S, France
Grygoriy Zholtkevych   V. N. Karazin Kharkiv National University, Ukraine

Poster and Demo Chair

Yaroslav Prytula   Ukrainian Catholic University, Ukraine

IT Talks Chairs

Aleksander Spivakovsky   Verkhovna Rada of Ukraine, Kherson State University,
                             Ukraine
Mikhail Zavileysky   DataArt, Russian Federation

Local Organization Chair

Mykola Nikitchenko   Taras Shevchenko National University of Kyiv,
                             Ukraine

Publicity Chair

Nataliya Kushnir   Kherson State University, Ukraine

Web Chair

Yevhen Alferov   German Climate Computing Center, Germany

Program Committee

Yevhen Alforov   German Climate Computing Center, Germany
Costin Badica   University of Craiova, Romania
Nikolaos Bardis   Hellenic Army Academy, Greece
Nick Bassiliades   Aristotle University of Thessaloniki, Greece
Sotiris Batsakis   University of Huddersfield, UK
Lukas Chrpa   Czech Technical University in Prague, Czech Republic
Gabriel Ciobanu   Alexandru Ioan Cuza University of Iasi, Romania
Nikolaos Doukas   Hellenic Army Academy, Greece
Vadim Ermolayev   Zaporizhzhia National University, Ukraine
David Esteban   TECHFORCE, Spain
Wolfgang Faber   University of Huddersfield, UK
Hans-Georg Fill   University of Bamberg, Germany
Adrian Giurca   Brandenburgische Technische Universität Cottbus,
                             Germany
Brian Hainey   Glasgow Caledonian University, UK
Natalya Keberle   Zaporizhzhia National University, Ukraine
Vyacheslav Kharchenko   National Technical University Kharkiv Aviation
                             Institute, Ukraine
Vitaliy Kobets   Kherson State University, Ukraine
Christian Kop   Alpen-Adria-Universität Klagenfurt, Austria
Kalliopi Kravari   Aristotle University of Thessaloniki, Greece
Vladimir Kukharenko   National Technical University Kharkiv Polytechnic
                             Institute, Ukraine
Frederic Mallet   Université Nice Sophia-Antipolis, France
Wolf-Ekkehard Matzke   MINRES Technologies GmbH, Germany

Heinrich C. Mayr	Alpen-Adria-Universität Klagenfurt, Austria
Mykola Nikitchenko	Taras Shevchenko National University of Kyiv, Ukraine
Tope Omitola	University of Southampton, UK
Yaroslav Prytula	Ukrainian Catholic University, Ukraine
Wolfgang Reisig	Humboldt Universität zu Berlin, Germany
Dumitru Roman	SINTEF/University of Oslo, Norway
Wolfgang Schreiner	Johannes Kepler University Linz, Austria
Vladimir A. Shekhovtsov	Alpen-Adria-Universität Klagenfurt, Austria
Oleksandr Sokolov	Nicolaus Copernicus University, Poland
Martin Strecker	Université de Toulouse, France
Ilias Tachmazidis	University of Huddersfield, UK
Vagan Terziyan	University of Jyväskylä, Finland
Mykola Tkachuk	National Technical University Kharkiv Polytechnic Institute, Ukraine
Leo van Moergestel	Utrecht University of Applied Sciences, The Netherlands
Paul Warren	Knowledge Media Institute, Open University, UK
Vitaliy Yakovyna	Lviv Polytechnic National University, Ukraine
Grygoriy Zholtkevych	V. N. Karazin Kharkiv National University, Ukraine

ICTERI 2017 Sponsors

Oleksandr Spivakovsky's Educational Foundation	http://spivakovsky.fund/
DataArt	http://www.dataart.com/
Taras Shevchenko National University of Kiev	http://www.knu.ua/en
BWT Group	http://www.groupbwt.com/
Springer	http://www.springer.com/
Logicify	http://logicify.com/

Contents

Modeling and Theoretical Frameworks

Availability Model of Critical Nuclear Power Plant Instrumentation and Control System with Non-Exponential Software Update Distribution

Bogdan Volochiy[1]📵, Vitaliy Yakovyna[1]📵,
Oleksandr Mulyak[1(✉)]📵, and Vyacheslav Kharchenko[2]📵

[1] National University Lviv Polytechnic, Lviv, Ukraine
bvolochiy@ukr.net, vitaliy.s.yakovyna@lpnu.ua,
mulyak.oleksandr@gmail.com
[2] National Aerospace University "KhAI", Kharkiv, Ukraine
v.kharchenko@csn.khai.edu

Abstract. This paper is the continuation of the research devoted to enhancing the adequacy of reliability model of Nuclear Power Plant (NPP) Instrumentation and Control (I&C) System considering software reliability. The reliability model of NPP I&C system is a basement from which the availability, safety, risk, and other important characteristics of the system could be assessed. The availability function of a critical NPP I&C system depends on the hardware and software reliability and maintenance. The high availability value of the critical I&C systems could be ensured by following: structural redundancy; maintenance of the system; using the N-version programming; software updates. Thus, the NPP I&C system reliability model to ensure its high level of adequacy and applicability has to take into account software and a hardware failure, as well as the non-exponential distribution of software updates that are implemented by K-phase Erlang Distribution.

Keywords: Instrumentation and Control (I&C) system
Discrete-continuous stochastic system · Reliability behavior
Structural-automated model · Markovian chain · Software reliability
Erlang distribution

1 Introduction

1.1 Motivation

Nowadays the development of fault-tolerant computer-based systems (FTCSs) is a part of weaponry components, space, aviation, energy, and other critical systems. One of the main tasks is to provide requirements of reliability, availability and functional safety. Thus the two types of possible risks are related to the assessment of risk and to ensure their safety and security.

Reliability (dependability) related design (RRD) [1–6] is the main part of the development of complex fault-tolerant systems based on computers, software (SW) and

© Springer International Publishing AG, part of Springer Nature 2018
N. Bassiliades et al. (Eds.): ICTERI 2017, CCIS 826, pp. 3–20, 2018.
https://doi.org/10.1007/978-3-319-76168-8_1

hardware (HW) components. The goal of RRD is to develop the structure of FTCS tolerating HW physical failure and SW designs faults and assure required values of reliability, availability and other dependability attributes. Two or more versions of software (developed by different developers or/and different programming languages and technologies, etc.) are used to ensure fault-tolerance software [7]. Therefore the use of structural redundancy for FTCS with multiple versions of software is mandatory. After commissioning software some bugs (design faults) remain in its code [8], this leads to shut-down of the FTCS. After detection the bugs, a software update is carried out. These factors have an influence on the availability of the FTCS and should be taken into account in the availability indexes. The efficiency of fault-tolerant hardware of FTCS is provided by maintenance and repair.

Real distribution of software debugging time has a significant impact on the availability model of FTCS as discrete-continuous stochastic Markov systems. For that approach, there is an important problem of improving models by considering the real distribution of procedure durations and time intervals between events in the process. Presented improvement allows automating the usage of K-phase Erlang Distribution for the Markovian chain development of the statistical representation of the process of FTCS exploitation.

Insufficient level of adequacy of the availability models of FTCS leads either to additional costs (while underestimating of the measures) or to the risk of total failure (when inflating their values), namely accidents, material damage and even loss of life. Reliability and safety are assured by using (selection and development) fault-tolerant structures at RRD of the FTCS and identifying and implementing strategies for maintenance. Adoption of wrong decisions at this stage leads to similar risks.

1.2   Related Works Analysis

Research papers, which focus on RRD, consider models of the FTCS [8–13]. Most models are primarily developed to identify the impact of one the above-listed factors on reliability indexes. The rest of the factors are overlooked. Papers [4, 5] describe the reliability model of FTCS which illustrates separate HW and SW failures. Paper [6] offer reliability model of a fault-tolerant system, in which HW and SW failures are differentiated and after corrections, in the program code the software failure rate is accounted for. Paper [8] describes the reliability model of the FTCS, which accounts for the software updates. In paper [10] the author outlines the relevance of the estimation of the reliability indexes of FTCS considering the failure of SW and recommends a method for their determination. Such reliability models of the FTCS produce an analysis of its conditions under the failure of SW. This research suggests that $MTTF_{system} = MTTF_{software}$. Thus, it is possible to conclude that the author considers the HW of the FTCS as absolutely reliable. Such condition reduces the credibility of the result, especially when the reliability of the HW is commensurable to the reliability of the SW. Paper [11] presents the assessment of reliability parameters of FTCS through modeling behavior using Markovian chains, which account for multiple software updates. Nevertheless, there was no evidence of the quantitative assessments of the reliability measures of presented FTCS.

In paper [12], the authors propose a model of FTCS using Macro-Markovian chains, where the software failure rate, duration of software verification, failure rate and repair rate of HW are accounted for. The presented method of Macro-Markovian chains modeling [12, 13] is based on logical analysis and cannot be used for profound configurations of FTCS due to their complexity and high probability of the occurrence of mistakes. Also, there is a discussion around the definition of requirements for operational verification of software of the space system, together with the research model of the object for availability evaluation and scenarios preference. It is noted that over the last ten years out of 27% of space devices failures, which were fatal or such that restricted their use, 6% were associated with HW failure and 21% with SW failure.

Software updates are necessary due to the fact that at the point of SW commissioning they may contain a number of undetected faults, which can lead to critical failures of the FTCS. Presence of HW faults relates to the complexity of the system, and failure to conduct overall testing, as such testing is time-consuming and needs substation financial support. To predict the number of SW faults at the time of its commissioning various models can be used, one, for example, is Jelinski-Moranda [14].

The K-phase Erlang method is used for developing the analytical stochastic models of functional and reliability behaviors of the technical system. Usage of this method for reliability predictions of a technical system is presented in paper [14]. Usage of this method for functional behavior for queuing system is presented in researchers [15; 16, pp. 137–144; 14, pp. 136–143].

In monographs [15, pp. 10–11, pp. 36–37; 17, pp. 196] states that any real distributions of the random variable are possible to present by "mix" of Erlang distributions $p_i(t_v)$:

$$p(t_v) = \sum_{i=1}^{k} q_i p_i(t_v) \quad for \quad t_v \geq 0 \ ,$$

where q_i – weighting coefficients, defining the share each of the Erlang distribution $p_i(t_v)$ which was used for presenting the real distribution.

1.3 Objectives and Structure of the Paper

The goal of the paper is to suggest the structural-automated model for developing Markovian chain of critical NPP I&C system with different redundancy types (first of all, structure and version) and real distribution of software update time, using the developed formal procedure and tool. The main idea is to decrease risks of Markovian chain (MC) development errors for systems with very large (dozens and hundreds) number of states. We propose a special notation, which allows one to support chain development step by step and to design final MC using software tools. The wider objective of the paper will be illustrated by a case study, where the availability model of critical NPP I&C system with version-structural redundancy and double software updates will be developed and analyzed.

To build the availability model we propose a newly developed reliability model of the critical NPP I&C system. The following factors are accounted for in this model: an overall reserve of critical NPP I&C system, as well as joint cold redundancy of main and diverse system modules of the system; the existence of two software versions; software double update; physical faults.

The structure of the paper is as follows. The second section of the paper is devoted to discussion on the nature of software defects, as well as to randomness of software failures. The discussion of this section results from the need of software failure rate to be included into the developed availability model, and from the software failures and updates point of view, which also are a part of the present study. The rationale for using the Erlang distribution for software updates is presented in the next section. The structure of the studied critical NPP I&C system is described in more details in the fourth section of the paper. The development of the mathematical model based on the Markovian chain and the implementation of the Erlang distribution of software update into the Markovian chain is described the in the fifth section. Simulation results of the influence of the Erlang distribution of software update duration on the availability of the studied critical NPP I&C system are presented and analyzed in Sect. 6. The last section concludes the paper and presents some directions for future research.

2   The Dependency of Software Failure Rates on the Frequency of Data Input Changing. The Randomness of Software Failures

Hardware aging occurs naturally over time, therefore, time is a generally accepted variable in functions for estimating hardware reliability. On the other hand, software failure will never occur if the software is not run. Therefore, in the context of software reliability, it is more practical to represent software runtime as the number of computational operations completed by the software. It is important that the test metrics and ways of running the software take into account the following: that statistics of software failures should be investigated when a number of tasks are performing with different input data. Performing a task repeated times with the same input data will not result in a software failure if the software did not fail the first time the task was completed. Therefore, according to [18], the number and nature of software failures are the result of internal defects and depends on the conditions in which the software is used.

In contrast to hardware failures which can occur at any time regardless of input data, software failure depends on the frequency with which data are input. In practice, the software can be considered such as some function f, which converts entry space into output space. The entry space is a set of all input conditions and the output space is the set of all output conditions [19]. Respective states are determined by a set of variables or typical software commands/transactions. According to standard IEC 60880, the input space which includes the branch of software performance is called the signal path [20]. In the period between two sets of incoming data being input, a software failure cannot occur if the software preliminary entry is performed and the software is in standby mode. Based on this, if the probability of software failure is calculated as 10^{-4} per software launch and the frequency of input data from sensors is one second, the resulting software failure rate is calculated as 10^{-4} s^{-1} or 0.36 h^{-1} (without taking into account the time required to create the output state), what can be unacceptable according to system reliability requirements, part of which is such software.

Failure is a concept in reliability theory and can be defined as an event, after the occurrence of which the characteristics of a technical object are outside of defined bounds [21]. According to [22], software failures are an event during which a software failure is detected. The signs of software disability are outlined in the technical documentation. The unrealistic results of software performance can be the result of temporary hardware failures or software defects. Software defects are the elements or parts of the code, usage of which leads to unrealistic results [22]. In contrast to hardware failures, software failures can be caused by:

- incorrect algorithms or the incorrect implementation of algorithms ("write element of a program");
- incorrect software documentation, which will lead to incorrect user actions;
- the input data which are being processed by the software;
- temporary failures of hardware which occur under external factors (ionizing radiation, temperature, humidity or another factor), which can sometimes be eliminated by a software restart.

In [23, 25] an attempt to build a comprehensive software fault classification has been presented. The authors, in general, consider two fault types, viz. Bohrbugs and Mandelbugs.

According to [23] Bohrbug is "a fault that is easily isolated and that manifests consistently under a well-defined set of conditions because its activation and error propagation lack "complexity" as set out in the definition of Mandelbug. Complementary antonym of Mandelbug". This type of software faults evidently results in software failure under the specific set of conditions and cannot be avoided by software or computer system restart. To achieve fault-tolerance against the Bohrbugs one should use diverse systems were identical in sense of functionality programs should be developed by different teams (see e.g. [7, 25–27]). While using a diverse system one should be aware of the probability of common software faults in both program versions. The general assumption of using diverse systems is they do not contain software faults that manifest under the same set of conditions – "common faults". However, this is not obvious to be true. To consider this effect one can use the "diversity metrics" which indicate the portion of common software faults in two versions of a program. In the present paper, we will use the value of the diversity metric to be equal to unity, which means two versions of the program do not contain common software faults.

Mandelbug is "a fault whose activation and/or error propagation are complex, where "complexity" can take two forms: (1) the activation and/or error propagation depend on interactions between conditions occurring inside the application and conditions that accrue within the system-internal environment of the application; (2) there is a time lag between fault activation and failure occurrence" [23]. Typically, a Mandelbug is difficult to isolate, and/or the failures caused by it are not systematically reproducible. Mandelbug is the complementary antonym of Bohrbug. Indeed Mandelbugs will necessary results in software failure under the same set of conditions, but this set is hard to identify due to complex nature of affecting factors, which are hard to reveal and reproduce (see e.g. [28]). In [24] such "complexity" is ascribed to:

(1) a time lag between the fault activation and the occurrence of a failure; or
(2) the influence of indirect factors, namely:
   a. interactions of the software application with its system-internal environment (hardware, operating system, other applications); or
   b. influence of the timing of inputs and operations (relative to each other, or in terms of the system runtime or calendar time); or
   c. influence of the sequencing of operations; sequencing is considered influential, if the inputs could have been run in a different order and if at least one of the other orders would not have led to a failure.

Mandelbugs, in turn, include two subtypes [23]: Heisenbugs and aging-related bugs.

Heisenbug is "a fault that stops causing a failure or that manifests differently when one attempts to probe or isolate it" [23]. This could result from e.g. initialization of unused memory to default values by debuggers or operating system during program restart or scheduling-related failures in multi-threaded programs may disappear when a debugger is used to single-step through a process or system-internal environment during program restart was changed [23].

The aging-related bug is "a fault that leads to the accumulation of errors either inside the running application or in its system-internal environment, resulting in an increased failure rate and/or degraded performance" [23]. Though it is well recognized that "software systems do not degrade over time unless modified", the reason of aging-related bugs could be in conditions, which may accrue either within the running application (e.g., round-off errors in program variables) or in the system-internal environment (e.g., unreleased physical memory due to memory leaks in the application) [23]. The class of aging-related bugs of an application may or may not overlap with the class of those software faults that are Heisenbugs with respect to a specific observation tool or method.

Therefore, the Mandelbugs may not manifest after program or computer system restart due to changes in the system-internal environment, and such restart could be effectively used to restore the operational state of the system after a software failure.

In [24] according to the relationships between the fault types, the authors consider each fault to be a Bohrbug, a non-aging-related Mandelbug, or an aging-related bug. According to Grottke, Nikora, and Trivedi, Bohrbugs basically correspond to solid [29] or hard [30] faults, while Mandelbugs are soft [29] or elusive [30] faults, which Gray [29] also refers to as Heisenbugs. However, there are subtle differences.

In this paper, the following types of software faults are considered: (1) Bohrbugs, which are eliminated by the diverse system and software updates after a Bohrbug failure; and (2) non-aging-related Mandelbugs, manifestation of which are eliminated by software restart procedure.

While developing the model of the fault-tolerance system the following assumptions on software faults are considered:

(1) The diversity metric is equal to unity, and software failure does not occur in both program versions simultaneously.

(2) During an update of one program, it is possible for the other program version to fail, and thus the outage of the fault-tolerance system will occur. The duration of this outage will influence the value of the availability function.

3 The Use of Erlang Distribution for Software Updates in Availability Model of Fault-Tolerant Computer-Based System with Version-Structural Redundancy

The duration of software updates is a random value and it is possible to present it by "mean time of new (next) software version development". On the one hand, this value depends on software engineering factors as mentioned below; on the other hand since the duration of software updates affects the availability function of the whole NPP I&C system, its edge value could be evaluated at system design stage based on the reliability analysis. The robustness of this measure should be found in the resolution of decision reliability syntheses tasks of the fault-tolerant computer-based system which is an integral part of the high availability critical infrastructure. The duration of new software version development depends on many factors such as: available staff with appropriated technology knowledge; qualification of developers; the complexity of the software and other factors. In previous papers [31, 32], it was assumed that the duration of software updates is a random variable with exponential distributions. However, it is more correct to consider software updates as a random variable with normal (or Gaussian) distribution. If an availability model is developed in the discrete-continuous stochastic system form, the duration of all procedures in the fault-tolerant computer-based system (included software updates) being analyses will be presented by exponential distributions. In this regard, the frequency with which software update durations occur in the vicinity of the mean is low compared to short software updates with duration near zero. This leads to decreasing adequacy of the availability model the studied object.

This paper provides detailed suggestions for using Erlang distributions for the duration of software updates that will increase the adequacy of models and provide more realistic availability predictions. Figure 1 shows the probability density function for exponential distribution and the probability density function for Erlang distributions with a shape parameter $k = 5$. The probability of the occurrence of software update durations near the mean value in availability model with Erlang distributions is higher than when using exponential distributions for software updates. In defined (given) interval, the area under the probability density function of the Erlang distribution (S1) is larger than are under the probability density function of the exponential distribution (S2). The accuracy of software update duration probability is increased by increasing the shape parameter k of the Erlang distributions.

Based on this analysis, we conclude that Erlang distributions of software update durations are appropriate to use for availability models of fault-tolerant computer-based systems in Markovian chain development. The main idea and instructions for implementing Erlang distributions with an arbitrary shape parameter (for any distributions) for the automated building of the Markovian chain were presented in paper [33].

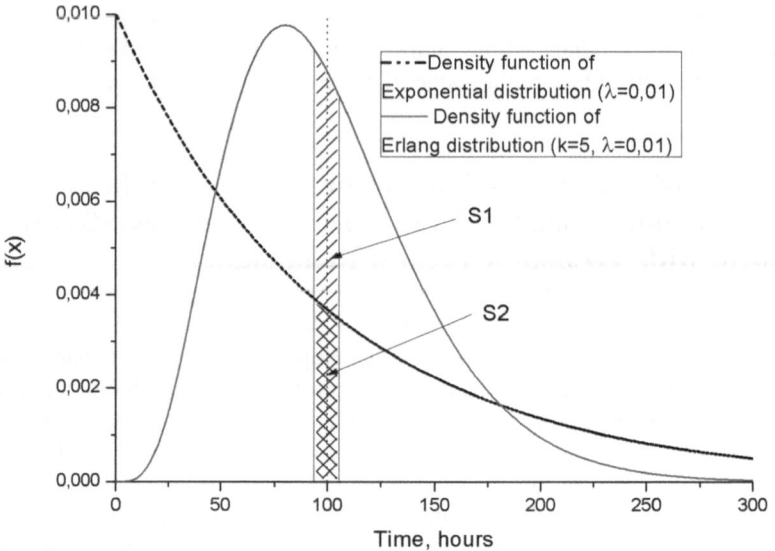

Fig. 1. Probability density function of Exponential and Erlang distributions with shape parameter equal 5

4   Industry Case: FPGA Platform Based Reactor Trip System of NPP

Here we provide the structure (Fig. 2) of researched safety critical NPP Instrumentation and Control system (I&C) based on the digital FPGA platform RadICS [34]. This is reactor trip system consisting of main and diverse systems [35]. Main and diverse systems have been developed using the FPGA safety controller (FSC) with three parallel channels on voting logic "2-out-of-3".

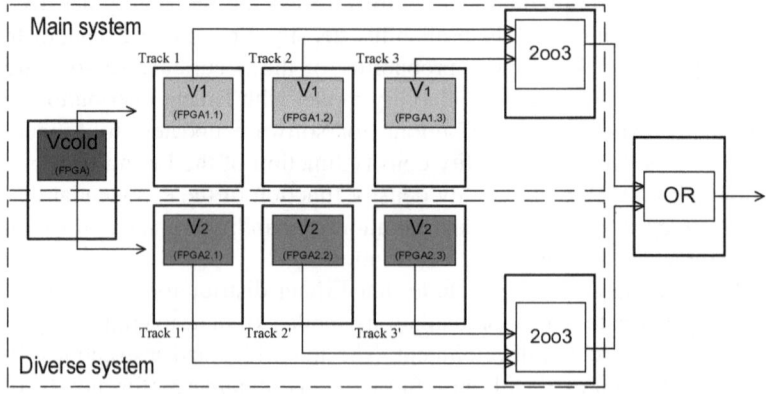

Fig. 2. Configuration of critical NPP I&C system

The output signals from main system (MS) and diverse systems (DS) are binary (signals "switch-off" of the reactor) and are joined according to with logic OR (1-out-of-2).

5 Markov Model of Critical NPP I&C System with K-Phase Erlang Distribution of Software Update

The method of formal and tool-based automated developing the Markovian chains for the researched critical NPP I&C systems are described in [9, 32]. It involves formalized representation of the object of study as "structural-automated model". The detailed availability model of critical NPP I&C systems was presented in our previous papers [31, 32]. In the current paper, we present modified structural-automated model considering the Erlang distributions of the software updates durations.

Structural-automated model of the critical NPP I&C systems for the automated development of the Markovian chains is presented in Table 1. Improvements for Structural-Automated Model of consideration the K-phase Erlang Distribution of software debugging duration are presented below (all improvements are marked by bold font).

The parameters of the critical NPP I&C systems Markov's model: n – number of modules that are the part of the MS; k – number of modules that are the part of the DS; mc –number of the modules in the cold standby; λ_{hw}– the failure rate that is in MS or DS and in the hot standby; λ_{sw11}, λ_{sw12} – the failure rate of first and second software versions; K_e – number of Erlang Distribution phase; T_{up1}, T_{up2} – mean time of the first and second software updates; T_{switch} – mean time of the module connections from standby; T_{not} – mean time of developers notifications after software failures; T_{rep}– mean time of hardware repair.

The number of software updates can be also changed. It is necessary to change vectors V4 and V5 the *event 7*, that are responsible for the number of updates. For example, if there are three software updates for the diverse system, the entry component of the event will be as follows:

(V5 = 2) AND (V7 = 1) AND (V10 = 1) AND (V12 > 0) AND (V11 < Ke)	Ke $(1/T_{up3})$	V12: = V12 + 1
(V5 = 2) AND (V7 = 1) AND (V10 = 1) AND (V12 = Ke)	Ke $(1/T_{up3})$	**V5: = 3;** V6: = 0; V10: = 0; V12: = 0

The developed availability model of the critical NPP I&C system gives the possibilities according to technology [9] for the automated develop of the Markovian chains. This construction provides a software module ASNA [36].

The Markovian chain, which take into account the following parameters of critical NPP I&C system: $n = 3$; $k = 3$; $m_c = 0$; λ_{hw}; λ_{sw11}, λ_{sw12}; T_{up1}, T_{up2}; T_{switch}; T_{rep}; $K_e = 1$, consists of 273 states and 893 transitions, and is presented in Fig. 3. Information is available on the status of each software module ASNA we have on file "vector.vs", which is written in the form:

Table 1. Structural-automated model of critical NPP I&C systems for the automated development of the Markovian chains

Terms and conditions of event	Formula for calculating the rate of events	Rule of modification the state vectors component
Event 1. Hardware failure of the MS module		
(V1 >= (n − 1)) AND (V6 = 0) AND (V10 = 0) **AND (V11 = 0) AND (V12 = 0)**	$V1 \cdot \lambda_{hw}$	V1: = V1 − 1; V8: = V8 + 1
Event 2. Software failure of the MS module		
(V1 >= (n − 1)) AND (V4 = 0) AND (V6 = 0) AND (V10 = 0) **AND (V11 = 0) AND (V12 = 0)**	λ_{sw11}	V4: = 0; V6: = 1
(V1 >= (n − 1)) AND (V4 = 1) AND (V6 = 0) AND (V10 = 0) **AND (V11 = 0) AND (V12 = 0)**	λ_{sw12}	V4: = 1; V6: = 1
Event 3. Completing the developer's notifications after software failures in the main system		
(V1 <= n) AND (V4 = 0) AND (V6 = 1) AND (V9 = 0) **AND (V11 = 0) AND (V12 = 0)**	$1/T_{not}$	V4: = 0; V6: = 1; V9: = 1; **V11: = V11 + 1**
(V1 <= n) AND (V4 = 1) AND (V6 = 1) AND (V9 = 0) **AND (V11 = 0) AND (V12 = 0)**	$1/T_{not}$	V4: = 1; V6: = 1; V9: = 1; **V11: = V11 + 1**
Event 4. Hardware failure of diverse system module		
(V2 >= (k − 1)) AND (V7 = 0) AND (V9 = 0) AND (V11 = 0) AND (V12 = 0)	$V2 \cdot \lambda_{hw}$	V2: = V2 − 1; V8: = V8 + 1
Event 5. Software failure of the diverse system module		
(V2 >= (k − 1)) AND (V5 = 0) AND (V7 = 0) AND (V9 = 0) **AND (V11 = 0) AND (V12 = 0)**	λ_{sw11}	V5: = 0; V7: = 1
(V2 >= (k − 1)) AND (V5 = 1) AND (V7 = 0) AND (V9 = 0) **AND (V11 = 0) AND (V12 = 0)**	λ_{sw12}	V5: = 1; V7: = 1
Event 6. Completing the developer's notifications after software failures in diverse system		
(V2 <= k) AND (V5 = 0) AND (V7 = 1) AND (V10 = 0) **AND (V11 = 0) AND (V12 = 0)**	$1/T_{not}$	V5: = 0; V7: = 1; V10: = 1; **V12: = V12 + 1**
(V2 <= k) AND (V5 = 1) AND (V7 = 1) AND (V10 = 0) **AND (V11 = 0) AND (V12 = 0)**	$1/T_{not}$	V5: = 1; V7: = 1; V10: = 1; **V12: = V12 + 1**
Event 7. Completing the procedure of software version updates in the main system		
(V4 = 0) AND (V6 = 1) AND (V9 = 1) AND (V11 > 0) AND (V11 < Ke)	$(1/T_{up1}) \cdot P_{cor}$	**V11: = V11 + 1**
(V4 = 0) AND (V6 = 1) AND (V9 = 1) AND (V11 = Ke)	$(1/T_{up1}) \cdot P_{cor}$	V4: = 1; V6: = 0; V9: = 0; **V11: = 0**

(*continued*)

Table 1. (*continued*)

Terms and conditions of event	Formula for calculating the rate of events	Rule of modification the state vectors component
(V4 = 1) AND (V6 = 1) AND (V9 = 1) AND (V11 > 0) AND (V11 < Ke)	**$(1/T_{up2}) \cdot P_{cor}$**	**V11: = V11 + 1**
(V4 = 1) AND (V6 = 1) AND (V9 = 1) AND (V11 = Ke)	$(1/T_{up2}) \cdot P_{cor}$	V4: = 2; V6: = 0; V9: = 0; **V11: = 0**
Event 8. Completing the procedure of software version updates in diverse system		
(V5 = 0) AND (V7 = 1) AND (V10 = 1) AND (V12 > 0) AND (V11 < Ke)	**$Ke(1/T_{up1})$**	**V12: = V12 + 1**
(V5 = 0) AND (V7 = 1) AND (V10 = 1) AND (V12 = Ke)	**Ke** $(1/T_{up1})$	V5: = 1; V6: = 0; V10: = 0; **V12: = 0**
(V5 = 1) AND (V7 = 1) AND (V10 = 1) AND (V12 > 0) AND (V11 < Ke)	**$Ke(1/T_{up2})$**	**V12: = V12 + 1**
(V5 = 1) AND (V7 = 1) AND (V10 = 1) AND (V12 = Ke)	**$Ke(1/T_{up2})$**	V5: = 2; V6: = 0; V10: = 0; **V12: = 0**
Event 9. Completing the maintenance procedure of the system		
((V1 <= n) OR (V2 <= k)) AND (V8 = 4) AND (V11 = 0) AND (V12 = 0)	$1/T_{rep}$	V2: = k; V1: = n; V8: = 0

State 1: V1 = 3; V2 = 3; V3 = 0; V4 = 0; V5 = 0; V6 = 0; V7 = 0; V8 = 0; V9 = 0; V10 = 0; V11 = 0; V12 = 0

State 2: V1 = 2; V2 = 3; V3 = 0; V4 = 0; V5 = 0; V6 = 0; V7 = 0; V8 = 1; V9 = 0; V10 = 0; V11 = 0; V12 = 0

....

State 481: V1 = 2; V2 = 1; V3 = 0; V4 = 1; V5 = 2; V6 = 1; V7 = 0; V8 = 3; V9 = 1; V10 = 0; V11 = 3; V12 = 0

The implementation of Erlang distributions of software update in the Markovian chains is described in Figs. 4 and 5. The part of the Markovian chain describing software and hardware failure, one software update and hardware repair is presented in Fig. 4. To implement Erlang distributions of software update duration the transition from state 4 to state 5 would be changed with the chain of five (shape parameter) stages. The result of these implementations is presented in Fig. 5. In the same manner, this idea was implemented in the structural-automated model.

For three phase parameters (K_e) of Erlang distribution for software updates durations were constructed three Markovian chains with a different dimension. The parameters of this Markovian chain are shown in Table 2.

The proposed structural-automated model of critical NPP I&C system for availability assessment can be easily transformed for other features of the object of study. It is enough to: add/remove basic event; attach/remove components of the state vector, and include/exclude parameters that describe the studied system. Based on information about the work of critical NPP I&C system an appropriate change in the model could be made (Fig. 2).

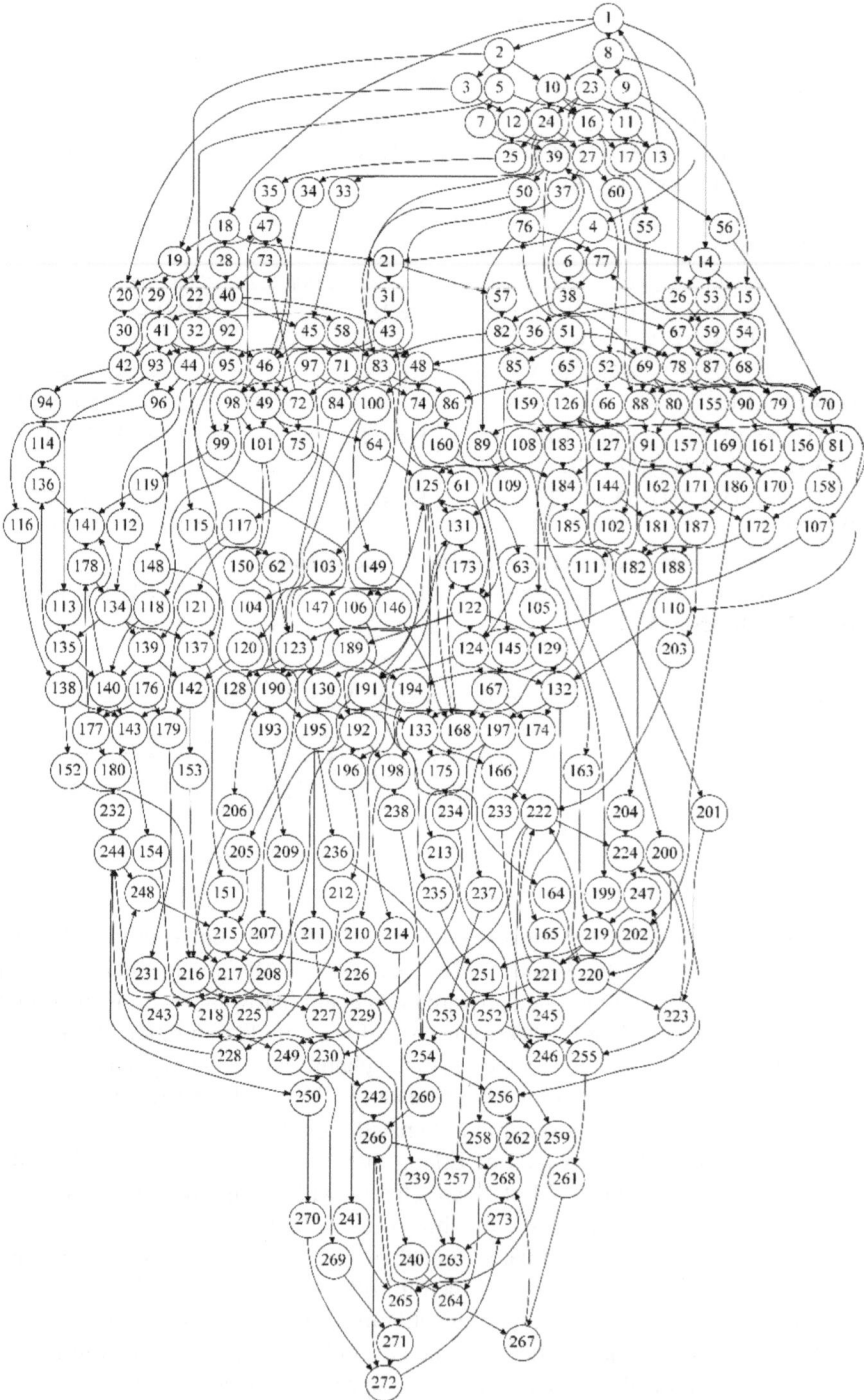

Fig. 3. The Markovian chains of the researched critical NPP I&C systems

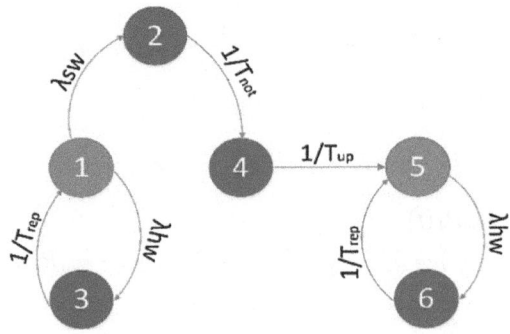

Fig. 4. Fragment of Markovian chain with describe operations critical NPP I&C system

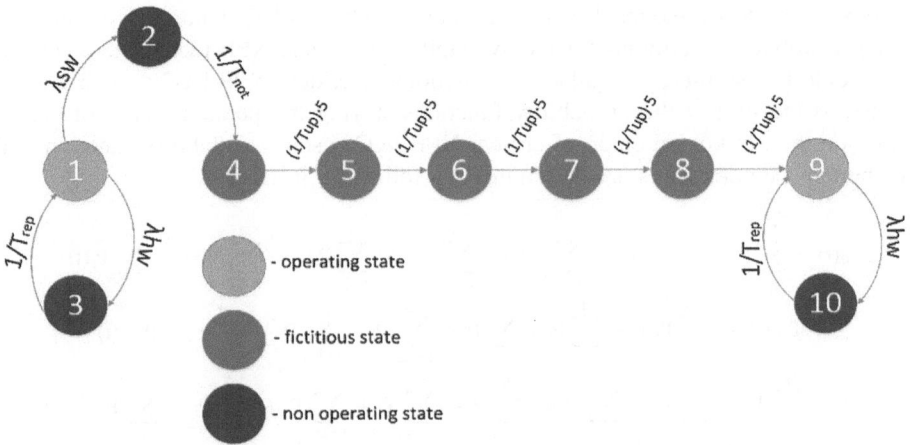

Fig. 5. Fragment of Markovian chain with describe operations critical NPP I&C system and 5-phase Erlang distribution of software update

Table 2. Parameters of Markovian chain with different phase number of Erlang distribution

n	k	K_e	Number of operation states	Number of non-operation states	Number of fictitious states	Total number of states in model
3	3	1	120	153	0	**273**
3	3	3	120	153	208	**481**
3	3	5	120	153	416	**689**

Based on the Markovian chain with an exponential distribution ($Ke = 1$) for critical NPP I&C system ("vector.vs") a system of differential equations was formed. Its solution allows us to estimate the function availability value of researched critical NPP I&C system. In the same manner, the systems of differential equation for a Markovian chain with Erlang distribution ($Ke = 3$, $Ke = 5$) of software updates were formed.

$$\frac{dP_1(t)}{dt} = -6 \cdot (\lambda_{hw} + \lambda_{sw11}) \cdot P_2(t) + \frac{1}{T_{repl}} \cdot (P_2(t) + P_3(t) + P_6(t) + P_7(t)$$

$$+ P_8(t) + P_9(t) + P_{11}(t) + P_{16}(t))$$

$$\frac{dP_2(t)}{dt} = -\frac{1}{T_{repl}} \cdot P_2(t) - 2 \cdot \lambda_{sw11} P_2(t) - 2 \cdot \lambda_{hw} \cdot P_2(t) - 3 \cdot \lambda_{hw} \cdot P_2(t)$$

$$+ 2 \cdot \lambda_{hw} P_1(t)$$

$$\frac{dP_3(t)}{dt} = -\frac{1}{T_{repl}} \cdot P_3(t) - 3 \cdot (\lambda_{hw} + \lambda_{sw11}) \cdot P_3(t) + 2 \cdot \lambda_{hw} P_2(t)$$

$$\vdots$$

$$\frac{dP_{273}(t)}{dt} = -\frac{1}{T_{repl}} \cdot P_{273}(t) + 2 \cdot \lambda_{hw} P_{156}(t) + 2 \cdot \lambda_{sw12} P_{272}(t)$$

Initial conditions for the system (2) are $P_1(t) = 1$; $P_2(t)\ldots P_{273}(t) = 0$.

Based on the developed Markovian chains with a different number of phase in Erlang distributions formulas for the availability of critical NPP I&C system calculations could be assembled. Availability functions of critical NPP I&C system are calculated as the sum of the probability functions staying in operation states of chains. Based on the Markovian chain of critical NPP I&C system availability function with different shape parameters are determined by following formulas:

$$A_{Ke=0}(t) = \sum_{i=1}^{12} P_i(t) + P_{14}(t) + \sum_{i=16}^{18} P_i(t) + \sum_{i=23}^{24} P_i(t) + \sum_{i=38}^{52} P_i(t) + \sum_{i=67}^{72} P_i(t) + \sum_{i=76}^{78} P_i(t)$$

$$+ P_{80}(t) + \sum_{i=82}^{83} P_i(t) + \sum_{i=87}^{88} P_i + \sum_{i=92}^{93} P_i + \sum_{i=122}^{144} P_i + \sum_{i=167}^{172} P_i + \sum_{i=176}^{177} P_i + P_{181}(t)$$

$$+ \sum_{i=183}^{184} P_i + \sum_{i=186}^{187} P_i + \sum_{i=189}^{192} P_i + \sum_{i=215}^{230} P_i + \sum_{i=243}^{246} P_i + \sum_{i=251}^{254} P_i + \sum_{i=263}^{267} P_i + \sum_{i=271}^{272} P_i$$

$$A_{Ke=3}(t) = \sum_{i=1}^{12} P_i(t) + P_{14}(t) + \sum_{i=16}^{18} P_i(t) + \sum_{i=23}^{24} P_i(t) + \sum_{i=42}^{43} P_i(t) + \sum_{i=64}^{76} P_i(t) + \sum_{i=91}^{96} P_i(t) + P_{100}(t)$$

$$+ P_{102}(t) + P_{104}(t) + \sum_{i=106}^{108} P_i(t) + \sum_{i=111}^{112} P_i + \sum_{i=116}^{117} P_i + \sum_{i=121}^{122} P_i + \sum_{i=170}^{173} P_i + \sum_{i=178}^{179} P_i$$

$$+ \sum_{i=200}^{205} P_i + \sum_{i=226}^{236} P_i + \sum_{i=259}^{264} P_i + \sum_{i=268}^{269} P_i + P_{273}(t) + \sum_{i=275}^{279} P_i + \sum_{i=281}^{284} P_i + \sum_{i=328}^{330} P_i + \sum_{i=355}^{358} P_i$$

$$+ \sum_{i=371}^{372} P_i + \sum_{i=393}^{398} P_i + \sum_{i=411}^{414} P_i + \sum_{i=419}^{422} P_i + \sum_{i=455}^{458} P_i + \sum_{i=471}^{472} P_i + \sum_{i=475}^{476} P_i$$

$$A_{Ke=5}(t) = \sum_{i=1}^{12} P_i(t) + P_{14}(t) + \sum_{i=16}^{18} P_i(t) + \sum_{i=23}^{24} P_i(t) + \sum_{i=46}^{47} P_i(t) + \sum_{i=88}^{100} P_i(t) + \sum_{i=115}^{120} P_i(t) + P_{124}(t)$$

$$+ P_{126}(t) + P_{128}(t) + \sum_{i=130}^{131} P_i(t) + \sum_{i=135}^{136} P_i + \sum_{i=140}^{141} P_i + \sum_{i=145}^{146} P_i + \sum_{i=218}^{221} P_i + \sum_{i=230}^{231} P_i$$

$$+ \sum_{i=272}^{277} P_i + \sum_{i=318}^{328} P_i + \sum_{i=351}^{356} P_i + \sum_{i=243}^{246} P_i + \sum_{i=360}^{361} P_i + P_{365}(t) + \sum_{i=367}^{368} P_i + \sum_{i=370}^{371} P_i + \sum_{i=373}^{376} P_i$$

$$+ \sum_{i=439}^{442} P_i + \sum_{i=491}^{494} P_i + \sum_{i=519}^{520} P_i + \sum_{i=561}^{566} P_i + \sum_{i=579}^{582} P_i + \sum_{i=587}^{590} P_i + \sum_{i=647}^{650} P_i + \sum_{i=675}^{676} P_i + \sum_{i=679}^{680} P_i$$

6 Simulation Results: The Influence of K-Phase Erlang Distribution of the Software Update Durations on Availability of the Critical NPP I&C System

With the assistance of the proposed model, the following questions can be answered: what are the duration values of the first and the second software update (ensuring the values of the availability function of critical NPP I&C system of the initial phase of its operation do not reach below the specified level)? What are the allowed duration values of the first and the second SW updates? Does the correlation between the first and the second SW update influence on the availability function? What is an influence on the availability function of the duration of SW updates by Erlang distribution?

The experiment is conducted for the condition where the duration of the first software update is significantly shorter than the duration of the second update and the distribution of software update duration presented by Erlang distribution with different shape parameters $K_e = 1$, $K_e = 5$, $K_e = 25$. The experiment is conducted with the following parameters critical NPP I&C system: $\lambda_{hw} = 1 \cdot 10^{-5}$ h^{-1}; $\lambda_{sw11} = 2 \cdot 10^{-4}$ h^{-1}, $\lambda_{sw12} = 1 \cdot 10^{-4}$ h^{-1}; $T_{rep} = 200$ h; $T_{up1} = 10$ h; $T_{up2} = 200$ h (Fig. 6).

The following results have been obtained by the proposed experiments:

1. Minimal levels of the availability functions for Markovian chains without Erlang distribution (Ke = 1) for the duration of software updates and Markovian chains with Erlang distributions (Ke = 5, Ke = 25) are changed. Analyzing the dependents of availability functions on the Fig. 3 could be concluded that real distribution of processes in the system has a significant effect on reliability indexes of critical NPP I&C system.
2. With the assistance of the proposed model, it is possible to choose the duration of software updates that help to ensure a minimum allowed level of the decrease of the availability function of the critical NPP I&C system.
3. In this research, we confirmed that the exponential distribution in discrete-continuous stochastic models usage provides the limiting value of efficiency indicators. This occurrence was described by J. Martin in his monograph [pp. 58–59, 37]. However, based on the proposed model we confirmed that exponential distributions provide the most optimistic availability measures. The Erlang distribution for software updates usage provides more realistic availability measure that is important during the operation of critical system and correction of software defects.

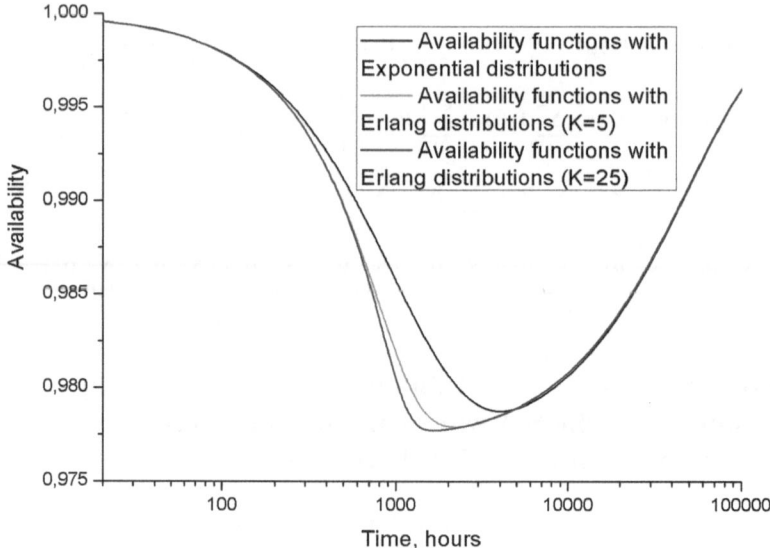

Fig. 6. Dependencies of availability function of the critical NPP I&C system on Erlang distributions (Ke = 1, Ke = 5, Ke = 25) of software updates duration.

7 Conclusion

This research presents a model of critical NPP I&C system with double software updates and real distribution of software updates duration (by presented Erlang distributions) to illustrate the automated development of Markovian chains using special technology and tool ASNA.

The presented model can be easily adapted to different configurations of critical NPP I&C system, which envisages different majority voting, hardware standby and plurality of software versions from different developers. In fact, this model can be adopted for an arbitrary number of software updates.

Future research has the potential to supplement this model with further factors: Erlang distribution for durations of hardware repair; unsuccessful restarting; unreliable commutation of elements and so on.

References

1. Mudry, P.A., Vannel, F., Tempesti, G., Mange, D.: A reconfigurable hardware platform for prototyping cellular architectures. In: IEEE International Parallel and Distributed Processing Symposium, pp. 96–103 (2007)
2. Viktorov, O.: Reconfigurable multiprocessor system reliability estimation. Asian J. Inf. Technol. **6**(9), 958–960 (2007)
3. Rajesh, S., Vinoth Kumar, C., Srivatsan, R., Harini, S., Shanthi, A.: Fault tolerance in multicore processors with reconfigurable hardware unit. In: 15th International Conference on High-Performance Computing, Bangalore, India, pp. 166–171 (2008)

4. Amerijckx, C., Legat, J.-D.: A low-power multiprocessor architecture for embedded reconfigurable systems. In: International Workshop on Power and Timing Modeling, Optimization and Simulation, pp. 83–93 (2008)
5. Zhu, C., Gu, Z., Dick, R., Shang, L.: Reliable multiprocessor system-on-chip synthesis. In: International Conference Hardware/Software Co-design and System Synthesis, pp. 239–244 (2007)
6. Gostelow, K.P.: The design of a fault-tolerant, real-time, multi-core computer system. In: Aerospace Conference, pp. 1–8. IEEE (2011)
7. Lyu, M.R. (ed.): Software Fault Tolerance. Wiley, New York (1995)
8. Korotun, T.M.: Models and methods for testing software systems. Program. probl. 2, 76–84 (2007). (In Russian)
9. Volochii, B.: Technology of modeling the information systems. Publishing NU "Lviv Polytechnic" (2004). (In Ukrainian)
10. Xiong, L., Tan, Q., Xu, J.: Effects of soft error to system reliability. In: Workshops of International Conference on Advanced Information Networking and Applications, pp. 204–209 (2011)
11. Ponochonvyi, J.L., Odarushchenko, E.B.: The reliability modeling non-redundant information and control systems with software updated. Radioelectron. Comput. Syst. 4(8), 93–97 (2004). (In Russian)
12. Kharchenko, V., Odarushchenko, O., Odarushchenko, V., Popov, P.: Selecting mathematical software for dependability assessment of computer systems described by stiff markov chains. In: Proceeding of International Conference on ICTERI, pp. 146–162 (2013)
13. Kharchenko, V., Ponochovny, Y., Boyarchuk, A.: Availability assessment of information and control systems with online software update and verification. In: Ermolayev, V., Mayr, H., Nikitchenko, M., Spivakovsky, A., Zholtkevych, G. (eds.) ICTERI 2014. CCIS, vol. 469, pp. 300–324. Springer, Cham (2014). https://doi.org/10.1007/978-3-319-13206-8_15
14. Cox, D.R.: Renewal Theory, p. 142. Methuen, London (1962)
15. Konig, D., Shtojan, D.: Methoden der Bedienungstheorie [Methods of Queueing Theory], p. 128. Vieweg, Braunschweig (1976). (In German)
16. Klejnrok, L.: Queueing Systems: Theory, vol. 1, p. 432. Wiley, New York (1976)
17. Rajnshke, K., Ushakov, I.A.: Assessment of the Reliability of the Systems via Graphs, 208 p. Radio I svjaz' Publ., Moskva (1988). (In Russian)
18. Lipaev V.: Software reliability, 232 p. Syntex, Moskov (1998) (In Russian)
19. Pham, H.: System Software Reliability. SSRE, p. 387. Springer, London (2006). https://doi.org/10.1007/1-84628-295-0
20. IEC 60880: Nuclear power plants - Instrumentation and control systems important to safety - Software aspects for computer-based systems performing category A functions, 217 p. (2006)
21. Polovko, A.: Fundamentals of Reliability Theory, p. 704. BHV-Peterburg, Saint Petersburg (2006). (In Russian)
22. DSTU 2844-94. Computer Software. Quality ensuring. Terms and definitions. Federal standard, 19 p. (1996). (In Ukrainian)
23. Grottke, M., Trivedi, K.S.: A classification of software faults. In: Supplemental Proceedings of Sixteenth International IEEE Symposium on Software Reliability Engineering, pp. 4.19–4.20 (2005)
24. Grottke, M., Nikora, A.P., Trivedi, K.S.: An empirical investigation of fault types in space mission system software. In: IEEE/IFIP International Conference on Dependable Systems and Networks (DSN), pp. 447–456 (2010)

25. Littlewood, B., Popov, P., Strigini, L.: Design diversity: an update from research on reliability modelling. In: Redmill, F., Anderson, T. (eds.) Aspects of Safety Management: Proceedings of the Ninth Safety-critical Systems Symposium, Bristol, UK 2001, pp. 139–154. Springer, London (2001). https://doi.org/10.1007/978-1-4471-0713-2_11
26. Ammann, P.E., Knight, J.C.: Data diversity: an approach to software fault tolerance. IEEE Trans. Comput. **C37**(4), 418–425 (1988)
27. Popov, P., Strigini, L., et al.: Estimating bounds on the reliability of diverse systems. IEEE Trans. Softw. Eng. **29**(4), 345–359 (2003)
28. Yakovyna, V., Nytrebych, O.: Discrete and continuous time high-order markov models for software reliability assessment. In: Proceedings of the 11th International Conference ICTERI 2015, Lviv, Ukraine, 14–16 May 2015. CEUR-WS.org, CEUR-WS.org/Vol-1356/paper_62.pdf
29. Gray, J.: Why do computers stop and what can be done about it? In: Proceedings of Fifth Symposium on Reliability in Distributed Systems, pp. 3–12 (1986)
30. Avižienis, A., Laprie, J.-C., Randell, B., Landwehr, C.: Basic concepts and taxonomy of dependable and secure computing. IEEE Trans. Dependable Secure Comput. **1**(1), 11–33 (2004)
31. Volochiy, B., Mulyak, O., Kharchenko, V.: Automated development of markovian chains for fault-tolerant computer-based systems with version structure redundancy. In: Proceedings of the 11th International Conference on ICT in Education, Research and Industrial Applications: Integration, Harmonization and Knowledge Transfer, vol. 1356, pp. 462–475 (2015)
32. Volochiy, B., Mulyak, O., Ozirkovskyi, L., Kharchenko, V.: Automation of quantitative requirements determination to software reliability of safety critical NPP I&C systems. In: Proceedings of the Second International Symposium on Stochastic Models in Reliability Engineering, Life Science and Operations Management (SMRLO 2016), pp. 337–346 (2016)
33. Fedasyuk, D.V., Volochiy, S.B.: Structural-automaton model of fault-tolerant systems for automated usage of Erlang distribution. Radio Electron. Comput. Syst. **3**(77), 78–92 (2016). (In Ukrainian)
34. Kharchenko, V., Sklyar, V., Volkoviy, A.: Development and verification of dependable multi-version systems on the basic of IP-cores. In: Proceedings of International Conference on Dependability of Computer Systems (2008)
35. Review Guidelines for Field-Programmable Gate Arrays in Nuclear Power Plant Safety Systems. NUREG/CR-7006, U.S. Nuclear Regulatory Commission, Washington, D.C., USA (2010)
36. Bobalo, J., Volochiy. B., Lozynskyi, O., Mandzii, B., Ozirkovskyi, L., Fedasuk, D., Shcherbovskyh, S., Jakovyna, V.: Mathematical models and methods for reliability analysis of electronic, electrical and software systems, Lviv Polytechnic Press, Lviv, 425 p. (2013). http://vlp.com.ua/node/10764. (In Ukrainian)
37. Martin, J.: System Analysis for Data Transmission, p. 823. IBM System Research Institute, Prentice Hall, Inc., Englewood Cliffs (1972)

Two Approaches to Modelling Logical Time in Cyber-Physical Systems

Grygoriy Zholtkevych$^{(\boxtimes)}$ and Hassan Khalil El Zein

Mathematics and Computer Science School, V.N. Karazin Kharkiv National University, 4, Svobody Sqr., Kharkiv 61022, Ukraine
g.zholtkevych@karazin.ua, dr.hassanelzein@icloud.com

Abstract. The paper is devoted to problems caused by the nonlinearity of logical time in distributed, especially cyber-physical, systems. Two approaches to the modelling of such systems are considered in the paper. The operational approach is based on the traditional model that defines the admissible system behaviour as a set of acceptable schedules of the system. The paper argues in favour of restricting possible sets of schedules by that sets of schedules that satisfy certain safety properties. The denotational approach is stated in the language of category theory. This abstraction level clarifies concepts used in the models. In particular, it is explained the feature of linear models as terminal objects with respect to some natural class of morphisms. Further, the interrelation between these two approaches is represented as a formal relation and discuss some properties of the relation that need to be studied.

Keywords: Cyber-physical system · Logical time · Clock
Denotational semantic model · Operational semantic model
Schedule · Safety property · Clock structure · Clock morphism

1 Introduction

Apparently, the class of cyber-physical systems (CPS for short) was defined by National Science Foundation of USA for the first time in 2012 [14, Synopsis of Program] as the class of "engineered systems that are built from and depend upon the synergy of computational and physical components". Moreover, this document specifies the perspectives of CPS: "The CPS of tomorrow will far exceed the simple embedded systems of today in capability, adaptability, resiliency, safety, security, and usability. CPS technology will transform the way people interact with engineered systems, just as the Internet transformed the way people interact with information. New smart cyber-physical systems will drive innovation and competition in sectors such as the power grid, transportation, buildings, medicine, and manufacturing".

In [15] this definition was refined and extended as follows: "CPS are engineered systems that are built from, and depend upon, the seamless integration of computational algorithms and physical components. Advances in CPS will

© Springer International Publishing AG, part of Springer Nature 2018
N. Bassiliades et al. (Eds.): ICTERI 2017, CCIS 826, pp. 21–40, 2018.
https://doi.org/10.1007/978-3-319-76168-8_2

enable capability, adaptability, scalability, resiliency, safety, security, and usability that will far exceed the simple embedded systems of today. CPS technology will transform the way people interact with engineered systems – just as the Internet has transformed the way people interact with information. New smart CPS will drive innovation and competition in sectors such as agriculture, energy, transportation, building design and automation, healthcare, and manufacturing just as the Internet has transformed the way people interact with information. Indeed, it is also clear that CPS technologies are central to achieving the vision of Smart & Connected Communities (S&CC), including "Smart Cities", which spans these multiple sectors and includes the important attributes of efficiency, safety, and security". Thus, comparing this texts we may say that the notion of CPS is a well-established concept and refer to a combined system of executive subsystems and network of controlling units (cyber components), which guarantee the wholeness of the system.

It should be emphasised that the development trend of modern technology is the integration of CPS-components through technology Internet of Things (IoT). Analysing trends of IoT- and CPS-technology Kate Carruthers notes [4]: "CPS include traditional embedded and control systems, and these will be transformed by new approaches from IoT. However, the challenge for IoT and CPS remains security and risk management. As less rigorously controlled systems are linked then risk becomes distributed and the provenance of software components becomes difficult to trace. This gives rise to questions around risk management and liability for breaches or damages".

Thus, we may state that any modern CPS should be considered as a safety-critical system. The necessity to use trustworthy strategies for development of systems of such a type is the first significant conclusion for the practice of system design.

The above reasons motivate our research, which is aimed to clarification of objective limits to the applicability of the clock model for the specification and computer-aided analysis of behavioural constraints for cyber components of CPS. The principal tool of our study is the clock model proposed by Lamport [9] (see also [3, Chap. 2] and [7, Chap. 3]) for studying distributed computing. A survey of examples of applying this model to study CPS can be found in [12].

2   Motivation and Refinement of Basic Concepts

The aim of this section is to clarify meaning basic concepts of the paper and motives to suggest them.

2.1   Conceptual Framework for Modelling Cyber-Physical Systems

Recall that in the article we use the term cyber-physical system to denote a heterogeneous complex consisting of natural objects and artificial subsystems that operate as a whole entity by using the special system of interacting controllers (cyber components). This informal description can be refined by the following

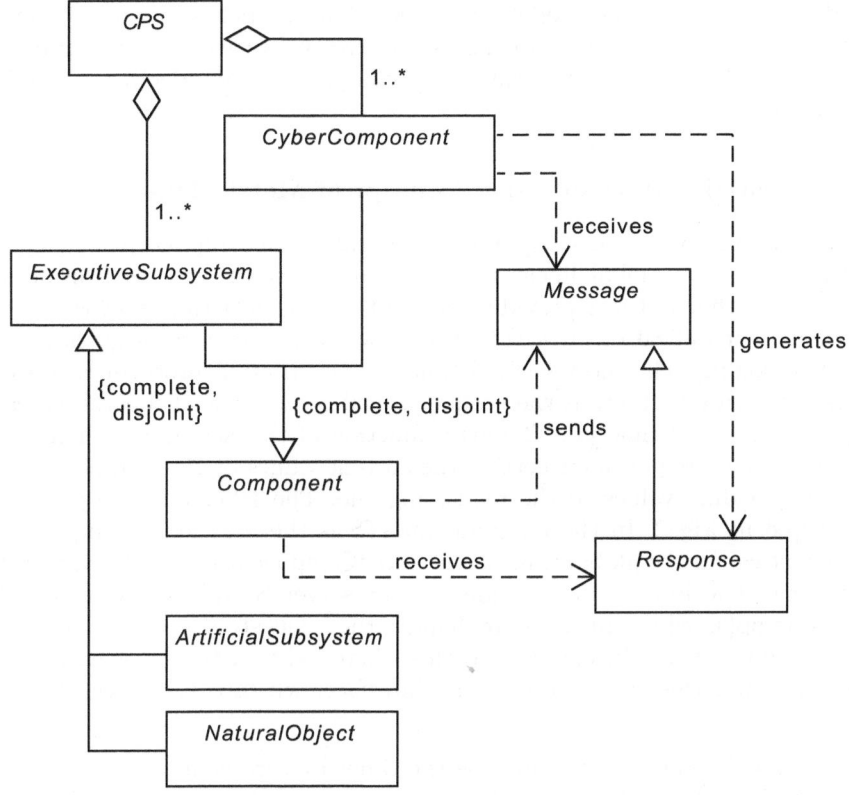

Fig. 1. CPS: conceptual framework

class diagram (Fig. 1) representing the abstract framework for CPS. This framework establishes that

– any *CPS* consists of at least one instance of class *ExecutiveSubsystem* and at least one instance of class *CyberComponent*;
– each of these instances is an instance of class *Component*;
– an instance of class *ExecutiveSubsystem* is either an instance of class *NaturalObject* or of class *ArtificialSubsystem*.

This model fixes that the message interchange between components of CPS is the only way to provide interaction of these components:

– each instance of class *Component* sends an instance of class *Message*, which are received by some instances of class *CyberComponent*;
– each instance of class *CyberComponent* generates a special message, which is an instance of class *Response*; of course, a response depends on messages received by the cyber-component that has generated this response;
– if the component receiving responses is an instance of class *ExecutiveSubsystem* then it executes the actions corresponding to the received response collection, otherwise, the behaviour is similar to the previous case.

The described conceptual model establishes that the behaviour of each cyber-component is determined only by a message stream, received by the component. In the situation, the concept of time is very important to understand whether a system operates correctly or not.

2.2   Potential Pitfalls of Using Concept of Metric Time

The most natural way reasoning about temporal relationships consists in accepting the concept of global linear time. The necessity of some synchronisation protocol, i.e. the protocol providing for setting all local timers in the system such that their indications would be the same, is the direct consequence of this way of reasoning. The most general time synchronisation protocol is based on the assumption that there is the unique special component of the system called the server of global time [5]. The main function of this server is to handle system components requests for getting the current values of global time and send the corresponding values to the requesting one. The scheme of the protocol is represented in Fig. 2. In the diagram, theGTS is the mentioned unique cyber-component called the global time server and aComponent is an arbitrary system component. The interface of the global time server contains only one method getTimestamp(), which provides to handle the request of getting the current stamp of global time. In contrast to this, there exists a timer for each system component and this timer provides an interface, which contains the following methods

resetTimer()	to initialise the timer by zero value;
getTimerValue()	to get the current value of the timer;
setTimer(value)	to set value as the current value of the timer.

Thus delay is length of the time interval between the events "a request has issued" and "the response has received". It is evident that delay is a random variable and its distribution is determined by features of the network connecting components of the system.

Let us calculate the probability density function of the synchronisation error provided that the delivery times of messages in the network are described by mutually independent random exponentially distributed quantities with an average T. Let us describe the mathematical model of the error occurrence of the synchronisation process based on the protocol represented in Fig. 2.

First of all, let us denote random variables representing delivery times of a timestamp query and of the corresponding response by τ_q and τ_r respectively. In Fig. 3, symbols t_q and t_r refer to members of the sample spaces of random variables τ_q and τ_r respectively, and symbol t^* refers to value of timestamp. One can easily see that delay $= t_q + t_r$ and the error of synchronisation err equals $\frac{1}{2} \cdot (t_q - t_r)$. Thus, the error of synchronisation is the random variable $\epsilon = \frac{1}{2} \cdot (\tau_q - \tau_r)$.

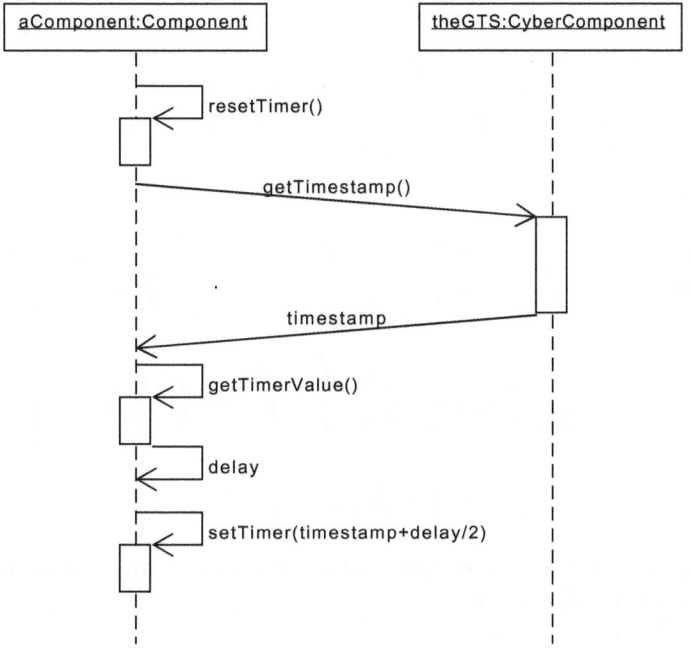

Fig. 2. Typical time synchronisation protocol

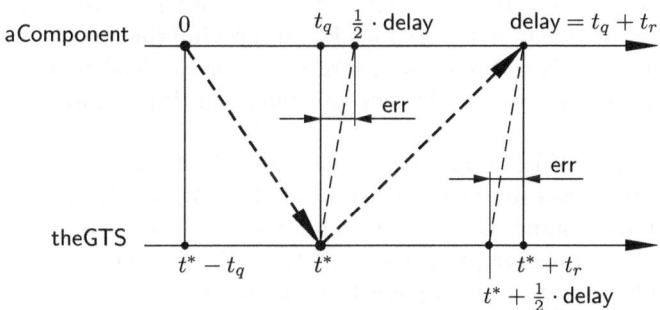

Fig. 3. Timing diagram for synchronisation process

Taking into account the assumption about independence of τ_q and τ_r we have

$$\Pr(\epsilon \leq x) = \iint\limits_{\substack{t_q, t_r \geq 0 \\ t_r \geq t_q - 2x}} \frac{1}{T^2} \cdot \exp\left(-\frac{t_q + t_r}{T}\right) \cdot dt_q \, dt_r.$$

Simple integration gives for $x < 0$

$$\Pr(\epsilon \leq x) = \frac{1}{T^2} \int_0^{+\infty} \exp\left(-\frac{t_q}{T}\right) \cdot \left(\int_{t_q-2x}^{+\infty} \exp\left(-\frac{t_r}{T}\right) \cdot dt_r\right) \cdot dt_q = \frac{1}{2} \cdot \exp\left(\frac{2x}{T}\right)$$

and for $x \geq 0$

$$\Pr(\epsilon \leq x) = \frac{1}{T^2} \int_0^{2x} \exp\left(-\frac{t_q}{T}\right) \cdot \left(\int_0^{+\infty} \exp\left(-\frac{t_r}{T}\right) \cdot dt_r\right) \cdot dt_q$$

$$+ \frac{1}{T^2} \int_{2x}^{+\infty} \exp\left(-\frac{t_q}{T}\right) \cdot \left(\int_{t_q-2x}^{+\infty} \exp\left(-\frac{t_r}{T}\right) \cdot dt_r\right) \cdot dt_q$$

$$= 1 - \frac{1}{2} \cdot \exp\left(-\frac{2x}{T}\right).$$

These formulas guarantee that the probability density function of the random variable ϵ has the following form

$$p_\epsilon(x) = \frac{1}{T} \cdot \exp\left(-\frac{2 \cdot |x|}{T}\right).$$

Note that T depends only on the characteristics of the system communication network, therefore, it can not be reduced by improving the software of the system cyber-components. Thus, the existence of the error can lead to a situation when the timestamp of some event appears less than the timestamp of an event that is its reason.

To demonstrate this, suppose that the event E_1 that occurred at time t_1^* of the global time causes an event E_2 at time $t_1^* + \Delta t^*$ of the global time where $\Delta t^* > 0$. Let us assume also that E_1 and E_2 connected with different system components then timestamps $t_1^* + e_1$ and $t_1^* + \Delta t^* + e_2$ are assigned to E_1 and E_2 respectively where e_1 and e_2 are the corresponding synchronisation errors. The inequality $t_1^* + e_1 > t_1^* + \Delta t^* + e_2$ means that the designated timestamps are contrary to a logical sequence of events. Therefore, let us calculate the probability of the inequality is fulfilled. Thus, taking into account the independence of ϵ_1 and ϵ_2 we have

$$\Pr(\epsilon_1 - \epsilon_2 > \Delta t^*) = \iint_{e_1-e_2>\Delta t^*} p_\epsilon(e_1) \cdot p_\epsilon(e_2) \cdot de_1 de_2$$

$$= \int_{-\infty}^{\infty} p_\epsilon(e_1) \cdot \left(\int_{-\infty}^{e_1-\Delta t^*} p_\epsilon(e_2) \cdot de_2\right) \cdot de_1$$

$$= \frac{1}{2} \cdot \left(1 + \frac{\Delta t^*}{T}\right) \cdot \exp\left(-2 \cdot \frac{\Delta t^*}{T}\right).$$

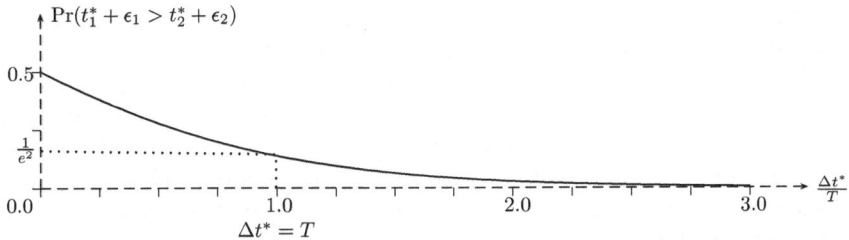

Fig. 4. The probability of pitfalls under using concept of metric time

Thus, the probability of raising a pitfall under using the global timestamps in the model being studied always greater than zero and what is more it is greater or equal $\frac{1}{e^2} \approx 0.1353$ if the time between event occurrences less or equal to the mean time of message delivery in the network. The dependence of this probability on the ratio of Δt^* to T is shown in Fig. 4.

In other words, for every hundred pairs of cause-caused events, the timestamps of 13 to 14 pairs on average contradict the order caused by the causal relationship under condition that the time interval between the events of the pair does not exceed the average time of delivery of messages on the network.

All of the above leads to the conclusion about the unreliability of a model based on the concept of the global linear time.

2.3 Modelling Logical Time Based on Logical Clock Concept

As we have discussed the existence of synchronisation errors can lead to violations causality relationships under modelling behaviour of distributed and, in particularly, cyber-physical systems. This anomaly prompted Lamport to introduce the notion of a logical clock (see [9]) to overcome the mentioned difficulties. In this paper, we base on [13] to define general concepts for mathematical modelling the logical time.

First of all, we agree that the behaviour of each CPS can be described by using "the temporal picture" that is formed by all event occurrences happening in the system and causal relationships between ones. Below these event occurrences are called **instants** and the set of all instants denoted usually by $\mathcal{I}$.

We also assume that there exists a finite set C of sources of instants, and the source of each moment is uniquely determined, i.e. there exists a surjective mapping clk: $\mathcal{I} \to C$. Elements of C are called **clocks** and in the context, each instant $i \in \mathcal{I}$ can be considered as a tick of the correspondent clock clk(i).

We suggest also that the relationship "happen not later" is a fundamental binary relationship between instants. This relationship defines the following derived binary relationships between instants: "happen simultaneously", "happen before", "are mutually excluded", and "are mutually independent".

If we have some full set of instants $\{i_1, i_2, \ldots, i_k\}$ that are happening simultaneously then we say that the subset $\{\text{clk}(i_1), \text{clk}(i_2), \ldots, \text{clk}(i_k)\}$ of clocks is a **message** about clock ticking, i.e. a message is a non-empty subset of C. The corresponding set of messages we denote below by $\boldsymbol{M}_C$.

A **schedule** (or more precisely a C-schedule) is an infinite sequence of messages. It is natural to denote the set of all C-schedules by $\boldsymbol{M}_C^\omega$. Each element of $\boldsymbol{M}_C^\omega$ models some individual behaviour of the system being studied.

The schedules are used to build the operational model of the CPS that distinguishes the correct and incorrect behaviours of the system components based on the observed sequences of messages.

The appropriate approach to determine the correctness of the logical time dependencies was apparently first used by Lamport [9], who introduced the concept "logical clock".

The clock model is designed to define and analyse the logical temporal relationships between the instants, i.e. event occurrences having different event types. The first class citizens of the model are clocks, which are considered as sources of monotypic instants. The uniqueness of the source for each event type means that all instants of the same event type are linearly ordered in time, i.e. for any pair of such instants, we can exactly establish what instant from this pair has happened before.

We are interested in studying such relationships between instants which do not depend on fortuitous aspects of behaviours of the system being studied, but which fix regularities of behaviours of the system. In other words, our interests are focused on relations of causality.

There are two approaches to study these relationships, namely, the approach based on representing admissible system behaviours by using schedules, and the approach based on representing admissible system behaviours by using special mathematical objects called a time structures.

The first approach (see Sect. 3) can be used to define the operational semantics of the specification languages, and the second approach (see Sect. 4) can be used to define the denotational semantics for languages describing the temporal requirements limiting possible system behaviours.

Thus, understanding the interrelationship between these two approaches is an important both theoretical and applied problem for the theory of CPS.

The first results concerning this problem were obtained in [18]. This paper develops the study presented in the mentioned paper. But our innovation consisting in to study the time structures not as isolated objects, but as objects of the special category clarifies more completely and correctly this interrelation.

3   Operational Model Based on Concept of Schedules

In this section we give a brief overview of the operational model of logical time, the creation of which goes back to the articles [8,9] Lamport, written in the seventies of last century, Later, the Lamport's ideas gained traction in the paper [1] of Alpern and Schneider.

3.1   Safety Properties

Note, we need to limit ourselves such properties of schedules whose violations, speaking not formally, can be recognised in a finite time. Lamport proposed to recognise a property of schedules (the set of schedules satisfying this property) as a safety property if any violation of this property can be detected by the way of observing the system during a finite time interval [8]. The following definition describes formally a safety property.

Definition 1. *A property P of C-schedules is a safety property if and only if for any C-schedule $\pi \notin P$ there exists $n \in \mathbb{N}_+$ such that any C-schedule π' satisfying equation $\pi[0:n] = \pi'[0:n]$ satisfies also condition $\pi' \notin P$.*

One can find the detailed discussion of the formal definition of safety properties in [1].

We consider that any acceptable behaviour of CPS is being described by the corresponding safety property. Safeness ensures that the corresponding property is physically correct because it can be checked using information obtained in the past and present. In other words, checking such a property does not require the presence of magical abilities like foresight.

3.2   Topology on M_C^ω

This subsection contains some facts of the general topology necessary to understand the topological nature of the notions of safeness. For more detailed acquaintance with the subject, you can refer to [1,16].

Proposition 1. *For any $n \in \mathbb{N}_+$ and $u \in M_C^+$, let us denote by $Z_n(u)$ the set*

$$Z_n(u) = \{\pi \in M_C^\omega \mid \pi[n:n+len(u)] = u\}$$

then the family $\left\{ Z_n(u) \mid n \in \mathbb{N}_+, \ u \in M_C^+ \right\}$ forms the base of Tikhonov topology on M_C^ω.

Proposition 2. *Let $\{\pi_n \mid n \in \mathbb{N}\}$ be a sequence of C-schedules and π be a C-schedule then $\pi = \lim\limits_{n \to \infty} \pi_n$ in Tikhonov topology if and only if for any $M \in \mathbb{N}_+$ there exists $N \in \mathbb{N}_+$ such that whenever $n > N$ the equation $\pi_n[0:M] = \pi[0:M]$ holds.*

Definition 2. *Let P be a subset of M_C^ω then P is called closed if for any schedule sequence $\{\pi_n \in P \mid n \in \mathbb{N}\}$ such that there exists $\pi = \lim\limits_{n \to \infty} \pi_n$ then $\pi \in P$ also.*

Now one can be sure that a property P is a safety property if and only if the set of schedules satisfying P is a closed set in Tikhonov topology. Thus, the problem how to specify some set of admissible system behaviours becomes the specification problem of a closed set in Tikhonov topology on the space of C-schedules.

4 Category of Time Structures

We try to describe the denotational approach to modelling of CPS behaviour in this section. We emphasize that if the approach specified above gives acceptable schedules in physical time, then the denotational approach describes a pure logical picture of relations between event occurrences without any references to physical time. In our opinion, this approach described firstly in the paper of Andre and Mallet [2] published in 2008.

4.1 Quasi-Ordered Sets

This subsection is given to introduce the mathematical basis for the denotational approach to semantic modelling of CPS behaviour. The principal source is [6]. It is well known that the quasi-ordered set is a set equipped with a binary relation that is reflexive and transitive.

As usual, for a quasi-ordered set $(X, \preccurlyeq)$ we define the following derived binary relations on X (see Table 1). Simple dependencies between the relations indicated in the table are gathered in the following statement.

Proposition 3. *For any $i, j \in X$, both the following hold*

(i) $\neg(i \# j)$ *and* $i \equiv j \vee i \parallel j$ *are the same;*
(ii) $i \preccurlyeq j$ *and* $i \prec j \vee i \equiv j$ *are the same.*

The proof of the proposition is a simple exercise in Boolean algebra.

Now, let $(X, \preccurlyeq)$ and $(Y, \preccurlyeq)$ be quasi-ordered sets and $f \colon X \to Y$ be a mapping then we say that f is conservative if for any $i, j \in X$,

(i) $i \preccurlyeq j$ implies $f(i) \preccurlyeq f(j)$ and
(ii) $i \# j$ implies $f(i) \# f(j)$.

The following is also true.

Proposition 4. *For quasi-ordered sets $(X, \preccurlyeq)$ and $(Y, \preccurlyeq)$ the mapping $f \colon X \to Y$ is conservative if and only if both the following are true.*

(i) $i \prec j$ *implies* $f(i) \prec f(j)$ *and*
(ii) $i \equiv j$ *implies* $f(i) \equiv f(j)$.

The proof of the proposition can be easily obtained by using Proposition 3.

Further, below we need in the concept of a principal ideal $(i]$ of an element i of a quasi-ordered set $(X, \preccurlyeq)$ that is defined as the subset $(i] = \{j \in X \mid j \preccurlyeq i\}$ of X.

Table 1. The derived relations on a quasi-ordered set

Name	Properties	Notation	Definition
Coincidence	Reflexive, antisymmetric, and transitive	$i \equiv j$	$i \preccurlyeq j \wedge j \preccurlyeq i$
Precedence	Irreflexive and transitive	$i \prec j$	$i \preccurlyeq j \wedge j \not\preccurlyeq i$
Exclusion	Symmetric	$i \# j$	$i \prec j \vee j \prec i$
Independence	Symmetric	$i \parallel j$	$i \not\preccurlyeq j \wedge j \not\preccurlyeq i$

4.2 Clock Structures

We start this section with the following formal definition.

Definition 3. *Let C be a finite set of clocks then a C-structure S^1 is a triple $(I, \gamma, \preccurlyeq)$ where*

I	*is the set of instants corresponding to the occurrences of events,*
$\preccurlyeq$	*is a quasi-order on I that models the causality relation between instants, and, finally,*
$\gamma \colon I \to C$	*is a surjective mapping that associates each instant with the clock that is the source of this instant*

provided that the following axioms met:
the axiom of unbounded liveness: *the set I is infinite;*
the axiom of finite causality: *for any $i \in I$, the corresponding principal ideal $(i]$ is finite;*
the axiom of total ordering for clock timelines: *for all $c \in C$, the restriction of "$\preccurlyeq$" on $I_c = \gamma^{-1}(c)$ is a linear order.*

This definition is a repetition of the corresponding definition given in [2,11].

Some simple conclusions from this definition are gathered in the following proposition.

Proposition 5. *Let $S = (I, \gamma, \preccurlyeq)$ be a C-structure then*

(i) *width of the ordered set $(I, \prec)$ is less than or equal to $|C|$;*
(ii) *for each $c \in C$, the set I_c is well-ordered;*
(iii) *for each $c \in C$, the ordinal type of I_c is less than or equal to ω;*
(iv) *there is at least one $c \in C$ such that its ordinal type equals ω;*
(v) *the set I is countable;*
(vi) *if $i, j \in I$ and $i \equiv j$ then either $i = j$ or $\neg(i \;\#\; j)$, i.e. any equivalence class for the relation "$\equiv$" is an antichain for the strict order "$\prec$";*
(vii) *if $i, j, i', j' \in I$, $i \prec j$, $i \equiv i'$, and $j \equiv j'$ then $i' \prec j'$;*
(viii) *each instant $i \in I$ is uniquely characterized by the pair $(\gamma(i), \mathrm{idx}(i))$ where $\mathrm{idx} \colon I \to \mathbb{N}$ is defined as follows*

$$\mathrm{idx}(i) = \left| \{ j \in I_{\gamma(i)} \mid j \prec i \} \right|.$$

We omit the proof because it uses standard reasoning.

4.3 Morphisms of Clock Structures

As usual, we define morphisms of C-structures to describe the relationship between them.

Definition 4. *Let S' and S'' be C-structures, I' and I'' be the corresponding sets of instants then a mapping $f \colon I' \to I''$ is called a C-morphism from S' into S'' if the following holds*

---

[1] Usually, one uses the term clock structure if C is uniquely determined by the context.

(i) $\gamma(i) = \gamma(f(i))$ *for any* $i \in I'$;
(ii) f *is a conservative mapping for quasi-ordered sets* $(I', \preccurlyeq)$ *and* $(I'', \preccurlyeq)$.

Note 1. Usually, we do not distinguish symbols used to denote the causality relations and the mappings associated instants with their sources for different clock systems.

Note 2. The fact that f is a C-morphism from S' into S'' is as usually denoted by $f\colon S' \to S''$.

The following statement establishes an important property of C-morphisms.

Proposition 6. *Any C-morphism is an injective mapping.*

Proof. Indeed, let us suppose that $f\colon I' \to I''$ be a morphism of C-structures $(I', \preccurlyeq, \gamma)$ and $(I'', \preccurlyeq, \gamma)$, $i \neq j \in I'$, and $f(i) = f(j)$. Then either $\gamma(i) \neq \gamma(j)$ or $\gamma(i) = \gamma(j)$ and $\mathrm{idx}(i) \neq \mathrm{idx}(j)$ (see Proposition 5, item (viii)).

Firstly, let us assume that $\gamma(i) \neq \gamma(j)$ but then we get $\gamma(f(i)) = \gamma(i) \neq \gamma(j) = \gamma(f(j))$ and, therefore, $f(i) \neq f(j)$. This contradicts to the assumption, hence the case is impossible.

Secondly, let us assume that $\gamma(i) = \gamma(j) = c$ and $\mathrm{idx}(i) \neq \mathrm{idx}(j)$. Let for definiteness $\mathrm{idx}(i) < \mathrm{idx}(j)$ then $\gamma(i) = \gamma(j)$ ensures $i \prec j$. But this means that $i \prec j$, i.e. $i \,\#\, j$ and, therefore, $f(i) \,\#\, f(j)$, i.e. we have that $f(i) \equiv f(j)$ is false and, hence, $f(i) = f(j)$ is false also. Thus, in this case, we also obtain a contradiction with the assumption. The case $\mathrm{idx}(j) < \mathrm{idx}(i)$ is analysed by the similar way. □

The following statement is evident.

Proposition 7. *For any finite set C, the class of C-structures together with the class of C-morphisms form a small category[2].*

Corollary 1 (of Proposition 6). *Any C-morphism is a monomorphism in the category of C-structures.*

The above results lead to the following classification of C-morphisms.

Definition 5. *A C-morphism $f\colon S' \to S''$ is called a covering C-morphism if the mapping $f\colon I' \to I''$ is surjective.*

The following proposition clarifies logical relations between different classes of C-morphisms.

Proposition 8. *Logical relations between the notions C-isomorphism, covering C-morphism, C-epimorphism, C-bimorphism, C-monomorphism, and C-morphism are shown in Fig. 5.*

---

[2] The necessary definitions and results from the theory of categories can be found in [10].

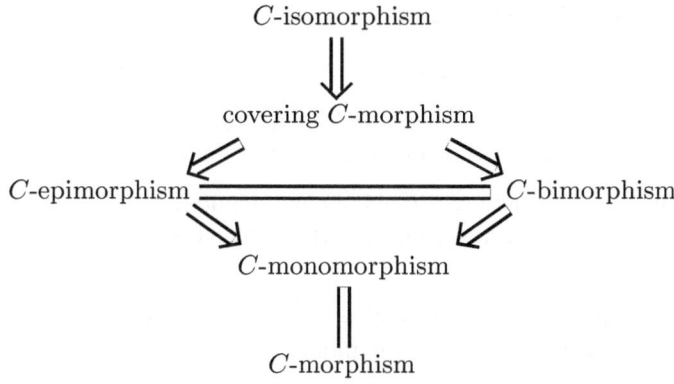

Fig. 5. Logical relations between different classes of C-morphisms

Proof. To prove the proposition it is sufficient to demonstrate that, firstly, there is a covering C-morphism that is not an isomorphism and, secondly, there is an C-epimorphism that is not a covering morphism.

To demonstrate the first position let us consider $C = \{c_1, c_2\}$ and two C-structures S' and S'' with $I' = I'' = \mathbb{N} \times \{c_1\} \bigcup \mathbb{N} \times \{c_2\}$, $\gamma(n, c) = c$, $(m, c') \preccurlyeq'$ (n, c'') if and only if $c' = c''$ and $m \leq n$, and $(m, c') \preccurlyeq'' (n, c'')$ if and only if $m \leq n$. It is evident that $f \colon I \to I$ defined as $f(n, c) = (n, c)$ is a covering C-morphism, but is not a C-isomorphism.

To demonstrate the second position let us consider a C-system S'' such that $i_* \equiv j_*$ for some $i_* \neq j_* \in I''$. Now, let us define $I' = I'' \setminus \{i_*\}$ and $i \preccurlyeq j$ in I' if and only if $i \preccurlyeq j$ in I''. In this case, the natural embedding $\iota \colon S' \to S''$ is a C-morphism, but it is not evidently a covering C-morphism. Let us take C-morphisms f and g from S'' into an arbitrary S such that $f\iota = g\iota$. If $f \neq g$ then f and g is not equal only on i_*. Taking into account that $i_* \equiv j_*$ one can get $f(i_*) \equiv f(j_*)$ and $g(i_*) \equiv g(j_*)$. Therefore, the equality $f(j_*) = g(j_*)$ implies $f(i_*) \equiv g(i_*)$. Note, that $\gamma(f(i_*)) = \gamma(i_*) = \gamma(g(i_*))$. The last together with $f(i_*) \equiv g(i_*)$ and axiom about total ordering for clock timelines implies $f(i_*) = g(i_*)$.

Thus, we obtain that $f\iota = g\iota$ implies $f = g$. It means that ι is an epimorphism. $\qquad\square$

5   Interrelation Between Operational and Denotational Approaches

This section contains some results concerning mutual relationships between operational and denotational models. Below we construct a relation between clock structures and schedules. This relation describes the possible ways of diving a clock structure into physical time. Properties of schedules represent these ways.

5.1   Some Needed Technique

Below we need the following notion.

Definition 6. *Let* $S = (I, \gamma, \preccurlyeq)$ *be a C-structure,* $A \subset I$, *and* $i \in A$ *then* i *is called a minimal instant in* A *if for any* $j \in A$ *the statement* $j \prec i$ *is false.*

The subset of minimal instants of A is below denoted by $\min A$. The following simple sentence demonstrates that $\min A$ is closed in A with respect to the relation "$\equiv$".

Proposition 9. *For a C-structure* $S = (I, \gamma, \preccurlyeq)$ *and* $A \subset I$, *the assumptions* $i \in \min A$, $j \in A$, *and* $i \equiv j$ *imply* $j \in \min A$.

Proof. Really, if $j \notin \min A$ then there exists $k \in A$ such that $k \prec j$. But, in this case, item (vii) of Proposition 5 guarantees $k \prec i$. This conclusion contradicts to $i \in \min A$.   □

We associate the sequence of layers $I^{(0)}, I^{(1)}, \ldots$ with any C-structure S in the following manner

$$I^{(0)} = \min I$$

$$I^{(n)} = \min \left(I \setminus \bigcup_{m=0}^{n-1} I^{(m)} \right) \quad \text{for } n > 0$$

where I is the instant set of S as usual.

Proposition 10. *The following properties hold*

(i) $|I^{(n)}| \leq |C|$ *for each* $n \in \mathbb{N}$;
(ii) *if* $i, j \in I^{(n)}$ *for some* $n \in \mathbb{N}$ *then either* $i \parallel j$ *or* $i \equiv j$;
(iii) *the sequence of layers is a covering of the set of instants;*
(iv) *if* $i \in I^{(n)}$ *for some* $n \in \mathbb{N}$, $j \in I$, *and* $j \equiv i$ *then* $j \in I^{(n)}$;
(v) *if* $i \in I^{(n+1)}$ *for some* $n \in \mathbb{N}$ *then there exists* $j \in I^{(n)}$ *such that* $j \prec i$.

Proof. (i) The assumption that $|I^{(n)}| > |C|$ for some $n \in \mathbb{N}$ leads to the existence of different i and j satisfying the condition $\{i, j\} \subset I_c \cap I^{(n)}$. But this contradicts to Definition 6.

(ii) Indeed, each the statement $i \# j$ contradicts to the statement that the both statements $i \in I^{(n)}$ and $j \in I^{(n)}$ are true. Now, one can apply item (i) of Proposition 3.

(iii) Suppose that there exists some $i \in I$ such that $i \notin I^{(n)}$ for any $n \in \mathbb{N}$ then using induction one can demonstrate that for each $n \in \mathbb{N}$ there exists $j_n \in I^{(n)}$ such that $j_n \prec i$. Taking into account that $I^{(m)} \cap I^{(n)} = \varnothing$ for $m \neq n$ we conclude that the set $\{j_n \mid n \in \mathbb{N}\}$ is infinite. But this set is a subset of $(i]$ and we have obtain the contradiction to Definition 3.

(iv) If $j \notin I^{(n)}$ then item (iii) ensures that $j \in I^{(m)}$ for some $m \neq n$. If $m < n$ then Proposition 9 guarantees $i \in I^{(m)}$ that is impossible taking into account disjunctivity of layers. Similarly, $n < m$ is impossible too. Thus, $m = n$.

(v) If $i \in I^{(n+1)}$ for some $n \in \mathbb{N}$ then $j \not\prec i$ for any $j \in I \setminus \left(\bigcup_{0 \leq k \leq n} I^{(k)} \right)$. If $j \not\prec i$ for all $j \in I^{(n)}$ also then $j \not\prec i$ for any $j \in I \setminus \left(\bigcup_{0 \leq k < n} I^{(k)} \right)$. This means that $i \in \bigcup_{0 \leq k < n} I^{(k)}$ and, therefore, $i \in I^{(n+1)}$ is false. This proves the item of the proposition. □

Corollary 2. *An instant i belongs to $I^{(n)}$ if and only if number of elements of each maximal chain in $(i]$ equals $n + 1$.*

Proof. It is being proved by induction with respect to n. □

Corollary 3. *Layer $I^{(n)}$ for each $n \in \mathbb{N}$ is a union of $\equiv$-equivalence classes of elements belonging the layer, moreover layer elements lying to different classes are independent.*

5.2   Linear Clock Structures

An important special class of clock structures is formed by so-called linear clock structures. This class was introduced in [18]. In the mentioned paper, it was also shown that linear clock structures are closely related to schedules.

Definition 7. *A C-structure $\mathcal{L} = (I, \gamma, \preccurlyeq)$ is called a linear C-structure if for any $i, j \in I$, statement $i \parallel j$ is false.*

Any linear clock structure holds the following important property.

Proposition 11. *Let $\mathcal{L} = (I, \gamma, \preccurlyeq)$ be a linear C-structure, $\mathcal{S}' = (I', \gamma, \preccurlyeq)$ be a C-structure, and $f \colon I \to I'$ be a covering C-morphism then f is a C-isomorphism.*

Proof. Indeed, taking into account that f is a covering C-morphism one can conclude that f is a bijection, hence there exists the unique mapping $g \colon I' \to I$ such that $g(f(i)) = i$ for each $i \in I$ and $f(g(i')) = i'$ for each $i' \in I'$.

Now let us demonstrate that g is a C-morphism.

If $i', j' \in I'$ and $i' \preccurlyeq j'$ then for $i = g(i')$ and $j = g(j')$ the linearity of I ensures either $j \prec i$ or $i \preccurlyeq j$.

The statement $j \prec i$ implies $j \# i$ and, therefore, $f(j) = j' \# f(i) = i'$, i.e. $j' \prec i' \vee i' \prec j'$. On the other hand, the statement $j \prec i$ implies $j \preccurlyeq i$ and, therefore, $j' \preccurlyeq i'$. But the assertions $i' \prec j'$ and $j' \preccurlyeq i'$ are evidently incompatible, hence $j' \prec i'$ is necessary true. Taking into account that $j' \prec i'$ and $i' \preccurlyeq j'$ are incompatible one can conclude that $i \preccurlyeq j$ is the unique acceptable variant. Thus, we proved that $g(i') \preccurlyeq g(j')$.

Further, if $i', j' \in I'$ and $i' \# j'$ then for $i = g(i')$ and $j = g(j')$ the linearity of I ensures $i \equiv j$ or $i \# j$. Taking into account that $i \equiv j$ ensures $i' \equiv j'$ we conclude that $i \equiv j$ contradicts to $i' \# j'$. Thus, we proved that $g(i') \# g(j')$.

Therefore, g is the inverse C-morphism for f. □

As it is below shown the proposition converse to Proposition 11 is also true.

5.3 Analogue of Szpilrajn Extension Theorem

The concept of extension is an important concept in ordered sets theory. Therefore we study its analogue for clock structures.

Definition 8. *Let $S = (I, \gamma, \preccurlyeq)$ be C-structures then a covering non-invertible C-morphism $e\colon I \to I'$ for some C-structure $S' = (I', \gamma, \preccurlyeq)$ is called an extension of S. Whenever S' is a linear C-structure we say that e is a linear extension of S.*

The following theorem refines Theorem 3 in [18].

Theorem (about Linear Extension). *Let $S = (I, \gamma, \preccurlyeq)$ be a C-structure and i_*, j_* be some pair of independent instants belonging to I then there exists a linear extension $e\colon S \to \mathcal{L}$ such that the condition $e(i_*) \prec e(j_*)$ holds.*

To prove the theorem we need in the following lemmas.

Lemma 1. *Let $S = (I, \gamma, \preccurlyeq)$ be a C-structure and i_*, j_* be two independent instants in I then there exists an extension $e\colon S \to S^*$ such that $e(i_*) \prec e(j_*)$.*

Proof. Let $\mathbf{1} = \{*\}$ be some singleton. Then let us define

$$I^* = I \times \mathbf{1}$$

$$\gamma(i, *) = \gamma(i) \quad \text{for any } i \in I$$

$$(i, *) \preccurlyeq (j, *) \text{ means either } i \preccurlyeq j \text{ or } i \preccurlyeq i_* \text{ and } j_* \preccurlyeq j \quad \text{for any } i, j \in I$$

$$e(i) = (i, *) \quad \text{for any } i \in I.$$

Let us check that "$\preccurlyeq$" defined on I^* is a quasi-order. Indeed, it is evident that this relation is reflexive. If now we have that $(i, *) \preccurlyeq (j, *)$ and $(j, *) \preccurlyeq (k, *)$ for some $i, j, k \in I$ then the next variants are only possible:

1. $i \preccurlyeq j$ and $j \preccurlyeq k$; these conditions ensure $i \preccurlyeq k$ and, hence, $(i, *) \preccurlyeq (k, *)$;
2. $i \preccurlyeq i_*$, $j_* \preccurlyeq j$, and $j \preccurlyeq k$; these conditions ensure $i \preccurlyeq i_*$ and $j_* \preccurlyeq k$, but this means that $(i, *) \preccurlyeq (k, *)$;
3. $i \preccurlyeq j$, $j \preccurlyeq i_*$, and $j_* \preccurlyeq k$; these conditions ensure $(i, *) \preccurlyeq (k, *)$ that is checked similarly to above.

Thus, "$\preccurlyeq$" is a quasi-order on I^*.

One can easily see that $(i_*, *) \preccurlyeq (j_*, *)$, but $(j_*, *) \not\preccurlyeq (j_*, *)$, i.e. $e(i_*) \prec e(j_*)$.

The construction ensures evidently that $i \# j$ implies $e(i) \# e(j)$.

And, finally, it is evident that $((i, *)] \subset (i] \bigcup (i_*]$. Therefore, the set $((i, *)]$ is finite for any $(i, *) \in I^*$.

Thus, $S^* = (I^*, \gamma, \preccurlyeq)$ is a C-structure, $e\colon S \to S^*$ is a covering C-morphism, and $e(i_*) \prec e(j_*)$. □

Lemma 2. *Let $S = (I, \gamma, \preccurlyeq)$ then for $I^* = I \times 1$; $\gamma(i, *) = \gamma(i)$; and $(i, *) \preccurlyeq (j, *)$ meaning $i \in I^{(m)}$, $j \in I^{(n)}$, and $m \leq n$ the triple $\mathcal{L} = (I^*, \gamma, \preccurlyeq)$ is a linear C-structure. Moreover, $e: S \to \mathcal{L}$ that is defined as $e(i) = (i, *)$ is a linear extension of S.*

Proof. Taking into account that $I^{(m)} \cap I^{(n)} = \varnothing$ if $m \neq n$ and item (iii) of Proposition 10 one can conclude that $\preccurlyeq$ is a correctly defined linear quasi-order on I^*, moreover items (iv) and (v) of Proposition 10 ensure that $i \preccurlyeq j$ implies $(i, *) \preccurlyeq (j, *)$ and $i \prec j$ implies $(i, *) \prec (j, *)$. Thus, $\mathcal{L}$ is a linear C-structure and e is a covering C-morphism. Therefore, e is a linear extension of S.   □

Proof (of Theorem about Linear Extension).
Let $e': S \to S'$ be the extension of S constructed in accordance with Lemma 1 end e'' be the linear extension of S' constructed in accordance with Lemma 2 then $e = e'' \circ e'$ is a linear extension of S.

Construction of e' ensures that $e'(i_*) \prec e'(j_*)$ and construction of e'' ensures that $i' \prec j'$ implies $e''(i') \prec e''(j')$. Thus, $e(i_*) \prec e(j_*)$.   □

Corollary 4. *Each C-structure S is uniquely defined by the family $\{e_\alpha\}$ of all its linear extensions in the following sense*

$$\text{if } i, j \in I \text{ then } i \preccurlyeq j \text{ iff } e_\alpha(i) \preccurlyeq e_\alpha(j) \text{ for all } e_\alpha.$$

Corollary 5. *If C-structure S satisfies the property "any covering C-morphism from S is a C-isomorphism" then this C-structure is linear.*

Note 3. Corollary 5 is the claimed inversion of Proposition 11.

Note 4. The obtained criterion for the linearity of a clock structure shows that all linear clock structures and only them are "weak terminal" with respect to covering clock morphisms.

5.4 Relation of Admissibility

Linear extensions of a clock structure can be considered as admissible realisations of the clock structure in the global time. In this subsection, the corresponding formal relation called admissibility is defined.

Let us assume that some finite set of clock are fixed. Then we associate the linear C-structure $\mathcal{L}_\pi = (I_\pi, \preccurlyeq, \gamma)$ with any C-schedule π in the following manner:

1. $I_\pi = \{(n, c) \in \mathbb{N} \times C \mid c \in \pi[n]\}$;
2. $\gamma_\pi(n, c) = c$ for $(n, c) \in I_\pi$;
3. $(m, a) \preccurlyeq (n, b)$ means $m \leq n$ for any (m, a) and (n, b) belonging to I_π.

Thus we can define the following relation.

Definition 9. *We say that a C-structure S admits a C-schedule π and denote this fact by $S \models \pi$ if there exists an extension $e \colon S \to \mathcal{L}_\pi$.*

Definition 9 leads us to the notion property of clock structure.

Definition 10. *A set of C-schedules P is a property of C-structure S^3 if for any $\pi \in P$ the condition $S \models \pi$ is fulfilled.*

Corollary 4 of Theorem about Linear Extension shows that any clock structure S can be uniquely specified by some property, which we call the **characteristic property of the structure** and denote by $[\![S]\!]$.

The following hypothesis is natural (see [17]).

Conjecture (about Safeness of Characteristic Properties). *The characteristic property of any clock structure is a safety property.*

Unfortunately, this conjecture is false as the following example shows.

Example (a counterexample for the conjecture). Let $C = a, b$, $I = \mathbb{N} \times C$, $(m, c') \preccurlyeq (n, c'')$ if and only if $c' = c''$ and $m \leq n$, and $\gamma(n, c) = c$ then we can define the C-structure $S = (I, \preccurlyeq, \gamma)$.

Let us define now the following sequence $\{\pi_n \mid n \in \mathbb{N}\}$ of C-schedules

$$\pi_n[k] = \begin{cases} \{a\} & \text{if } 0 \leq k < n \text{ or } k = n + 2m + 1 \text{ for } m \in \mathbb{N} \\ \{b\} & \text{if } k = n + 2m \text{ for } m \in \mathbb{N} \end{cases}$$

One can easily see that $\lim_{n \to \infty} \pi_n = \pi$ where $\pi[k] = \{a\}$ for all $k \in \mathbb{N}$.

Evidently that for each π_n there exists the linear extension of S onto $\mathcal{L}_{\pi_n}$, but does not exist any linear extension of S onto $\mathcal{L}_\pi$.

6   Conclusion

The problems of the interaction of components for an important class of complex systems, so-called cyber-physical systems, are studying in the paper. In the article, the difficulties of describing synchronisation processes of the system component behaviours in terms of physical (metric) time have been demonstrated. The presence of these difficulties has become the principal reason for the authors to focus their study on the concept of logical time as the base for investigating the synchronisation processes.

The principal tool of studying logical time in the paper is the clock model first described and been used by Lamport to investigate the interaction of processes in distributed systems. Such a choice has motivated by rich expressive means of the model, which provides the specification process both synchronous and asynchronous inter-component interactions. The successful practice of using this model for specification temporal guarantees and constraints for system behaviour on the base of Clock Constraint Specification Language has been also taken into account.

---

[3] Symbolically, $S \models P$.

Two approaches to modelling logical time for a cyber-physical system have been considered in the paper.

The first approach is based on the notion "schedule", which is used to model an acceptable sequence of occurrences of system events. Each set of schedules can be considered as a specification of the required property of system behaviour. In this context, the key notion is a safety property that corresponds to such a specification of system behaviour whose violations can be detected during a finite time. This approach is traditional to study the behaviour of distributed systems.

The second approach had been proposed to define the denotational semantics of Clock Constraint Specification Language. This approach, in contrast to mentioned above one, considers the time as a set of instants classified with using some set of logical clocks. Under such a consideration, each instant represents some event occurrence. Taking into account that the set-theoretic language has insufficient expressiveness to represent some features of the model being studied in the paper, our efforts have been focused on developing the corresponding category-theoretic language. The category of time structures defined in the paper has become the foundation for the language. Sets of instants equipped by the causality relation and the mapping that associates each instant with the clock corresponding to it are objects of this category. Using the category-theoretic language has given a possibility to refine and make more rigorous this model due to the suited definition of morphisms.

The theorem about linear extension under such an approach is becoming more expressive. This theorem, which has been proved in the paper, is a bridge between two approaches being analysed.

In the last part of the paper, Theorem about Linear Extension has been applied to study interdependence between time structures and properties of schedules. It has been shown that properties of time structures are identified by sets of schedules. It is also clear that there exist sets that are not characteristic properties of the corresponding time structure.

The counterexample described at the end of Subsect. 5.4 raises the important question about consistency two approaches to modelling logical time. We understand that this example is degenerate in some sense. Therefore, the formulation of the conjecture should be improved.

We hope that further study will shine a spotlight on this problem and will lead to formulating the weakest necessary requirements for the languages of the behaviour constraint specification based on the clock model for cyber-physical systems.

References

1. Alpern, B., Schneider, F.B.: Defining liveness. Inf. Process. Letts. **21**, 181–185 (1985)
2. André, C., Mallet, F.: Clock constraints in UML MARTE. Research Report 6540, INRIA (2008)

3. Cachin, C., Guerraoui, R., Rodrigues, L.: Introduction to Reliable and Secure Distributed Programming, 2nd edn. Springer, Heidelberg (2011). https://doi.org/10.1007/978-3-642-15260-3
4. Carruthers, K.: Internet of Things and beyond: cyber-physical systems. IEEE IoT Newsl. (2016). http://iot.ieee.org/newsletter/may-2016/internet-of-things-and-beyond-cyber-physical-systems.html
5. Cristian, F.: Probabilistic clock synchronization. Distrib. Comput. **3**, 146–158 (1989)
6. Harzheim, E.: Ordered Sets. Springer Science & Business Media, New York (2006). https://doi.org/10.1007/b104891
7. Kshemkalyani, A.D., Singhal, M.: Distributed Computing: Principles, Algorithms, and Systems. Cambridge University Press, Cambridge (2008)
8. Lamport, L.: Proving the correctness of multiprocess programs. IEEE Trans. Softw. Eng. **2**, 125–143 (1977)
9. Lamport, L.: Time, clocks, and the ordering of events in a distributed system. CACM **21**(7), 558–565 (1978)
10. Mac Lane, S.: Categories for the Working Mathematician, 2nd edn. Springer New York Inc., New York (1998). https://doi.org/10.1007/978-1-4757-4721-8
11. Mallet, F.: Clock constraint specification language: specifying clock constraints with UML/MARTE. Innov. Syst. Softw. Eng. **4**(3), 309–314 (2008)
12. Mallet, F.: MARTE/CCSL for modeling cyber-physical systems. In: Drechsler, R., Kühne, U. (eds.) Formal Modeling and Verification of Cyber-Physical Systems, pp. 26–49. Springer, Wiesbaden (2015). https://doi.org/10.1007/978-3-658-09994-7_2
13. UML Profile for MARTE: Modeling and Analysis of Real-Time Embedded Systems. Formal/2011-06-03. OMG (2011)
14. The National Science Foundation: Cyber-Physical Systems (CPS). Program Solicitation NSF 12–520. NSF, Arlington, VA (2012)
15. The National Science Foundation: Cyber-Physical Systems (CPS). Program Solicitation NSF 17–529. NSF, Arlington, VA (2017)
16. Willard, S.: General Topology. Dover Publication Inc., Mineola (1998)
17. Zholtkevych, G., El Zein, H.K.: Logical time models to study cyber-physical systems. In: Ermolayev, V., et al. (eds.) Information and Communication Technologies in Education, Research, and Industrial Applications, vol. 1844, pp. 488–503. CEUR-WS (2017)
18. Zholtkevych, G., Mallet, F., Zaretska, I., Zholtkevych, G.: Two semantic models for clock relations in the clock constraint specification language. In: Ermolayev, V., Mayr, H.C., Nikitchenko, M., Spivakovsky, A., Zholtkevych, G. (eds.) ICTERI 2013. CCIS, vol. 412, pp. 190–209. Springer, Cham (2013). https://doi.org/10.1007/978-3-319-03998-5_10

Extended Floyd-Hoare Logic over Relational Nominative Data

Mykola Nikitchenko[1](✉) ⓘ, Ievgen Ivanov[1],
Artur Korniłowicz[2] ⓘ, and Andrii Kryvolap[1]

[1] Taras Shevchenko National University of Kyiv,
64/13, Volodymyrska Street, Kyiv 01601, Ukraine
nikitchenko@unicyb.kiev.ua, ivanov.eugen@gmail.com, krivolapa@gmail.com
[2] Institute of Informatics, University of Białystok,
Ciołkowskiego 1M, 15-245 Białystok, Poland
arturk@math.uwb.edu.pl

Abstract. The classical Floyd-Hoare logic is defined for the case of total pre- and postconditions and partial programs (i.e. programs can be undefined on some input data, but conditions must be defined on all data). In this paper we propose an extension of this logic for the case of partial conditions and partial programs over structured data. These data are based on two constructing primitives: naming and relational structuring and are called relational nominative data. They can conveniently represent many data structures used in programming. The semantics of the proposed logic is represented by special algebras of partial functions and predicates over relational nominative data. Operations of these algebras are called compositions. We present an inference system for the mentioned logic and propose an approach to its formalization in Mizar proof assistant. The obtained results can be used in software verification.

Keywords: Formal methods · Software verification
Floyd-Hoare logic · Proof assistant · Nominative data · Partial table
Relational database

1 Introduction

Floyd-Hoare logic [1–3] is a formal system widely used for reasoning about program correctness. It is based on the notion of a Floyd-Hoare triple (assertion) which consists of a precondition, a program, and a postcondition and means the following requirement: when input data satisfies the precondition, the program output must satisfy the postcondition, if the program terminates. Specification of program properties in terms of Floyd-Hoare triples is natural and reasoning is convenient thanks to a compositional proof system. A survey of the important results on properties of the Hoare's proof system (soundness, completeness in specific senses) and its extensions was given in [3].

In the classical Floyd-Hoare logic predicates (pre- and postconditions) are assumed to be total (defined on all data) and programs can be partial (in the

ⓒ Springer International Publishing AG, part of Springer Nature 2018
N. Bassiliades et al. (Eds.): ICTERI 2017, CCIS 826, pp. 41–64, 2018.
https://doi.org/10.1007/978-3-319-76168-8_3

sense that if a program does not terminate, its resulting value is undefined). The ability to deal with partiality is an important aspect, because partial operations frequently arise in programming. In most programming languages some basic operations on data such as arithmetic division are already partial. Furthermore, partiality of programs may be caused by non-termination which can arise from loop constructs and/or recursion. For similar reasons partiality can arise in software specifications.

In [4] the following classification of partiality phenomena in software specifications was proposed: *non-termination*, i.e. if evaluation of an expression does not terminate, its value is assumed to be undefined and the operation is considered partial; *error value*, i.e. if some values of an operation's argument are illegal (e.g. division by zero, Pop operation applied to an empty stack, etc.), the result of the operation on such values is assumed to be undefined and the operation is considered partial; and *nondeterminism*, i.e. if a result of an operation on an argument value is not determined uniquely by the specification of this operation (operation is underspecified), the result of application of the operation to such a value is assumed to be undefined and the operation is considered partial. Other opinions on the meanings of partiality in software specifications can be found in [5–7].

In [5] a taxonomy of the ways of dealing with partiality in software specification languages and logics was proposed. Among different approaches notable are excluding partial functions from consideration and providing alternative notations (e.g. graph of a partial function), using a three-valued (many-valued) logic, where the third value represents an undefined result, or making all function applications denote [5]. It should be noted that almost all approaches that try to not allow partial programs and/or predicates that describe program guards or properties explicitly and reduce or translate them to the classical case of total functions and predicates have drawbacks analyzed in detail in [4–6].

A more natural and potentially fruitful approach is to allow partiality in both programs and program specifications and construct non-classical proof systems allowing explicit reasoning about properties of such programs and specifications. This approach is applied in this paper to Floyd-Hoare logic. More specifically, in the classical Floyd-Hoare logic the predicates describing program pre- and postconditions are assumed to be total. But obviously, it is desirable to be able to use partial operations in pre- and postconditions of programs, where partiality may be interpreted in one of the senses proposed in [4]. So it is desirable to obtain an extension of Floyd-Hoare logic that is able to deal with both partial programs and partial predicates.

We consider such an extension in this paper. In the previous works [8,9] we have considered extensions of Floyd-Hoare logic to partial mappings over data represented as partial mappings on named values (called nominative sets) and proposed the corresponding inference systems and investigated their soundness and extensional and intensional completeness. However, nominative sets (which can be considered as partial functions from names to values) naturally represent only a flat data organization in low-level programming. Using Floyd-Hoare logic with partial mappings over nominative sets for reasoning about programs which operate on complex data structures (e.g. trees) is inconvenient, because one needs to take into account many low-level details about data structure implementation. For this reason, in this paper we propose an extension of Floyd-Hoare logic for the case of partial conditions and partial programs on more general class of data. These data are based on two primitives: hierarchical naming and relational structuring and are called relational nominative data. As was shown in [10] hierarchically nominative data are sufficient for representing many data structures (like multidimensional arrays, lists, trees, etc.) that are frequently used in programming. Relational structuring permits to represent partial tables and relations used in relational databases.

To develop such an extension we will adopt the *composition-nominative approach* [11] to program formalization. This approach aims to propose a mathematical basis for development of formal methods of analysis and synthesis of software systems and is grounded on several principles [12], including the *Development principle* (from abstract to concrete), the *Principle of integrity of intensional and extensional aspects*, the *Principle of priority of semantics over syntax*, *Compositionality principle*, and the *Nominativity principle*. The latter Nominativity principle states that *nominative data* adequately represent various forms of data that are processed and stored in computing systems. Nominative data can be considered as a special class of hierarchically organized data. There exist several types of nominative data [12] (with simple or complex names and with simple or complex values), but all of them are based on naming relations that associate names and values. In the composition-nominative approach on the abstract level a computing system is modeled as a partial function that maps nominative data (input data) to nominative data (output data). Such functions are called *binominative*. Properties of data are represented as partial predicates on nominative data. Nominative functions and predicates can be composed in many ways, e.g. by sequential composition, branching, and so on. Operations that construct composed systems from constituents are called *compositions*. A set of compositions together with a set of functions obtained from a chosen set of basic functions by applications of compositions forms an algebraic system (*program algebra*) which is a semantic model of a programming language. The syntax of this language follows naturally from this semantic model: programs are represented as terms of the described algebra.

In accordance with the composition-nominative approach the semantic component of our Floyd-Hoare logic extension will be based on program algebra (a set of functions and predicates on nominative data which can be obtained from some chosen basic functions and predicates using a specific set of compositions). In this paper we generalize the notion of nominative data by adding a new constructing primitive that introduces finite relations (sets of nominative data) as name values. Obtained data are called relational nominative data. Such data permit to model relations considered in relational databases. Thus, the carrier sets of our program algebra will consist of partial functions and predicates over relational nominative data with complex names and complex values [10].

We will treat a Floyd-Hoare triple as a composition with two predicates on relational nominative data and a program (a partial binominative function which belongs to the carrier set of the program algebra) as arguments. The predicates represent pre- and postconditions and the result of the composition is a predicate. However, the classical definition of Floyd-Hoare triple validity leads to Floyd-Hoare composition that is not monotone [8]. Monotonicity is one of the key properties used for reasoning about programs. It is also important for reasoning about loop-free programs and using them as approximations of programs with loops. This explains the need of a special definition of Floyd-Hoare composition for the extension of Floyd-Hoare logic on partial predicates which is monotone, but converges to the classical definition, if predicates are total. Such a definition was presented in [8] and we will adapt it to the case considered in this paper.

To make our Floyd-Hoare logic extension practically applicable for program verification one can implement it in a proof assistant software [13].

Many well known proof assistants (e.g. Isabelle, Coq, PVS, etc.) provide a substantial support for reasoning about total functions, programs, predicates and are convenient for either formulating the classical Floyd-Hoare logic axiomatically, or embedding it in their logics. For example, Isabelle proof assistant includes the "Hoare" HOL (Higher-Order Logic)-based theory that provides an implementation of Hoare logic for a simple imperative programming language with WHILE loops following [14,15]. However, a support of reasoning about programs using partial pre- and postconditions is generally not developed.

We propose an approach to formalization of our extended Floyd-Hoare logic which supports partial pre- and postconditions in the proof assistant Mizar [16,17]. This proof assistant is based on first-order logic and axiomatic set theory (Tarski-Grothendieck set theory [18]). The Mizar system has its own proof verifier[1] used to verify the logical correctness of proofs written in the Mizar language – a declarative language designed to write mathematical documents. It contains rules for writing traditional mathematical items (e.g. definitions, theorems, proof steps, etc.) and also provides syntactic constructions to launch specialized procedures (e.g. term identifications, term reductions [22], flexary connectives [23], definitional expansions [24]) which increase the computational power of the verifier (e.g. equational calculus [25,26], processing properties of functors and predicates [27–29]). An important component of the Mizar system is its library of formalized mathematical theories called Mizar Mathematical Library (MML). It contains developments on various domains of mathematics, including set theory, calculus, topology, lattice theory [30], group theory, category theory, algebra [31], rough sets [32], and others.[2] Consequently, Mizar has well developed tools for working with partial functions and predicates and is well-suited for our purposes. Besides, the Mizar system has a degree of proof

---

[1] Research on using specialized external systems to increase computational power of the Mizar system is also conducted [19–21].

[2] Due to the size, the MML is a subject of research on optimization of theorems and definitions [33]. It includes the improvement of legibility of proofs [34–36] and removing duplications.

automation support such as discovery of a list of proven facts that imply the current goal which may be used as basis for implementing software verification in a semi-automatic mode.

To simplify and partially automate application of Floyd-Hoare logic to proving program properties it is convenient to have a corresponding system of inference rules. The traditional inference system for the language WHILE [37] is sound and extensionally complete for the classical Floyd-Hoare logic with total predicates [37] (extensional completeness means that pre- and postconditions may be arbitrary predicates; intensional completeness means that pre- and postconditions should be presented by formulas of a given language). Soundness and completeness are important for practical applicability of an inference system (if a system is not sound, assertions that can be inferred using this system may be false; if a system is not complete, some of the valid assertions could be impossible to infer). However, this inference system is not sound and complete for partial predicates as was shown in [8].

To deal with the soundness and completeness problems we will modify the traditional inference system for the language WHILE and introduce additional constraints on inference rules that correspond to the new definition of validity of Floyd-Hoare assertions, and investigate its soundness and extensional completeness. The obtained results extend the results concerning inference systems for Floyd-Hoare logic with partial predicates over flat (non-hierarchical) data obtained in [8,9].

The paper is organized in the following way. In Sect. 2 we describe the notion of relational nominative data and define main operations on them. In Sect. 3 we describe our semantics based on Floyd-Hoare logic. In Sect. 4 we specify the syntax of our extended Floyd-Hoare logic. In Sect. 5 we propose an inference system for our logic and consider problems of its soundness and completeness. In Sect. 6 we describe an approach to formalization of our extended Floyd-Hoare logic in Mizar. In Sect. 7 we describe the related work. In Sect. 8 we give conclusions.

2   Algebra of Relational Nominative Data

In the composition-nominative approach data are treated as nominative data. There are several types of nominative data, but all of them are based on naming relations. The simplest type of nominative data is the class of *nominative sets* which are partial mappings from a set of names (program variables) to a set of basic values. Other types of nominative data represent hierarchical data organizations [10]. Here we present the definition of relational nominative data. Before giving such definitions, let us introduce the following notation.

To distinguish total functions from partial we will use the symbol $\xrightarrow{p}$ for partial functions and $\xrightarrow{t}$ for total. We will also use the symbol $\xrightarrow{n}$ for partial functions with finite graphs. For any partial function $f : D \xrightarrow{p} D'$ on some set D:

- $f(d) \downarrow$ denotes that f is defined on $d \in D$;
- $f(d) \downarrow = d'$ denotes that f is defined on $d \in D$ with a value $d' \in D'$;
- $f(d) \uparrow$ denotes that f is undefined on $d \in D$;
- $\mathrm{dom}(f) = \{d \in D \mid f(d) \downarrow\}$ is the domain of a function (note that in different branches of mathematics there exist different definitions of the domain of a partial function; we will adopt the convention used in recursion theory).

We will denote by $f_1(d_1) \cong f_2(d_2)$ the *strong equality*, i.e. the condition that $f_1(d_1) \downarrow$ if and only if $f_2(d_2) \downarrow$, and if $f_1(d_1) \downarrow$, then $f_1(d_1) = f_2(d_2)$.

For any nonempty set V we will denote by V^+ the set of all nonempty finite sequences (*words*) of elements of V. For any word $u \in V^+$ we will denote by $|u|$ its length. If $u, v \in V^+$, we will denote by uv the concatenation of u and v. We will write $u \le v$, if u is a prefix of v, and $u < v$, if $u \le v$, $u \ne v$.

For any set of names V and a set of basic values (atoms) A the corresponding class $^V A$ of *nominative sets* is defined as

$$^V A = V \xrightarrow{p} A.$$

We chose V to denote the set of names because we are oriented on mathematical logic where V is practically standard notation for a set of variables (names). We will use the following notations for nominative sets:

- $[v_1 \mapsto a_1, \ldots, v_n \mapsto a_n]$, where $v_1, \ldots,$ v_n are names from V and $a_1, \ldots,$ a_n are atoms from A, denotes a nominative set with the graph $\{(v_1, a_1), \ldots, (v_n, a_n)\}$;
- $[v_i \mapsto a_i | i \in I]$, where I is some set of indices, means a nominative set with the graph $\{(v_i, a_i) \mid i \in I\}$;
- $v \mapsto a \in d$, where d is a nominative set, means that $d(v) \downarrow = a$, i.e. the value of the variable v in d is a;
- $[]$ denotes the empty nominative set (a nowhere defined function).

Relational nominative data are built over classes of names V and basic values A using a naming construction of the form $[v_1 \mapsto d_1, \ldots, v_n \mapsto d_n]$, and a relational construction of the form $\{d_1, \ldots, d_n\}$ where $v_1, \ldots, v_n$ are different names from V and $d_1, \ldots, d_n$ are either atoms or other relational nominative data.

Relational nominative data are classified in accordance with the following parameters [10]: *names* can be simple (unstructured) or complex (structured), *values* can be simple (unstructured) or complex (structured). Within the class of complex structured values we distinguish the class of relational values of the form $\{d_1, \ldots, d_n\}$. To define the notion of a complex name we will use the Development principle (from abstract to concrete) and consider the simplest case of name construction: complex names are *sequences* of simple names which satisfy the associativity property [10]. More specifically, we will assume that complex names are constructed with the help of concatenation operation (which is associative). We will adopt the following *Principle of associative construction and processing of complex names* [10]: complex names are constructed from simple names using concatenation, and data with complex names must be processed by operations that take into account associativity of names. Moreover, we will require that data with complex names satisfy the *Principle of unambiguous associative naming* [10]: one complex name must have at most one corresponding value in any given data.

Let us give the formal definition of the class $RND(V, A)$ of relational nominative data with complex names and complex values. We will assume that V and A are fixed nonempty sets of *simple names* and *basic values*. We will call the elements of V^+ *complex names*.

First, we define

$$RNDs(V, A) = \bigcup_{k \geq 0} RNDs_k(V, A),$$

where

$$RNDs_0(V, A) = A \cup \{[]\},$$

$$RNDs_{k+1}(V, A) = RNDs_k(V, A) \cup (V^+ \xrightarrow{n} RNDs_k(V, A)) \cup R(RNDs_k(V, A)).$$

Here $\xrightarrow{n}$ denotes a constructor of nominative sets and R denotes a construction of finite relations:

$$R(X) = \{Y \subseteq X \mid Y \text{ is finite}\}.$$

The class $RNDs(V, A)$ uses complex names in its construction, but possible ambiguity of naming is not taken into consideration. Thus, we add additional restrictions to obtain the class $RND(V, A)$.

Naming structure can be represented by oriented trees with arcs labeled by names and leafs labeled by atoms, empty nominative set, or relations. We will call any finite sequence of names $p = (v_1, v_2, \ldots, v_k)$ a *path*. A *path in a given data* $d \in RNDs(V, A)$ is a path $(v_1, v_2, \ldots, v_k)$ such that the value of the expression $(\ldots((d(v_1))(v_2))\ldots(v_k))$ is defined (it corresponds to a path from the root to some vertex in a tree). If $pt = (v_1, v_2, \ldots, v_k)$ is a path in d, we will say that $(\ldots((d(v_1))(v_2))\ldots(v_k))$ is the value of pt in d and denote it as $d(v_1, v_2, \ldots, v_k)$.

A *terminal path* is a path with atomic, empty value or relational value.

Data of the class $RND(V, A)$ are elements of the set $RNDs(V, A)$ such that for any d and any two paths $(u_1, u_2, \ldots, u_k)$ and $(v_1, v_2, \ldots, v_l)$ in d, neither of which is a prefix of another, words $u_1 u_2 \ldots u_k$ and $v_1 v_2 \ldots v_l$ are incomparable in the sense of prefix relation (*principle of unambiguous associative naming*). This principle should be applied to all subdata within d.

In [10] it was shown how conventional data structures can be represented by different kinds of relational nominative data.

Let $Nd(V, A) = (V^+ \xrightarrow{n} RND(V, A)) \cap RND(V, A)$ and

$$Rd(V, A) = R(RND(V, A))$$

be the subclasses of $RND(V, A)$ called classes of nominative and relational data respectively.

The main operations on nominative data consist of operations over nominative data and operations over relational data. Operations over nominative data are operations of *denaming* (taking a value of a name), *naming* (assigning a new value to a name), and *overlapping* (overwriting).

The *nominative rank* of $d \in RND(V, A)$ is the greatest length of terminal paths in d. For any word $u \in V^+$ and any data $d \in RND(V, A)$ let us denote

$$d/u = [v_1 \mapsto d(v) \mid d(v) \downarrow, v = uv_1, v_1 \in V^+]$$

(*division* of d by u).

Definition 1. *Associative denaming*

$$v \Rightarrow_a: RND(V, A) \xrightarrow{p} RND(V, A)$$

is an operation with a parameter $v \in V^+$. On $Rd(V, A)$ it is undefined, and on $Nd(V, A)$ is defined by induction on the length of v as follows:

- *if $|v| = 1$, then $v \Rightarrow_a (d) = d(v)$, if $d(v) \downarrow$; $v \Rightarrow_a (d) = d/v$ if $d(v) \uparrow$ and $d/v \neq [], and $v \Rightarrow_a (d) \uparrow$ otherwise.*
- *if $|v| = n > 1$, then $v \Rightarrow_a (d) \cong v_1 \Rightarrow_a (x \Rightarrow_a (d))$,*
  where $v = xv_1$, $x \in V$, $v_1 \in V^{n-1}$ (principle of associative denaming).

For example,

$$uv \Rightarrow_a ([u \mapsto [vw \mapsto 1, u \mapsto 2]]) = [w \mapsto 1].$$

It is easy to check that $v \Rightarrow_a$ satisfies the following property (associativity)

$$u \Rightarrow_a (d) \cong u_n \Rightarrow_a (u_{n-1} \Rightarrow_a (\dots u_1 \Rightarrow_a (d) \dots))$$

for all complex names $u, u_1, u_2, \dots, u_n \in V^+$ such that $u = u_1 u_2 \dots u_n$.

Definition 2. *Naming is an operation*

$$\Rightarrow v : RND(V, A) \xrightarrow{t} RND(V, A)$$

with a parameter $v \in V^+$ such that

$$\Rightarrow v(d) = [v \mapsto d].$$

Overlapping can be considered as an operation which updates values in the first argument with the values from the second argument. It joins two data and resolves name conflicts in favor of its second argument. We will define two kinds of overlapping: global and local. Global overlapping can be used for formalization of procedure calls and the local overlapping formalizes the assignment operator in programming languages.

Definition 3. *Global overlapping is a binary operation*

$$\nabla_a : RND(V, A) \times RND(V, A) \xrightarrow{p} RND(V, A)$$

defined inductively by the nominative rank of the first argument as follows.

Let $Nd_k(V, A)$ be the class of data with the nominative rank not greater than k.

Induction base. If $d_1 \in Nd_0(V, A)$, then

$$d_1 \nabla_a d_2 \cong \begin{cases} d_2, & d_1 = [] \text{ and } d_2 \in Nd(V, A) \backslash A; \\ undefined, & \text{in other cases} \end{cases}$$

Induction step. Assume that the value $d_1 \nabla_a d_2$ is defined for all d_1, d_2 such that $d_1 \in Nd_k(V, A)$. Let $d_1 \in Nd_{k+1}(V, A)$ and $d_1 \notin Nd_k(V, A)$. Then $d_1 \nabla_a d_2 = d$, where $d \in Nd(V, A)$ is defined by its values on names $u \in V^+$:

- *$d(u) = d_2(u)$, if $u \in \text{dom}(d_2)$ and u does not have a proper prefix which belongs to $\text{dom}(d_1)$;*
- *$d(u) = d_1(u) \nabla_a(d_2/u)$, if $d_1(u) \downarrow$ and $d_1(u) \notin A$, and u is a proper prefix of some element of $\text{dom}(d_2)$;*
- *$d(u) = d_2/u$, if $d_1(u) \downarrow$ and $d_1(u) \in A$, and u is a proper prefix of some element of $\text{dom}(d_2)$;*
- *$d(u) = d_1(u)$, if $d_1(u) \downarrow$ and u is not comparable (in the sense of prefix relation) with any element of $\text{dom}(d_2)$;*
- *$d(u) \uparrow$, otherwise.*

The following examples illustrate this operation:

1. $[u \mapsto d_1] \nabla_a [v \mapsto d_2] = [u \mapsto d_1, v \mapsto d_2]$, if u, v are incomparable in the sense of prefix relation;
2. $[uv \mapsto d_1] \nabla_a [u \mapsto d_2] = [u \mapsto d_2]$, i.e. a value of a name in the second argument overwrites the value of extension of this name in the first argument;
3. $[u \mapsto d_1] \nabla_a [uv \mapsto d_2] = [u \mapsto (d_1 \nabla_a [v \mapsto d_2])]$ $(d_1 \notin A)$, i.e., a value of a name in the second argument modifies values of prefixes of this name in the first argument.

Definition 4. *Local overlapping is an operation*

$$\nabla_a^v : RND(V, A) \xrightarrow{p} RND(V, A)$$

with a parameter $v \in V^+$ such that

$$d_1 \nabla_a^v d_2 \cong d_1 \nabla_a(\Rightarrow v(d_2)).$$

For example, $[u \mapsto 1] \nabla_a^v [w \mapsto 2] = [u \mapsto 1, v \mapsto [w \mapsto 2]]$.

Now we define operations that operate also on relational data. Therefore we consider two cases: data is a nominative data and data is a relational data. Nominative data are often considered as sets.

Definition 5. *Union $\cup$ is an operation*

$$\cup : RND(V, A) \times RND(V, A) \xrightarrow{p} RND(V, A)$$

defined for any $d_1, d_2 \in RND(V, A)$ in the following way:

- $d_1 \cup d_2 = [v \mapsto d' | v \mapsto d' \in d_1$ *or* $v \mapsto d' \in d_2]$, *if* $d_1, d_2 \in Nd(V, A)$ *and names from* $\mathrm{dom}(d_1)$ *and* $\mathrm{dom}(d_2)$ *are pairwise incomparable;*
- $d_1 \cup d_2 = \{d' | d' \in d_1$ *or* $d' \in d_2\}$, *if* $d_1, d_2 \in Rd(V, A)$;
- *undefined in other cases.*

An example of the union of elements of $Nd(V, A)$: if

$$d_1 = [x_1 \mapsto 1, x_2 \mapsto 2], \quad d_2 = [x_3 \mapsto 3, x_4 \mapsto 4],$$

then $d_1 \cup d_2 = [x_1 \mapsto 1, x_2 \mapsto 2, x_3 \mapsto 3, x_4 \mapsto 4]$.
An example of the union of elements of $Rd(V, A)$: if

$$d_1 = \{[u \mapsto 1, v \mapsto 2], [u \mapsto 3, v \mapsto 4]\},$$

$$d_2 = \{[u \mapsto 5, v \mapsto 6], [u \mapsto 7, v \mapsto 8]\},$$

then $d_1 \cup d_2 = \{[u \mapsto 1, v \mapsto 2], [u \mapsto 3, v \mapsto 4], [u \mapsto 5, v \mapsto 6], [u \mapsto 7, v \mapsto 8]\}$.

Definition 6. *Difference $\setminus$ is an operation*

$$\setminus : RND(V, A) \times RND(V, A) \xrightarrow{p} RND(V, A)$$

defined for any $d_1, d_2 \in RND(V, A)$ in the following way:

- $d_1 \setminus d_2 = [v \mapsto d' | v \mapsto d' \in d_1$ *and* $v \mapsto d' \notin d_2]$, *if* $d_1, d_2 \in Nd(V, A)$;
- $d_1 \setminus d_2 = \{d' | d' \in d_1$ *and* $d' \notin d_2\}$, *if* $d_1, d_2 \in Rd(V, A)$;
- *undefined in other cases.*

An example of the difference of elements of $Nd(V, A)$: if

$$d_1 = [x_1 \mapsto 1, x_2 \mapsto 2], \quad d_2 = [x_1 \mapsto 1, x_4 \mapsto 4],$$

then $d_1 \setminus d_2 = [x_2 \mapsto 2]$.
An example of the difference of elements of $Rd(V, A)$: if

$$d_1 = \{[u \mapsto 1, v \mapsto 2], [u \mapsto 3, v \mapsto 4]\},$$

$$d_2 = \{[u \mapsto 1, v \mapsto 2], [u \mapsto 5, v \mapsto 6]\},$$

then $d_1 \setminus d_2 = \{[u \mapsto 3, v \mapsto 4]\}$.

Definition 7. *Product $\otimes$ is an operation*

$$\otimes : RND(V, A) \times RND(V, A) \xrightarrow{p} RND(V, A)$$

defined for any $d_1, d_2 \in RND(V, A)$ in the following way:

- $d_1 \otimes d_2 = \{d_1' \cup d_2' \mid d_1' \in d_1, d_2' \in d_2\}$, if $d_1, d_2 \in Rd(V, A)$;
- *undefined in other cases.*

An example of the product of elements of $Rd(V, A)$: if

$$d_1 = \{[u \mapsto 1, v \mapsto 2], [u \mapsto 3, v \mapsto 4]\}, d_2 = \{[w \mapsto 3]\},$$

then $d_1 \otimes d_2 = \{[u \mapsto 1, v \mapsto 2, w \mapsto 3], [u \mapsto 3, v \mapsto 4, w \mapsto 3]\}$.

Definition 8. *Projection $\pi^{v_1,\ldots,v_n}$ is an operation*

$$\pi^{v_1,\ldots,v_n} : RND(V, A) \xrightarrow{p} RND(V, A)$$

with parameters $v_1, \ldots, v_n \in V^+$ such that $v_1, \ldots, v_n$ are pairwise incomparable names, defined for any $d \in RND(V, A)$ in the following way:

- $\pi^{v_1,\ldots,v_n}(d) = [v \mapsto d(v)\mid v \in \{v_1, \ldots, v_n\}, v \in \text{dom}(d)]$, *if $d \in Nd(V, A)$;*
- $\pi^{v_1,\ldots,v_n}(d) = \{\pi^{v_1,\ldots,v_n}(d')\mid d' \in d, d' \in Nd(V, A)\}$, *if $d \in Rd(V, A)$;*
- *undefined in other cases.*

An example of the projection of elements of $Nd(V, A)$: if

$$d = [x_1 \mapsto [a \mapsto 1, b \mapsto 2], x_2 \mapsto [a \mapsto 1, c \mapsto 2], x_3 \mapsto []],$$

then $\pi^{x_1,x_3}(d) = [x_1 \mapsto [a \mapsto 1, b \mapsto 2], x_3 \mapsto []]$.

An example of the projection of elements of $Rd(V, A)$: if

$$d = \{[u \mapsto 1, v \mapsto 2], [u \mapsto 3, v \mapsto 4]\},$$

then $\pi^v(d) = \{[v \mapsto 2], [v \mapsto 4]\}$.

Definition 9. *Deleting $\delta^{v_1,\ldots,v_n}$ is an operation*

$$\delta^{v_1,\ldots,v_n} : RND(V, A) \xrightarrow{p} RND(V, A)$$

with parameters $v_1, \ldots, v_n \in V^+$ defined for any $d \in RND(V, A)$ in the following way:

- $\delta^{v_1,\ldots,v_n}(d) = [u \mapsto d(u) \mid u \in \text{dom}(d), u \notin \{v_1, \ldots, v_n\}]$, *if $d \in Nd(V, A)$;*
- $\delta^{v_1,\ldots,v_n}(d) = \{\delta^{v_1,\ldots,v_n}(d') \mid d' \in d, d' \in Rd(V, A)\}$, *if $d \in Rd(V, A)$;*
- *undefined in other cases.*

An example of an application of deletion to elements of $Nd(V, A)$: if

$$d = [x_1 \mapsto [a \mapsto 1, b \mapsto 2], x_2 \mapsto [a \mapsto 1, c \mapsto 2], x_3 \mapsto []],$$

then $\delta^{x_2}(d) = [x_1 \mapsto [a \mapsto 1, b \mapsto 2], x_3 \mapsto []]$.

An example of an application of deletion to elements of $Rd(V, A)$: if

$$d = \{[u \mapsto 1, v \mapsto 2], [u \mapsto 3, v \mapsto 4]\},$$

then $\delta^u(d) = \{[v \mapsto 2], [v \mapsto 4]\}$.

Definition 10. *Renaming* $r_{u_1,\ldots,u_n}^{v_1,\ldots,v_n}$ *is an operation*

$$r_{u_1,\ldots,u_n}^{v_1,\ldots,v_n} : RND(V,A) \xrightarrow{p} RND(V,A)$$

with parameters $v_1,\ldots,v_n, u_1,\ldots,u_n \in V^+$ *such that* $v_1,\ldots,v_n$ *are pairwise incomparable names, defined for any* $d \in RND(V,A)$ *in the following way:*

- $r_{u_1,\ldots,u_n}^{v_1,\ldots,v_n}(d) = \delta^{v_1,\ldots,v_n}(d) \cup [v \mapsto d(u) \mid u \in \mathrm{dom}(d)], \text{ if } d \in Nd(V,A);$
- $r_{u_1,\ldots,u_n}^{v_1,\ldots,v_n}(d) = \{r_{u_1,\ldots,u_n}^{v_1,\ldots,v_n}(d') \mid d' \in d, d' \in Rd(V,A)\}, \text{ if } d \in Rd(V,A);$
- *undefined in other cases.*

An example of application of renaming to elements of $Nd(V,A)$: if

$$d = [x_1 \mapsto [a \mapsto 1], x_2 \mapsto [a \mapsto 1, b \mapsto 2]],$$

then $r_{x_1,x_2}^{y_1,x_1}(d) = [x_2 \mapsto [a \mapsto 1, b \mapsto 2], y_1 \mapsto [a \mapsto 1], x_1 \mapsto [a \mapsto 1, b \mapsto 2]]$.
An example of application of renaming to elements of $Rd(V,A)$: if

$$d = \{[v \mapsto 2], [v \mapsto 4]\},$$

then $r_v^u(d) = \{[v \mapsto 2, u \mapsto 2], [v \mapsto 4, u \mapsto 4]\}$.

Definition 11. *Natural join* $\bowtie$ *is an operation*

$$\bowtie: RND(V,A) \times RND(V,A) \xrightarrow{p} RND(V,A)$$

defined for any $d_1, d_2 \in RND(V,A)$ *in the following way:*

- $d_1 \bowtie d_2 = d_1 \cup d_2,$
  if $d_1, d_2 \in Nd(V,A)$ *and* $d_1(v) = d_2(v)$ *for any* $v \in \mathrm{dom}(d_1) \cap \mathrm{dom}(d_2);$
- $d_1 \bowtie d_2 = \{d_1' \bowtie d_2' \mid d_1' \in d_1, d_2' \in d_2, d_1' \bowtie d_2' \text{ is defined}\},$
  if $d_1, d_2 \in Rd(V,A);$
- *undefined in other cases.*

An example of the natural join of elements of $Nd(V,A)$: if

$$d_1 = [x \mapsto 1, y \mapsto 2], \quad d_2 = [y \mapsto 2, z \mapsto 3],$$

then $d_1 \bowtie d_2 = [x \mapsto 1, y \mapsto 2, z \mapsto 3]$.
An example of the natural join of elements of $Rd(V,A)$: if

$$d_1 = \{[u \mapsto 1, v \mapsto 2], [u \mapsto 3, v \mapsto 4]\},$$

$$d_2 = \{[v \mapsto 2, w \mapsto 3]\},$$

then $d_1 \bowtie d_2 = \{[u \mapsto 1, v \mapsto 2, w \mapsto 3]\}$.

Definition 12. *Division* $\div$ *is an operation*

$$\div : RND(V,A) \times RND(V,A) \xrightarrow{p} RND(V,A)$$

defined for any $d_1, d_2 \in RND(V,A)$ *as:*

$$d_1 \div d_2 \cong \bigcup\{d \in RND(V,A) \mid d \otimes d_2 \subseteq d_1\}.$$

An example of the division of elements of $Rd(V, A)$: if

$$d_1 = \{[u \mapsto 1, v \mapsto 1], [u \mapsto 1, v \mapsto 2], [u \mapsto 2, v \mapsto 1]\},$$

$$d_2 = \{[v \mapsto 2]\},$$

then $d_1 \div d_2 = \{[u \mapsto 1]\}$.

Definition 13. *An algebra of relational nominative data $RNDA(V, A)$ is an algebra with the carrier $RND(V, A)$ and the operations*

$$\Rightarrow v, v \Rightarrow_a, \nabla_a^v, \cup, \backslash, \otimes, \pi^{v_1,\ldots,v_n}, \delta^{v_1,\ldots,v_n}, r_{u_1,\ldots,u_n}^{v_1,\ldots,v_n}, \bowtie, \div.$$

3   Semantics of Extended Floyd-Hoare Logic

We treat programs as being defined over nominative data.

Let $Bool = \{F, T\}$ be the set of Boolean values, $Pr^{V,A} = RND(V, A) \xrightarrow{p} Bool$ be the set of *partial predicates*. They can be used to represent semantics of conditions in programs.

Let $FPrg^{V,A} = Nd(V, A) \xrightarrow{p} Nd(V, A)$. The elements of $FPrg^{V,A}$ are called *binominative functions*. They can be used to represent semantics of programs.

Multi-sorted algebras on sets of partial predicates and partial binominative functions can be used to define semantics of program logics [11,38]. The operations of such algebras will be called *compositions*.

There are many possible ways to define compositions that provide means to construct complex programs from simpler ones. We have chosen the following compositions to include them as basic to the logics of program level (level of binominative functions):

- parametric assignment composition AS^x which corresponds to assignment operator := ;
- composition of identical program *id* which corresponds to the *skip* operator of the WHILE language;
- composition of sequential execution •;
- conditional composition *IF* which corresponds to the *if-then-else* operator;
- cycle (loop) composition *WH* which corresponds to the *while-do* operator;
- superpositions $S_F^{\bar{x}}$ which correspond to procedure calls.

We also need compositions that provide the possibility to construct different kinds of expressions (functions) and conditions (predicates) that are program components. Thus, we will include into the list of compositions superposition compositions.

Finally, to construct predicates describing properties of programs we define the Floyd-Hoare composition *FH*. It takes a precondition, a postcondition, and a program as inputs and yields a predicate that represents respective Floyd-Hoare assertion. We will also define a composition of *preimage predicate transformer* inspired by weakest precondition introduced by Dijkstra [39].

Let us give definitions of the mentioned compositions.

Definition 14. *Disjunction is a binary composition*

$$\vee : Pr^{V,A} \times Pr^{V,A} \xrightarrow{t} Pr^{V,A}$$

such that for all $p, q \in Pr^{V,A}$ and $d \in RND(V, A)$:

$$(p \vee q)(d) = \begin{cases} T, \text{ if } p(d) \downarrow = T \text{ or } q(d) \downarrow = T, \\ F, \text{ if } p(d) \downarrow = F \text{ and } q(d) \downarrow = F, \\ \text{undefined in other cases.} \end{cases}$$

Definition 15. *Negation is a unary composition*

$$\neg : Pr^{V,A} \xrightarrow{t} Pr^{V,A}$$

such that for all $p \in Pr^{V,A}$ and $d \in RND(V, A)$:

$$(\neg p)(d) = \begin{cases} F, \text{ if } p(d) \downarrow = T, \\ T, \text{ if } p(d) \downarrow = F, \\ \text{undefined in other cases.} \end{cases}$$

We will consider *conjunction* $p \wedge q$ of predicates p, q as an abbreviation for $\neg(\neg p \vee \neg q)$.

Definition 16. *Existential quantification over hierarchical data is a unary composition*

$$\exists x : Pr^{V,A} \xrightarrow{t} Pr^{V,A}$$

with a parameter $x \in V^+$ such that for all $p \in Pr^{V,A}$ and $d \in RND(V, A)$:

$$(\exists x \, p)(d) = \begin{cases} T, \text{ if } p(d\nabla_a^x d') \downarrow = T \text{ for some } d' \in RND(V, A), \\ F, \text{ if } p(d\nabla_a^x d') \downarrow = F \text{ for all } d' \in RND(V, A), \\ \text{undefined in other cases.} \end{cases}$$

For each $n = 1, 2, 3, \ldots$ denote by $\bar{U}_n(V)$ the set of all tuples $(x_1, \ldots, x_n) \in (V^+)^n$ of n complex names such that $x_1, x_2, \ldots, x_n$ are pairwise incomparable in the sense of prefix relation $\le$.

Also, let us denote $\bar{U}(V) = \bigcup_{n=1}^{\infty} \bar{U}_n(V)$.

Definition 17. *For each $n = 1, 2, 3, \ldots$, superposition of n functions into a function is a $n+1$-ary composition*

$$S_F^{\bar{x}} : (FPrg^{V,A})^{n+1} \xrightarrow{t} FPrg^{V,A}$$

with a parameter $\bar{x} = (x_1, \ldots, x_n) \in \bar{U}_n(V)$ such that for all $f, g_1, \ldots, g_n \in FPrg^{V,A}$ and $d \in RND(V, A)$:

$$S_F^{\bar{x}}(f, g_1, \ldots, g_n)(d) \cong f(d\nabla_a[x_1 \mapsto g_1(d), \ldots, x_n \mapsto g_n(d)]).$$

Definition 18. *For each* $n = 1, 2, 3, \ldots$, *superposition of* n *functions into a predicate is a* $n+1$-*ary composition*

$$S_P^{\bar{x}} : Pr^{V,A} \times (FPrg^{V,A})^n \xrightarrow{t} Pr^{V,A}$$

with a parameter $\bar{x} = (x_1, \ldots, x_n) \in \bar{U}_n(V)$ *such that for all* $p \in Pr^{V,A}$, $g_1, \ldots, g_n \in FPrg^{V,A}$, *and* $d \in RND(V, A)$:

$$S_P^{\bar{x}}(p, g_1, \ldots, g_n)(d) \cong p(d\nabla_a[x_1 \mapsto g_1(d), \ldots, x_n \mapsto g_n(d)]).$$

Definition 19. *Denomination is a null-ary composition* $'x : FPrg^{V,A}$ *with a parameter* $x \in V^+$ *such that for each* $d \in RND(V, A)$:

$$'x(d) \cong x \Rightarrow_a (d).$$

Definition 20. *Assignment over hierarchical data is a composition*

$$AS^x : FPrg^{V,A} \xrightarrow{t} FPrg^{V,A}$$

with a parameter $x \in V^+$ *such that for each* $f \in FPrg^{V,A}$ *and* $d \in RND(V, A)$:

$$AS^x(f)(d) \cong d\nabla_a^x f(d).$$

Definition 21. *Identity program composition is a null-ary composition* $id : FPrg^{V,A}$ *such that for each* $d \in RND(V, A)$:

$$id(d) = d.$$

Definition 22. *Sequential execution is a binary composition*

$$\bullet : FPrg^{V,A} \times FPrg^{V,A} \xrightarrow{t} FPrg^{V,A}$$

such that for all $f, g \in FPrg^{V,A}$ *and* $d \in RND(V, A)$:

$$(f \bullet g)(d) \cong g(f(d)).$$

Definition 23. *Branching is a ternary composition*

$$IF : Pr^{V,A} \times FPrg^{V,A} \times FPrg^{V,A} \xrightarrow{t} FPrg^{V,A}$$

such that for all $r \in Pr^{V,A}$ *(condition)*, $f, g \in FPrg^{V,A}$ *(branches bodies), and* $d \in RND(V, A)$:

$$IF(r, f, g)(d) = \begin{cases} f(d), & \text{if } r(d) \downarrow = T \text{ and } f(d) \downarrow, \\ g(d), & \text{if } r(d) \downarrow = F \text{ and } g(d) \downarrow, \\ \text{undefined in other cases.} \end{cases}$$

Definition 24. *While cycle is a binary composition*

$$WH : Pr^{V,A} \times FPrg^{V,A} \xrightarrow{t} FPrg^{V,A}$$

such that for each $p \in Pr^{V,A}$ (condition), $f \in FPrg^{V,A}$ (loop body), and $d \in RND(V, A)$:

$$WH(p, f)(d) \downarrow= f^{(n)}(d),$$

if $n \geq 0$ such that $p(f^{(i)}(d)) \downarrow= T$ for all $i = 0, 1, \ldots, n-1$ and $p(f^{(n)}(d)) \downarrow= F$, where $f^{(i)}$ denotes $\underbrace{f \bullet f \bullet \cdots \bullet f}_{i}$ and $f^{(0)} = id$; and $WH(p, f)(d) \uparrow$, otherwise.

Definition 25. *Monotone Floyd-Hoare composition*

$$FH : Pr^{V,A} \times FPrg^{V,A} \times Pr^{V,A} \xrightarrow{t} Pr^{V,A}$$

is a composition such that for all $p, q \in Pr^{V,A}$ (pre- and postcondition), $f \in FPrg^{V,A}$ (program), and $d \in RND(V, A)$:

$$FH(p, f, q)(d) = \begin{cases} T, \text{ if } p(d) \downarrow= F \text{ or } q(f(d)) \downarrow= T, \\ F, \text{ if } p(d) \downarrow= T \text{ and } q(f(d)) \downarrow= F, \\ \text{undefined in other cases.} \end{cases}$$

Definition 26. *Predicate transformer composition is a binary composition*

$$PC : FPrg^{V,A} \times Pr^{V,A} \xrightarrow{t} Pr^{V,A}$$

such that for all $q \in Pr^{V,A}$, $f \in FPrg^{V,A}$, and $d \in RND(V, A)$:

$$PC(f, q)(d) = \begin{cases} T, \text{ if } f(d) \downarrow \text{ and } q(f(d)) \downarrow= T, \\ F, \text{ if } f(d) \downarrow \text{ and } q(f(d)) \downarrow= F, \\ \text{undefined in other cases.} \end{cases}$$

Predicate transformer composition is the same as *Glushkov prediction operation* (sequential execution of a function and a predicate). We call this composition (defined for partial predicates) as preimage predicate transformer composition in order to relate it to the *weakest precondition* predicate transformer [39]. Note that $FH(p, pr, q) = p \rightarrow PC(pr, q)$.

The Floyd-Hoare composition is called monotone, because it satisfies the following property, as was shown in [8]:

$$p \subseteq p', q \subseteq q', f \subseteq f' \Rightarrow FH(p, f, q) \subseteq FH(p', f', q'),$$

where inclusion $\subseteq$ is understood as inclusion of the graphs of functions and predicates.

We also need to raise the level of $RNDA(V, A)$ operations to the level of compositions. It means, that operations $\Rightarrow v$, $v \Rightarrow_a$ we treat as nullary compositions of the type $FPrg^{V,A}$, operations $\cup$, $\setminus$, $\bowtie$ as binary compositions of the type $FPrg^{V,A} \times FPrg^{V,A} \xrightarrow{t} FPrg^{V,A}$, and $\pi^{v_1,\ldots,v_n}$, $\delta^{v_1,\ldots,v_n}$, $r^{v_1,\ldots,v_n}_{u_1,\ldots,u_n}$ as unary compositions of the type $FPrg^{V,A} \xrightarrow{t} FPrg^{V,A}$. We will use the same symbols both for data algebra operations and compositions.

Definition 27. *A relational nominative program algebra $RNPA(V, A)$ is a two-sorted algebra $< Pr^{V,A}, FPrg^{V,A};\ \vee, \neg, \exists x, S_P^{\bar{x}}, S_F^{\bar{x}},' x, id, AS^x, \bullet, IF, WH,\ FH,$ $PC,\ \Rightarrow v, v \Rightarrow_a, \nabla_a^v, \cup, \backslash, \otimes, \pi^{v_1,...,v_n}, \delta^{v_1,...,v_n}, r_{u_1,...,u_n}^{v_1,...,v_n}, \bowtie, \div >$.*

This algebra is the semantic base of our extension of Floyd-Hoare logic to partial predicates and (hierarchical) nominative data with complex names and complex values.

4   Syntax and Interpretation

Algebra $RNPA(V, A)$ has strong expressive power that is not required for our goal: to construct a special program logic. Therefore we restrict syntactically the class of terms of this algebra. The idea is to consider programs as binominative functions constructed with the help of compositions $id, AS^x, \bullet, IF, WH,$ $S_F^{\bar{x}}$. Functions of other types (including relational data) can be represented by functional expressions. Formulas represent nominative predicates. The signature of the constructed logic is $\Sigma = (V, Ps, FEs, Prgs)$ where $Ps, FEs, Prgs$ are sets of predicates, functions, and program symbols.

Let us give definitions of the sets of program texts Pt^{Σ}, formulas Fr^{Σ}, functional expressions FEx^{Σ}, and Floyd-Hoare assertions $FHFr^{\Sigma}$.

The sets Pt^{Σ}, FE^{Σ}, and Fr^{Σ} are defined inductively (here we use the symbols of compositions in the purely syntactic sense, i.e. they are currently not associated with semantics, also, for parameters from V^+ respective restrictions hold):

1. if $prs \in Prs$, then $prs \in Fr^{\Sigma}$;
2. if $fes \in FEs$, then $fes \in FE^{\Sigma}$;
3. if $prgs \in Prgs$, then $prgs \in Pt^{\Sigma}$;
4. if $\Phi, \Psi \in Fr^{\Sigma}$, then $\Phi \vee \Psi, \neg\Phi, \exists x \in Fr^{\Sigma}$;
5. if $fe, fe_1, fe_2 \in FEs$, then $\Rightarrow v, v \Rightarrow_a, 'x, fe_1 \nabla_a^v fe_2, fe_1 \cup fe_2, fe_1 \backslash fe_2,$ $\otimes, \pi^{v_1,...,v_n}(fe), \delta^{v_1,...,v_n}(fe), r_{u_1,...,u_n}^{v_1,...,v_n}(fe), fe_1 \bowtie fe_2 \in FE^{\Sigma}$;
6. if $\Phi \in Fr^{\Sigma}$ and $fe \in FE^{\Sigma}$, then $\sigma(\Phi, fe) \in FE^{\Sigma}$;
7. if $n \geq 1$, $\Phi \in Fr^{\Sigma}$, $fe_1, \ldots, fe_n \in FE^{\Sigma}$, and $\bar{x} \in \bar{U}_n(V)$, then $S_P^{\bar{x}}(\Phi, fe_1, \ldots, fe_n) \in Fr^{\Sigma}$;
8. if $n \geq 1$, $fe, fe_1, \ldots, fe_n \in FE^{\Sigma}$, and $\bar{x} \in \bar{U}_n(V)$, then $S_F^{\bar{x}}(fe, fe_1, \ldots, fe_n) \in FE^{\Sigma}$;
9. if $n \geq 1$, $prg \in Pt^{\Sigma}$, $fe_1, \ldots, fe_n \in FE^{\Sigma}$, and $\bar{x} \in \bar{U}_n(V)$, then $S_F^{\bar{x}}(prg, fe_1, \ldots, fe_n) \in Pt^{\Sigma}$;
10. if $x \in V^+$ and $fe \in FE^{\Sigma}$, then $AS^x(fe) \in Pt^{\Sigma}$;
11. $id \in Pt^{\Sigma}$;
12. if $prg_1, prg_2 \in Pt^{\Sigma}$, then $pr_1 \bullet pr_2 \in Pt^{\Sigma}$;
13. if $\Phi \in Fr^{\Sigma}$ and $prg_1, prg_2 \in Pt^{\Sigma}$, then $IF(\Phi, prg_1, prg_2) \in Pt^{\Sigma}$;
14. if $\Phi \in Fr^{\Sigma}$ and $prg \in Pt^{\Sigma}$, then $WH(\Phi, prg) \in Pt^{\Sigma}$.

The set $FHFr^{\Sigma}$ is the set of all formulas of the form $\{p\}f\{q\}$, where $p,$ $q \in Fr^{\Sigma}$ and $f \in Pt^{\Sigma}$.

Definition 28. *Let* $\Sigma = (V, Ps, FEs, Prgs)$ *be a logic signature and* A *be an arbitrary set. Then an interpretation* J *is a tuple* $(RNPA(V, A), I_{Ps}, I_{FEs},$ $I_{Prgs})$, *where* $I_{Ps} : Ps \xrightarrow{t} Pr^{V,A}$ *is an interpretation mapping for predicate symbols,* $I_{FEs} : FEs \xrightarrow{t} FPrg^{V,A}$ *and* $I_{Prs} : Prs \xrightarrow{t} FPrg^{V,A}$ *are interpretation mappings for function and program symbols, respectively.*

For any interpretation $J = (RNPA(V, A), I_{Ps}, I_{FEs}, I_{Prgs})$ we will denote by J_{Fr}, J_{FE}, and J_{Pt} the *formula, function, and program text interpretation mappings*

$$J_{Fr} : Fr^{\Sigma} \xrightarrow{t} Pr^{V,A},$$

$$J_{FE} : FE^{\Sigma} \xrightarrow{t} FPrg^{V,A},$$

$$J_{Pt} : Pt^{\Sigma} \xrightarrow{t} FPrg^{V,A}$$

which are the standard extensions of I_{Ps}, I_{FEs}, and I_{Prgs} to Fr^{Σ}, FE^{Σ}, and Pt^{Σ} respectively (defined by structural induction). Also, we will denote by J_{FHFr} the *interpretation mapping of Floyd-Hoare assertions* $J_{FHFr} : FHFr^{\Sigma} \xrightarrow{t} Pr^{V,A}$ defined as follows:

$$J_{FHFr} (\{p\}f\{q\}) = FH(J_{Fr} (p), J_{Pt}(f), J_{Fr} (q)).$$

In this paper we will not define interpretations explicitly expecting that they are clear from the context. For any $P \in Fr^{\Sigma}$ or $P \in FHFr^{\Sigma}$ we will denote by P_J or $(P)_J$ the predicate that corresponds to P under interpretation J. We will omit the index J when it is clear from the context.

We will use the following notation for any predicate p:
$p^T = \{d \mid p(d) \downarrow = T\}$ is the truth domain of a predicate p;
$p^F = \{d \mid p(d) \downarrow = F\}$ is the falsity domain of p.

Definition 29. *A formula* $P \in Fr^{\Sigma}$ *or a Floyd-Hoare assertion* $P \in FHFr^{\Sigma}$ *is valid (irrefutable) in an interpretation* J *(denoted as* $J \models P$*), if* $P_J^F = \emptyset$.

Definition 30. *A formula* $P \in Fr^{\Sigma}$ *or a Floyd-Hoare assertion* $P \in FHFr^{\Sigma}$ *is logically valid (denoted as* $\models P$*), if it is valid in every interpretation.*

Let us define the *logical consequence relation* $\models \subseteq Fr^{\Sigma} \times Fr^{\Sigma}$ as

$$p \models q \Leftrightarrow \models p \rightarrow q,$$

where $p \rightarrow q$ means $\neg p \vee q$ for any $p, q \in Fr^{\Sigma}$.

We will also need the following *special logical consequence relations*

$$\models_T, \models_F \subseteq Fr^{\Sigma} \times Fr^{\Sigma}$$

such that

- $p \models_T q \Leftrightarrow p_J^T \subseteq q_J^T$ for every interpretation J;
- $p \models_F q \Leftrightarrow q_J^F \subseteq p_J^F$ for every interpretation J.

5 Inference System for a Floyd-Hoare Logic with Partial Predicates

To make the program logic which we have defined applicable to software verification problems it is necessary to present an inference system. Such an inference system could be based on the inference system for the classical Floyd-Hoare logic with total predicates for the language WHILE [37], but it is known be unsound in the case of partial predicates [8] which is considered in the paper. For this reason additional constraints need to be added to achieve a sound inference system.

We will write $\vdash_X p$ to denote that a formula p is *derived* in some inference system X. An inference system X is *sound*, if $\vdash_X p \Rightarrow \models p$ for each formula p, and is *complete*, if $\models p \Rightarrow \vdash_X p$ for each p. Completeness can be treated in extensional or intensional approaches. For *extensional completeness* [37] pre- and postconditions can be arbitrary predicates. *Intensional completeness* requires that pre- and postconditions are presented by formulas in a given language.

The classical inference system for the language WHILE [37] can be presented in semantic form as follows ($x \in V$):

$$R\_AS \ \overline{\{S_P^x(p,h)\} \ AS^x(h) \ \{p\}} \qquad R\_SKIP \ \overline{\{p\} \ id \ \{p\}}$$

$$R\_SEQ \ \frac{\{p\} \ f \ \{q\}, \{q\} \ g \ \{r\}}{\{p\} \ f \bullet g \ \{r\}} \qquad R\_IF \ \frac{\{r \wedge p\} \ f \ \{q\}, \{\neg r \wedge p\} \ g \ \{q\}}{\{p\} \ IF(r,f,g) \ \{q\}}$$

$$R\_WH \ \frac{\{r \wedge p\} \ f \ \{p\}}{\{p\} \ WH(r,f) \ \{\neg r \wedge p\}} \qquad R\_CONS \ \frac{\{p'\} \ f \ \{q'\}}{\{p\} \ f \ \{q\}} \ p \to p', q' \to q$$

This inference system is sound and extensionally complete for total predicates, but for partial predicates it is not sound [8,9], because rules R_SEQ, R_WH, and R_CONS do not guarantee a valid derivation from valid premises.

There can be different solutions for this problem. Here we will restrict the class of assertions to the class of T-increasing assertions [9].

An assertion $\{p\}f\{q\}$ is *T-increasing* if $p \models_T PC(f,q)$. In this case the truth domain of p is included in the preimage of the truth domain of q under f.

It is important to note that for partial predicates T-increasing assertions are logically valid, i.e. $p \models_T PC(f,q)$ implies $\models \{p\}f\{q\}$.

Now we extend the inference system TI [9], oriented on T-increasing assertions, to the system RN. This extension takes into account that the language works with complex names and new superposition compositions appeared in our program language.

In this new system RN rules R_AS, R_SKIP, R_SEQ, R_IF, R_WH remain the same, but $v \in V^+$ in the rule R_AS since we consider complex names. To these rules the following new rules specifying superpositions into a program (procedure calls) are added:

$$R\_SFID \ \overline{\{S_P^{\bar{x}}(p,g_1,\ldots,g_n)\}S_F^{\bar{x}}(id,g_1,\ldots,g_n)\{p\}}$$

$$R\_SF \ \frac{\{p\}S_F^{\bar{x}}(id,g_1,\ldots,g_n) \bullet f\{q\}}{\{p\}S_F^{\bar{x}}(f,g_1,\ldots,g_n)\{q\}}$$

Also, we have to change the consequence rule R_CONS to the following rule:

$$R\_CONS' \ \frac{\{p'\}\ f\ \{q'\}}{\{p\}\ f\ \{q\}} \ \ ,p \models_T p', q' \models_T q$$

Proposition 1. *The inference system RN is sound for the class of T-increasing assertions.*

To prove the proposition we should demonstrate that axioms specify T-increasing assertions, and that given T-increasing assertions as premises the rules specify T-increasing assertions as consequences.

These properties can be proved analogously to [8, Theorem 4].

Proposition 2. *The inference system RN is extensionally complete for the class of T-increasing assertions.*

The prove is analogous to the standard proofs based on the notion of weakest precondition (see, for example, [37]) but taking into account partiality of predicates we use preimage predicate transformer (preimage composition) instead of the weakest precondition. Such a proof is given in [9, Theorem 4.1]. To prove our proposition we should additionally consider rules for superpositions with complex names. Details are omitted here.

In the system RN a new unconventional consequence relation $\models_T$ is used. Its main semantic properties were studied in [40]. Further investigation will permit to substitute this consequence relation by the corresponding inference relation $\vdash_T$. Let us also note that relational operations were not directly used in RN. The functions over relational data can be used inside arguments of assignment and superposition compositions. They will be specified explicitly in the predicate logic for relational nominative data. A detailed investigation of such logic is planned for the forthcoming publications.

6 Towards Formalization of Extended Floyd-Hoare Logic in Mizar

We proposed a formalization of nominative data in Mizar in [41–44]. In the mentioned work different types of nominative data were defined as Mizar *modes* with set parameters V and A which meant the sets of basic names and atomic values, respectively. We can use this formalization as a basis for formalization of the extended Floyd-Hoare logic for programs over relational nominative data. The following steps have to be done to achieve this.

(1) Define the mode of binominative functions over $Nd(V, A)$. This gives us a formalization of $FPrg^{V,A}$ defined above.
(2) Similarly define the modes of partial predicates over $RND(V, A)$.
(3) Formalize Pt^Σ (program texts), Fr^Σ (formulas), FE^Σ (functional expressions), and $FHFr^\Sigma$ (Floyd-Hoare assertions) as Mizar modes.

(4) Formalize the interpretation mapping in accordance with Definition 28.
(5) Formalize the relation of validity in an interpretation in accordance with Definition 29 and the relation of validity in accordance with Definition 30.
(6) Formalize the logical consequence relation $p \models q$ and the special logical consequence relations $p \models_T q$ and $p \models_F q$ for $p, q \in Fr^{\Sigma}$.
(7) Formulate the inference rules of the RN inference system described in Sect. 5 as Mizar schemes and formally prove their semantic validity.

Finally, the proven inference rules can be used to prove semantics properties of programs defined by concrete program texts (elements of Pt^{Σ}).

7 Related Work

Logical approaches to program specification and reasoning about program properties were used in the works by Floyd [1] and Hoare [2]. These approaches were based on axiomatic systems with total predicates and used triples of a precondition, program, and a postcondition. Later, it became evident that partiality of predicates and programs needs to be taken into account which gave rise to three-valued logics which represented undefinedness of a predicate by a special third value. In particular, such logics were studied by Łukasiewicz, Kleene, Bochvar and others. At the same time many other extensions of Floyd-Hoare logic were proposed as a basis for program verification, including Dynamic logic and Separation logic. In Dynamic logic [45] special modalities that allow usage of program texts and specifications alongside are used. A Floyd-Hoare assertion $\{p\}pr\{q\}$ can be replaced with a formula $p \rightarrow [pr]q$, where $[pr]q$ indicates that if a program pr terminates, then q necessarily holds. For deterministic programs, $[pr]q$ is equal to our preimage composition which also allows use of specifications and program texts together. Separation logic [46] was introduced to deal with widespread usage of heap and pointers in programming. This logic has special means for specifying heap properties. But only a heap function that maps memory addresses to values is assumed to be partial. In other aspects only total predicates are considered.

The ways of dealing with partiality in current software specification languages (VDM, RSL, Z, etc.) are described in [4]. Most approaches use either a many-valued logic or underspecification for dealing with partiality.

8 Conclusions

We have proposed an extension of Floyd-Hoare logic for the case of partial conditions and programs on hierarchically organized data called relational nominative data. Such data can conveniently represent many data structures used in programming. We have proposed a special inference system for our logic, investigated its soundness and extensional completeness and proposed an approach to its formalization in the Mizar system. In the future works we plan to implement the proposed approach and apply the results to software verification tasks.

References

1. Floyd, R.: Assigning meanings to programs. Math. Asp. Comput. Sci. **19**, 19–32 (1967)
2. Hoare, C.: An axiomatic basis for computer programming. Commun. ACM **12**(10), 576–580 (1969)
3. Apt, K.: Ten years of Hoare's logic: a survey - part I. ACM Trans. Program. Lang. Syst. **3**(4), 431–483 (1981). http://doi.acm.org/10.1145/357146.357150
4. Hähnle, R.: Many-valued logic, partiality, and abstraction in formal specification languages. Log. J. IGPL **13**(4), 415–433 (2005). http://dx.doi.org/10.1093/jigpal/jzi032
5. Jones, C.: Reasoning about partial functions in the formal development of programs. In: AVoCS 2005. Electronic Notes in Theoretical Computer Science, vol. 145, pp. 3–25. Elsevier (2006). https://doi.org/10.1016/j.entcs.2005.10.002
6. Gries, D., Schneider, F.B.: Avoiding the undefined by underspecification. In: van Leeuwen, J. (ed.) Computer Science Today. LNCS, vol. 1000, pp. 366–373. Springer, Heidelberg (1995). https://doi.org/10.1007/BFb0015254
7. Duzi, M.: Do we have to deal with partiality? Misc. Log. **5**, 45–76 (2003)
8. Kryvolap, A., Nikitchenko, M., Schreiner, W.: Extending Floyd-Hoare logic for partial pre- and postconditions. In: Ermolayev, V., Mayr, H.C., Nikitchenko, M., Spivakovsky, A., Zholtkevych, G. (eds.) ICTERI 2013. CCIS, vol. 412, pp. 355–378. Springer, Cham (2013). https://doi.org/10.1007/978-3-319-03998-5_18
9. Nikitchenko, M., Kryvolap, A.: Properties of inference systems for Floyd-Hoare logic with partial predicates. Acta Electrotech. Inform. **13**(4), 70–78 (2013)
10. Skobelev, V., Nikitchenko, M., Ivanov, I.: On algebraic properties of nominative data and functions. In: Ermolayev, V., Mayr, H., Nikitchenko, M., Spivakovsky, A., Zholtkevych, G. (eds.) Communications in Computer and Information Science, ICTERI, vol. 469, pp. 117–138. Springer, Cham (2014). https://doi.org/10.1007/978-3-319-13206-8_6
11. Nikitchenko, M., Shkilniak, S.: Mathematical logic and theory of algorithms. Publishing house of Taras Shevchenko National University of Kyiv, Ukraine (2008). (in Ukrainian)
12. Nikitchenko, M.: Composition-nominative aspects of address programming. Cybern. Syst. Anal. **45**, 864 (2009). https://doi.org/10.1007/s10559-009-9159-4
13. Wiedijk, F. (ed.): The Seventeen Provers of the World. Foreword by Dana S. Scott. LNAI, vol. 3600. Springer, Heidelberg (2006). https://doi.org/10.1007/11542384
14. Gordon, M.: Mechanizing programming logics in higher order logic. In: Birtwistle, G., Subrahmanyam, P. (eds.) Current Trends in Hardware Verification and Automated Theorem Proving, pp. 387–439. Springer, New York (1989). https://doi.org/10.1007/978-1-4612-3658-0_10
15. Von Wright, J., Hekanaho, J., Luostarinen, P., Langbacka, T.: Mechanizing some advanced refinement concepts. Form. Methods Syst. Des. **3**(1), 49–81 (1993). https://doi.org/10.1007/BF01383984
16. Bancerek, G., Byliński, C., Grabowski, A., Korniłowicz, A., Matuszewski, R., Naumowicz, A., Pąk, K., Urban, J.: Mizar: state-of-the-art and beyond. In: Kerber, M., Carette, J., Kaliszyk, C., Rabe, F., Sorge, V. (eds.) CICM 2015. LNCS (LNAI), vol. 9150, pp. 261–279. Springer, Cham (2015). https://doi.org/10.1007/978-3-319-20615-8_17
17. Grabowski, A., Korniłowicz, A., Naumowicz, A.: Four decades of Mizar. J. Autom. Reason. **55**(3), 191–198 (2015). http://dx.doi.org/10.1007/s10817-015-9345-1

18. Trybulec, A.: Tarski Grothendieck set theory. Formaliz. Math. **1**(1), 9–11 (1990)
19. Naumowicz, A.: Interfacing external CA systems for Gröbner bases computation in Mizar proof checking. Int. J. Comput. Math. **87**(1), 1–11 (2010). http://dx.doi.org/10.1080/00207160701864459
20. Naumowicz, A.: SAT-enhanced MIZAR proof checking. In: Watt, S.M., Davenport, J.H., Sexton, A.P., Sojka, P., Urban, J. (eds.) CICM 2014. LNCS (LNAI), vol. 8543, pp. 449–452. Springer, Cham (2014). https://doi.org/10.1007/978-3-319-08434-3_37
21. Naumowicz, A.: Automating Boolean set operations in Mizar proof checking with the aid of an external SAT solver. J. Autom. Reason. **55**(3), 285–294 (2015). http://dx.doi.org/10.1007/s10817-015-9332-6
22. Korniłowicz, A.: On rewriting rules in Mizar. J. Autom. Reason. **50**(2), 203–210 (2013). http://dx.doi.org/10.1007/s10817-012-9261-6
23. Korniłowicz, A.: Flexary connectives in Mizar. Comput. Lang. Syst. Struct. **44**, 238–250 (2015). http://dx.doi.org/10.1016/j.cl.2015.07.002
24. Korniłowicz, A.: Definitional expansions in Mizar. J. Autom. Reason. **55**(3), 257–268 (2015). http://dx.doi.org/10.1007/s10817-015-9331-7
25. Nelson, G., Oppen, D.C.: Fast decision procedures based on congruence closure. J. ACM **27**, 356–364 (1980). http://doi.acm.org/10.1145/322186.322198
26. Grabowski, A., Korniłowicz, A., Schwarzweller, C.: Equality in computer proof-assistants. In: Ganzha, M., Maciaszek, L.A., Paprzycki, M. (eds.) Proceedings of the 2015 FedCSIS. Annals of Computer Science and Information Systems, vol. 5, pp. 45–54. IEEE (2015). https://doi.org/10.15439/2015F229
27. Naumowicz, A., Byliński, C.: Improving MIZAR texts with *properties* and *requirements*. In: Asperti, A., Bancerek, G., Trybulec, A. (eds.) MKM 2004. LNCS, vol. 3119, pp. 290–301. Springer, Heidelberg (2004). https://doi.org/10.1007/978-3-540-27818-4_21
28. Korniłowicz, A.: Enhancement of MIZAR texts with transitivity property of predicates. In: Kohlhase, M., Johansson, M., Miller, B., de de Moura, L., Tompa, F. (eds.) CICM 2016. LNCS (LNAI), vol. 9791, pp. 157–162. Springer, Cham (2016). https://doi.org/10.1007/978-3-319-42547-4_12
29. Naumowicz, A., Korniłowicz, A.: Introducing Euclidean relations to Mizar. [47], pp. 245–248. https://doi.org/10.15439/2017F368
30. Grabowski, A.: Mechanizing complemented lattices within Mizar type system. J. Autom. Reason. **55**(3), 211–221 (2015). http://dx.doi.org/10.1007/s10817-015-9333-5
31. Grabowski, A., Korniłowicz, A., Schwarzweller, C.: On algebraic hierarchies in mathematical repository of Mizar. In: Ganzha, M., Maciaszek, L.A., Paprzycki, M. (eds.) Proceedings of the 2016 FedCSIS. Annals of Computer Science and Information Systems, vol. 8, pp. 363–371. IEEE (2016). https://doi.org/10.15439/2016F520
32. Grabowski, A., Jastrzębska, M.: Rough set theory from a math-assistant perspective. In: Kryszkiewicz, M., Peters, J.F., Rybinski, H., Skowron, A. (eds.) RSEISP 2007. LNCS (LNAI), vol. 4585, pp. 152–161. Springer, Heidelberg (2007). https://doi.org/10.1007/978-3-540-73451-2_17
33. Grabowski, A., Schwarzweller, C.: On duplication in mathematical repositories. In: Autexier, S., Calmet, J., Delahaye, D., Ion, P.D.F., Rideau, L., Rioboo, R., Sexton, A.P. (eds.) CICM 2010. LNCS (LNAI), vol. 6167, pp. 300–314. Springer, Heidelberg (2010). https://doi.org/10.1007/978-3-642-14128-7_26

34. Pąk, K.: Improving legibility of natural deduction proofs is not trivial. Log. Methods Comput. Sci. **10**(3), 1–30 (2014). http://dx.doi.org/10.2168/LMCS-10(3:23)2014

35. Pąk, K.: Automated improving of proof legibility in the Mizar system. [48], pp. 373–387. https://doi.org/10.1007/978-3-319-08434-3_27

36. Pąk, K.: Improving legibility of formal proofs based on the close reference principle is NP-hard. J. Autom. Reason. **55**(3), 295–306 (2015). http://dx.doi.org/10.1007/s10817-015-9337-1

37. Nielson, H., Nielson, F.: Semantics with Applications - A Formal Introduction. Wiley, Hoboken (1992)

38. Nikitchenko, M., Tymofieiev, V.: Satisfiability in composition-nominative logics. Cent. Eur. J. Comput. Sci. **2**(3), 194–213 (2012). https://doi.org/10.2478/s13537-012-0027-3

39. Dijkstra, E.: A Discipline of Programming, 1st edn. Prentice Hall PTR, Upper Saddle River (1997)

40. Nikitchenko, M., Shkilniak, S.: Semantic properties of T-consequence relation in logics of quasiary predicates. Comput. Sci. J. Mold. **23**(2(68)), 102–122 (2015)

41. Ivanov, I., Korniłowicz, A., Nikitchenko, M.: Formalization of nominative data in Mizar. In: Proceedings of TAAPSD 2015, pp. 82–85. Taras Shevchenko National University of Kyiv, Ukraine, 23–26 December 2015

42. Ivanov, I., Nikitchenko, M., Kryvolap, A., Korniłowicz, A.: Simple-named complex-valued nominative data - definition and basic operations. Formaliz. Math. **25**(3), 205–216 (2017). http://dx.doi.org/10.1515/forma-2017-0020

43. Korniłowicz, A., Kryvolap, A., Nikitchenko, M., Ivanov, I.: Formalization of the algebra of nominative data in Mizar. [47], pp. 237–244. https://doi.org/10.15439/2017F301

44. Korniłowicz, A., Kryvolap, A., Nikitchenko, M., Ivanov, I.: Formalization of the nominative algorithmic algebra in Mizar. In: Świątek, J., Borzemski, L., Wilimowska, Z. (eds.) ISAT 2017. AISC, vol. 656, pp. 176–186. Springer, Cham (2018). https://doi.org/10.1007/978-3-319-67229-8_16

45. Harel, D., Tiuryn, J., Kozen, D.: Dynamic Logic. MIT Press, Cambridge (2000)

46. Reynolds, J.C.: Separation logic: a logic for shared mutable data structures. In: Proceedings of the 17th LICS, pp. 55–74 (2002)

47. Ganzha, M., Maciaszek, L.A., Paprzycki, M. (eds.): Proceedings of FedCSIS 2017. Annals of Computer Science and Information Systems, vol. 11. IEEE, Prague, Czech Republic, 3–6 September 2017

48. Watt, S.M., Davenport, J.H., Sexton, A.P., Sojka, P., Urban, J. (eds.): CICM 2014. LNCS (LNAI), vol. 8543. Springer, Cham (2014). https://doi.org/10.1007/978-3-319-08434-3

ICT in Teaching, Learning, and Education Management

Rankings of Students Based on Experts' Assessment and Levels of the Likelihood of Learning Outcome Acquirement

Aleksandra Mreła[1][(✉)] and Oleksandr Sokolov[2]

[1] Faculty of Technology, Kujawy and Pomorze University in Bydgoszcz,
Toruńska Street 55-57, 85-023 Bydgoszcz, Poland
a.mrela@kpsw.edu.pl
[2] Faculty of Physics, Astronomy, and Informatics,
Nicolaus Copernicus University in Toruń,
Grudziądzka Street 5, 87-100 Toruń, Poland
osokolov@is.umk.pl

Abstract. The paper presents methods of preparing students' rankings based on the results of final secondary school examination test in mathematics in Poland with the proposal of methods for calculating the levels of the likelihood of learning outcome acquirement. The currently used method is based on the percentage of earned points and does not take into account levels of acquirement of learning outcomes by students. The data used in this article contains results of students who earned the same number of points, so the structure of this uniform group with respect to learning outcomes will be presented. All chosen methods of preparing rankings are based on the experts' assessment of levels of verification of learning outcomes by items and methods of this assessment fuzzification. According to the applied method, the rankings show some difference.

Keywords: Ranking of students · Fuzzification · Quality assurance
Learning outcome acquirement

1 Introduction

Development of information technologies has contributed significantly to the teaching methods and students' assessment. IT can help in the process of individualization of studying. Computer programs can choose the tasks from the task base with respect to some rules. The most important problem is to define these rules. Nowadays, the education is concentrated on learning outcomes, their acquirement by students and levels of their verification, so the computer programs should calculate the levels of acquirement of the assumed learning outcomes for the given curriculum. Tutorial programs, interactive tests, different monitoring studies and state programs for automated evaluation of knowledge and skills should take this into consideration.

Testing has been applied widely in distance education and during the implementation of the Bologna Process for student's self-education. The automated testing application has been expanded to manufacturing, where personnel management is transformed into a continuous process of training (of course, with the subsequent

© Springer International Publishing AG, part of Springer Nature 2018
N. Bassiliades et al. (Eds.): ICTERI 2017, CCIS 826, pp. 67–88, 2018.
https://doi.org/10.1007/978-3-319-76168-8_4

testing and assessment of trainees). The distinct feature of such systems is that the role of a teacher in the process of learning and assessment is much narrower, and the results have been evaluated automatically which has been caused by the requirement for simultaneous estimation of a large number of trainees, and by the ideology of auto-mated learning itself – self-consistent learning and independent evaluation. One of the major tasks is the comparability of the results of different tests, ranging from students level of knowledge, the formation of the final scoring for the test sets. Use of so-called "raw" scores, i.e., totals for the successful implementation of items resulting from the test might be applied to the very limited extent (if testing is limited to the identifying of the level of knowledge on a particular topic and cannot be integrated with other results). The effectiveness of the test score depends not only on the quality of the test but also on the methods of comparison and interpretation of primary (raw) score of a test group.

Therefore one can assume it is important to analyze the existing methods of comparison and integration of scores of various tests, study the quality of the students' group assessment, understanding the diversity of evaluation points as a quality criterion for estimating methods. There are a lot of methods of comparing results of tests, however recently more effort has been put on learning outcomes not only the score received by students or trainees.

In 1999 the Polish Government decided to take part in the Bologna Process [1] and because of that all Polish educational institution at the beginning of the process of designing curricula define learning outcomes which students have to acquire during their studies and their teachers have to verify their acquirement by the students.

The mathematics curriculum in Polish secondary schools was approved by the Polish Ministry of Education [2]. This curriculum considers 5 learning outcomes which students are taught during three-year studies. At the end of the studies, students take the written final secondary school examination.

The examination is dived into two parts, the first one consists of 25 items of multiple choice for which students can earn 1 point for answering correctly and the second part consists of 9 items for solving which students can earn more than 1 point. In this paper, the data we use to discuss the methods of preparing rankings, refers only to results of the first part of this examination.

The data is comprised of results from the final secondary school examination in mathematics in one of the Polish secondary schools in 2015. This examination was written by 149 students. For solving the first part of this examination students can earn up to 25 points. This paper presents a discussion on the group of 18 students who earned the number of points equal to 18, so they all achieved the same position in the ranking of students based on the number of earned points or the average mean.

Sometimes we might encounter situations when there is a need to distinguish between these students, for example, we would like to choose 5 out of these 18 students. So this ranking does not help us choose 5 better students unless we decide to apply more criteria. Apart from values-levels of acquirement of learning outcomes, it is important to analyze the likelihood of the achieving these results.

In this paper we will discuss methods of preparing rankings [10, 11] of students taking into consideration the results of the test in mathematics and experts' assessment of levels of verification of learning outcomes by test items and we discuss the results of

18 students who answering the first 25 items of the final secondary school examination in mathematics earned total score 18 points in one of the Polish high schools.

In order to calculate levels of acquiring learning outcomes by students, we will use the theory of fuzzy sets which was introduced by Zadeh [23] in 1965. In 1975 he generalized the concept of type 1 fuzzy sets and introduced type 2 fuzzy sets [24].

The scientific objective of the paper is to compare different methods of preparing students' rankings based on levels of learning outcome's acquirement. As an example, in the paper, the rankings of the group of students who earned the same number of marks (18) during the final secondary school examination were prepared.

The concept of using fuzzy logic for development of educational systems and preparing rankings is not new. In 1995 Biswas proposed two methods of evaluation of students [6], called Fuzzy Evaluation Method (FEM) and its generalization (GFEM), which were based on fuzzy approach. To establish more reliable educational systems, different variations of the concept of the fuzzy set were used and on this basis, there were designed new methods of evaluating students and preparing rankings. For example, the idea of soft fuzzy sets, which Molodtsov introduced [18] and Ahmad and Kharal developed [4], was used. Majumdar presented the new technique for preparing the class ranking of students which was based on generalized fuzzy soft sets [17]. In [8], the method of preparing the ranking of students based on generalized fuzzy soft matrix theory was presented. This method used socio-economic backgrounds and the authors defined the social difficulty coefficient.

Hameed and Sorensen showed that the system for evaluation of students using Gaussian membership functions with the standard deviation equals 0.4 or more was more reliable [14]. Moreover, they showed that Gaussian membership functions "provides a system with less degree of freedom and hence more robustness". Huapaya [15] defined the diagnosis model of the educational system based on fuzzy logic which was able to represent interpretable knowledge and was based on 27 intuitive fuzzy rules.

Ingoley [16] proposed the methods which were depended on the complexity of questions, difficulty and, importance of questions for students. The final marks are used to prepare new rankings. According to authors the system proposed by them was "fairer, transparent and beneficial to all students". It is also important to find criteria for assessment of educational systems. Csaba defined four conditions which should be fulfilled by based-on-fuzzy-logic methods of preparing students evaluation [7].

Rankings are prepared not only for evaluation of students but also in different areas of science, social science and practice, for example, there were prepared rankings of universities ([12]), the efficiency of washing machines ([22]) and football teams ([25]).

In the paper, we are building rankings using four kinds of relations: crisp, fuzzy type 1, fuzzy type 2 and relations built on the results the Item Response Theory.

2   Crisp Relations

To build the relations between learning outcomes and items we will use the description of four learning outcomes $LO_1 - LO_4$ written in [2]:

- LO_1 – Student interprets mathematical texts. After solving the tasks, student interprets the achieved result.
- LO_2 – Student uses simple, well-known mathematical objects.
- LO_3 – Student chooses a mathematical object to the simple situation and estimates the pertinence of model critically.
- LO_4 – Student applies strategy which results clearly from the content of the task.

On the basis of principles of assessment published in [3], where for each learning outcome the experts indicate items prepared for verifying its acquirement by students, the crisp relation R_1 between learning outcomes and items was prepared, so the value of this relation $R_1(LO_j, I_k)$ for learning outcome LO_j, where $j = 1, \ldots, 4$ and item I_k, where $k = 1, \ldots, 25$, is equal to 1 if the experts decided that item I_k can verify the acquirement of learning outcome LO_j, or it is equal to 0, otherwise.

Figure 1 presents the membership functions of the relation between learning outcomes and items (bars show the value equal to 1).

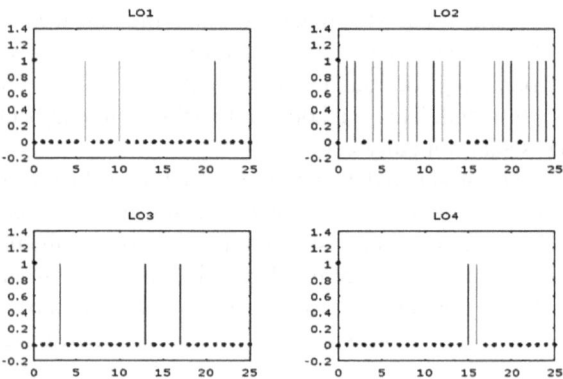

Fig. 1. The membership functions of the relation between learning outcomes $LO_1 - LO_2$ and items $I_1 - I_{25}$.

The value $R_2(I_k, S_i)$ of relation R_2 between item I_k, where $k = 1, \ldots, 25$ and student S_i, where $i = 1, \ldots, 18$, is equal to 1 if the student answered this item correctly or it is equal to 0, otherwise.

To calculate values of relation R_3 between learning outcomes and students, S-T-composition is used. Let us recall the definition of S-T composition [21].

Let $R_1 = \{(LO_j, I_k), \mu_{R_1}(LO_j, I_k)\} \subset \{learning\,outcomes\} \times \{items\}$ and $R_2 = \{(I_k, S_i), \mu_{R_2}(I_k, S_i)\} \subset \{items\} \times \{students\}$ be two fuzzy relations with the membership functions μ_{R_1} and μ_{R_2}, respectively. The S-T composition of these two relations R_1 and R_2 is relation $R_1 \circ R_2 \subset \{learning\,outcomes\} \times \{students\}$ with the membership function defined as follows:

$$\mu_{R_1 \circ R_2}(LO_j, S_i) = S_{k=1,\ldots,25}(T(\mu_{R_1}(LO_j, I_k), \mu_{R_2}(I_k, S_i))).$$

In [19] there is shown that for educational purposes when after solving following items correctly the levels of learning outcome acquirement should be higher, the algebraic T-norm and S-norm are better than the most popular T-norm minimum and S-norm maximum, so we will use S-T composition with algebraic T-norm and S-norm. Thus

$$\mu_{R_1 \circ R_2}(LO_j, S_i) = 1 - (1 - \mu_{R_1}(LO_j, I_1) \cdot \mu_{R_2}(I_1, S_i)) \cdot \ldots$$
$$\cdot (1 - \mu_{R_1}(LO_j, I_{25}) \cdot \mu_{R_2}(I_{25}, S_i)). \tag{1}$$

Table 1 presents values of relation $R_1 \circ R_2$.

Table 1. Levels of acquirement of learning outcomes by students.

Students	Learning outcomes			
	LO1	LO2	LO3	LO4
S1–S9; S11–S18	1	1	1	1
S10	1	1	1	0

In this case, all these students acquired learning outcomes $LO_1 - LO_4$ on the level 1 except student S10 whose level of acquirement of learning outcome LO_4 was 0. Thus we cannot distinguish between these students with the exception of S10 and we cannot prepare the ranking.

It is interesting to find a measure for describing the likelihood of calculating levels of acquirement of learning outcomes by students.

Assume that n_j is the number of items defined for the verification of the acquirement of learning outcome LOj and $m_{i,j}$ is the sum of levels of acquirement of learning outcome LO_j by student S_i (which is equal to the number of these items for which student Si answered correctly), where $i = 1, \ldots, 18$ and $k = 1, \ldots, 25$. Let $L_{i,j}$ denote the likelihood of acquirement of learning outcome LO_j by student S_i which is defined as follows:

$$L_{i,j} = \frac{m_{i,j}}{n_j} \quad \text{for } i = 1, \ldots, 18 \text{ and } j = 1, \ldots, 4. \tag{2}$$

It can be noticed that, in the case of learning outcome LO_4, there are only 2 items defined for verification the acquirement of this learning outcome, so there are only 3 levels of the likelihood of acquirement of this learning outcome. The situation is much better in the case of learning outcome LO_2 because there were defined 17 items for its verification. Moreover, student S10 did not acquire learning outcome LO_4 so the likelihood is equal to 0. The likelihood of acquirement of the given learning outcome for students who answered correctly all items designed for its verification is equal to 1.

Furthermore, let L_i, where $i = 1, 2, \ldots, 18$, be a level of the likelihood of all learning outcomes acquirements for student S_i, which is calculated in the following way:

$$L_i = \sum_{j=1}^{4} L_{i,j} \text{ for each } i = 1, 2, \ldots, 18 \tag{3}$$

The levels of the likelihood of all learning outcomes acquirement for all students are presented in Table 2.

Table 2. Levels of the likelihood of all learning outcomes acquirement.

Student	Value	Student	Value
S1	2.88	S10	2.44
S2	3.32	S11	2.32
S3	2.6	S12	2.6
S4	2.76	S13	2.04
S5	3.04	S14	2.76
S6	2.64	S15	3.04
S7	2.28	S16	2.6
S8	3.4	S17	3.32
S9	3	S18	2.6

After calculating the levels of the likelihood of all learning outcomes acquirement, the new ranking of students can be produced (Table 3).

Table 3. Ranking of students.

Position	Student	Position	Student
1	S8	8	S6
2	S2, S17	9	S16
3	S5	10	S3, S12, S18
4	S15	11	S10
5	S9	12	S11
6	S1	13	S7
7	S4, S14	14	S13

It can be observed that the ranking distinguishes 14 groups of students.

Now we introduce the concept of the ideal ranking, which lets each person be located in the unique place in the ranking. This ideal ranking will be based on the levels of the likelihoods. Thus for further analysis of levels of the likelihood, the levels of the likelihood are sorted (Fig. 2A) and standardized, that means let m and s be the average and standard deviation of the set of all levels of the likelihood of all learning outcomes acquirement (data from Table 2) and let x be an element of this set, then y is called the standardized value of x if

$$y = \frac{x - m}{s}.$$

Now we calculate the interval to which all standardized levels of the likelihood belong. Thus it can be noticed that all levels of the likelihood, after standardization and rounding, belong to the interval $[-2, 2]$ and there are 18 students, so the ideal ranking line should pass through points (the worst student, -2) and (the best student, 2). Thus the gradient of this line is equal to $\frac{4}{17}$, so $y = \frac{4}{17}x - 2\frac{4}{17}$. The graph of sorted levels of the likelihood and the ideal ranking line is presented in Fig. 2B. It is interesting to observe the differences between consecutive levels of the likelihoods (Fig. 2C) which are relatively high. Moreover, the distance between levels of the likelihoods and the ideal ranking line is calculated in the following way:

$$d = \sqrt{\sum_{i=1}^{18} (x_i - y_i)^2}, \tag{4}$$

where x_i is the level of the likelihood, y_i – the level of ideal ranking and $i = 1, \ldots, 18$.

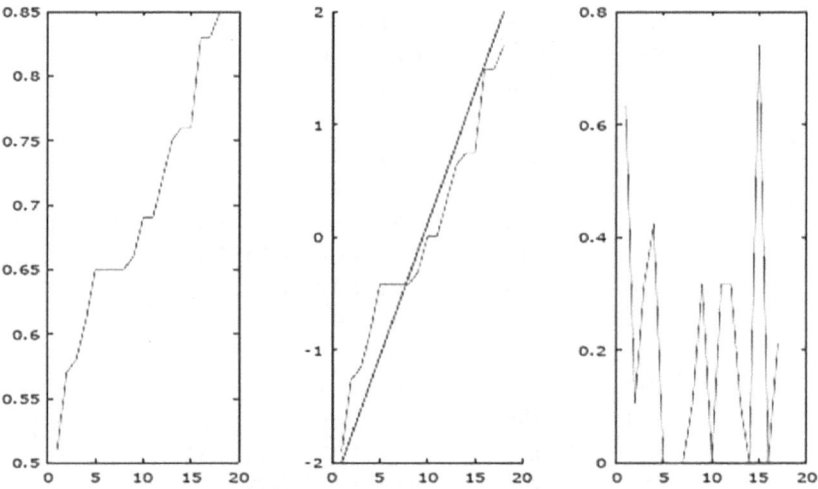

Fig. 2. Likelihoods of all learning outcomes acquirement in the case of crisp relations. **A.** The sorted values. **B.** The standardized values with the ideal ranking line. **C.** The distances between consecutive standardized values.

This distance d can be treated as an error of ranking because if the ranking was ideal, then all students would be on the ideal ranking line, so d would be 0. In the case of crisp relations, $d = 0.92799$.

3   The Item Response Theory

The Item Response Theory (IRT) [5] treats mathematical ability (understanding mathematics and skills in solving tasks) as a latent trait which cannot be measured. Let this ability of a person be denoted by θ. Under this model, the probability $P(\theta)$ of the event that a person's ability level is θ is equal to $P(\theta) = \frac{1}{1+e^{-a(\theta-b)}}$, where a is the discrimination parameter and b is the difficulty parameter. This theory describes the method of measuring this ability on the basis of results of the test which was solved by the group of students [5, 13, 20]. To find parameters a and b of the model of the ITR, iteration and statistical methods are applied [20].

According to the algorithm [20], the mathematical abilities described in learning outcomes $LO_1 - LO_4$ (all together) and then in these learning outcomes taken into account separately were calculated and put on Table 4.

Table 4. Levels of mathematical abilities according to IRT.

Students	Learning outcomes				
	$LO_1 - LO_4$	LO_1	LO_2	LO_3	LO_4
S1	3.15	2.64	1.01	0.78	0
S2	−1.15	2.64	0.66	0.78	1.83
S3	3.15	−0.89	1.41	2.35	0
S4	0.96	0.87	1.41	−0.75	1.83
S5	3.15	0.87	1.01	0.78	1.83
S6	0.96	2.64	1.41	−0.75	0
S7	3.15	−0.89	1.9	0.78	0
S8	0.96	0.87	0.66	2.35	1.83
S9	−1.15	2.64	1.01	−0.75	1.83
S10	0.96	2.64	1.41	0.78	−1.82
S11	3.15	0.87	1.9	−0.75	0
S12	3.15	−0.89	1.41	2.35	0
S13	0.96	−0.89	2.56	−0.75	0
S14	0.96	0.87	1.41	−0.75	1.83
S15	0.96	2.64	1.01	−0.75	1.83
S16	0.96	0.87	1.41	0.78	0
S17	3.15	2.64	0.66	0.78	1.83
S18	0.96	2.64	1.41	−0.75	0

On the basis of these values, the rankings of students were prepared and they are presented in Table 5.

Table 5. The rankings of students.

Position	The basis for the ranking				
	$LO_1 - LO_4$	LO_1	LO_2	LO_3	LO_4
1	S1, S3, S5, S7, S11, S12, S17	S1, S2, S6, S9, S10, S15, S17, S18	S13	S3, S8, S12	S2, S4, S5, S8, S9, S14, S15, S17
2	S4, S6, S8, S10, S13, S14, S15, S16, S18	S4, S5, S8, S11, S14, S16	S7, S11	S1, S2, S5, S7, S10, S16, S17	S1, S3, S6, S7, S11, S12, S13, S16, S18
3	S2, S9	S3, S7, S12, S13	S3, S4, S6, S10, S12, S14, S16, S18	S4, S6, S9, S11, S13, 14, S15, S18	S10
4			S1, S5, S9, S15		
5			S2, S8, S17		

The main problem with levels of mathematical abilities is too few values (too many students achieved the same level of this ability) in order to prepare rankings and differentiate students. For example, when we take into account all learning outcomes ($LO_1 - LO_4$) there are only 3 positions in the ranking, in the first position there are 7 students (S1, S3, S5, S7, S11, S12, S17), on the second one there are 9 students (S4, S6, S8, S10, S13, S14, S15, S16, S18) and on the third one there are 2 students (S2, S9).

The similar situation we encounter if we take as the basis of the ranking learning outcomes LO_1, LO_3 and LO_4 (there are only 3 positions) and only for learning outcome LO_2 there are 6 positions.

If we have more requirements according to the ranking, e.g. assume that learning outcome LO_1 is the most important, then LO_2, LO_3, and the least important learning outcome is LO_4, then we can distinguish students and using the lexicographical order we can prepare the ranking of the students presented in Table 6.

Table 6. Rankings of students.

Position	Student	Position	Student
1	S10	8	S4, S14
2	S6, S18	9	S5
3	S1	10	S8
4	S9, S15	11	S13
5	S2, S17	12	S7
6	S11	13	S3, S12
7	S16	14	–

Now we can differentiate students and prepare the ranking. Remembering that the most important learning outcome was LO_1, the students who were in the first position in the ranking based on this learning outcome are in the first 5 positions, so we differentiated them. It is interesting that student S10 who did not acquire learning outcome LO_4 takes the first position in the ranking. Students, who took the third position in the ranking based on learning outcome LO_1, take positions 11–13.

Table 4 presents levels of learning outcome acquirements for $LO_1 - LO_4$ which will be also called the level of the likelihood of given learning outcomes acquirement. The level of all learning outcomes acquirement will be calculated with the use of formula (3). Levels of the likelihood of all learning outcomes acquirement are presented in Table 7.

Table 7. Levels of the likelihood of all learning outcomes acquirement

Student	Value	Student	Value
S1	4.43	S10	3.01
S2	5.91	S11	2.02
S3	2.87	S12	2.87
S4	3.36	S13	0.92
S5	4.49	S14	3.36
S6	3.3	S15	4.73
S7	1.79	S16	3.06
S8	5.71	S17	5.91
S9	4.73	S18	3.3

After calculating the levels of the likelihoods of all learning outcomes acquirement, the next ranking of students can be prepared (Table 8).

Table 8. Ranking of students.

Position	Student	Position	Student
1	S2, S17	8	S16
2	S8	9	S10
3	S9, S15	10	S3, S12
4	S5	11	S11
5	S1	12	S7
6	S4, S14	13	S13
7	S6, S18	–	–

The ranking distinguishes 13 groups of students.

Similarly, as in the case of crisp relations, the graph of sorted levels of the likelihood of all learning outcome acquirements is prepared (Fig. 3A), then the standardized levels of the likelihood with the ideal ranking line are presented in Fig. 3B. In

Fig. 3C, there are shown distances between consecutive levels of the likelihood of all learning outcomes acquirement, which are even higher than in the case of crisp relations.

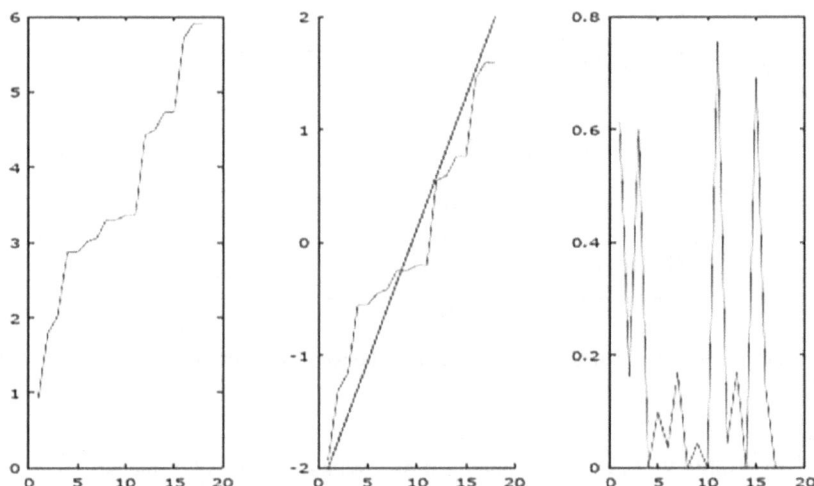

Fig. 3. Likelihoods of all learning outcomes acquirement in the case of IRT. **A.** The sorted values. **B.** The standardized values with the ideal ranking line. **C.** The distances between consecutive standardized values.

In the case of the Item Response Theory, the error d is equal to 1.0908, so it is higher than in the case of crisp relations.

4 First Type Fuzzification

Now, we will fuzzify the relation between learning outcomes and items by letting the experts who define levels of verifying learning outcomes by items to use values from the interval [0,1]. The membership functions of the relation between the given learning outcome and items are presented in Fig. 4.

Now using the crisp relation between students and items and type 1 fuzzy relation between learning outcomes and items we can calculate, using the S-T composition (1), type 1 fuzzy relation between learning outcomes and students which values denote levels of acquirement learning outcomes by students. The values of this relationship are presented in Table 9.

Now we can prepare rankings on the basis of levels of acquirement of each learning outcome $LO_1 - LO_4$ (separately) by the students. However, since they should acquire all learning outcomes, we prepare the ranking based on all of them using the lexicographical order. Assume that learning outcome LO_1 is the most important, then LO_2, LO_3 and finally LO_4. After using this information we can prepare the ranking of students in Table 10.

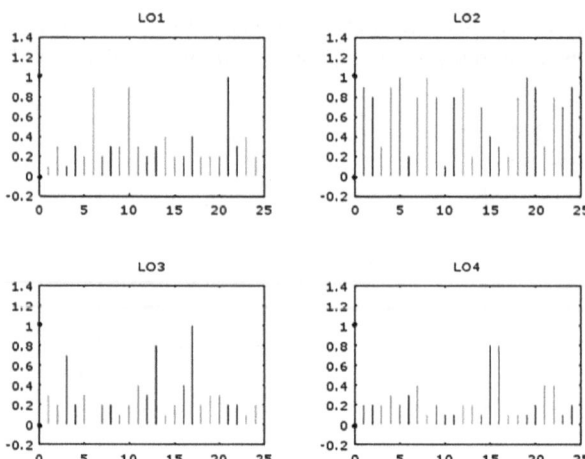

Fig. 4. The membership functions of the relation between learning outcomes $LO_1 - LO_4$ and items $I_1 - I_{25}$.

Table 9. Levels of acquirement of learning outcomes by students.

Students	Learning outcomes			
	LO_1	LO_2	LO_3	LO_4
S1	0.79	0.68	0.67	0.66
S2	0.83	0.73	0.74	0.79
S3	0.63	0.71	0.73	0.62
S4	0.71	0.73	0.59	0.77
S5	0.72	0.74	0.68	0.79
S6	0.77	0.68	0.55	0.63
S7	0.56	0.69	0.58	0.60
S8	0.75	0.72	0.78	0.77
S9	0.80	0.72	0.61	0.78
S10	0.79	0.63	0.64	0.41
S11	0.67	0.69	0.52	0.63
S12	0.60	0.71	0.72	0.62
S13	0.55	0.66	0.52	0.57
S14	0.72	0.73	0.59	0.78
S15	0.80	0.72	0.61	0.78
S16	0.72	0.66	0.69	0.60
S17	0.81	0.74	0.70	0.79
S18	0.78	0.67	0.57	0.64

At first, we can notice that the students take different positions in the ranking, only two students S9 and S15 have got the same position in the ranking. Now the best student is S2 and the poorest student is S13.

Table 10. Ranking of students.

Position	Student	Position	Student
1	S2	10	S14
2	S17	11	S16
3	S9, S15	12	S4
4	S1	13	S11
5	S10	14	S3
6	S18	15	S12
7	S6	16	S7
8	S8	17	S13
9	S5	–	–

This ranking shows that student S2 is the best one when learning outcome LO_1 is the most important one. Of course, if we choose the different order of importance of learning outcomes, the ranking will be different. The possibility of preparing different rankings according to specific criteria is really important for recruitment officers because they need candidates with specific abilities and skills.

Comparing the fuzzification and the IRT method we can see that the IRT takes into consideration only the difficulties of items and the examinee's abilities. Our method enables to calculate the levels of learning outcomes' acquirement taking into consideration one, a few or all learning outcomes.

The likelihoods $L_{i,j}$ of acquirement of learning outcome LO_j by student S_i are calculated as follows:

$$L_{i,j} = \frac{r_{i,j}}{v_j} \text{ for } j = 1,\ldots,4 \text{ and } i = 1,2,\ldots,18,$$

where $r_{i,j}$ denote the sum of levels of acquirement of learning outcome LO_j by student S_i and v_{LOi} denote the maximal value of levels of acquirement of learning outcome LO_j (for the student who answered all items correctly). Let L_i, where $i = 1,2,\ldots,18$, be a level of the likelihood of learning outcomes acquirements for each student S_i, which is calculated with the formula (3). The levels of the likelihood of all learning outcomes acquirement for all students are presented in Table 11.

Table 11. Levels of the likelihood of all learning outcomes acquirement

Student	Value	Student	Value
S1	2.88	S10	2.81
S2	3.03	S11	2.79
S3	2.83	S12	2.86
S4	2.88	S13	2.74
S5	2.97	S14	2.97
S6	2.79	S15	2.92
S7	2.75	S16	2.86
S8	2.94	S17	2.92
S9	2.87	S18	2.90

The levels of the likelihood of all learning outcomes acquirement can be the basis for preparing the new ranking of students can be produced (Table 12).

Table 12. Ranking of students.

Position	Student	Position	Student
1	S2	8	S12, S16
2	S5, S14	9	S3
3	S8	10	S10
4	S15, S17	11	S6, S11
5	S18	12	S7
6	S1, S4	13	S13
7	S9	–	–

The ranking distinguishes 13 groups of students. Similarly, like in the previous cases, the graphs of sorted levels of the likelihood of all learning outcome acquirement is prepared (Fig. 5A), the graph of these values standardized with the ideal ranking line is shown in Fig. 5B and the differences between consecutive levels of the likelihood of all learning outcomes acquirement are introduced in Fig. 5C.

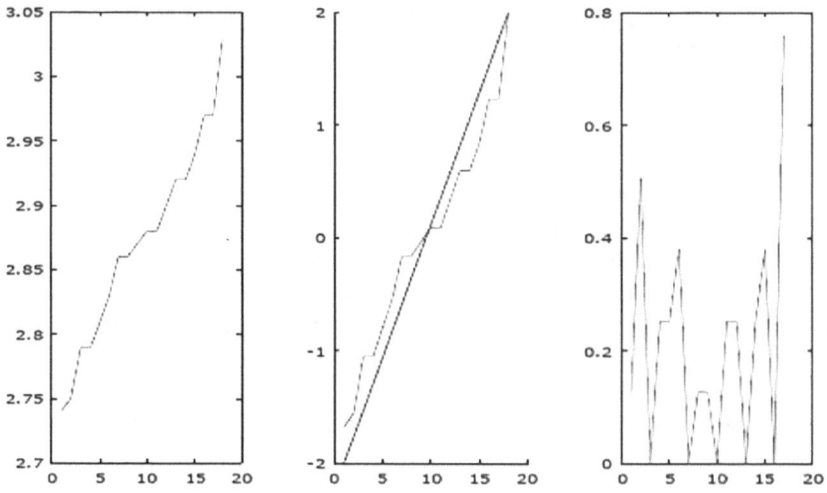

Fig. 5. Likelihoods of all learning outcomes acquirement in the case of first type fuzzification. **A.** The sorted values. **B.** The standardized values with the ideal ranking line. **C.** The distances between consecutive standardized values.

As it can be noticed, only one difference is high, the others are relatively low. In the case of fuzzy 1 relations, the error d is equal to 0.83943 (the lowest level in comparison with crisp relations and the method based on the IRT).

5 Second Type Fuzzification

Now, we fuzzify further the relation between learning outcomes and items by letting the experts who defined levels of verifying learning outcomes define their own value belonging to the interval [0,1]. Hence the sample membership functions of the relation between the given learning outcome and items are presented in Fig. 6.

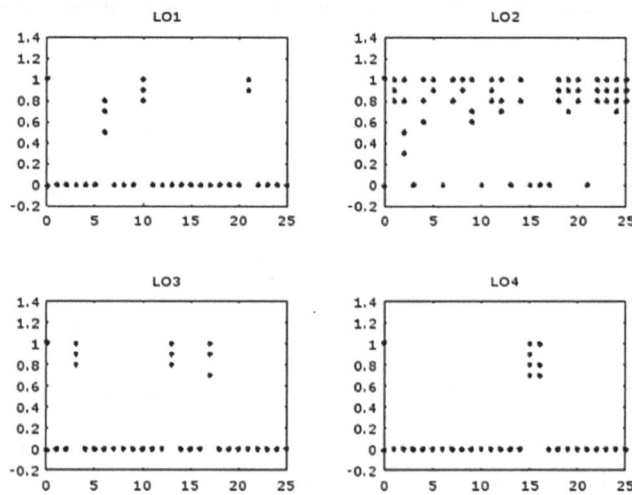

Fig. 6. The membership functions of the relation between learning outcomes $LO_1 - LO_4$ and items $I_1 - I_{25}$.

In order to prepare another ranking of students, we will use type 2 fuzzy relations [21, 24].

Let $m_{j,k}$ and $s_{j,k}$ denote the average mean and standard deviation of values set by experts for learning outcome LO_j and item I_k. Let each secondary membership function of the relation between learning outcome and item be defined the Gauss function $\mu_1(x, LO_j, I_k) = exp\left(-(x - m_{j,k})^2/s_{j,k}\right)$ for each j, k, and $x \in A$. Since the domain of all Gaussians is the set of real numbers, we have decided to choose some values for the calculations, so let A = $\{-0.5, -0.49, \ldots, 0, \ldots, 1.6\}$ be the basic membership for all secondary membership functions for $j = 1, \ldots, 4$, $i = 1, \ldots, 18$ and $k = 1, \ldots, 25$.

Since students can earn 0 or 1 points, so the secondary membership functions of the type 2 fuzzy relation between items and students can be the Gauss functions defined as follows: function $\mu_2(x, S_i, I_k) = exp\left(-(x - m_{i,k})^2/s_{i,k}\right)$ for each i, k and $x \in A$, where $m_{i,k} = 0 \, or \, 1$ and $s_{i,k} = 0.1$.

Now let the S-T composition between relations R_1 and R_2 be defined according to formula (1) for each x, so

$$\mu_{R_3}(x, LO_j, S_i) = 1 - \left(1 - \mu_{R_1}(x, LO_j, I_1) \cdot \mu_{R_2}(x, I_1, S_i)\right) \cdot \ldots \cdot \left(1 - \mu_{R_1}(x, LO_j, I_{25})\right)$$
$$\cdot \mu_{R_2}(x, I_{25}, S_i))$$

for each j, i. After the S-T composition, the sample secondary membership functions of the type 2 fuzzy relation between learning outcomes and students are presented in Fig. 7.

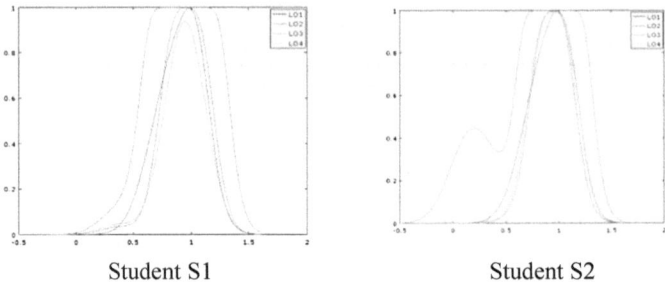

Student S1   Student S2

Fig. 7. The membership functions of the relation type 2 fuzzy relation between learning outcomes LO1–LO4 and students.

The next step is to find the method of comparing the results of students on the basis of the calculated secondary membership functions of the relation between learning outcomes and students. We can use the defuzzification methods, for example [9], to achieve type 1 fuzzy sets, which was discussed in the previous section or proceed with the type 2 fuzzy sets. Let the level of acquirement of learning outcome LO_j by student S_i be equal to first coordinate $x_{j,i}$ of the maximal point of the secondary membership function. Moreover, as we can see (Fig. 7) some of the functions are "slim" and some are "wide". Hence we can assume that if the function is "slim", so the likelihood of the result is higher and when the function is "wide", so the likelihood is smaller.

Thus the level of the likelihood of acquiring learning outcome LO_j by student S_i, called the range, is defined as follows:

$$range(j, i) = A(a_2) - A(a_1),$$

where $a_1 = min_{x \in A} \mu_{R_3}(x, LO_j, S_k) > 0.5$ and $a_2 = max_{x \in A} \mu_{R_3}(x, LO_j, S_k) > 0.5$.

Thus for student S_i and learning outcome LO_j we get the pair $(x_{j,i}, range(j, i))$. Hence we got the set of values of acquiring learning outcomes with their ranges. The pairs of these values for learning outcomes LO_1 and LO_2 and all students are put to Table 13.

Table 13. Levels of acquirement of learning outcomes LO_1 and LO_2 with their ranges.

Students	Learning outcomes			
	LO_1-value	LO_1-range	LO_2-value	LO_2-range
S1	0.98	0.49	0.96	0.8
S2	0.98	0.49	0.97	0.78
S3	0.98	1.32	0.95	0.82
S4	0.98	1.26	0.97	0.79
S5	0.98	1.26	0.96	0.79
S6	0.98	0.49	0.97	0.81
S7	0.07	0.38	0.96	0.81
S8	0.86	0.32	0.96	0.79
S9	0.98	0.49	0.96	0.8
S10	0.98	0.49	0.95	0.81
S11	0.98	1.26	0.95	0.82
S12	0.07	0.38	0.95	0.79
S13	0.07	0.38	0.94	0.82
S14	0.98	1.26	0.96	0.79
S15	0.98	0.49	0.95	0.81
S16	0.86	0.32	0.97	0.81
S17	0.98	0.49	0.95	0.8
S18	0.98	0.49	0.97	0.81

To prepare the ranking we have to defuzzify the achieved results [21]. We assume that the first value should be greater and for students who achieved the same first values, the second one should be smaller. Thus on this basis, we can prepare the ranking of students according to each learning outcome but as in the previous sections, we will present the ranking based on the lexicographic order assuming that learning outcome LO_1 is most important, than LO_2, LO_3, and LO_4. Hence we achieve the following ranking of students presented in Table 14.

Table 14. Ranking of students.

Position of students			
Position	Student	Position	Student
1	S2	10	S5
2	S6, S18	11	S11
3	S9	12	S3
4	S1	13	S16
5	S17	14	S8
6	S15	15	S7
7	S10	16	S12
8	S4	17	S13
9	S14	–	–

Comparing the rankings presented in Tables 10 and 14 we can notice that the first and last positions are the same and position of other students are similar. However, using the type 2 fuzzy relations we have more information because we can also describe the likelihood of acquirement of the learning outcomes by given students.

Even if this ranking did not differentiate students S6 and S18, it is not worse than the previous rankings. Moreover, we have got more information about the likelihood of acquirement of learning outcomes. After summing all levels of the likelihood of learning outcome acquirement in the way as before, the levels of the likelihood of all learning outcomes acquirement are calculated and presented in Table 15.

Table 15. Levels of the likelihood of all learning outcomes acquirement

Student	Value	Student	Value
S1	2.21	S10	2.22
S2	2.06	S11	2.25
S3	2.18	S12	2.25
S4	1.92	S13	2.25
S5	1.93	S14	1.93
S6	2.22	S15	1.9
S7	2.25	S16	2.22
S8	1.89	S17	1.9
S9	1.89	S18	2.22

The levels of the likelihood of all learning outcomes can be the basis for preparing the new ranking of students can be produced (Table 16).

Table 16. Ranking of students.

Position	Student	Position	Student
1	S8, S9	6	S3
2	S15, S17	7	S1
3	S4	8	S6, S10, S16, S18
4	S5, S14	9	S7, S11, S12, S13
5	S2	–	

The ranking distinguishes only 9 groups of students. Similarly, like in the previous cases, the graphs of sorted levels of the likelihood of all learning outcomes acquirements is prepared (Fig. 8A), of these values standardized with the ideal ranking line (Fig. 8B) and the differences between standardized consecutive levels of the likelihood of all learning outcomes acquirement (Fig. 8C).

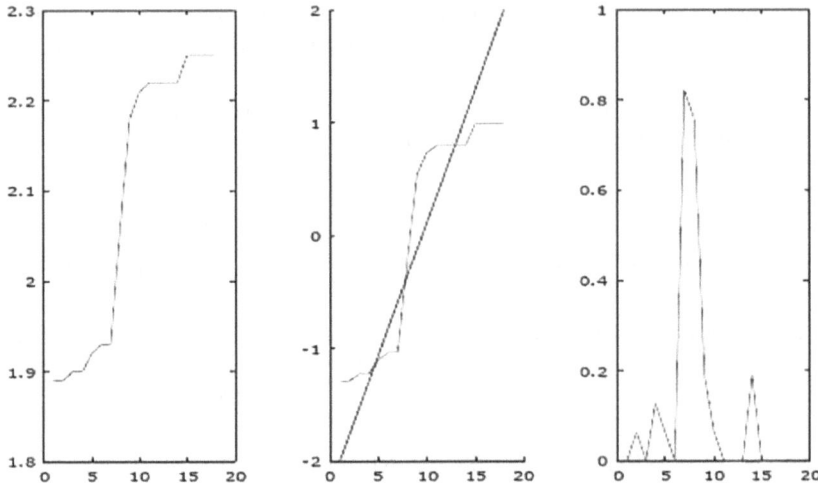

Fig. 8. Likelihoods of all learning outcomes acquirement in the case of second type fuzzification. **A.** The sorted values. **B.** The standardized values with the ideal ranking line. **C.** The distances between consecutive standardized values.

As it can be observed, only one difference is high. The error d is equal to 1.1049 (the highest value).

6 Conclusions

Nowadays rankings of students are prepared very often. For example, in Poland, all universities to admit students for the first year course prepare the ranking of candidates based on the results of the final secondary school examination and the grades of specific subjects. Universities could choose students based on the levels of acquirement of learning outcomes, not only on the average mean. All students discussed in the paper are in the same position after the first part of the examinations.

The paper presents different methods of preparing rankings based on the IRT algorithm and three different level of fuzzification of the relation between learning outcomes and items: crisp (two different position in the ranking), type 1 (we can prepare the ranking using additionally the lexicographical order of levels of acquirement of learning outcomes by students) and type 2 (the ranking based on the lexicographical order of levels of acquirement of learning outcomes by students gives additionally the information about the likelihood of this learning outcome acquirement).

The IRT method takes into account only difficulties of items and examinee's abilities described as learning outcomes. Moreover, when we prepared the ranking based on examinee's abilities of all discussed learning outcomes we have got only 3 positions.

The ranking prepared on the basis of the crisp relation between learning outcomes and items had only 2 positions. After the first and second fuzzifications, we have got the rankings with 17 positions and in the case of type 2 fuzzy relations, we have got more information (the levels of the likelihood of learning outcomes acquirement). In the case of type 2 fuzzy relations there are wider possibilities of using the experts' knowledge to prepare the rankings of students.

The second kind of methods for preparing rankings of students is based on the levels of the likelihoods of all learning outcomes acquirement (Table 17), where = indicates students in the same position.

Table 17. Comparison of rankings of students based on levels of the likelihood of all learning outcomes acquirement

Position	Crisp relations	ITR	Type 1 fuzzy relations	Type 2 fuzzy relations
1	S8	S2 =	S2	S8 =
2	S2 =	S17 =	S5 =	S9 =
3	S17 =	S8	S14 =	S15* =
4	S5	S9 =	S8	S17* =
5	S15	S15 =	S15 =	S4
6	S9	S5	S17 =	S5 =
7	S1	S1	S18	S14 =
8	S4=	S4=	S1 =	S2
9	S14=	S14 =	S4 =	S3
10	S6	S6* =	S9	S1
11	S16	S18* =	S12 =	S6
12	S3 =	S16	S16 =	S10
13	S12 =	S10	S3	S16 =
14	S18 =	S3 =	S10	S18 =
15	S10	S12 =	S6 =	S7* =
16	S11	S11	S11 =	S11*=
17	S7	S7	S7	S12* =
18	S13	S13	S13	S13* =
d	0.92799	1.0908	0.83943	1.1049

where = indicates the first group of students with the same level of the likelihood,
* = indicates the second group of students with the same level of the likelihood.

As it can be noticed, these methods can differentiate students (13–14 positions for 18 students) in the cases of crisp and type 1 fuzzy relations and the IRT, in the case of type 2 fuzzy relations there are only 9 positions. The error d indicates that the levels of the likelihood for type 1 fuzzy relations ranking are the closest to the ideal ranking line for this specific example.

The next step is to find more precise measure than the range to calculate the likelihood of learning outcome acquirement by students, for example, the area between x-axis and Gauss functions.

References

1. European Higher Educational Area. www.ehea.info. Accessed 12 July 2016
2. Rozporządzenie Ministra Edukacji Narodowej z dnia 23 grudnia 2008 r. w sprawie podstawy programowej wychowania przedszkolnego oraz kształcenia ogólnego w poszczególnych typach szkół. http://isap.sejm.gov.pl. Accessed 12 July 2016
3. Zasady oceniania rozwiązań zadań, Egzamin maturalny w roku 2014/2015, Centralna Komisja Egzaminacyjna. www.cke.edu.pl. Accessed 12 July 2016
4. Ahmad, B., Kharal, A.: On fuzzy soft sets. Adv. Fuzzy Syst. **2009**, 6 p. (2009). Article ID 586507. https://doi.org/10.1155/2009/586507
5. Baker, F.B.: The Basics of Item Response Theory. ERIC Clearinghouse on Assessment and Evaluation, USA (2001)
6. Biswas, R.: An application of fuzzy sets in students' evaluation. Fuzzy Sets Syst. **74**, 187–194 (1995)
7. Csaba, J.Z.: Survey on four fuzzy set theory based student evaluation methods. In: Proceedings of Kecskemét College, Faculty of Technology (GAMF), Kecskemét, HU, vol. XXIII, pp. 121–130 (2008). ISSN: 1587-4400
8. Dayan, F., Zulqarnain, M., Hassan, N.: A ranking method for students of different socio economic backgrounds based on generalized fuzzy soft sets. Int. J. Sci. Res. (IJSR) **6**(9), 2015–2018 (2017)
9. Dobrosielski, W.T., Szczepański, J., Zarzycki, H.: A proposal for a method of defuzzification based on the golden Ratio—GR. In: Atanassov, K.T., et al. (eds.) Novel Developments in Uncertainty Representation and Processing. AISC, vol. 401, pp. 75–84. Springer, Cham (2016). https://doi.org/10.1007/978-3-319-26211-6_7
10. Duch, W., Wieczorek, T., Biesiada, J., Blachnik, M.: Comparison of feature ranking methods based on information entropy. In: Proceedings of International Joint Conference on Neural Networks (IJCNN), Budapest 2004, pp. 1415–1420. IEEE Press (2004)
11. Duch, W., Winiarski T., Biesiada J., Kachel, A.: Feature ranking, selection and discretization. In: Proceedings of Joint International Conference on Artificial Neural Networks (ICANN) and International Conference on Neural Information Processing (ICONIP), Istanbul, pp. 251–254 (2003)
12. Erdoğan, M., Kaya, İ.: A type-2 fuzzy MCDM method for ranking private universities in İstanbul. In: Proceedings of the World Congress on Engineering, WCE 2014, London, U.K. 2–4 July, vol. 1 (2014)
13. Hambleton, R.K., Swaminathan, H.: Item Response Theory, Principles and Applications. Springer Science + Business Media, LLC, New York (1991). https://doi.org/10.1007/978-94-017-1988-9
14. Hameed, I.A., Sorensen, C.G.: Fuzzy systems in education: a more reliable system for student evaluation. In: Azar, A.T. (ed.) Fuzzy systems. InTech, London (2010). http://www.intechopen.com/books/fuzzy-systems/fuzzy-systems-in-education-a-more-reliable-system-for-student-evaluation
15. Huapaya, C.: Proposal of fuzzy logic-based students´ learning assessment model. In: XVIII Congreso Argentino de Ciencias de la Computación (2012)
16. Ingoley, S., Bakal, J.W.: Use of fuzzy logic in evaluating students' learning achievement. Int. J. Adv. Comput. Eng. Commun. Technol. (IJACECT), **1**(2), 47–54 (2012)
17. Majumdar, P., Samanta, S.K.: A generalised fuzzy soft set based student ranking system. Int. J. Adv. Soft Comput. Appl. **3**(3) November 2011. www.i-csrs.org
18. Molodtsov, D.: Soft set theory first results. Comput. Math App. **37**, 19–31 (1999)

19. Mreła, A., Sokolov, O., Katafiasz, T.: Types of fuzzy relations' composition applied to the validation of learning outcomes at mathematics during final high school examination. In: Mreła, A., Wilkoszewski, P. (eds.): Nauka i technika u progu III tysiąclecia, Wydawnictwo Kujawsko-Pomorskiej Szkoły Wyższej w Bydgoszczy, Bydgoszcz, pp. 119–132 (2015)
20. Нейман, Ю.М, Хлебников, В.А.: Введение в теорию моделирования и параметризации педагогических тестов. Прометей, М. (2000)
21. Rutkowski, R.: Metody i techniki sztucznej inteligencji. PWN, Warsaw (2009)
22. Yadav, A.K., Reza, A., Srivastava, S.: A comparative study for ranking the efficiency of washing machines based on fuzzy set theory. Int. J. Innov. Res. Sci., Eng. Technol. 3(4), 11678–11684 (2014)
23. Zadeh, L.A.: Fuzzy sets. Inf. Control 8, 338–353 (1965)
24. Zadeh, L.A.: The concept of a linguistic variable and its application to approximate reasoning–1. Inf. Sci. 8, 199–249 (1975)
25. Zeng, W., Li, J.: Fuzzy logic and its application in football team ranking. Sci. World J. 2014, 1–6 (2014). https://doi.org/10.1155/2014/291650. Article ID 291650

Training of E-learning Managers
at Universities

Nataliia Morze[1](✉) (iD), Olena Glazunova[2] (iD),
and Olena Kuzminska[2] (iD)

[1] Boris Grinchenko Kyiv University, Kiev, Ukraine
n.morze@kubg.edu.ua
[2] National University of Life and Environmental Sciences of Ukraine,
Kiev, Ukraine
{o-glazunova, o.kuzminska}@nubip.edu.ua

Abstract. The article offers the theoretical-and-methodic aspects and practical experience outcomes of implementing the master's program "E-learning management" for the students of pedagogical specialities of the University, which forms professional competences in the field of innovative methods, Web-services 2.0, e-learning expertise, projecting of e-environment, IT-infrastructure management, as well as develops soft skills. It suggests the solution to the training of specialists, who will have an ability not only to use ICT in their academic activities, but will also master the competences of e-learning. The article features the model of professional competences of e-learning manager, the content of the training program, methods, forms and training tools, efficiency indicators. Examples of competency tasks for measuring levels of professional competencies according to the developed model are given. Experimental verification of the developed model was carried out at Borys Grinchenko Kyiv University. The results of measuring the level of professional competence of e-learning managers before and after training in the master's program "E-learning management" have been analyzed and statistically confirmed. Defined outlines the directions of research results dissemination.

Keywords: Competence education · Management of E-learning
Professional competence · Model · Instructional design

1 Introduction

The expansion of technology changes the way knowledge is acquired and disseminated – in the future, online education professionals will be increasingly in demand. Moreover, by the year 2020 new professions will appear. As a rule, such professions are hybrids by their form: for example, they imply combination of the human intelligence with the machine one. In education, for instance, this may be a coordinator of the educational platform, educational production manager, online coach.

The research results testify to the fact that nowadays the majority of higher educational institutions (HEIs) are implementing e-learning [1]. The universities have IT-infrastructure, e-libraries, e-research centers (e.g., http://www.oerc.ox.ac.uk), e-environments are being developed [2, 3], the issues of e-learning specialists training, e-sciences, e-democracies, implementation of e-management approach at the university environment are being studied [4].

At the same time, not enough attention is paid to the teachers training regarding the effective e-learning implementation into the educational process with the aim of ensuring quality of education. Teachers receive an episodic ICT training and training of applying ICT in the educational process.

The topical task of many HEIs is training specialists, who do not only possess professional competences, but also can:

- analyze market offers of accessible information systems and technologies of building and developing the IT-structure and information educational e-environment;
- test, implement and assess IT-technologies for the e-learning system;
- choose forms and tools of presenting educational e-content;
- elaborate instructions as regards the use of electronic resources and e-content;
- organize the educational process based on using informational educational e-environment and assess its efficiency;
- effectuate the monitoring the usage and satisfaction of the educational process participants by the components of the information educational e-environment;
- manage the educational process through the usage of resources of information educational e-environment for the provision of high-quality educational services 24 * 7 * 365, etc.

The solution to the problem of the efficient teacher training towards future professional activities under the conditions of educational informatization process may lie in the implementation of corresponding specialized master's programs. The aim of the present article is to substantiate and analyze results of the experimental study by means of implementing "E-learning management" into the educational process of master's program, conducted on the basis of Borys Grinchenko Kyiv University.

2   Literature Review

The majority of researchers in the field of e-learning implementation pay attention to the students' ability to use IT. The E-Learning Competency Framework for Teachers and Trainers is comprised of 10 groups of competences, which should be formed for the effective use of ICT [5]. Among them: preparation for the training sessions, students' support, student's progress assessment, learning environment management, participation in the organization of teaching process, management of the personal professional development, communication. Martin examines on the topic of technology in teacher preparation through the theoretical lens of Technology, Pedagogy and Content Knowledge (TPACK) which has shown potential to emphasize the teacher's understanding of how technologies can be used effectively as a pedagogical tool [6]. Keengwe and Kidd [7] generalize best e-learning practices; Weigel [8] defines in what way the instructor may help the students to develop skills in the sphere of scientific researches, problem solution, critical thinking and knowledge management by means of web-tools for the common work by using virtual spaces, "knowledge rooms", in which the students cooperate. The ISTE National Educational Technology Standards [9] provide a framework for rethinking education, adapting to a constantly changing technological landscape and preparing students to enter an increasingly global economy.

European universities have introduced master's programs in educational technology, for example, in Tartu, Estonia.

At the same time the researchers in the sphere of ICT usage in the educational process pay attention to the problem of staff training for the organization of e-learning, including the corporate sector. The European Institute for e-Learning (EIfEL) has developed a framework for e-learning competencies for teachers and trainers [10]. Cardos and Tiron-Tudor [11] defined, that one of the most important competences, that an e-learning manager should master, is the ability to manage the project on e-learning implementation as his continuous activity. Keramida [12] defines six top skills that e-learning managers should have: general understanding of e-learning functioning; sustention of e-learning in the relevant state in accordance with the tendencies in the field, leadership skills; communicative skills, assets management and resources placement; time management skills. Leadership, interpersonal, technical, presentation skills (soft skills) are defined among the e-learning project managers by Dhondi [13].

3 E-learning Managers Training: Preconditions and Realization

3.1 Needs Assessment and Research Setting

The authors' experience regarding the e-learning implementation, taking into account that Borys Grinchenko Kyiv University is the participant of European University Association [1, p. 79], and analysis of the international and national experience form the basis for defining the peculiarities of e-learning managers training program, which [14]:

- is based on the world-wide approaches to the specialists training in the field of electronic learning, foresees the award of the corresponding documents to graduates (takes into consideration the experience of specialists training in different countries, in particular, in Poland, Slovakia, Portugal, the Czech Republic, Russia, Spain);
- envisages learning of contemporary Internet-services, ways of managing the educational process on their basis, organization of the formal, non-formal and informal learning on the basis of contemporary ICT, implementation of team project activities, defense of the master's thesis in the form of a Startup;
- is based on competence principles;
- ensures the implementation of fundamentals of adaptive learning, formation of soft skills, and learning approaching the real "production" process.

The analysis of the needs of different categories of subjects of educational activity regarding the training of e-learning specialists in Ukraine was carried out by the authors in the form of e-survey. There were 531 survey respondents (Fig. 1), of which 93% recognized the need for systematic implementation of e-learning in educational institutions, but 86.7% rated it as inadequate training courses conducted by state educational institutions on effective introduction of e-learning in the educational process.

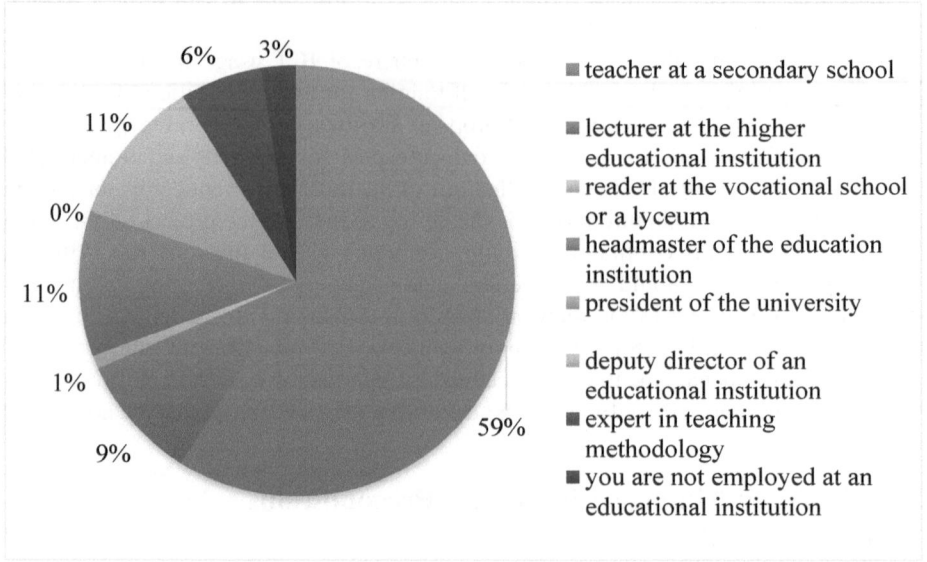

Fig. 1. Respondents of the survey (Source: Own work)

The problems, most often arising in the process of implementing e-learning, are listed in such a way (Fig. 2):

- the lack of development of the modern IT infrastructure of the institution;
- low level of teachers' (lecturers') proficiency in modern Web 2.0 services and technologies;
- failure to understand the ways of motivating teachers and lecturers to use e-learning;
- failure to understand the clear steps for the implementation of e-learning, more specifically, distance e-learning;
- low level of mastering the methods of forming 21-st century skills in your pupils and students;
- complexity in the development of modern e-educational environment.

Research hypothesis was assumed that the introduction of the master's program "E-learning management", which forms the professional competence of future teachers of educational, technical, design, research activities using ICT, improves the quality of teacher training for the education system in conditions of informatization. The main tasks of research are to:

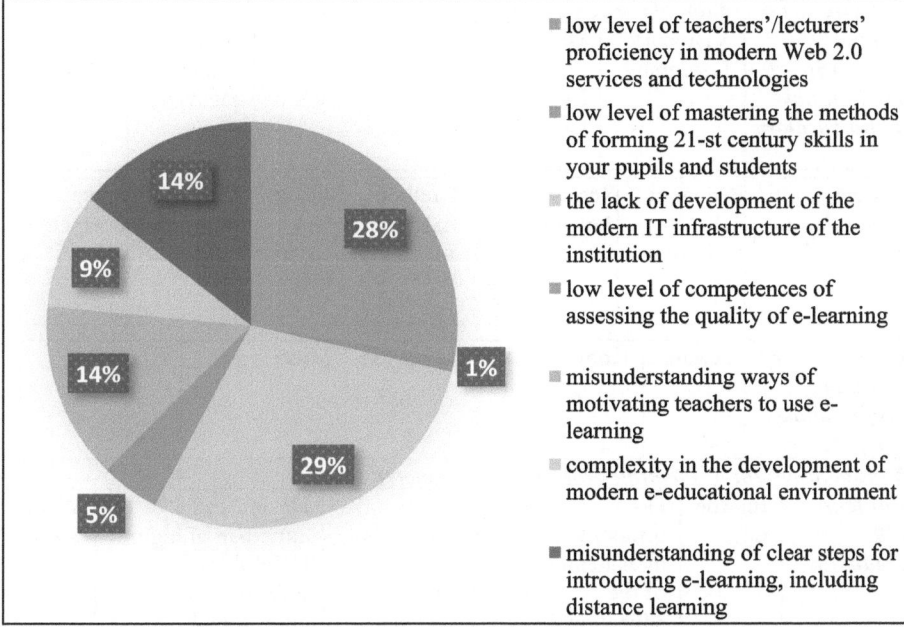

- low level of teachers'/lecturers' proficiency in modern Web 2.0 services and technologies
- low level of mastering the methods of forming 21-st century skills in your pupils and students
- the lack of development of the modern IT infrastructure of the institution
- low level of competences of assessing the quality of e-learning
- misunderstanding ways of motivating teachers to use e-learning
- complexity in the development of modern e-educational environment
- misunderstanding of clear steps for introducing e-learning, including distance learning

Fig. 2. The problems, most often arising in the process of implementing e-learning: replies of respondents (Source: Own work)

1. Theoretically substantiate and verify experimental model of professional competences of the e-learning manager.
2. Develop methodical approaches of training e-learning managers, based on developed model of competences (contents, methods, forms and tools).
3. Identify indicators of effectiveness of training future e-learning managers, develop a system of competency tasks.

3.2   The Model of Professional Competences of an E-learning Manager

Based on the analysis of sources and practical experience, a model for the formation of professional competences of the e-learning manager (Fig. 3) was developed, which includes the purpose, components; content, forms, methods and means of training; indicators and evaluation tools, assessment levels, the result.

Based on the analysis of Standards and other reference documents the authors are guided by the ISTE standards for administrators in the educational system (Table 1).

On the basis of this standard, the requirements were specified and a system of professional competences of e-learning management specialists was formed. The European ICT Professional Profiles and the European e-Competence Framework (hereinafter referred to as e-CF) were used as the basis for developing the model of the system of professional competences of the e-learning manager (Table 2).

ICT profiles are structured in 6 directions: business management, technical management, design, development, maintenance and support [15]. Each direction contains

Purpose	Formation of the competent e-learning manager					
ISTE standards for educational administrators	Visionary Leadership	Digital Age Learning Culture	Excellence in Professional Practice		Systemic Improvement	Digital Citizenship
System of professional competences	Pedagogical activities (1P)	Research and development activities (2R)	Methodical activities (3M)	Management activities (4Mg)	Project activities (5Pr)	Specific competences (6S)
Levels of forming professional competences	Awareness (1)	Knowledge (2)	Experience (3)		Mastery (3)	Expert (5)
Methodic system of forming professional competences						
Content (30 credits):	Internetics	IT-infrastructure management of the educational institution	Innovative methods, technologies and monitoring of the electronic education quality		Design and expertise of high technology information educational environment	Work practice
Methods	Discussions brainstorming	Role games	Educational and social projects	Work practice classes	Practices in educational institutions	
Forms	Classroom activities	Individual work	Team work activities		Distance learning	
Tools and resources	Online courses (Moodle)	MOOC	Google Academy, Microsoft Academy		Professional online tools	
Methods of competences assessment	Surveys	Tests	Competency-based tasks	Expert assessment	Self-assessment, peer assessment	
Result	Competent e-learning manager					

Fig. 3. Model of forming the system of a competent e-learning manager (Source: Own work)

ICT profiles that meet the European e-Competence Framework. In response to the large number of qualification frameworks in the sphere of information and communication technologies and portfolio descriptions used by European businesses, the European e-Competence Framework (e-CF) was created [16]. The European e-Competence Framework is a framework that can be used and acknowledged by both the companies that produce ICT services and products, and institutions that use ICTs in their core activities. Currently, version 3.0 of the European e-Competence Framework is relevant. It focuses on the competences required to develop, execute and manage IT projects and processes, on the use of information and communication technologies, decision-making, strategy development, and forecast of new scenarios.

Table 1. ISTE standards for administrators in the educational system (Source: http://www.iste. org/standards/for-administrators)

Component	Characteristic
Visionary Leadership (VL)	Administrators inspire and lead development and implementation of a shared vision for comprehensive integration of technology to promote excellence and support transformation throughout the organization
Digital Age Learning Culture (DALC)	Administrators create, promote and sustain a dynamic, digital age learning culture that provides a rigorous, relevant and engaging education for all students
Excellence in Professional Practice (EPX)	Administrators promote an environment of professional learning and innovation that empowers educators to enhance student learning through the infusion of contemporary technologies and digital resources
Systemic Improvement (SI)	Administrators provide digital age leadership and management to continuously improve the organization through the effective use of information and technology resources
Digital Citizenship (DC)	Administrators model and facilitate understanding of social, ethical and legal issues and responsibilities related to an evolving digital culture

Table 2. Components of the system of professional competences of the e-learning manager

Component	Characteristic
Pedagogical activities (1P)	1.1. Ability to use modern methods and technologies of the learning environment organization and realization, which envisage the use of ICT on different educational levels in different educational institutions 1.2. Readiness to use modern technologies, which envisage the use of ICT, diagnostics and assessment of the educational process quality 1.3. Ability to form the educational electronic environment and use their skills in the process of realizing the tasks of innovative educational policy 1.4. Ability to supervise the research work of students by means of contemporary ICT
Research and development activities (2R)	2.1. Ability to analyze the results of scientific researches and apply them in the process of solving specific educational and research tasks, including the ICT-based ones 2.2. Readiness to apply individual creative abilities for the unique research tasks solving by applying contemporary ICT 2.3. Readiness to carry out independent scientific research by applying cutting edge science methods and ICT
Methodical activities (3M)	3.1. Readiness to elaborate and realize models, methods, technologies and means of learning, which envisage the use of ICT, to the outcomes analysis of their usage in educational institutions of different types 3.2. Ability to systematization, generalization and distribution of experimental methods (domestic and foreign) and readiness to disseminate realization by means of contemporary ICT

(continued)

Table 2. (*continued*)

Component	Characteristic
Management activities (4Mg)	4.1. Readiness to study the state and potential of the managed system and its macro- and micro-environment by means of using the complex of strategic and operational analyses methods, including the ICT-based 4.2. Ability to carry out research, project, organization and evaluation of realization of management process through the usage of innovative management technologies, which conform to general and specific regularities of the managed system development and envisage the use of ICT 4.3. Ability to organize the teamwork for the tasks solution of educational institution development, realization of research and development activities by means of contemporary ICT 4.4. Readiness to use individual and group technologies of decision-making in the educational institution management, based on national and foreign experience by means of contemporary ICT
Project activities (5Pr)	5.1. Readiness to the fulfill instructional design of the educational environment, including the electronic one, educational programs and individual educational trajectories by means of contemporary ICT 5.2. Ability to design forms and methods of education quality control as well as different types of test-and-measurement materials, including the IT-based ones 5.3. Readiness to design new educational content, technologies and specific methods of learning, which envisage the use of ICT
Specific competences (6S)	6.1. Awareness of the ICT role in education and readiness to initiate innovation in the sphere of IT usage in the educational process 6.2. Ability to use instructional technologies and means in the ICT-saturated educational environment 6.3. Ability to the select effective ICT-tools and services for building individual educational trajectories for those, who study; affording access to full-value education of different categories, for those, who study, according to their abilities, individual aptitudes and interests; for widening the possibilities of specialization for those, who study 6.4. Ability to design balance dedicational components based on IT-technologies application, conducting experimental approbation, further integration into the educational process 6.5. Ability to use different approaches of social media in education via social interaction of students and instructors (teachers), understanding the possibilities and skills of social media application for the experience exchange increase among instructors (teachers) 6.6. Understanding the organization concept and managing the educational institution as an organization, that is constantly developing: the staff are constantly acquiring new knowledge and mastering new ICT, developing their abilities, thus, contributing to the institution success in general 6.7. Understanding the significance of digital literacy for the society in general and education, in particular 6.8. Knowledge of tools usage didactics and ICT services in specific subject fields 6.9. Knowledge of methods of cost estimating for the realization of educational process

The basis of e-CF is not a description of job responsibilities, but a system of competences, since this approach is more flexible. At present, companies with identical job titles refer to different job descriptions. Moreover, the title of the position and the job description often inadequately reflect the requirements of a particular workplace. The business environment in the ICT sector is very complex and subject to constant changes; the complexity and changes make fixed and rigid structures, connected with the work of ICT professionals, ineffective, thus, making it impossible to describe job responsibilities within the international environment. Competencies, on the contrary, are general and quite comprehensive in order to be integrated with any organizational structure.

Defining competences helps respond to changes and plan such changes in the future. Moreover, different combinations of competences may create descriptions of various positions that organizations need, while ensuring flexibility. The structure of the e-CF is based on 4 descriptors. These descriptors reflect different requirements related to levels of business planning, human resources management, in addition to job descriptions.

Taking into account the results of respondents' surveys in the educational process in Ukraine, the analysis of literary sources, and the experience of organizing the training of e-learning managers, 4 descriptors for the model of the system of professional competencies of the e-learning manager were formed (Table 2).

Descriptor 1: 6 components of competences that correspond to the main business processes in which e-learning managers will be involved: teaching activity – research and development activity – methodical activity – project activity – management – specific activity.

Descriptor 2: A set of indicators for each component of the e-learning manager's competences.

Descriptor 3: The professional level of each competence provides a correlation with the European specification – levels e-1 to e-5 correspond to the levels 3 to 5 of the EQF (European Qualification Framework).

Descriptor 4: Examples of knowledge and skills that fit each competence are identified as optional framework components for specimen provision. They are not exhaustive.

In each component (pedagogical activity – research and development activity – methodical activity – project activity – management – specific activity), a certain amount of competences is defined (total – 25). Each of them is further described in the form of a general description, a description of the appropriate abilities for qualifying levels (1–5), examples of knowledge and skills. Table 3 provides an example of a model fragment of professional competences of the e-learning manager for the competence "Project Activity".

The development of such a model is the basis for defining the content modules of the master's program "E-learning management", since 80.2% of surveyed respondents identified the need for such specialists to be trained in the master's program of higher education.

Table 3. A fragment of the model of the system of professional competences of the e-learning manager

Descriptor 1 competence	5. Project activities (5Pr)				
Descriptor 2 (title and general description)	5.1. Instructional design of the educational environment Readiness for instructional design of the educational environment, including electronic, academic programs and individual educational trajectories with the help of modern ICT				
Descriptor 3 formation level 1–5	Level 1 (awareness)	Level 2 (knowledge)	Level 3 (experience)	Level 4 (mastery)	Level 5 (expert)
	Baseline level of the structure of e-learning	Knows which components are used to organize e-learning environment	Can project e-learning environment in line with the requirements of the educational institution	Can project all components of the e-learning environment in line with the development of modern ICT	Suggests unconventional innovative solutions for the organization of e-learning environment applying ICT and advanced educational technologies

3.3   Training of E-learning Managers at the University

Formation of professional competences (Table 2) is accomplished on the basis of a complex approach, which includes: creation of favorable innovation-oriented educational environment and educational communications support system, improvement of the educational and research-and-development content, as well as the infrastructure of the educational institution. The University (www.kubg.edu.ua) has the above-mentioned preconditions for e-learning managers training:

- the curriculum and working programs of the discipline of this specialty are elaborated on the basis of e-learning manager competences;
- the researchers who are directly involved in this sphere are invited to teach in line with the program of e-learning managers training;
- the masters are selected by the specialties "Education Science", to study by the master's program "E-learning management";
- the hybrid cloud-oriented educational environment is formed, which includes e-courses (EEC – electronic educational courses) on the LMS Moodle platform, corporate accounts in Microsoft and Google clouds, access to tools and services, which are the subject matter [17], in particular, services for the organization of independent and individual work, establishment of educational communication, creation of electronic didactic materials, control and diagnostics of students' academic progress [18], tools of organizing independent research activities, common applications and virtual classrooms.

The content of training was formed taking into account the standards and recommendations on quality assurance in the European Higher Education Area [19] on the basis of educational disciplines providing basic, professional and specialized competences in accordance with the model of the system of competences of the e-learning manager. During training the students are offered to master four key disciplines (Table 4). Detailed description of these disciplines given in [20].

Table 4. Recommended list of subjects of the curriculum of students' training by the master's program "E-learning management"

№	Name of the subject/code (URL-address EEC)	Credits/hours number
1.	Internetics and applied information technologies in education/DLC.1.01 (http://e-learning.kubg.edu.ua/course/view.php?id=2593)	8/240
2.	IT-infrastructure management of the educational institution/DLC.1.04 (http://e-learning.kubg.edu.ua/course/view.php?id=2636)	4/120
3.	Innovative methods, technologies and monitoring of the electronic education quality/DLC.1.02 (http://e-learning.kubg.edu.ua/course/view.php?id=2682)	6/180
4.	Design and expertise of high technology information educational environment/DLC.1.03 (http://e-learning.kubg.edu.ua/course/view.php?id=2683)	6/180
5.	Work practice (by the specialization)/PP.1.01	4,5/135
6.	Qualification examination by the specialization/BA.1.01	1,5/45

Table 5 provides an example of implementation of the model for developing a system of professional competences of e-learning managers in the process of training by the master's program "E-learning management".

The formation of students' professional and specific competences, personal characteristics and skills of interpersonal cooperation (soft skills) was carried out based on the embedded model [21]. Teaching by this model does not need any additional resources – soft skills are formed in the process of holding discussions, brainstorming, team work activities, role games, organization of educational and social projects, holding work practice classes and practices in educational institutions, etc.

The tentative foundation of e-learning managers training within the framework of mastering program "E-learning management" is offered as an electronic educational course (EEC), placed at LMS Moodle.

For the critical assessment and processing of the course materials the students may use resources of the platform LMS Moodle, that is: Forum (discussion, recognition of educational problems); Test (achievement tests of the input knowledge of the students and assessment of the intermediate outcomes); File, Hyperlink (visualization, instructions, additional data, etc.); Pages (list of useful resources for studying); Lesson

Table 5. An example of implementation of the model for forming the competence system of the e-learning manager in the discipline "Innovative methods, technologies and monitoring of the quality of e-learning"

Component	Characteristic
Module title (*summary*)	Educational policy in the field of using ICT in the educational institution *Theory of innovation and tools of innovation processes in education. Innovative methods and technologies in education. Educational trends and educational policy of the educational institution*
Coplience with ISTE standard	– VLa.: inspire and facilitate among all stakeholders a shared vision of purposeful change that maximizes use of digital resources to meet and exceed learning goals, support effective instructional practice – VLb.: engage in an ongoing process to develop, implement and communicate technology infused strategic plans with shared vision – SIa.: lead purposeful change to maximize the achievement of learning goals through the appropriate use of technology and media-rich resources – SId.: establish and leverage strategic partnerships to support systemic improvement
Resources	– National strategy of development of education in Ukraine for the period till 2021. – [Electronic resource]. – Access mode: http://zakon4.rada.gov.ua/laws/show/344/2013 – Information technologies in education. UNESCO Institute. – Access mode: http://ru.iite.unesco.org/policy_and_research/ – Research of NMC Horizon Project. – Access mode: http://www.nmc.org/nmc-horizon/ – Intel® "Transformation of ICT-policy in education". Textbook. – Access mode: http://edutransform.org/wp-content/uploads/2015/04/Intel_EduPolicy_Guide_Ukraine.pdf – ICT in Education policy [Electronic resource]. – Access mode: https://ictedupolicy.org/
Tools	Electronic educational course (EEC) based on LMS Moodle, thematic forums and blogs, online bookkeeping services, services for building a timeline, Google documents, social networks
Methods (activity)	– searching (performing target searches of information on the Internet) – research (analysis of the leading countries in the field of informatization of education, construction of an information society, critical evaluation of Internet resources) – problem education (construction of an ICT-plan for the development of an educational institution)
Forms (activity)	– individual work (search of materials, construction of a road map of the school) – pair work (peering estimation) – collective work (defense of the mini project)
Result	ICT-plan for the development of an educational institution for 5 years (text document, timeline, presentation)

(*continued*)

Table 5. (*continued*)

Component	Characteristic
Methods of assessment	– assessment of competency-based tasks – testing (as part of EEC) – case analysis (competency tasks) – non-formal learning (MOOC, Microsoft Image Academy) – surveys (online forms) and interviews
Formed competences	(2R) 2.1. Ability to analyze the results of scientific research and apply them in solving specific educational and research tasks, based on modern ICTs inclusive (1P) 1.1. Ability to apply modern methods and technologies for the organization and implementation of the educational process involving the use of ICT at various educational levels in various educational institutions (3M) 3.2. Ability to systematize, synthesize and disseminate methodological experience (domestic and foreign) and readiness for implementation of dissemination with the help of modern ICTs (4Mg) 4.4. Readiness to use individual and group decision-making technologies in the management of an educational institution, based on domestic and foreign experience, with the help of modern ICTs (6S) 6.1. Understanding the role of ICT in education and readiness to initiate innovations in the use of ICT in the educational process

(material learning, self-checks through tests); Tasks (drilling of practical abilities and skills, experimental activities).

For the organization of the team work and establishment of communication not only the resources of centralized platform LMS Moodle (recommended by the University) were used, but also Google Apps cloud services and Microsoft Office 365 tools (Borys Grinchenko Kyiv University has corresponding license agreements).

At the same time the offered tools do not restrict the students, as the use of other social services allows the students to widen their personal educational environment and enrich it in the process of carrying out their research activities. Selection of tools and services by the students was effectuated independently, based on the aim of educational activities and taking into account Pedagogy Wheel [22], also based on Top 200 Tools for Learning 2016 (http://c4lpt.co.uk/top100tools/) and the assessment of the selected services expediency was carried out by the SAMR-model [23].

For monitoring the training level and students' readiness to study the disciplines of the mentioned specialization at the stage of input testing we defined basic knowledge, abilities and skills of working with office applications. Correction was conducted during the term by way of additional training at Microsoft Imagine Academy, as well as providing additional training regarding the implementation of ICT into the pedagogical activities (Teaching with Technology Microsoft Imagine Academy). The students independently defined tasks and trajectory of non-formal education in MOOC.

The Masters had a chance "to check" the formation of professional and specific competences and soft skills during their working practice at the educational institutions.

In particular, the tasks of practical preparation foresaw the ability to apply the acquired aptitudes and skills on information education expertise, preparation of recommendations on the improvement of ICT-policy of the educational institution, provision of recommended practices regarding the use of contemporary information technologies and services for the organization of pedagogical activities, etc. (https://goo.gl/TXp8Rn). The methods of survey and observation were applied for conducting reflection and monitoring of the formation of the above-mentioned competences of students.

The assessment of acquisition by the students of cognitive and communicative skills in the process of mastering the disciplines of specialization (Table 4.) was effectuated by means of solving competency-based tasks, developing individual (e.g., compiling an e-textbook for the student) and team (e.g., creation of the knowledge map on the defined topic) projects.

The technology of carrying out such projects foresaw specific stages of activities, as a result of which the students developed communicative, interpersonal, leadership skills, skills of working in the team, and time management skills.

3.4 Assessment Tools: Competency-Based Tasks

Assessment of students' acquisition of cognitive and communicative skills in the process of mastering disciplines of master's program "E-learning management" (Table 4) was carried out by way of solving competency-based tasks. The technology of performing such project tasks envisaged activities at certain stages, which resulted in the development of communicative, interpersonal, leadership skills, teamwork and time management skills, presented in the works by the authors of the article [20].

Competency-based tasks were used, both during the study of individual disciplines, and during the professional examination. For example, when studying the discipline "Designing and Expertise of High-Tech Information Educational Environment", the following task was proposed for assessing the level of competence in "Designing an e-learning environment": "An average secondary school is building an e-learning environment. The first step was to create a site. Based on the study of the functional of the site, it is necessary to analyze which school processes require the use of resources and services of the e-learning environment. Design infrastructural, software, information components of the e-educational environment for certain processes".

This task gives an opportunity to evaluate students' skills to analyze the proposed resource, as well as to identify the needs of an educational institution and form a functional e-educational environment. In accordance with Bloom's taxonomy [24], educational objectives for analysis and synthesis are achieved. The levels of formation of the aforementioned competence in accordance with the descriptor 3 are described in Table 3. The assessment of the performance of the competency-based task was carried out in accordance with the description of the above-mentioned levels.

Below is an example of a competency-based task offered for final assessment [20]. This task is complex and combines several competences specified in the model (Fig. 3).

Case study (basic discipline "Innovative methods, technologies and monitoring of e-learning quality"): under the current conditions, the problem of equal access to education for all citizens of our country is actualized. You were involved in the development of proposals for the provision of educational services to various categories of citizens.

- Suggest a model of e-learning of one category, taking into account the specifics of your institution. To achieve this:
- Identify the category of potential listeners (children in treatment, residents of temporarily occupied territories, rural areas, people with special needs, citizens registered on the labor exchange, etc.) and justify their choice;
- Formulate goals and objectives, purpose of learning (specific, understandable and achievable);
- Analyze the domestic and world experience of organizing e-learning for a specific category of listeners;
- Propose innovative methods to be used in the educational process to ensure the quality of educational services.

Implementation tools (basic discipline "Internetics and Applied Information Technologies in Education"): provide examples of learning resources and communication services that can be used for a selected category of potential learners.
Analysis of the conditions of implementation:

1. Basic discipline "IT Infrastructure Management": assess the IT infrastructure of the educational institution where you study (work) from the position of the "Help your neighbor" project. Justify your offer.
2. Basic discipline "Designing and Expertise of High-Tech Information Educational Environment": evaluate the structure and functionality of the educational e-environment of the educational institution where you study (work) from the point of view of the "Help your neighbor" project. Determine limitations for project implementation. Suggest an e-environment model for project implementation. Justify your offer.

Present the result in the form of a business plan. The structure of the document is to be developed individually.

Since the components of the competences of the proposed model (Fig. 3) were not specified in the task, the students had to independently determine them and assess their own acquisition level. To do this, the following task was proposed: Determine which competences are needed to solve this problem, evaluate your level. To do this, fill out the online form (https://goo.gl/5nGiw4) and Table 6.

Students fulfilling their competency-based tasks during the professional examination assessed the development of their own professional competences in pedagogical, research-and-development, methodical, project activities, as well as specific competences on a 5-point scale from 1 to 5. Concurrently, students' competences were assessed by teachers using developed indicators, for example, indicators for determining Level 5 of competence acquisition. The project activity (Table 3) is comprised of: test results for understanding the structure of the e-environment and the basic principles of its functioning (quantitative indicator); the completeness of the analysis of the proposed e-environment, the quality of the design of the e-environment, the correspondence of the e-environment designed by students to the objectives defined (qualitative indicators). The results of self-assessment and assessment by educators

Table 6. Assessment of the level of competences for solving the problem (example of filling)

Competence name	Discipline (example of the topic or task/competence characteristic)	Level (1.5)
1. Professional competences in the sphere of pedagogical activity (1P)	D.: Realization of the model of the inverted class in the study of natural science (1.1)	4
6. Specific (6S)	B.: designing the structure of the electronic educational environment (6.4)	3

Note: *I. Disciplines are indicated by the letters*: A. IT Infrastructure Management; B. Designing and expertise of high-tech information educational environment; C. Innovative methods, technologies and monitoring of e-learning quality; D. Internet and Applied Information Technologies.
II Competence: Components and Characteristics (Fig. 3).
III Level (Fig. 3): Awareness (1), Knowledge (2), Experience (3), Mastery (4), Expert (5).

were compared and presented in [23], and the statistical verification of the hypothesis about the equality of averages according to Student's T-test criterion proved the adequacy of self-assessment of students in relation to acquired competences.

4   Training Outcomes by the Speciality

The pedagogical experiment on the implementation of a new master's program "E-learning management" for Master's speciality "Education Science" was held at Borys Grinchenko Kyiv University in the one academic years (2016–2017). The total number of students was 56. The objective of the experiment was to determine the level of students' competences (from 1 to 5) to training in the master's program "E-learning management" and further training. For each component of the competency model, students' knowledge, skills and abilities were assessed on the basis of the above-mentioned assessment tools before and after the experiment.

To measure the level of professional competences development of students, a system of tasks was developed, similar to the professional testing of Microsoft Certified Educator (Technology Literacy for Educators: pp. 62–193, https://www.microsoft.com/ru-ru/learning/exam-62-193.aspx). The test for the definition of professional competences in accordance with the developed model (Table 2) consisted of 20 tasks: 3 assignments to determine the level of acquiring each of 6 components of the professional competences of e-learning managers and 2 complex tasks. Each task has a description of the case; these are practical situations and a series of questions to determine the level of mastery of non-predictable competences. We offer an example of a task for determining the level of acquiring Management activities (4 Mg), in particular 4.3 and 4.4.

Case: In the educational institution where you work, a re-rebranding project on forming a positive image of the school (department, university) has been launched. This project involves updating the site for more information on the educational institution and establishing cooperation between the participants in the educational process.

Participants in the project include the participants in the educational process (pupils, students, educators) and external experts. As an e-learning manager, you are the coordinator of this project. What decisions will you make in the following situations?

1. You need to determine the site assignment of the educational institution (*Level 1 – Awareness*)
   A. Business card
   B. Showcase achievements
   C. Information system
   D. Interaction platform
2. You understand the need for external experts to be involved. What methods do you use for this? (*Level 2 – Knowledge*)
   A. Place an ad on the institution's website
   B. Search in professional social networks
   C. Visit professional conferences
   D. Set a task for pupils (students)
3. You agree with a web design expert for conducting a workshop for your students. How can you make the learning process more effective? (*Level 3 – Experience*)
   A. Offer an expert to send you a workshop plan and post it on the site for review
   B. Prepare a preliminary questionnaire for students to determine their level of interest and willingness to study
   C. Ask students to put questions to the expert and send them by mail
   D. Create a wiki page where you can submit information about an expert and suggest writing personal questions
4. You plan to organize work on the project. What tasks should be performed in the first place? (*Level 4 – Mastery*)
   A. Create a closed community, using e-mail as communication tools
   B. Create a closed community using cloud services
   C. Create a public community in social networks
   D. Invite students to use their own tools and place the results in a shared document
5. You are asked to create a positive online image of an educational institution involving limited financial resources. What technology, in your opinion, is better to choose for this? Justify your answer. (*Level 5 – Expert*)
   A. Outsourcing
   B. Crowdsourcing
   C. Crowdfunding
   D. Your option

The assessment results for the relevant components of the competency model before and after the experiment are presented in Table 7. The table shows that, the number of students, whose competences have developed, has increased for each component of the competency model.

Since the results of the experiment contain non-metric variables, that is, the variables relating to the nominal scale (experiment, components) or to the order scale (levels), for mapping the relationship between the results of the experiment, the correlation tables, χ^2 (xi-square) and Spearman correlation coefficients were used (SPSS Statistics was used as a tool). It is worth noting that since the experiment variable has

Table 7. Results of the experiment on obtaining professional competences according to levels

Components	Number of students with the level of professional competences from 1 to 5 (%)									
	Before experiment					After experiment				
	1	2	3	4	5	1	2	3	4	5
Pedagogical activities (1P)	10	23	38	29	0	0	8	38	51	3
Research and development activities (2R)	21	36	29	14	0	2	11	36	48	3
Methodical activities (3M)	16	27	45	12	0	4	12	31	49	4
Management activities (4Mg)	29	37	24	10	0	10	18	36	35	1
Project activities (5Pr)	34	27	23	16	0	14	26	39	19	2
Specific competences (6S)	45	32	13	10	0	10	22	31	34	3

only 2 categories: before/after, we can treat it as an ordinal. This will further determine the coefficient of rank correlation τ (tau) – Kendall.

During the statistical processing of the results of the experiment, the correlation tables for each component (components) were constructed. Since the listing of the result is significant, the result for the component "Research and development activities" is given as an example (Table 8). In addition to the correlation table, we additionally build a histogram grouped by experimental data before and after training.

Table 8. Crosstabs "experiment * levels * components"

Components				Levels					Total
				1	2	3	4	5	
Research and development activities	Experiment	Before	Count	12	20	16	8	0	56
			Expected count	6.5	13.0	18.0	17.5	1.0	56.0
			% within experiment	21.4%	35.7%	28.6%	14.3%	0.0%	100.0%
		After	Count	1	6	20	27	2	56
			Expected count	6.5	13.0	18.0	17.5	1.0	56.0
			% within experiment	1.8%	10.7%	35.7%	48.2%	3.6%	100.0%

Analyzing the values of the table and the graphs (Fig. 4), we can observe the displacement of the value of frequencies at levels in the direction of higher values depending on the conducted experiment. In particular, we see that after the experiment (value "after"), the percentage distribution has changed: far more students have levels 3 and 4. In addition, 3.6% received Level 5 in contrast to "before" the experiment, when nobody got such a high rating.

A similar situation is observed in other components. This makes it possible to assume that statistical interdependence exists between the experiment and the level of competence (*experiment* × *levels*).

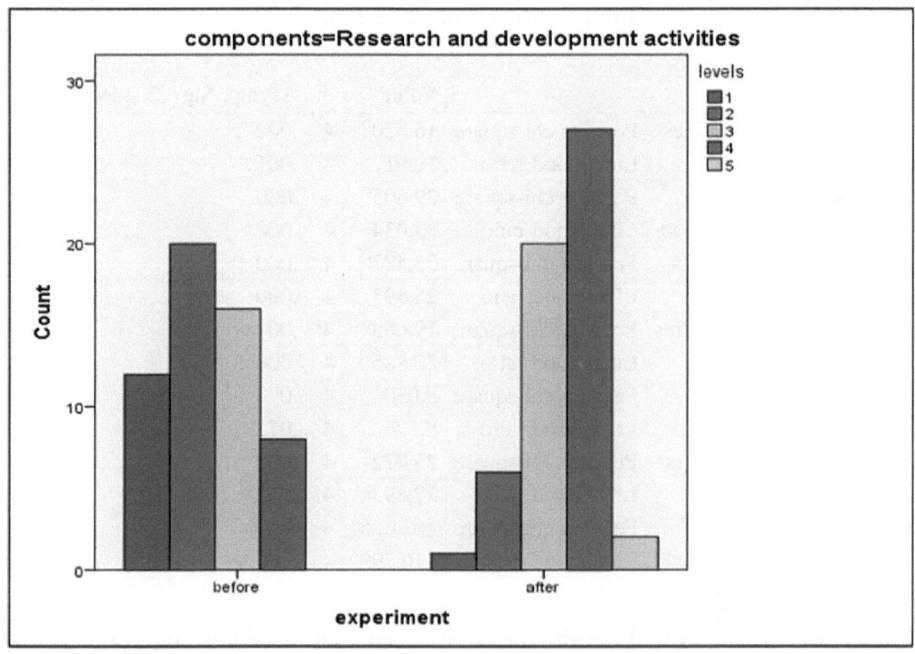

Fig. 4. Experiment data for the component "Research and development activities" (Source: Own work)

However, this statement is based on the "visual assessment". To prove this statistically, tests have been carried out that will allow us to answer the question whether there is any relationship in general, whether there exists intensity and nature (direction) of this dependence. The χ2-Pearson criterion provides the answer to the first question. For our case null hypothesis of the χ2-test suggests that the experiment does not have any effect on the level of achievement of competences. That is, it signifies the homogeneity of the estimates obtained before the experiment (value "before") and after (value "after").

Listing of the χ2 test result for components is shown in Table 9.

Analyzing the result, we see significant values of χ2 (Pearson Chi-Square). In particular, we analyze the value of the p-value (Asymp. Sig.) of probability of type 1 error: the probability of rejecting the null hypothesis with its correctness. At $p > 0,05$, it is considered that the differences between the observed values and the expected values are insignificant. Otherwise, the assumption of the independence of two nominal variables is rejected and it is concluded that the two classifications (variables) depend on each other. As it can be seen from the corresponding p-value of this criterion (critical value of p-value: 0.05), the probability that the null hypothesis is true is extremely small. That is, we can conclude that the effect of the experiment is significant. The only exception is the results for the "Project activities" component, for which the probability value is 0.09, which exceeds the critical value of p-value.

Table 9. Results of χ2-Pearson test

Chi-square tests				
Components		Value	df	Asymp. Sig. (2-sided)
Pedagogical activities	Pearson chi-square	16,520[b]	4	.002
	Likelihood ratio	19,917	4	.001
Research and development activities	Pearson chi-square	29,605[c]	4	.000
	Likelihood ratio	33,034	4	.000
Methodical activities	Pearson chi-square	23,487[c]	4	.000
	Likelihood ratio	25,593	4	.000
Management activities	Pearson chi-square	19,688[d]	4	.001
	Likelihood ratio	20,885	4	.000
Project activities	Pearson chi-square	8,030[d]	4	.090
	Likelihood ratio	8,576	4	.073
Specific competences	Pearson chi-square	25,772[c]	4	.000
	Likelihood ratio	27,893	4	.000
Total	Pearson chi-square	102,685[a]	4	.000
	Likelihood ratio	110,799	4	.000

The next step is to find out the direction and closeness of this connection. To do this, we define the Spearman Correlation coefficients and the Kendall's tau-c inversions (Table 10).

As we see from the listing, according to both coefficients of correlation, the variables positively correlate, which confirms the assumptions made in the analysis of tables of correlation. Analyzing the tightness of communication, for the components

Table 10. Listing of nonparametric correlations

Components		Value	Asymp. std. error[a]	Approx. T[b]	Approx. Sig.
Pedagogical activities	Kendall's tau-c	.386	.091	4.227	.000
	Spearman correlation	.357	.083	4.005	.000[c]
Research and development activities	Kendall's tau-c	.565	.082	6.909	.000
	Spearman correlation	.510	.073	6.211	.000[c]
Methodical activities	Kendall's tau-c	.484	.088	5.510	.000
	Spearman correlation	.440	.079	5.137	.000[c]
Management activities	Kendall's tau-c	.461	.091	5.049	.000
	Spearman correlation	.413	.082	4.758	.000[c]
Project activities	Kendall's tau-c	.250	.102	2.457	.014
	Spearman correlation	.225	.091	2.416	.017[c]
Specific competences	Kendall's tau-c	.526	.087	6.023	.000
	Spearman Correlation	.470	.078	5.585	.000[c]
Total	Kendall's tau-c	.432	.038	11.468	.000
	Spearman correlation	.388	.034	10.893	.000[c]

"Research and development activities" and "Specific competences" it is significant (exceeds 0.5). For others it is weak. In this case, regression for all components except "Project activities" is significant (Approx. Sig. < 0.05), which confirms the hypothesis of the impact of the experiment on the level of competence.

Thus, the results show a significant increase in the level of professional competence of future e-learning management specialists. Taking into account Spearman coefficients for various components of competence, we have the opportunity to adjust training while teaching academic disciplines by the specialty, for example, to pay attention to the formation of project competences which are rather important for future e-learning managers who need not only to be able to create and methodically competently use ICTs in e-learning, but also to design the components of e-environment, the content components of the e-learning system, etc.

5   Conclusions

Analysis of the research results testifies to the significant effect of the implemented master's program "E-learning management" within the framework of Masters' training by the specialty "Education Sciences".

The model of professional competencies of e-learning managers, based on ISTE, European e-Competence Framework, is developed and substantiated theoretically. It includes a system of components (Pedagogical, Research and development, Methodical, Management, Project activities, Specific competences), levels (Awareness, Knowledge, Experience, Mastery, Expert), methods, forms and e-environments for learning organization.

To determine the level of professional competencies of masters, a system of competency tasks was proposed. It is based on the components of the developed model. The analysis of the results of the pedagogical experiment showed an increase in the level of professional competencies in all components of the model of competencies, with the exception of "Project activities".

In the perspective of further research, it is possible to adjust the training of future e-learning managers for the component "Project activities" through the implementation of educational, scientific, interdisciplinary projects.

References

1. Gaebel, M., Kupriyanova, V., Morais, R., Colucci, E.: E-learning in European Higher Education Institutions. European University Association. Results of a mapping survey conducted in October–December 2013 (2014). http://www.eua.be/Libraries/publication/e-learning_survey
2. Morze, N., Kuzminska, O., Protsenko, G.: Public information environment of a modern university. In: ICT in Education, Research and Industrial Applications: Integration, Harmonization and Knowledge Transfer. CEUR Workshop Proceedings, pp. 264–272 (2013). http://ceur-ws.org/Vol-1000/ICTERI-2013-p-264-272.pdf

3. Morze, N.V., Smyrnova-Trybulska, E., Glazunova, O.: Design of a university learning environment for SMART education. In: Smart Technology Applications in Business Environments, pp. 221–248. IGI Global (2017)
4. Al-Ani, M.: E-university environment based on E-management. Int. J. Comput. Eng. Res. 5(4), 1–6 (2015). https://www.researchgate.net/profile/Muzhir_Al-Ani/publication/275462223_ E-University_Environment_Based_on_E-management/links/553cb6fd0cf29b5ee4b8aa06.pdf
5. The eLearning Competency Framework for Teachers and Trainers, European Institute of E-Learning. http://www.eife-l.org/competencies/ttframework. Accessed 25 Sept 2017
6. Martin, B.: Successful implementation of TPACK in teacher preparation programs. Int. J. Integrating Technol. Educ. 4(1), 17–26 (2015). http://airccse.org/journal/ijite/papers/ 4115ijite02.pdf
7. Keengwe, J., Kidd, T.: Towards best practices in online learning and teaching in higher education. J. Online Learn. Teach. 6(2), 533 (2010)
8. Weigel, V.: Deep Learning for a Digital Age: Technology's Untapped Potential to Enrich Higher Education. Jossey-Bass, 169 p. (2002). https://eric.ed.gov/?id=ED457787
9. ISTE National Educational Technology Standards (2016). http://www.iste.org/standards/ standards. Accessed 25 Sept 2017
10. The eLearning Competency Framework for Teachers and Trainers, European Institute of E-Learning. http://www.eife-l.org/competencies/ttframework. Accessed 25 Sept 2017
11. Cardos, V.D., Tiron-Tudor, A.: Managerial skills of an e-learning manager. Ann. Fac. Econ. 4(1), 135–140 (2009). http://EconPapers.repec.org/RePEc:ora:journl:v:4:y:2009:i:1:p:135-140
12. Keramida, M.: Top 6 Skills of an Outstanding eLearning Project Manager (2016). https:// elearningindustry.com/top-6-skills-outstanding-elearning-project-manager
13. Dhondi, P.: Skills of a Successful E-learning Project Manager (2014). http://blog. commlabindia.com/elearning-design/skills-of-elearning-project-manager
14. Morze, N., Balyk, N., Smirnova-Trybulska, E.: The analysis of foreign and domestic training programs for managers of e-learning. Edukacja Humanistyczna: Pedagogium 2(31), 123–138 (2014). (in Russian). http://wshtwp.pl/eh-2014-2/
15. ICT Profiles. http://www.ecompetences.eu/ict-professional-profiles/. Accessed 25 Sept 2017
16. European e-Competence Framework 3.0 (EN). http://www.ecompetences.eu/wp-content/ uploads/2014/02/European-e-Competence-Framework-3.0_CEN_CWA_16234-1_2014.pdf. Accessed 25 Sept 2017
17. Glazunova, O., Voloshyna, T.: Hybrid cloud-oriented educational environment for training future IT specialists. In: Information and Communication Technologies in Education, Research, and Industrial Applications, Communications in Computer and Information Science, vol. 1614, pp. 157–167 (2016). http://ceur-ws.org/Vol-1614/paper_64.pdf
18. Kuzminska, O., Mazorchuk, M.: Models and tools for information support of test development process in learning management systems. In: Information and Communication Technologies in Education, Research, and Industrial Applications, Communications in Computer and Information Science, vol. 1614, pp. 632–639 (2016). http://ceur-ws.org/Vol-1614/paper_83.pdf
19. Standards and Recommendations for Quality Assurance in the European Higher Education Area. http://www.enqa.eu/wp-content/uploads/2013/06/ESG_3edition-2.pdf. Accessed 25 Sept 2017
20. Morze, N., Buinytska, O., Kuzminska, O., Glazunova, O., Protsenko, G., Vorotnykova, I.: E-learning managers training at universities: projection, design and efficiency indicators. In: ICT in Education, Research and Industrial Applications: Integration, Harmonization and Knowledge Transfer. CEUR Workshop Proceedings, pp. 229–244 (2017). http://ceur-ws. org/Vol-1844/10000229.pdf

21. Saravanan, V.: Sustainable employability skills for engineering professionals. Indian Rev. World Lit. English **5**(2), 1–9 (2009). https://pdfs.semanticscholar.org/9cb6/e933fef43504a7eee78e3bafb82da6e33d53.pdf
22. Carrington, A.: The Padagogy wheel – it's not about the apps, it's about the pedagogy (2015). http://www.teachthought.com/critical-thinking/blooms-taxonomy/the-padagogy-wheel/
23. Resources to support the SAMR Model. http://www.schrockguide.net/samr.html. Accessed 25 Sept 2017
24. Valcke, M., De Wever, M., Bram, C., Deed, C.: Supporting active cognitive processing in collaborative groups. The potential of Bloom's taxonomy as a labeling tool. Internet High. Educ. **12**, 165–172 (2009). https://doi.org/10.1016/j.iheduc.2009.08.003

Developing a Self-regulation Environment in an Open Learning Model with Higher Fidelity Assessment

Juan Pablo Martínez Bastida$^{(\boxtimes)}$, Olena Havrykenko ,
and Andrey Chukhray

National Aerospace University, KhAI, Kharkiv, Ukraine
jpbastida@gmail.com, lm77191220@gmail.com,
achukhray@gmail.com

Abstract. Automation of pedagogical interventions in Model-tracing cognitive tutors (MTCT) strongly depends on chained paradigms like a proper modeling of the knowledge involved behind the student's actions. Knowledge is tracked for inferring its degree of mastery that convey to a constructive learning process. In this paper is presented a methodology based on a probabilistic model for generating pedagogical interventions under a self-regulated environment. The foundations for developing it are explicitly detailed up to their implementation, passing through the modeling of the cognitive and meta-cognitive student knowledge. Probabilistic model is encoded in a Bayesian network topology that increases fidelity assessment by independently diagnosing degree of mastery of the relevant knowledge components and allowing a straightforward interpretation of the knowledge involved in a student's actions. Moreover, it is also interwoven with other processes for inferring decisions that will influence in the way pedagogical interventions are generated and promoting a self-regulated behavior. Preliminary results to assess effectiveness of the proposed approach are also presented by implementing it in a MTCT called TITUS.

Keywords: Bayesian inference · Probabilistic reasoning · Model-tracing Cognitive tutor · Pedagogical intervention · Self-regulation Learning

1 Introduction

Up to now, several Intelligent Tutoring Systems (ITS) have been widely documented, described and implemented in the worldwide scientific literature for tutoring in the task domain such as physics [2, 3], mathematics [5, 15], different topics in the programming field [14, 22], and engineering subjects [17] to consider a few. But a persistent absence of ITS for learning and developing knowledge and skills about fault-tolerant systems is actual and presented in the literature. Humanity strongly depends on a large amount of complex systems and technical processes that have a deep impact on our everyday life. We do not only use them, but our lives depend on them. Thus, the necessity to develop ITS that may improve and accelerate the formation of the future designers and developers that will include fault-tolerant principles [10, 11] into their solutions is of great importance. However, designing effective tutors has been an arduous and stressful

© Springer International Publishing AG, part of Springer Nature 2018
N. Bassiliades et al. (Eds.): ICTERI 2017, CCIS 826, pp. 112–131, 2018.
https://doi.org/10.1007/978-3-319-76168-8_6

task and taking into account that intrinsically is an interdisciplinary process. A process that might start by selecting a closed or open learning model [5] that will determine the way tasks are presented to trainees. How learning program is structured [1, 4–9], the manner assessment is carried out [8], how other kinds of pedagogical interventions are generated and supplied [12–16], the way graphic interface is designed [2], and many other important factors that should be taken into account during the prototyping and deployment phase of an ITS. Thus, diversity helps to improve and enforce ITS development processes, but it is also a weakness because it creates gaps between researches, developers, or specialists and the models and methodologies, creating poor conditions that do not promote the development of solutions in any task domain.

The aim of this work is focused on bringing closer a set of models and methods that are involved in the dynamical generation of pedagogical interventions in ITSs, specifically Model Tracing Cognitive Tutors (MTCT) [1–3, 25, 26]. Pedagogical interventions are actively based on the analysis and interpretation of uncertainty information and data mining also called as cognitive model (CM) so far, that are obtained while trainees use the tutor.

Cognitive models are an integral part of developing MTCTs [1, 2, 26]. Various MTCTs have successfully been applied over the last decades, they are capable to trace student's steps (student's actions), while she/he is interacting with the cognitive tutor in order to provide a positive impact on learners [1–3, 5, 6, 25]. CMs require a proper understanding of the knowledge involved in each step, problem-solving strategies or principles in a given learning domain. In addition, a CM should be able to interpret student's recurrent behavioral patterns and tendencies that reflect a way of thinking in order to provide constructive pedagogical interventions. Therefore, a MTCT is always "interested" in the way a student processes and assimilates the relevant knowledge components, resulting in the so-called learner's meta-cognitive model. This model is built by tracing and analyzing the actions when a student commits steps to accomplish certain task, but steps can be recurrent in terms of the way that knowledge is required, in other words, how tasks are presented [18–22]. Thus, interpretation for *fidelity assessment* of mastery in students is a very important feature that involves uncertainty information. *Fidelity assessment* in education can be understood like a parameter that helps us to frame how close the CM reflects the student's metal state that stablishes a strong link between her/his cognitive degree of mastery in certain learning domain and her/his actions [4]. This is a key feature that characterizes ITSs from more traditional educational procedures or systems, its ability to interpret students actions to maintain an individual model of the student's reasoning and learning.

Actually, Open Learner Models (OLMs) and Self-regulated Learning (SRL) have gained more interest from researcher [5]. ITS scientific community is focused on maintaining or enhancing effectiveness of tutors at domain-level learning [4, 5]. Whereas metacognitive support features and other pedagogical interventions, like feedback supplied by MTCTs enforce self-assessment that leads to a better learning process, but it does not assure learning effectiveness [4]. Therefore, development of efficient features in order to promote self-assessment and study choice is a vast field of study. Furthermore, OLMs add ITSs characteristics for supporting students' self-assessment and study choice by incorporating tools for promoting SRL.

Moreover, fidelity assessment of mastery in a student and keep track of it require uncertainty reasoning, since this assessment leads to monitor cognitive processes that are not always explicitly observable. Probabilistic models encoded in a novel Bayesian network (BN) topology is presented for increasing fidelity assessment by independently diagnosing misused relevant knowledge components and allowing a straightforward interpretation of the knowledge involved in a student task [23]. BN is interwoven with other processes for inferring decisions that will influence in the way pedagogical interventions are generated.

In the present work, we explore a few features of an OLM to support self-assessment in conjunction with "help-seeking" meta-cognitive skills development. This work is based on the hypothesis that some students are less able to look for help when they need it. They do not get closer to a person to get it, e.g. the teacher or other means of information, communication or learning support, due to the lack of meta-cognitive skills for "help-seeking" besides that, a help-seeking student becomes a better learner [3]. We believe, these features can foment a SRL process and improve domain-level learning outcomes. We also discuss details and considerations in fidelity prototyping and evaluation stages, including in between the employed models and methodologies. Different principles, approaches and paradigms were implemented in the development of a MTCT called TITUS [10] for the purpose of this study. Mainly, TITUS supports the base of learning by doing, self-assessment and help-seeking meta-cognitive approaches [3, 15]. The learning program was built in accordance with the signal-parametric approach for fault-tolerant systems [10, 11]. An engine for generating pedagogical interventions supported by a rule-based CM is discussed as well. Preliminary results to assess performance of the proposed approach are presented at Sect. 7, and challenges of future work at Sect. 8.

2 Prototyping and Designing Markup

One of the challenges that researchers and developers have to face is the proper establishment of the knowledge involved in learners' cognitive processes as close as possible. The higher comprehension of the knowledge involved in a cognitive process (cognitive fidelity), the better prototyping fidelity is carried out that promotes SRL [5] (e.g. a better development of tasks, better pedagogical interventions, task designations, self-assessment, self-explanation). Higher cognitive fidelity helps cognitive task analysis [2] that in fact, it is used for pedagogical model development. Thus, prototyping and cognitive fidelities lead to understand the skills, knowledge and conceptions involved in a given domain.

Cognitive Tutors generally provide a constraint-based step-by-step couching program, students train and develop knowledge and skills in basis of task or problem-solving practices. A Cognitive Tutor that is in compliance with SRL principles commonly have the following features [2, 5, 9]: (1) a rich set of task-problems, (2) personalized learning program, (3) detailed assessment for each relevant knowledge component in the given domain, (4) includes tools for promoting self-assessment, (5) provide tools for monitoring learning progress, (6) prompts hints in recurrent misused knowledge components and promotes problem-solving strategies, (7) from simple to error-specific feedback. A common feature also included in OLMs is letting students have control over task-problem selection. TITUS does not provide a control selection feature itself; this is a deferred feature for future study. However, the rest of features above exposed have been implemented in TITUS.

In this section, we outline the major components of TITUS; its general architecture is given on Fig. 1. TITUS obtains valuable information from students, which is helpful to know what to teach, whom it teaches and the way it teaches. TITUS has been developed as a computer application; the complete lecture notes of the studying program have been included and can be accessed on demand.

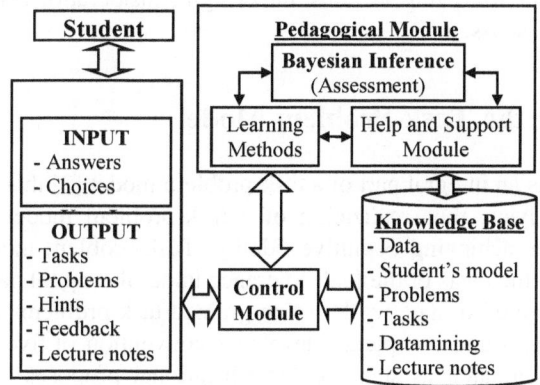

Fig. 1. General architecture of TITUS

The *user interface* is the environment where the student will execute his actions and attempts to solve different kinds of tasks-problems as well as it functions like a graphical portal that can depict hints and feedbacks among other required information.

The *control module* is on charge to process and administrates the flow of information from and to the other blocks in TITUS. The necessary pedagogical processes are involved with the *learning methods block* and the *help and support modules*; here is where the pedagogical decisions or actions are made in accordance to the answers of the tasks-problems. The *task analyzer* (step analyzer), a part of the *Bayesian inference block*, constantly monitors the student's answers and returns the proper support, (i.e. hints, feedbacks, by means of the *help and support module*).

The *knowledge base* is constituted by the expert knowledge in the task domain and information that is saved while TITUS is being used by the students. This information is required, updated and recycled as well. It also contains the complete cognitive model, task-problems model in base of the knowledge components, lessons notes that will be required on demand or automatically by the own system. The *knowledge base* records the complete state of the system as well as the student's performance, and that is how the system creates the student's CM. This model is a database that contains information about the student: the correct answers, wrong answers, attempts by task-problem, time for answering, and other important variables.

This data is used to perform assessments of the student's, but also, it is used to determine the proper pedagogical actions and decisions to maintain a continuous and productive learning process. For instance, it needs to know when the student's mastery has been obtained so it can advance the student to the next learning module or difficult level, and BNs can manage this uncertainty. Nevertheless, it also maintains an OLM that let students take part and decide the learning path. Prototyping fidelity has become such important term in modeling cognitive processes, without it, a proper representation of the knowledge components involved in certain problem-solving environment cannot be marked-up. This decreases cognitive fidelity and blocks cognitive task analysis, thus *assessment fidelity* becomes unreliable, and it compromises the other functionalities. In the following sections, the design considerations and development of such features are discussed.

3   Structuring the Task-Problem Model

Cognitive fidelity is an integral part of a task-problem model [2] that helps carrying out cognitive task analysis, thus realization of a task-problem model for selection and assessment requires achieving cognitive fidelity. Task-problem model in TITUS has been developed on the basis of the fault-tolerance under the signal parametric approach [10, 11]. It is structured in a network of fine-grained task-problems properly classified in sequential modules and complexity levels. A convention of five complexity levels are commonly instantiated as standard for educational proposes [6] (i.e. very easy, easy, average, difficult, and very difficult). Each module has a minimal requirement of two task-problems per complexity level with the aim to have alternatives of choice. Moreover, all the set of task-problems in a module must cover the complete set of relevant knowledge components (KCs) included in it.

Set of task-problems (following simply referred like the tasks) in every module should be developed as an interwoven network over the relevant KCs that it contains. Thus, it is preferable that every KC should be trained at least by two different tasks. This relationship between a KCs and tasks increases the probability of mastering them by increasing the times of possible situations that students might employ them. This is well known because it is the classic approach that is commonly implemented in classrooms. *Task Model (MT)* is represented in (1) and its boundaries in (2)–(4), where T is a task, KW defines a knowledge component, i is the task identifier, $j \in [1, 5]$ represents the levels of complexity, k is the module for the task T, and l is the identification number for the knowledge component. An example of the MT above explained is depicted on Fig. 2.

$$MT : \{T_{ijk}\} \rightarrow \{KW_{kl}\} \tag{1}$$

$$\forall k, \forall j \{T_{ijk}\} \neq \emptyset, \|T_{ijk}\| \geq 2 \tag{2}$$

$$\forall k, \forall j, \forall l \{T_{ijk}\} = MT^{-1}(KW_{kl}) \neq \emptyset, \|T_{ijk}\| \geq 2 \tag{3}$$

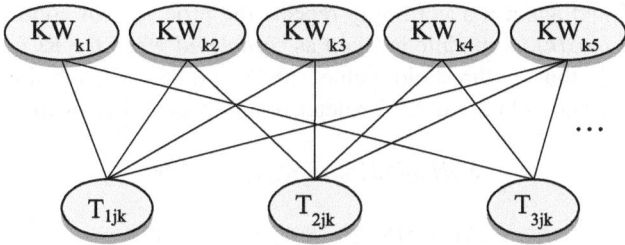

Fig. 2. Task model structure (example)

$$\forall k \ \cup MT\left(T_{ijk}\right) = \{KW_{kl}\} \tag{4}$$

On the other hand, the *student model* (*MS*) is constantly updated while the student is working with TITUS, for this reason, *MS* is a dynamic representation of the degree of mastery in the student. *MS* can be represented by (5) and (6), where S represents the student, q is his identifier, $P \subset \Re$ in the interval [0,1] that represents the probability of mastery, N is the attempts (steps) realized.

$$MS1 : \{S_q\} \times \{T_{ijk}\} \to N \tag{5}$$

$$MS2 : \{S_q\} \times \{KW_{kl}\} \to P \tag{6}$$

The prior information is initialized if a student S_q uses TITUS for the first time, thus for each $S_q : \forall i, \forall j, \forall k \ MS1 \left(S_q, T_{ijk}\right) = \{0\}, \forall l, \forall k \ MS2\left(S_q, KW_{kl}\right) = \{0.5\}$. After this, first module is selected and complexity level is set to the middle one. Therefore, a next task (*NT*) with KCs that have lower probabilities of mastery among tasks in a module (*MT*) is chosen by means of (7).

$$NT = MT^{-1}\left(KW_{kl} \ \middle|\ MS2\left(S_q, KW_{kl}\right) \to min\right) \tag{7}$$

If $\|NT\| > 1$, thus, search of the next task will be based on attempts *NT'*, represented by (8). In case $\|NT'\| > 1$, it will be implemented by (9) and a task will randomly be selected (*NT**). This case is certainly possible at the first time a student uses TITUS.

$$NT' = \left(NT \ \middle|\ MS1\left(S_q, T_{ijk}\right) \to min\right) \tag{8}$$

$$NT^* = RAND(NT) \tag{9}$$

Processes described by (7)–(9) will repeat meanwhile the student has not mastered the KCs in the current module; only then, the tutor passes to the closest following module: $K + 1$ and again it accordingly repeats the processes of choosing a next task meanwhile $k < max(k)$. A module is taken as completed when the KCs that conform it are all mastered, thus a threshold value (pKW = 0.85) helps estimating that [9]. Expressions (10) and (11) are used for determining probability of mastery.

$$MIN\left[MS2\left(S_q, KW_{kl}\right)\right] > pKW \tag{10}$$

$$AVG\left[MS2\left(S_q, KW_{kl}\right)\right] > pKW \tag{11}$$

4 Probabilistic Assessment

A probabilistic model is a feasible tool to englobe knowledge implications in uncertain situations. It might approximate cognitive processes involved in the resolutions of task-problems. They are directly related in the analysis of the possible solutions in base of the given context. Evidence in such models depicts a level of knowledge mastery about a specific situation, but the challenge is to deliver this kind of inference over a context domain.

Bayesian networks (BNs) are probabilistic models that have widely been employed in ITSs [5, 6]. BNs based on the Knowledge Tracing approach equally affect prior probabilities of mastery in KCs. Thus, when multiple KCs are involved in a task-problem solution and one of them is incorrect, all probabilities of mastery will be equally decreased in every involved KC, without taking in account if they were or were not misused. This presents a low-fidelity assessment model due to an improper representation of the cognitive process in the task solution.

A BN presented on Fig. 3 implements a *Diagnostic Model* (DM) that improves fidelity assessment of mastery in the case exposed above. This topology assumes that each cognitive task-problem process depends on individual KCs. Thus, the set of relevant KCs are individual cognitive processes when a student attempts to complete a task. KCs can be applied independently one from another, so their posterior probability of mastery should be assessed separately.

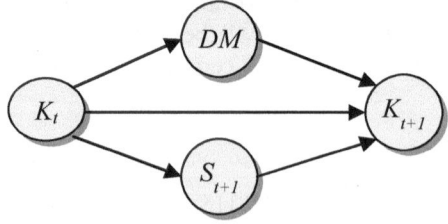

Fig. 3. BN with diagnostic model for Knowledge Tracing

BN on Fig. 3, consists of four nodes: K_t, S_{t+1}, DM and K_{t+1}, where K_t is the probability of mastery of certain KC or skill at t time; S_{t+1} is a step (student's action) at moment $t + 1$; DM is a diagnostic model that is directly linked to the step and influences the assessment of mastery; and K_{t+1} is the probability of mastery at $t + 1$ moment. $\neg K_t$, $\neg S_{t+1}$, $\neg DM$ and $\neg K_{t+1}$ are the respective complementary probabilities of mastery.

The probability $P(K_{t+1})$ of mastery certain knowledge component at a moment t after a student's correct step is obtained with (12). Conditional probabilities $P(K_t|S_{t+1}, \neg DM)$ and $P(\neg K_t|S_{t+1}, \neg DM)$ in (12) are obtained with (13) and (14) respectively, where α is a normalization coefficient. The evidences in a student's actions are denoted by $P(S_{t+1}) = 1$ (correct step) and $P(DM) = 0$ (deactivated).

$$
\begin{aligned}
P(K_{t+1}) = {} & P(K_t|S_{t+1}, \neg DM)P(K_{t+1}|K_t, S_{t+1}, DM)P(S_{t+1})P(DM) \\
& + P(\neg K_t|S_{t+1}, \neg DM)P(K_{t+1}|\neg K_t, S_{t+1}, DM)P(S_{t+1})P(DM) \\
& + P(K_t|S_{t+1}, \neg DM)P(K_{t+1}|K_t, S_{t+1}, \neg DM)P(S_{t+1})P(\neg DM) \\
& + P(\neg K_t|S_{t+1}, \neg DM)P(K_{t+1}|\neg K_t, S_{t+1}, \neg DM)P(S_{t+1})P(\neg DM) \\
& + P(K_t|S_{t+1}, \neg DM)P(K_{t+1}|K_t, \neg S_{t+1}, DM)P(\neg S_{t+1})P(DM) \\
& + P(\neg K_t|S_{t+1}, \neg DM)P(K_{t+1}|\neg K_t, \neg S_{t+1}, DM)P(\neg S_{t+1})P(DM) \\
& + P(K_t|S_{t+1}, \neg DM)P(K_{t+1}|K_t, \neg S_{t+1}, \neg DM)P(\neg S_{t+1})P(\neg DM) \\
& + P(\neg K_t|S_{t+1}, \neg DM)P(K_{t+1}|\neg K_t, \neg S_{t+1}, \neg DM)P(\neg S_{t+1})P(\neg DM)
\end{aligned}
\tag{12}
$$

$$
\begin{aligned}
P(K_t|S_{t+1}, \neg DM) &= \alpha \sum_{K_{t+1}} P(K_t, S_{t+1}, \neg DM, K_{t+1}) \\
&= \alpha \sum_{K_{t+1}} P(K_t)P(S_{t+1}|K_t)P(\neg DM|K_t)P(K_{t+1}|K_t, S_{t+1}, \neg DM)
\end{aligned}
\tag{13}
$$

$$
\begin{aligned}
P(\neg K_t|S_{t+1}, \neg DM) &= \alpha \sum_{K_{t+1}} P(\neg K_t, S_{t+1}, \neg DM, K_{t+1}) \\
&= \alpha \sum_{K_{t+1}} P(\neg K_t)P(S_{t+1}|\neg K_t)P(\neg DM|\neg K_t)\, P(K_{t+1}|\neg K_t, S_{t+1}, \neg DM)
\end{aligned}
\tag{14}
$$

Therefore, a *step analyzer* assesses each relevant KC in the actual step in order to determine the corresponding pedagogical actions. Conditional Probability Tables (CPT) for nodes K_t, K_t, S_{t+1}, DM and K_{t+1} are the following shown in Tables 1, 2, 3, and 4. According to Tables 1, 2, 3, and 4, it is possible to obtain the posterior probability of mastery by employing Eqs. (10)–(12). Probabilities $P(K_t|S_{t+1}, DM)$ and $P(K_t|S_{t+1}, DM)$ are computed in (15) and (16) respectively.

$$
P(K_t|S_{t+1}, \neg DM) = \alpha(0.5 * 0.9 * 0.9 * 1 + 0.5 * 0.9 * 0.9 * 0) = \alpha * 0.405
\tag{15}
$$

Table 1. CPT for node K_t.

Mastered	0.5
Unmastered	0.5

Table 2. CPT for node S_{t+1}.

K_t	Mastered	Unmastered
Mastered	0.9	0.1
Unmastered	0.1	0.9

Table 3. CPT for node DM.

K_t	Mastered	Unmastered
Activated	0.1	0.2
Deactivated	0.9	0.8

Table 4. CPT for node K_{t+1}.

K_t	Mastered			
S_{t+1}	Correct		Incorrect	
DM	Activated	Deactivated	Activated	Deactivated
Mastered	1	1	0.6	0.7
Unmastered	0	0	0.4	0.3
K_t	Unmastered			
S_{t+1}	Correct		Incorrect	
DM	Activated	Deactivated	Activated	Deactivated
Mastered	0.6	0.6	0	0
Unmastered	0.4	0.4	1	1

$$P(\neg K_t | S_{t+1}, \neg DM) = \alpha(0.5 * 0.1 * 0.8 * 0.6 + 0.5 * 0.1 * 0.8 * 0.4) = \alpha * 0.04 \tag{16}$$

From (15) and (16), we can obtain: $\alpha(0.405 + 0.04) = 1$; $\alpha = 2.24719$; $P(K_t|S_{t+1}, DM) = 0.910112$; $P(K_t|S_{t+1}, DM) = 0.089888$. Finally, $P(K_{t+1})$ and $P(\neg K_{t+1})$ are obtained by (17) and (18). They denote the posterior probabilities of mastery and non-mastery.

$$P(K_{t+1}) = 0.910112 * 1 * 1 * 1 + 0.089888 * 0.6 * 1 * 1 + 0.910112 * 1 *$$
$$1 * 0 + 0.089888 * 0.6 * 1 * 0 + 0.910112 * 0.6 * 0 * 1 + 0.089888 * 0 * \tag{17}$$
$$0 * 1 + 0.910112 * 0.7 * 0 * 0 + 0.089888 * 0 * 0 * 0 = 0.964045(11)$$

$$P(\neg K_{t+1}) = 1 - P(K_{t+1}) = 0.035955 \tag{18}$$

In order to develop and implement the proposed Probabilistic Assessment model, GeNIe© and SMILE [24] were used. An example of an implemented assessment model for a task-problem is depicted on Fig. 4. The case when a student has misused all KCs in a task-problem is shown on Fig. 4(a), thus both DMs have been activated, and equally decreasing their probabilities of mastery. A case when only one relevant KC was misused is presented on Fig. 4(b). It can be observed that student's step was "Other" because the *step analyzer* determined that knowledge component K23_0 was misused and it activated the corresponding DM23, resulting in a less posterior probability of mastery in K23_1.

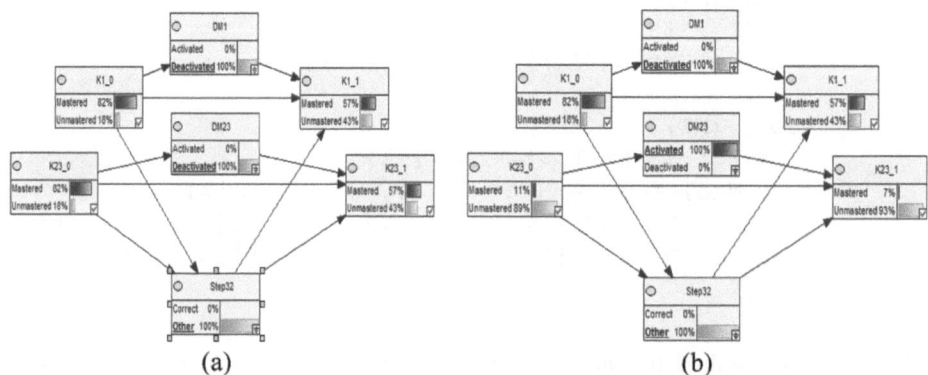

(a)   (b)

Fig. 4. Experimental test of the probabilistic assessment in GeNIe© [24]

5   Assigning Complexity Level and Generating Pedagogical Feedback

Once a task has been chosen, TITUS expects the student's action. After the student has committed it, the *step analyzer* is triggered and assesses probability of mastery of the relevant KCs in the task: $Sol_i(NT) \in \{0,1\}$, $NT \in \{ NT, NT', NT^* \}$, and updates the attempt counter as well. The complexity level is adjusted according to the piecewise statement in (19).

$$j = \begin{cases} j+1, if(Sol_i(NT) = 1)(j < max(j)) \\ j-1, if(Sol_i(NT) = 0)(j > min(j)) \\ j, other\ cases \end{cases} \qquad (19)$$

Pedagogical feedback is a "service" that may be offered at the moment the student makes steps. Although, a hint could be supplied before, during or after committing a step to support or assist students. Hints are intended to avoid frustration or remarking repetitive misconceptions or error patterns.

However, in this work, it is only proposed a general method for supplying pedagogical feedback after the student has submitted a step.

Nevertheless, it can be used as a base for developing other supporting pedagogical methodologies, but this would increase complexity of the software to make it capable of tracking every minimal student's action even over the tutor's GUI for interpreting and "translate" it into a pedagogical intervention. The method for the *pedagogical feedback support* (see below) is executed when the student's step is submitted and the *step analyzer* has already assessed the relevant KCs involved in the current task.

```
∀k Sol_i (NT), NT ∈ { NT, NT', NT*}
Start
    Analyze: ∀l{KW_kl} : {Sol_i (NT)} → [T_ijk]
        {Sol_i (NT)} ↔ 1
            MS1 : {S_q}x{T_ijk}→({N_ikr}+1)
            Give: {min(FB_l)} : {Sol_i (NT)} →1

        {Sol_i (NT)} ↔ 0
            MS1 : {S_q}x{T_ijk}→({N_ikw}+1)
            ({N_ikw} = 1) → {min(FB_l)}, {T_ijk} → [k]
            Give: ∀l {FB_l} = 2 : {N_ikw} ∈ [2, 3], {T_ijk}→[k]
            Give: ∀l {FB_l} = 3 : {N_ikw} > 3, {T_ijk} → [k]
End
```

In addition, method for the *pedagogical feedback support* computes how many times the student has properly employed a specific KC (N_{ikr}); how many times she/he has misused it (N_{ikw}), and accordingly the inner loop returns some classification of feedback (FB_l) $\in$ {1: minimal feedback, 2: hint about error, 3: specific error feedback}. For the first time a KC is misused, a minimal feedback ($FB_l \rightarrow 1$) is returned, such as "correct" or "incorrect". For the second and third time, it will return an error-specific hint or feedback ($FB_l \rightarrow 2$), i.e. "You should pay more attention on the value of the transfer coefficient" or "The class of fault you have chosen is not correct", "Static characteristics for this class of fault are depicted on the figure, identify them", etc. It has been determined second level feedback should be given twice as a very simple mechanism to minimize feedback abuse. Nevertheless, other more advanced mechanisms may be implemented.

On the fourth and over, a misuse of a relevant KC has occurred, the tutor will return and error-specific feedback that will lead the student to review and study the corresponding theory or related information to overcome the deficiencies on the corresponding KCs, in order to prevent this from occurring again and supporting a constructive learning process. The tutor gives only delayed *pedagogical feedback support* in accordance with the policies explained above and it will only give them right after the student had submitted his step.

6   TITUS and the Self-assessment and Help-Seeking Support

A fully functional Intellectual Technical Tutor System (TITUS) for learning the fault tolerant principles under the signal-parametric approach [10, 11] with self-assessment support and adaptive study choice based in probabilistic models was implemented. TITUS was developed to implement and test the performance of the proposed prototyping models and methodologies. The training program has 3 sequential modules and

29 relevant knowledge components. Thus, for training the complete set of KCs, 43 tasks were developed and grouped by level of complexity. Moreover, some of these tasks have more than one variant; this feature increases the set of tasks up to 212 different tasks that the TITUS may present to the student. The GUI is depicted on Fig. 5.

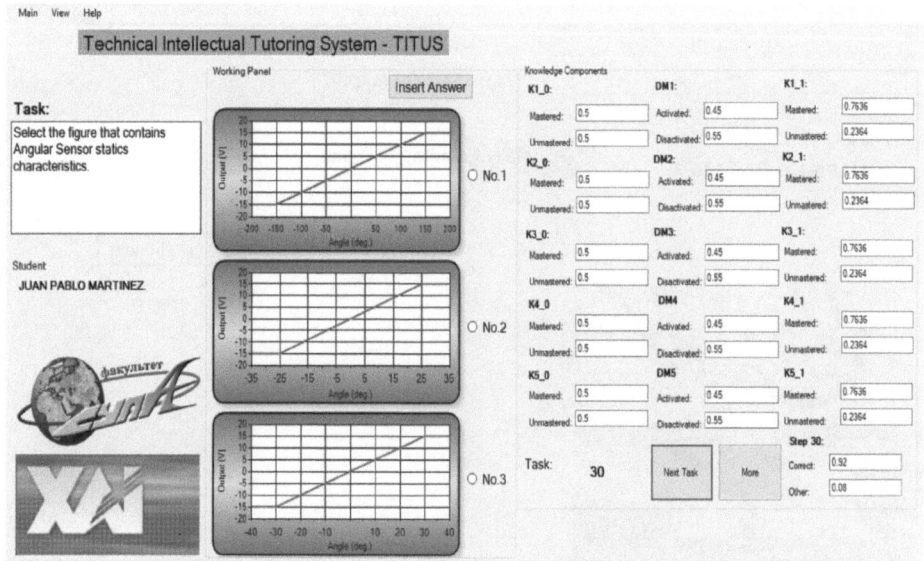

Fig. 5. Graphic user interface in TITUS

TITUS main window depicts the tasks to learner on the half-left side of it. Task required on Fig. 5, trains five knowledge components that are shown on the right side and students can monitor the probability of mastery for the relevant knowledge components in the task-problem.

They also may change the displayed task-problem clicking the "Next Task" button. These features in TITUS, promotes the principles of OLM and SRL. However, TITUS provides a hybrid engine that let student the freedom of choosing a next task-problem to do, but also it can select by itself a proper task-problem to show in accordance to student's performance. Therefore, the study choice either is taken by the student or by the tutor, and it promotes SRL as an open option for selecting the next task-problem. We believe that flexibility in tools and support given by the tutor, increments students' interest and reduces frustration.

For instance, a student could be on the situation that a task-problem like on Fig. 6 is depicted. KCs required for the task on Fig. 6 are the same as on Fig. 5, but Fig. 5 have a *friendlier* student presentation. It is possible to appreciate the big differences in the presentation of the task-problem, and the way KCs are required. This might generate stress in learners and higher levels of frustration in the case a student might be stuck.

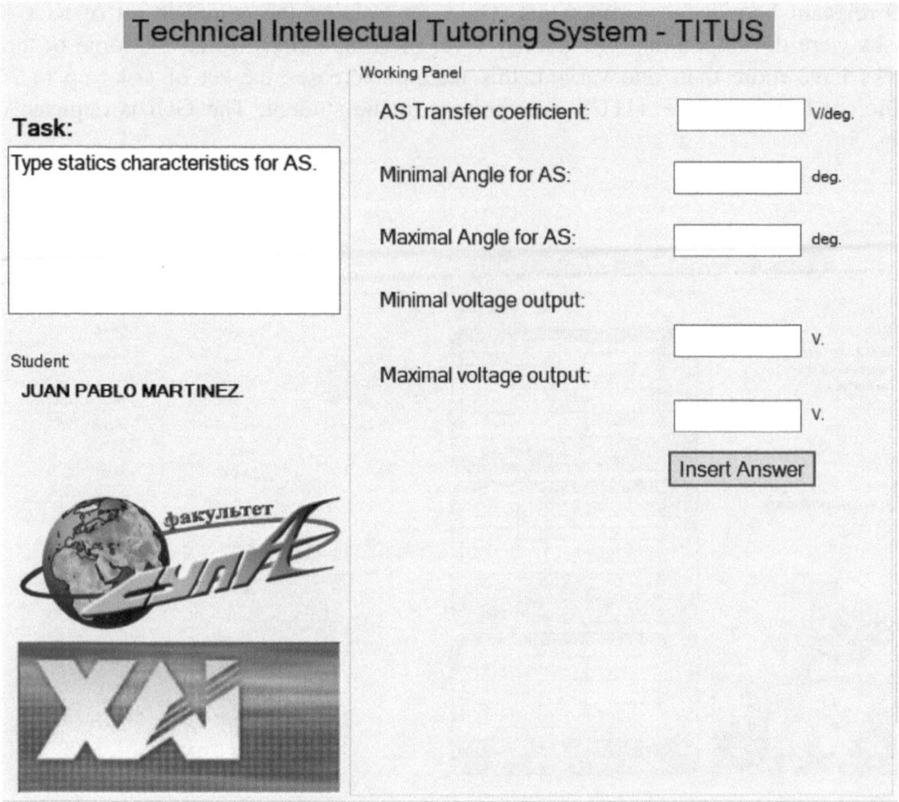

Fig. 6. Graphic user interface in TITUS (example 2)

In order to reduce the possibility of being blocked and frustrated, TITUS also is provided with at feedback service. Feedback is given in accordance to student performance and the process for delivering it, was discussed on Sect. 5.

When a student has repeatedly misused a KC, TITUS will guide her/him to a help window. It will specify where exactly to look for the information to overcome the misconceptions. The help window has all the necessary theory of the task domain. Help window is shown on Fig. 7. This information is also summarized and cataloged in modules in accordance with the curriculum in TITUS. Student must then read and work with self-seeking skills. Self-seeking skills do not only serve to find information but for developing other metacognitive skills like problem solving patterns.

Unfortunately in this work does not have a help-abuse support. Nevertheless we are looking forward to implemented in near future this support by implementing datamining techniques, face expression recognition, and implementing it into the probabilistic model in order to increase assessment fidelity.

The tutor also provide a set of tools for a more detailed assessment that may be used by students or human tutors. On Fig. 8 is depicted the window to depict information about student's performance.

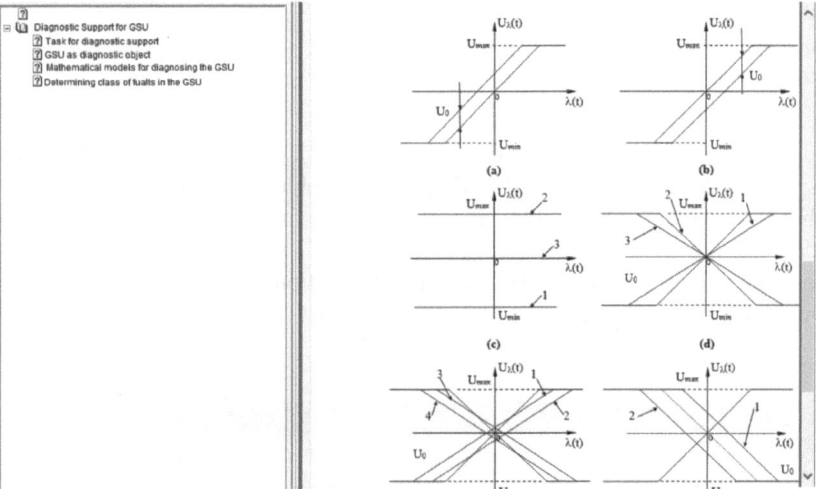

Fig. 7. Help window

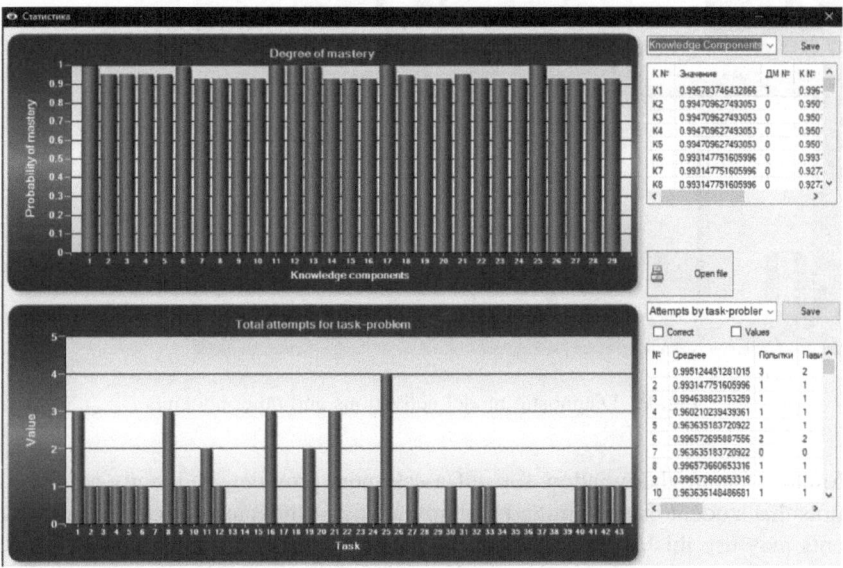

Fig. 8. Window for self-assessment

Window on Fig. 8 let us monitor different kind of information about student's performance:

- Degree of mastery for each KC;
- Times Diagnostic Models were activated;

- Attempts by task-problem;
- Correct attempts;
- Other attempts;
- Spent time.

For instance, on Fig. 9 we can observe which DMs were activated because the corresponding KCs were misused during a task-problem solving, and under it, a plot that shows how many errors were committed in certain task-problems. This might help to understand the relationship between conflicted KCs and tasks that train them in order to perform future adjustments or implementations in delivering pedagogical interventions.

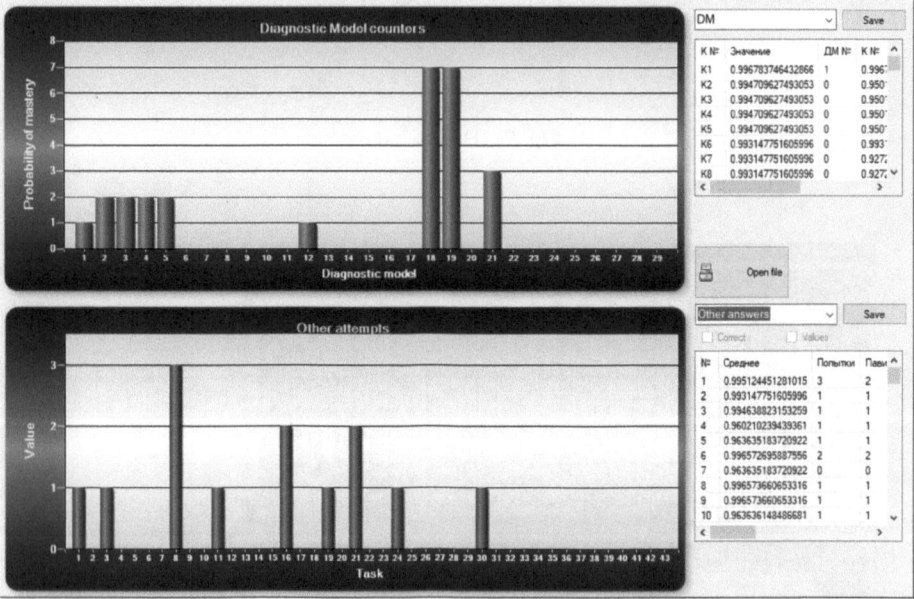

Fig. 9. Diagnostic model activations and other attempts

Another feature that window for self-assessment provides, is directly compare total attempts that student has committed and how many of them are correct. In other words, students may use this or be guided to detect their own wrong actions, in conjunction with the others features above discussed to perform the corrective actions to overcome those deficiencies. This feature can be seen on Fig. 10 on the downer plot. The number of times correct attempts were committed by the student are presented on green color.

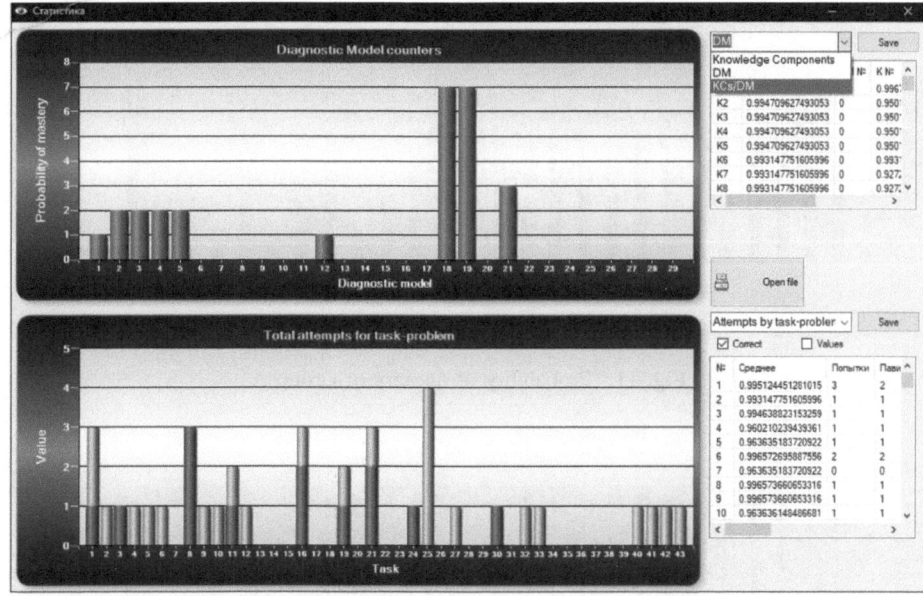

Fig. 10. Comparison of right/other attempts graph (Color figure online)

7 Implementation and Experimental Results

Experimental results for evaluating the effectiveness of the pedagogical interventions provided by TITUS, were obtained by means of the analysis of 38 students' performance, separated in two groups as follows:

1. 19 students used TITUS without any kind of pedagogical support and a closed learning model during the learning process (Group A);
2. 19 students used TITUS with a full implementation of the pedagogical support and OLM with SRL (Group B);

Experimental results from Group A are depicted on Fig. 11. Average degree of mastery for each of the 29 knowledge components in the task domain is clearly below the threshold *pKW*, and it states that mastery of the knowledge components in the task domain is less probably. On the other hand, when Group B used TITUS, the probability of mastery for every KC considerably increased, and this result is shown on Fig. 12. Times when student misused a knowledge component are shown on Fig. 13.

Attempts on Fig. 14 say which tasks resulted problematic for students, but also show the adaptability of the proposed approach and how it was developed according to the student's performance. Table 5 shows the average degree of mastery by groups, where the Group which used a fully featured MTCT clearly obtained a better performance at the end of the test in comparison with the group that did not obtained any kind of pedagogical support from the tutor.

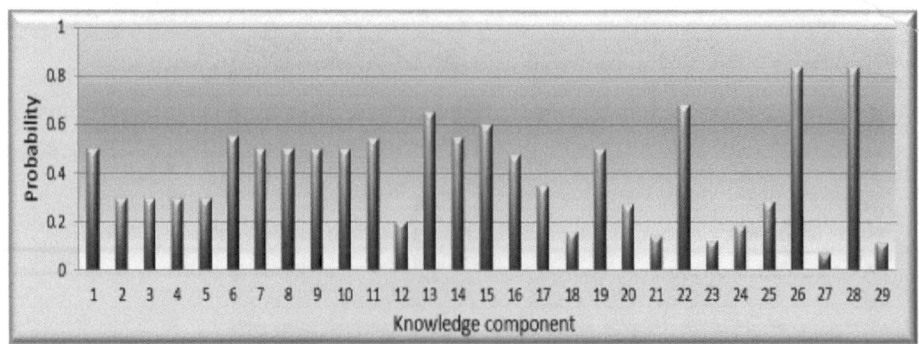

Fig. 11. Probability of mastery of Group A

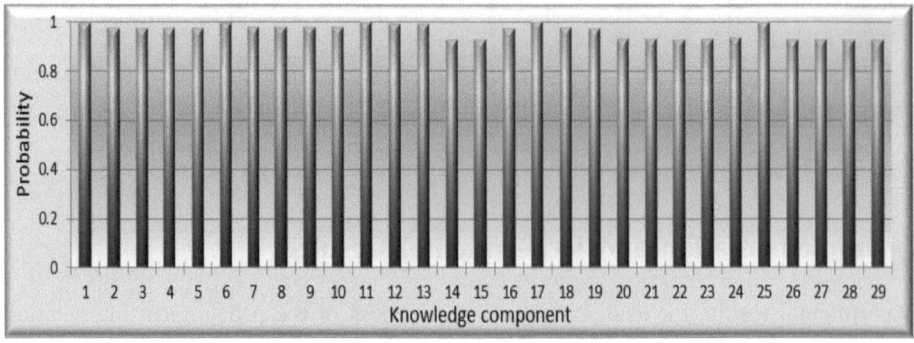

Fig. 12. Probability of mastery of Group B

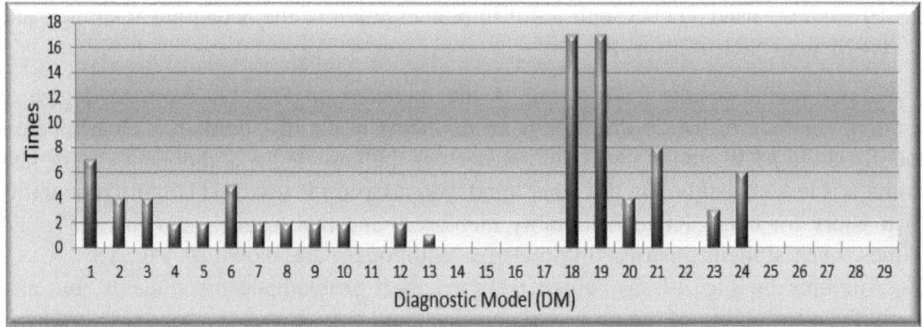

Fig. 13. Times DMs were activated for each knowledge component

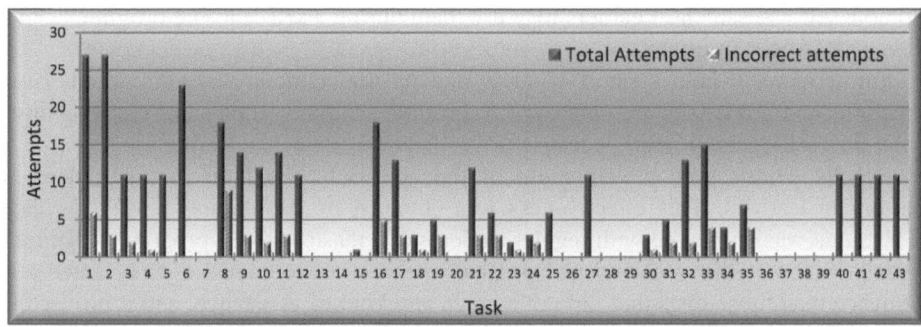

Fig. 14. Total and incorrect attempts for each task

Table 5. Average probability of mastery the KCs in tested groups

Group	Average probability
A	0.4068
B	0.9662

8 Conclusions

This paper proposes an approach for developing pedagogical intervention support under an Open Learning Model that is based on Self-Regulation Learning principles. It supports students to master the concepts and basic theory about fault-tolerant systems under the signal-parametric approach, by means of several pedagogical means.

It was presented the design of a task-problem model and the considerations that were taken in account to its construction and implementation. It was defined in three modules; each module has a set of task-problems with different levels of difficulty. Task-problem model is a set to task-problem with an interwoven net of Knowledge Components over the task domain. Structural considerations and characteristics were also discussed.

An assessment model based on probabilistic models presented as a Bayesian network for providing pedagogical interventions was presented as well. It helps to provide learners a cognitive pedagogical support, like hints and feedbacks. It has the ability to build a cognitive model from each student and provide individual pedagogical interventions based on it, in order to actively adapt the learning process according to the student's performance. Selection of study path is provided on-demand by the student that let her/him to decide to "scape" the current task-problem requirement in the current module. At the same time, the cognitive tutor also provide a selection task-problem engine that permits the tutor to automatically choose a task among the 212 possible ones.

This automatic process is directly related to the probabilistic assessment and the analysis of other datamining features that conform a more fine-grained assessment. Different kind of support tools were developed and discussed as well, in order to promote self-assessment. Learners may use them during a self-learning program or in a classic classroom program.

Furthermore, a help support window and its implications were discussed. How directions and guidelines are employed to promote students to develop metacognitive skills for "self-seeking help", because active learners are better learners.

Results demonstrate effectiveness of the approach based on the increment of mastery in learners. This effectiveness was obtained by developing a MTCT called TITUS that was employed with regular students in a master degree program of the task domain. Students that received pedagogical interventions obtained a 42% better performance than those ones that did not receive any kind of assistance, and it proves the positive educational impact in students when the proposed approach is implemented in a MTCT. In the near future, we expect to develop an extended version of the BN model and pedagogical feedback support by including for instance, help abuse and detections of frustration by means of visual analysis, among others.

References

1. Paquette, L., Lebeau, J.F., Beaulieu, G., Mayers, A.: Designing a knowledge representation approach for the generation of pedagogical interventions by MTTs. Int. J. Artif. Intell. Educ. **25**, 118–156 (2015)
2. Aleven, V., Nkambou, R., Bourdeau, J., Mizoguchi, R.: Rule-based cognitive modeling for intelligent systems. In: Nkambou, R., Bourdeau, J., Mizoguchi, R. (eds.) Advances in Intelligent Tutoring Systems, pp. 33–62. Springer, Heidelberg (2010). https://doi.org/10.1007/978-3-642-14363-2_3
3. Aleven, V., McLaren, B., Roll, I., Koedinger, K.: Toward meta-cognitive tutoring: a model of help-seeking with a cognitive tutor. Int. J. Artif. Intell. Educ. **16**, 101–130 (2016)
4. Wieber, F., Thürmer, J.L., Gollwitzer, P.M.: Promoting the translation of intentions into action by implementation of intentions: behavioral effects and physiological correlates. Front. Hum. Neurosci. **9**, 395 (2015). https://doi.org/10.3389/fnhum.2015.00395
5. Long, Y., Aleven, V.: Active learners: redesigning an intelligent tutoring system to support self-regulated learning. In: Hernández-Leo, D., Ley, T., Klamma, R., Harrer, A. (eds.) EC-TEL 2013. LNCS, vol. 8095, pp. 490–495. Springer, Heidelberg (2013). https://doi.org/10.1007/978-3-642-40814-4_44
6. Pelánek, R., Jarusek, P.: Student modeling based on problem solving time. Int. J. Artif. Intell. Educ. **25**, 493–519 (2015)
7. Conati, C., Gertner, A., VanLehn, K.: Using Bayesian networks to manage uncertainty in student modeling. User Model. User-Adap. Inter. **12**, 371–417 (2002)
8. VanLehn, K.: Intelligent tutoring systems for continuous, embedded assessment. In: Dwyer, C. (ed.) The Future of Assessment: Shaping Teaching and Learning, pp. 113–138. Lawrence Erlbaum Associates, New York (2008)
9. VanLehn, K., Burleson, W., Girard, S., Chavez-Echeagaray, M.E., Gonzalez-Sanchez, J., Hidalgo-Pontet, Y., Zhang, L.: The affective meta-tutoring project: lessons learned. In: Trausan-Matu, S., Boyer, K.E., Crosby, M., Panourgia, K. (eds.) ITS 2014. LNCS, vol. 8474, pp. 84–93. Springer, Cham (2014). https://doi.org/10.1007/978-3-319-07221-0_11
10. Martinez Bastida, J.P., Chukhray, A.G.: An active diagnostic algorithm for a gyroscopic sensors unit. In: 2016 II International Young Scientists Forum on Applied Physics and Engineering (YSF), pp. 29–32, Kharkiv (2016). https://doi.org/10.1109/ysf.2016.7753793

11. Kulik, A.S.: Fault diagnosis in dynamic systems via signal-parametric approach. In: IFAC/IMACS Symposium of Fault Detection, Supervision and a Technical Process, SAFE PROCESS 1991, vol. 1, pp. 157–162, Baden-Baden (1991)
12. VanLehn, K., Burleson, W., Chavez Echeagaray, M.E., Christopherson, R., Gonzalez Sanchez, J., Hastings, J., Hidalgo Pontet Y., Zhang, L.: The affective meta-tutoring project: how to motivate students to use effective meta-cognitive strategies. In: Proceedings of the 19th International Conference on Computers in Education, ICCE 2011, Chian Mai, Thailand, pp. 128–130 (2011)
13. Aleven, V.: Rule-based cognitive modeling for intelligent systems. In: Nkambou, R., Bourdeau, J., Mizoguchi, R. (eds.) Advances in Intelligent Tutoring Systems, pp. 33–62. (2010)
14. Russel, S., Norving, P.: Artificial Intelligence: A Modern Approach. Prentice Hall, USA (2010). 1132 p.
15. Arroyo, I., Woolf, B.P., Burelson, W., Muldner, K., Rai, D., Tai, M.: A multimedia adaptive tutoring system for mathematics that addresses cognition, metacognition and affect. Int. J. Artif. Intell. Educ. **24**, 387–426 (2014). https://doi.org/10.1007/s40593-014-0023-y
16. Walker, E., Rummel, N., Koedinger, K.R.: Adaptive intelligent support to improve peer tutoring in algebra. Int. J. Artif. Intell. Educ. **24**, 33–61 (2014). https://doi.org/10.1007/s40593-013-0001-9
17. Dzikovska, M., Steinhauser, N., Farrow, E., Moore, J., Campbell, G.: BEETLE II: deep natural language understanding and automatic feedback generation for intelligent tutoring in basic electricity and electronics. Int. J. Artif. Intell. Educ. **24**, 284–332 (2014). https://doi.org/10.1007/s40593-014-0017-9
18. Biswas, G., Segedy, J.R., Bunchongchit, K.: From design to implementation to practice a learning by teaching system: Betty's brain. J. Artif. Intell. Educ. **26**, 350–364 (2016). https://doi.org/10.1007/s40593-015-0057-9
19. Pelánek, R., Jarusek, P.: Student modeling based on problem solving times. J. Artif. Intell. Educ. **25**, 493–519 (2015). https://doi.org/10.1007/s40593-015-0048-x
20. Shanabrook, D.H., Arroyo, I., Woolf, B.P., Burleson, W.: Visualization of student activity patterns within intelligent tutoring systems. In: Cerri, S.A., Clancey, W.J., Papadourakis, G., Panourgia, K. (eds.) ITS 2012. LNCS, vol. 7315, pp. 46–51. Springer, Heidelberg (2012). https://doi.org/10.1007/978-3-642-30950-2_6
21. Chi, M., VanLehn, K., Litman, D.: Do micro-level tutorial decisions matter: applying reinforcement learning to induce pedagogical tutorial tactics. In: Aleven, V., Kay, J., Mostow, J. (eds.) ITS 2010. LNCS, vol. 6094, pp. 224–234. Springer, Heidelberg (2010). https://doi.org/10.1007/978-3-642-13388-6_27
22. Wang, Y., Heffernan, N.: Leveraging first response time into the knowledge tracing model. In: Proceedings of the International Conference on Educational Data Mining, pp. 176–179. (2012)
23. Chukhray, A.G.: Methodology for learning algorithms, monography. National Aerospace University, KhAI, Kharkiv, Ukraine, 336 p. ISBN 978–966-662-548-2 (2013)
24. Decision Systems Laboratory GeNIe 2.0. Decision Systems Laboratory, University of Pittsburg (2013). http://genie.sis.pitt.edu
25. Anderson, J.R., Corbett, A.T., Koedinger, K.R., Pelletier, R.: Cognitive tutors: lessons learned. J. Learn. Sci. **4**(2), 167–207 (1995)
26. Bessing, S.B., Gilbert, S.B., Ourada, S., Ritter, S.: Authoring model-tracing cognitive tutors. Int. J. Artif. Intell. Educ. **19**, 189–210 (2009)

ICT Evaluation and Applications

Cross-Evaluation of Automated Term Extraction Tools by Measuring Terminological Saturation

Victoria Kosa[1](✉), David Chaves-Fraga[2],
Dmitriy Naumenko[3], Eugene Yuschenko[3],
Carlos Badenes-Olmedo[2], Vadim Ermolayev[1],
and Aliaksandr Birukou[4]

[1] Department of Computer Science, Zaporizhzhia National University,
Zhukovskogo St. 66, Zaporizhzhia, Ukraine
victoriya1402.kosa@gmail.com, vadim@ermolayev.com
[2] Ontology Engineering Group, Universidad Politécnica de Madrid,
Madrid, Spain
{dchaves, cbadenes}@fi.upm.es
[3] BWT Group, Mayakovskogo St. 11, Zaporizhzhia, Ukraine
admin@groupbwt.com
[4] Springer-Verlag GmbH, Tiergartenstrasse 17, Heidelberg, Germany
aliaksandr.birukou@springer.com

Abstract. This paper reports on cross-evaluating the two software tools for automated term extraction (ATE) from English texts: NaCTeM TerMine and UPM Term Extractor. The objective was to find the most fitting software for extracting the bags of terms to be the part of our instrumental pipeline for exploring terminological saturation in text document collections in a domain of interest. The choice of these particular tools from the bunch of the other available is explained in our review of the related work in ATE. The approach to measure terminological saturation is based on the use of the THD algorithm developed in frame of our OntoElect methodology for ontology refinement. The paper presents the suite of instrumental software modules, experimental workflow, 2 synthetic and 3 real document collections, generated datasets, and set-up of our experiments. Next, the results of the cross-evaluation experiments are presented, analyzed, and discussed. Finally the paper offers some conclusions and recommendations on the use of ATE software for measuring terminological saturation in retrospective text document collections.

Keywords: Automated term extraction · Software tool
Experimental Cross-Evaluation · Terminological saturation
Retrospective document collection · OntoElect

1 Introduction

Automated term extraction (ATE, also known as recognition – ATR) from textual documents is an established sub-field in text mining. Its results are further used for different important purposes, for example as inputs in ontology learning. Many research activities are undertaken currently to improve the quality of extraction results. These activities focus on different aspects, including: new or improved extraction algorithms; combining linguistic and statistical approaches to extraction; developing new or refined metrics which allow higher quality extraction; developing new extraction tools which yield better results and scale to fit current dataset size requirements. The mainstream criteria used to assess the quality of extracted results are adopted from information retrieval and based on recall and precision metrics. However, to the best of our knowledge, there were no reports on approaches to assess the completeness of the document collection from which extraction is performed. Recall measures just inform about how completely the set of terms was extracted from the available data but does not hint if the data itself was complete to contain all significant terms characterizing the domain. In other words, there is no way so far to check if the collection of documents chosen for term extraction is representative. Therefore the approaches to measure the representativeness of document collections are timely. In this context, it is also important to know what would be a minimal representative subset of documents.

The research presented in this paper[1] develops the methodological and instrumental components for measuring the representativeness of high-quality collections of textual documents. It is assumed that the documents in a collection cover a single and well circumscribed domain and have a timestamp associated with them – so can be ordered by publication time. A typical example of such a collection is the set of the full text papers of a professional journal or conference proceedings series. The main hypothesis, put forward in this work, is that a sub-collection can be considered as representative to describe the domain, in terms of its terminological footprint, if any additions of extra documents from the entire collection to this sub-collection do not noticeably change this footprint. Such a sub-collection is further considered as complete and could be used e.g. for learning an ontology from it. In fact, this approach to assess the representativeness does so by evaluating terminological saturation in a document collection.

In this approach we are concerned about automated term extraction, as doing so manually is not feasible for any realistic document collection pretending to cover a professional domain. Therefore, it is important to know if terminological saturation depends on a term extraction method, implemented in a software tool. For finding this out, the presented research project cross-evaluated the two software tools. The choice of these particular tools from the bunch of the other available is explained in our review of the related work in Sect. 2.

The approach to measure terminological saturation is based on the use of the THD algorithm developed in frame of our OntoElect methodology for ontology refinement [2]. This part of OntoElect is outlined in Sect. 3.

Sections 4, 5, and 6 present our contributions.

We focused our experiments on a single but important factor that may influence terminological saturation – the choice of an ATE software tool. Further, we presented

---

[1] This paper is based on [1] in terms of its idea and research agenda presented as its research hypothesis and questions in Sect. 2. The rest constitutes the new result elaborated after the submission and publication of [1].

our generic workflow to support different series of experiments answering different research questions in our project [1]. We also developed the suite of instrumental software modules to support our experimental workflow. We provided a more detailed experimental set-up, based on the generic workflow, for studying the influence of the choice of the term extraction software. This contribution is presented in Sect. 4.

For evaluating the aspect of the choice of a term extraction software, we cross-evaluated the two selected software tools, UPM Term Extractor[2] versus NaCTeM TerMine[3], on two synthetic and three real document collections of full-text papers from different domains. Section 5 presents the document collections and datasets, and further elaborates on the details of the experimental set-up. The results of our cross-evaluation experiments are presented and discussed in Sect. 6.

Finally, we summarize our results in Sect. 7, which concludes the paper.

2 Motivation and Related Work

Extracting terminology from texts is a complicated and laborious process which requires a substantial part of highly qualified human effort. Despite that it is more and more often used in many important applications, e.g. for engineering ontologies [2, 3]. So, knowing the smallest possible representative document collection for a domain is very important to efficiently develop ontologies with satisfactory domain coverage. Therefore, laying out a method to determine a terminologically saturated subset of documents of the minimal size within a collection is topical. It is also important to make this method as efficient and automated as possible to lower the overhead on the core knowledge engineering workflow.

In our project we put forward a hypothesis that terminological saturation in a collection of documents is a complex thing which may depend on several aspects. These aspects are taken into account while answering the following research questions:

- **Q1**: Which of the term extraction software tools yield better saturated sets of terms?
- **Q2**: Which would be the proper direction in forming the datasets to check saturation: chronological, reverse-chronological, bi-directional, random selection? Which direction is the most appropriate to cope with potential terminological drift in time?
- **Q3**: Would the size of a dataset increment influence saturation measurements? Is there an optimal size of an increment for the purpose?
- **Q4**: Would frequently cited documents form a minimal representative subset of documents? Do these documents indeed provide the biggest terminological contribution to the document collection?
- **Q5**: Is the method for assessing completeness based on saturation measurements valid? Does it indeed provide a correct indication of statistical representativeness?

---

[2] UPM Term Extractor could be downloaded from https://github.com/ontologylearning-oeg/epnoi-legacy. It has to be further installed locally for use.

[3] The batch service of NaCTeM TerMine is available at http://www.nactem.ac.uk/batch.php. Access needs to be requested.

The answers to the outlined research questions **Q1–Q4** are sought based on conducting experiments using different document collections coming from different domains and communities. Thus, the setting of the experiments should consider these aspects.

In this paper we aim at finding out the answer to our research question **Q1**: which relevant term extraction software yields the best (smallest) saturated sub-sets of documents? Therefore, the rest of the paper is focused around this aspect.

We review the related work along the following lines. We compare existing ATE approaches in terms of the quality of their results. We also consider as relevant those methods (ATE algorithms plus metrics) which are domain-independent, unsupervised, and allow assessing the significance of extracted terms. Further we check if the selected methods are implemented as software tools which are publicly available for our experiments. We also pay attention to whether the tools return data for term significance evaluations that are essential for our saturation measurements.

2.1 Methods for Automated Term Extraction

Despite being important for practice, ATE is still far from being reliable. New approaches to ATE are being proposed and still demonstrate their precision at the level below 80% [4]. So, these can hardly be used in industry. Several reviews have been performed to compare and cross-evaluate ATE methods, e.g. [5]. Perhaps, [4] and [20] are the most recent work on that.

In the majority of approaches to ATE, e.g. [6] or [7], processing is done in two consecutive phases: Linguistic Processing and Statistical Processing. Linguistic processors, like POS taggers or phrase chunkers, filter out stop words and restrict candidate terms to n-gram sequences: nouns or noun phrases, adjective-noun and noun-preposition-noun combinations. Statistical processing is then applied to measure the ranks of the candidate terms. These measures are [5] either the measures of 'unithood', which focus on the collocation strength of units that comprise a single term; or the measures of 'termhood' which point to the association strength of a term to domain concepts.

For 'unithood', the metrics are used such as mutual information [8], log likelihood [9], t-test [6, 7], the notion of 'modifiability' and its variants [7, 10]. The metrics for 'termhood' are either term frequency-based (unsupervised approaches) or reference corpora-based (semi-supervised approaches). The most used frequency-based metrics are TF/IDF (e.g. in [4, 11]), weirdness [12] which compares the frequency of a term in the evaluated corpus with that in the reference corpus, domain pertinence [14]. More recently, hybrid approaches were proposed, that combine 'unithood' and 'termhood' measurements in a single value. A representative metric is c/nc-value [13]. C/nc-value-based approaches to ATE have received their further evolution in many works, e.g. [6, 14, 15] to mention a few.

Linguistic Processing is organized and implemented in a very similar fashion in all the ATE methods, except some of them that also include filtering out stop words. Stop words (terms) could be filtered out also at a cut-off step after statistical processing. So, in our review and selection we further look at the second phase of Statistical Processing only. Statistical Processing is sometimes further split in two consecutive sub-phases of term candidate scoring, and ranking. For term candidates scoring, reflecting its like-lihood of being a term, known methods could be distinguished by being based on (c.f. [4]) measuring occurrences frequencies (including word association), assessing occurrences contexts, using reference corpora, e.g. Wikipedia [16], topic modeling [17].

A cut-off procedure, takes the top candidates, based on scores, and thus distin-guishes significant terms from insignificant (or non-) terms. Many cut-off methods rely upon the scores, coming from one scoring algorithm, and establish a threshold in one or another way. Some others that collect the scores from several scoring algorithms use (weighted) linear combinations [18], voting [2, 5], or (semi-)supervised learning [19]. In our set-up, we do cut-offs after term extraction based on voting, as explained in Sect. 3. So, the ATE algorithms/solutions which perform cut-offs together with scoring are not relevant for our experimental setting.

Based on the evaluations in [4, 5, 20] the most widely used ATE algorithms, for which their performance assessments are published, are listed in Table 1. The table also provides the assessments on the aspects that we use for selection.

Comments:
Domain Independence: "+" stands for a domain-independent method; "-" marks that the method is either claimed to be domain-specific by its authors, or is evaluated only on one particular domain. A domain-independent method is sought as our aim is to develop a domain-independent technique.
Supervision: "U" – unsupervised; "SS" – semi-supervised. An unsupervised method is sought as our aim is to develop an unsupervised technique.
Term Significance: "+" – the method returns a value for each retained term which could further be used as a measure of its significance compared to the other terms. "-" – marks that such a measure is not returned or the method does the cut-off itself.
Cut-off: "+" – the method does cut-offs itself and returns only significant terms; "-" – the method does not do cut-offs.

For us, only the methods are relevant that do not do cut-offs and return significance values. Our THD algorithm does cut-offs at a later stage.
Precision and Run Time: The values are based on the comparison of the two cross-evaluation experiments reported in [4] / [20]. Empty cells in the table mean that there was no data for this particular method in this particular experiment. [4] used ATR4S – open-source software written in Scala. It evaluated 13 different methods, implemented in ATR4S, on 5 different datasets, including GENIA. [20] used JATE 2.0, free software written in Java. It evaluated 9 different methods, implemented in JATE, on 2 different datasets, including GENIA. So, the results on GENIA are the baseline for comparing the Precision. Two values are given for each reference experiment: preci-sion on GENIA; average precision. Both [4, 20] experimented with c-value method which was the slowest on average for [20]. So, the execution times for c-value were used as a baseline to normalize the rest in the Run Time column.

After analyzing the findings listed in Table 1, we support the conclusion of [20] stating that "*c-value* is the most reliable method as it obtains consistently good results, in terms of precision", evenly on the two different mixes of datasets – [4, 20]. We also

Table 1. The comparison of the most widely used ATE metrics and algorithms

Method [Source]	Domain-independence (+/-)	Supervision (U/SS)	Metrics	Term Significance	Cut-off (+/-)	Precision (GENIA; average)	Run Time (%/c-value)
TTF [21]	+	U	Term (Total) Frequency	+	-	0.70; 0.35	0.34
ATF [20]	+	U	Average Term Frequency	+	-	0.71; 0.33	0.37
						0.75; 0.32	0.35
TTF-IDF [22]	+	U	TTF+Inverse Document Frequency	+	-	0.82; 0.51	0.35
RIDF [23]	+	U	Residual IDF	-		0.71; 0.32	0.53
						0.80; 0.49	0.37
C-value [13]	+	U	c-value, nc-value	+	-	0.73; **0.53**	1.00
						0.77; **0.56**	1.00
Weirdness [12]	+/-	SS	Weirdness	-		0.77; 0.47	0.41
						0.82; 0.48	1.67
GlossEx [18]	+	SS	Lexical (Term) Cohesion, Domain Specificity	-		0.70; 0.41	0.42
TermEx [14]	+	SS	Domain Pertinence, Domain Consensus, Lexical Cohesion, Structural Relevance	-	+	0.87; 0.46	0.52
PU-ATR [16]	-	SS	nc-value, Domain Specificity	-	+	0.78; 0.57	809.21

note that *c-value* is one of the slowest in the group of unsupervised and domain-independent methods, though its performance is comparable with the fastest ones. Still, *c-value* outperforms the domain-specific methods, sometimes significantly, as it is in the case with PU-ATR. Hence, we have chosen *c-value* as the method for our cross-evaluation experiments. We were therefore looking further at the tools which implemented *c-value* and were publicly freely available.

2.2 Available Software Implementations

For choosing the software tools that implement the *c-value* method for ATE we looked at the descriptions of term extraction tools at several web resources like at http://inmyownterms.com/terminology-extraction-tools/ or https://en.wikipedia.org/wiki/Terminology_extraction. In addition to the reference implementations mentioned before, ATR4S [4] and JATE 2.0 [20], we have identified the following freely available ATE software tools as outlined in Table 2.

Table 2. Free ATE Software Tools (Listed Alphabetically)

Name / Owner	Website	Short description	Algorithm / Metric	Domain	Constraints
BioTex / LIRMM	http://tubo.lirmm.fr/biotex/	Extracts biomedical terms from free text		Biomedical	Domain-specific
FiveFilters / Medialab-Prado	http://fivefilters.org/term-extraction/	Extracts terms through a web service; relies on a PHP port of Topia's Term Extraction; a simple alternative to Yahoo Term Extraction service	Occurrence (TTF) and word count in a term	independent	Web service, size of text constrained
TaaS (TaaS EU Project)	https://term.tilde.com/	Identifies term candidates in documents and extracts them automatically. Uses CollTerm (linguistic) or Kilgray (statistical) services	Frequency-based	independent	Does not provide term significance scores
TerMine / NaCTeM	http://www.nactem.ac.uk/software/termine/	Extracts terms from plain English texts, provides the Batch mode (access to be requested for non-UK academic users)	*c-value*	independent	The service requests to avoid heavy bulk processing
TermFinder / Translated.net	https://labs.translated.net/terminology-extraction/	A Web application that extracts terms from the inserted text. Compares the frequency of words in a given document with their frequency in the language (generic corpus).	Poisson statistics, Maximum Likelihood Estimation and IDF	requires language corpus	Returns the score of a term as a numeric value (%)
TBXTools [24] / Universitat Oberta de Catalunya	https://sourceforge.net/projects/tbxtools/	A Python toolset using NLTK (Natural Language Toolkit)	TTF	Independent, multilingual, requires language corpus	Deletes n-grams with stop words
UPM Term Extractor [25] / Dr Inventor EU project	https://github.com/ontologylearning-oeg/epnoi-legacy	A Java software for extracting terms and relations from scientific papers.	*c-value*	Independent	Takes text input data of at most 15 Mb

For the final selection of the tools for our cross-evaluation we:

- Decided not to consider ATR4S and JATE 2.0, at list at this stage, because it was not fully clear how to extract the *c-value* method implementation from these suites
- Selected the tools that use the *c-value* method – which are NaCTeM TerMine and UPM Term Extractor

3   OntoElect Saturation Metric and Measurement Pipeline

OntoElect methodology [2] seeks for maximizing the fitness of the developed ontology to what the domain knowledge stakeholders think about the domain. Fitness is measured as the stakeholders' "votes" which allows assessing stakeholders' commitment to the ontology under development, reflecting how well their sentiment about the requirements is met. The more votes are collected – the higher the commitment is expected to be. If a critical mass of votes is acquired (say 50% + 1, which is a simple majority vote), the ontology is considered to satisfactorily meet the requirements. All the constituents of OntoElect as a processing technique are formally presented in [2].

It is well known that direct acquisition of requirements from domain experts is not very realistic as they are expensive and not really willing to do the work falling out of their core activity. So, in OntoElect, we are focused on the indirect collection of the stakeholders' votes by extracting these from high quality and reasonably high impact documents authored by the stakeholders.

An important feature to be ensured for knowledge extraction from text collections is that a dataset needs to be statistically representative to cover the opinions of the domain knowledge stakeholders satisfactorily fully. OntoElect suggests a method to measure the terminological completeness of a document collection by analyzing the *saturation* of terminological footprints of the incremental slices of the collection, as e.g. reported in [26]. The full texts of the documents from the retrospective collection are grouped in datasets in the increasing order of their timestamps. As pictured in Fig. 1a, the first dataset $D1$ contains the first portion (*inc*) of documents. The second dataset $D2$ contains the first dataset $D1$ plus the second incremental slice (*inc*) of documents. Finally, the last dataset Dn contains all the documents from the collection.

At the next step of the OntoElect workflow the bags of terms $B1$, $B2$, …, Bn are extracted from the datasets $D1$, $D2$, …, Dn, using TerMine software, together with their

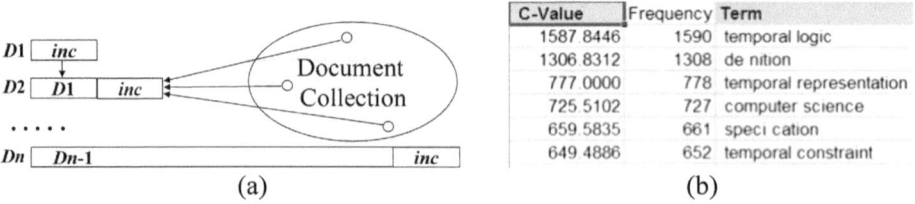

C-Value	Frequency	Term
1587.8446	1590	temporal logic
1306.8312	1308	de nition
777.0000	778	temporal representation
725.5102	727	computer science
659.5835	661	speci cation
649.4886	652	temporal constraint

(a)   (b)

Fig. 1. (a) Incrementally enlarged datasets in OntoElect; (b) An example of a bag of terms extracted by TerMine.

significance (c-value) scores. Please see an example of a bag of terms extracted by TerMine in Fig. 1b.

At the subsequent step, every extracted bag of terms Bi, $i = 1, ..., n$ is processed as follows:

- Normalized scores are computed for each individual term: *n-score = c-value/max(c-value)*
- Individual term significance threshold *(eps)* is computed to retain those terms that are within the majority vote. The sum of *n-scores* having values above *eps* form the majority vote if this sum is higher that ½ of the sum of all *n-scores*.
- The cut-off at *n-score < eps* is done.
- The result is saved in Ti – the bags of retained terms.

After this step only significant terms, whose *n-scores* represent the majority vote, are retained in the bags of terms. Ti are then evaluated for saturation by measuring pair-wise terminological difference between the subsequent bags Ti and $Ti + 1$, $i = 0, ..., n - 1$. It is done by applying the THD algorithm [2]. We provide it also here in Fig. 2 for reader convenience.

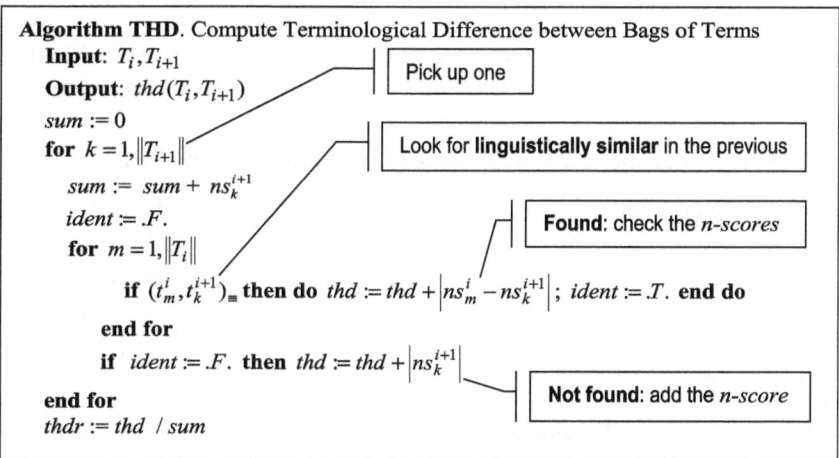

Fig. 2. THD algorithm [2] for comparing a pair of bags of retained terms. It has been modified, compared to [2], for computing the *thdr* value.

In fact, THD accumulates, in the *thd* value for the bag $Ti + 1$, the *n-score* differences if there were linguistically the same terms in Ti and $Ti + 1$. If there was no the same term in Ti, it adds the *n-score* of the orphan to the *thd* value of $Ti + 1$. After *thd* has been computed, the relative terminological difference *thdr* receives its value as *thd* divided by the sum of *n-scores* in $Ti + 1$.

Absolute *(thd)* and relative *(thdr)* terminological differences are computed for further assessing if $Ti + 1$ differs from Ti more than by the individual term significance threshold *eps*. If not, it implies that adding an increment of documents to Di for producing $Di + 1$ did not contribute any noticeable amount of new terminology. So, the subset $Di + 1$ of the overall document collection may have become terminologically saturated. However, to obtain more confidence about the saturation, OntoElect suggests that some more subsequent pairs of Ti and $Ti + 1$ are evaluated. If stable saturation is observed, then the process of looking for a minimal saturated sub-collection could be stopped. Sometimes, however, a terminological peak may occur after saturation has been observed in the previous pairs of T. Normally this peak indicates that a highly innovative document with a substantial number of new terms has been added in the increment.

To finalize this concise presentation of the OntoElect approach, it is worth noting that it is domain independent and unsupervised – due to the use of TerMine for term extraction. The shortcomings of this reliance on TerMine are revealed in our experimental study (Sect. 6).

One of the tasks for our research, on which we focus in this paper, is trying OntoElect pipeline with the alternative term extraction tool – UPM Term Extractor – and cross-evaluate the results versus those obtained using NaCTeM TerMine.

4   Experimental Workflow and Software Tools

In this section we present our generic experimental workflow and the suite of instrumental software tools which have been developed to support our experiments.

4.1   Generic Experimental Workflow and Instrumental Software

Our generic experimental workflow, outlined in Fig. 3, is based on the OntoElect processing pipeline (Sect. 3). In particular, this workflow will be applied (using Configure Experiment step) to perform all the cross-evaluation experiments described below (Sect. 6).

The workflow covers the preparatory phase, experiment configuration, the generation of the datasets, term extraction, saturation measurement, and the analysis and comparison of the results. Some of the steps in these phases can only be performed manually, like Configure Experiment, Analyze Saturation, and Compare Results. These steps are not too laborious, however, and the effort does not noticeably grow with the number of documents. To support the rest of the steps, the instrumental software has been developed and offered for public use – as described in [27].

The **preparatory** phase includes:

- The **generation of the catalogue** for the chosen document collection using the information available at the publisher's web site. This catalogue includes all the metadata for the documents, including their abstracts, and also the numbers of their citations acquired from Google Scholar[4]. This step is supported by the **Catalogue Generator** module.

---

[4] http://scholar.google.com/.

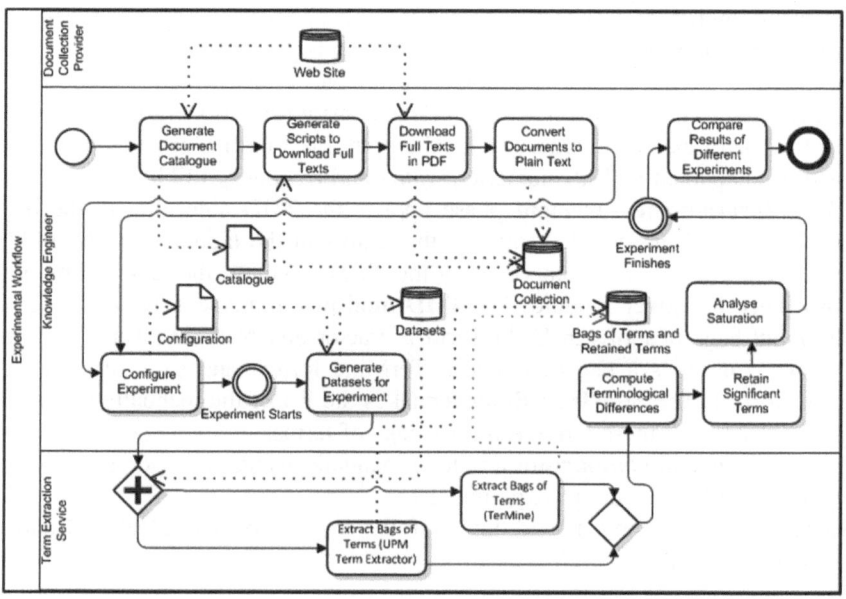

Fig. 3. Experimental workflow

- The **download** of the **full texts** of the papers, usually in PDF format, based on the information in the catalogue. This step may require the permission granted by the owner of the collection to bulk-download their full texts. This step is supported by the **Full Text Downloader** module.
- The **conversion** of the full texts of the downloaded documents to the **plain text** format for further term extraction is supported by the **PDF to Plain Text Convertor** module.

The **configuration** phase is the choice of the experimental setting and the parameters of the datasets to be generated. The experimental setting is defined by the series – i.e. by the research question we wish to answer. The parameters are hence defined by the objective of the series. These parameters are: the order of adding documents to a dataset, the size of an increment, the software tool used for term extraction.

The **datasets generation** phase takes these parameters and the document collection in the plain text format. The datasets are then generated (Sect. 3), to be further taken by term extraction. The texts are added to the increments in the order chosen as the parameter of the experiment. This phase is supported by the **Dataset Generator** module.

The phase of **term extraction** applies the chosen software tool to the generated datasets: $D1, D2, \ldots$ In result, it outputs the bags of extracted terms $B1, B2, \ldots$ In the context of reported experiments, this phase is supported by the use of the two software tools: **UPM Term Extractor** and **NaCTeM TerMine**. UPM Term Extractor has been developed in the Dr Inventor project. The tool takes a collection of documents (PDF or plain text) in English or a dataset generated from this collection (plain text) and returns the bag of extracted terms as a CSV file. Each term is provided in a separate line with its *c-value*. NaCTeM TerMine is a publicly available service which is used in a batch mode[5]. It takes an English plain text (ANSI) document (dataset) as a file to upload and returns the bag of extracted terms as a CSV output. Each term is provided in a separate line and accompanied with its numeric *c-value* and *frequency* (TTF).

The **saturation measurement** phase applies the THD algorithm to the bags of terms as explained in Sect. 3. It outputs the results in the tabular form (see [27] for more details). This phase is supported by the **THD** modules, the **Convertor** module, and **StopTermRemover** module. The **THD modules** implement the THD algorithm for the input bags of terms in UPM Term Extractor and NaCTeM TerMine formats. The **Convertor** takes a bag of terms in TerMine format and saves it in the UPM Extractor format. The **StopTermRemover** takes the list of the manually selected stop terms and deletes all these terms from the bags of terms.

The **analysis** and **comparison** are done manually using any appropriate software tool. We use MS Excel in our experiments.

Hence, our experimental workflow is fully covered by the developed and used instrumental software.

4.2   Planned Series of Experiments

Different series of experiments, using this workflow, are planned to be conducted in the presented project [1].

The **first series** are planned for experimental cross-evaluation of the selected ATE software tools. Based on the datasets with the increments of reasonable size, term extraction is done separately using the UPM Term Extractor and NaCTeM TerMine. The results are compared in terms of saturation measures. This may allow answering our research question **Q1** (c.f. Sect. 2).

For this we set-up the first series of experiments to cross-evaluate UPM Term Extractor versus NaCTeM TerMine. In this subsection we present the configuration of these experimental series and the measurements in more detail.

We plan to perform this cross-evaluation by applying the experimental workflow to the three selected real document collections coming from different domains. Before applying the tools to the real document collections we check if they perform adequately on the two specifically crafted synthetic collections representing the boundary cases – for immediate saturation and no saturation. All the document collections are presented in more detail in Sect. 5.

To cross-evaluate term extraction tools we look at:

- How quickly the bags of terms, extracted from the incrementally growing datasets, saturate terminologically in terms of *thd* versus *eps*. We also measure *thdr*. The results are measured for all the document collections, independently for each tool, and then compared.

---

[5] Batch mode for TerMine is freely accessible at http://www.nactem.ac.uk/batch.php for academic purposes, provided that the permission by NaCTeM is granted for non-UK users.

- If the tools extract the similar bags of terms from each of the document collections in which saturation has been observed. The similarity between the extracted bags of terms is also measured using *thd* versus *eps* approach by applying the THD module to the pairs (*B1*, *B1m*), (*B2*, *B2m*), ..., (*Bn*, *Bnm*), where *Bi* is the bag of terms extracted by the first chosen tool (UPM Term Extractor) and *Bim* is the bag of terms extracted by the second chosen tool (NaCTeM TerMine).

5   Document Collections and Datasets

In this section we describe the data used in our experiments. These data come from two synthetic and three real document collections[6].

5.1   Synthetic Document Collections

Our synthetic collections have been prepared to evaluate the boundary cases: one in which terminological saturation should happen immediately; and the other one in which terminological saturation should not happen. These cases help us evaluate if saturation metric is adequate at these two extremes. If so, there is more confidence that it is also adequate for real document collections.

1DOC is the document collection containing just one paper. As this paper, we used the source of [24]. It has been converted to plain ANSI text format manually. From the plain text, the datasets $D1$, $D2$, ..., $D20$ have been generated, as described in Sect. 3, and the increment for each subsequent dataset was the text of this one paper. So, $D1$ contained one copy of this paper text, $D2$ – two copies of the same text, ..., $D20$–20 copies of the same text. It is straightforward that, if the OntoElect approach to measuring saturation is correct, the saturation in this case should be observed quite quickly with *thd* close to 0, as all the increments are identical.

The intuition behind crafting the RAW collection is opposite to the previous case. To avoid saturation, a collection is required in which all the increments are substantially terminologically different. To have that, the documents dealing with different topics, coming from different fields, and therefore using very different terminology need to be put together. For constructing RAW 80 articles from English Wikipedia have been randomly selected such that no two of them are about a similar topic and the size of an article is not too small. The articles have been downloaded in 1-column PDF format. Further, these PDF files have been converted to plain ASCII texts using our PDF to Plain Text Convertor. The texts have not been cleaned to keep the possibility for checking how does the noise injected by Wikipedia into the PDF printouts influences saturation. Based on the plain texts, 20 datasets have been generated, $D1$, $D2$, ..., $D20$, with increments comprising 4 randomly taken documents from the collection.

---

[6] All the five collections in plain text and the datasets generated of these texts are publicly available at: https://www.dropbox.com/sh/64pbodb2dmpndcy/AACoDO0iBKP6Lm4400uxJQ6Ca?dl=0.

5.2   Real Document Collections

Our real document collections are all composed of the papers published at the peer-reviewed international venues in three different domains: the TIME collection contains the full text papers of the proceedings of the TIME Symposia series[7]; the DMKD collection is composed of the subset of full text articles from the Springer journal on Data Mining and Knowledge Discovery[8]; the DAC collection comprises the subset of full text papers of the Design Automation Conference[9].

The domain of the TIME collection is Time Representation and Reasoning. The publisher of these papers is IEEE. This collection has been acquired in our previous research [24]. It contains all the papers published in the TIME symposia proceedings between 1994 and 2013, which are 437 full text documents. These papers have been processed manually, including their conversion to plain texts and cleaning of these texts. So, the resulting datasets were not very noisy. We have chosen the increment for generating the datasets to be 20 papers. So, based on the available texts, we have generated 22 incrementally enlarged datasets $D1$, $D2$, ..., $D22$.

The domain of DMKD collection is Data Mining and Knowledge Discovery, which falls into our broader target domain of Knowledge Management as its essential part. It was provided by Springer based on their policy on full text provision for data mining purposes[10]. To the DMKD document collection, we have included 300 papers published in the Journal of Data Mining and Knowledge Discovery between 1997 and 2010. All the papers in their full texts were automatically processed using our instrumental pipeline. In difference to the TIME collection, no manual cleaning of document texts was applied. For generating the datasets, the increment has been chosen to be 20 papers. So, based on the available documents we have generated 15 incrementally enlarged datasets $D1$, $D2$, ..., $D15$.

The domain of the DAC collection is Engineering Design Automation. The publisher of these papers is IEEE. For this collection, we have chosen 506 papers published between 2004 and 2010. The papers of DAC have been automatically converted to plain text using our instrumental software. We deliberately skipped manual cleaning of the plain texts to be able to compare the results between very noisy (DAC) and not very noisy (TIME) datasets generated from the papers having the same publisher and, therefore, the same source layout (IEEE). Similarly to TIME, we have chosen the increment for generating the datasets to be 20 papers. So, based on the available texts, we have generated 26 incrementally enlarged datasets $D1$, $D2$, ..., $D26$.

5.3   Summary of Data Features

The characteristics of all the five document collections and datasets are summarized in Table 3.

---

[7] http://time.di.unimi.it/TIME_Home.html.

[8] https://link.springer.com/journal/10618.

[9] http://dac.com/.

[10] https://www.springer.com/gp/rights-permissions/springer-s-text-and-data-mining-policy/29056.

Table 3. The features of the used document collections and datasets

Collection	Type	Paper type and layout	No Doc	Noise	Processing	Inc	No datasets
1DOC	Synthetic	Journal, ACM 1-column	1	Manually cleaned	Manual	1 paper	20
RAW	Synthetic	Wikipedia 1-column	80	Not cleaned, moderately noisy	Automated	4 papers	20
TIME	Real	Conference, IEEE 2-column	437	Manually cleaned	Manual conversion to plain text, automated dataset generation	20 papers	22
DMKD	Real	Journal, Springer 1-column	300	Not cleaned, moderately noisy	Automated	20 papers	15
DAC	Real	Conference, IEEE 2-column	506	Not cleaned, quite noisy	Automated	20 papers	26

For all real collections, the documents have been added to the datasets in their chronological order of publication. For the RAW collection the documents have been added in random order.

6   Experiments and Discussion

In this section we report and discuss the results of our experiments on the datasets generated from the five data collections presented in Sect. 5, particularly on the results of the phases of term extraction, saturation measurement, analysis and comparison.

In the experiment with each collection we: (i) extracted the bags of terms from the prepared datasets using TerMine and UPM Extractor; (ii) measured saturation for both sets of the bags of terms using the corresponding THD modules; (iii) measured comparative saturation for the pairs of the bags of terms $(B1, B1m)$, $(B2, B2m)$, ..., (Bn, Bnm) – as described in Sect. 4.2; (iv) built the diagrams and analyzed the results.

In addition to the above activities, for the RAW collection we also looked at the effect of removing stop terms after doing term extraction. By removing these stop terms, which represented the injection of noise by Wikipedia and also the text fragments from the figures, we denoised the output. The lists of the stop terms were prepared manually based on the extractions from the last dataset $D20$. These stop terms were further automatically removed from all the datasets using our Stop Term Remover module. So, for the RAW collection we also compared noisy and denoised bags of terms.

6.1   Terminological Saturation in Synthetic Collections

Due to collections design (Sect. 5), the results on 1DOC are expected to demonstrate quick and steady saturation and the results on RAW have to be far from being saturated.

For the bags of terms extracted from 1DOC, the results of measuring saturation look as follows.

We first processed the bags of terms extracted by TerMine. The results of measuring individual term significance thresholds (*eps*) and terminological differences (*thd*, *thdr*) are visualized in Fig. 4(a)[11]. We then measured terminological differences between the bags of terms extracted by UPM Extractor. The results of measuring individual term significance thresholds (*eps*) and terminological differences (*thd*, *thdr*) are pictured in Fig. 4(b).

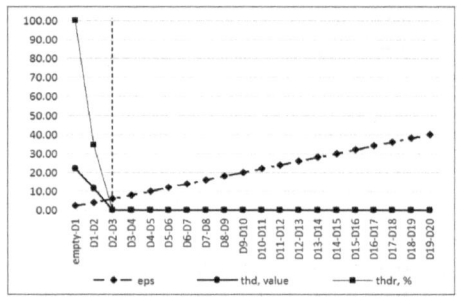
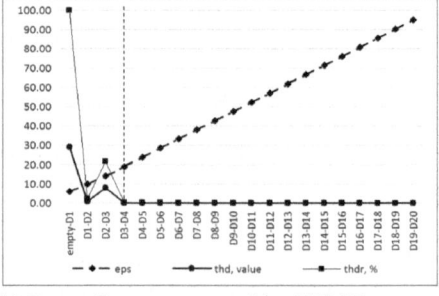

(a) Bags of terms extracted by TerMine   (b) Bags of terms extracted by UPM Extractor

Fig. 4. Visualization of saturation measurements on the 1DOC datasets

The dashed vertical line in Fig. 4(a) points to the bag of terms (extracted from *D*3) in which saturation indicator has been observed for the first time as *thd* went below *eps*. In fact, and as expected, we further observe steady saturation with the same number of extracted terms and increasing individual term significance threshold *eps*. The values of *thd* and *thdr* drop down to become statistically equal to zero starting from *T*2–*T*3. The dashed vertical line in Fig. 4(b) points to the bag of terms (extracted from *D*4) in which saturation indicator has been observed for the first time as *thd* went below *eps*. Very similarly to the case of TerMine, and as expected, we further observed very stable saturation with the same number of extracted terms and increasing individual term significance threshold *eps*. The values of *thd* and *thdr* drop down to become statistically equal to zero starting from *T*3–*T*4.

The differences in saturation measurements for the bags of terms extracted by TerMine and UPM Extractor are as follows: (i) UPM Extractor generated bigger bags of terms with *c-value* > 1: 3 019 terms versus 1 208 in the TerMine case; (ii) idividual term significance thresholds (*eps*) were about 2.5 times higher for UPM Extractor; (iii) the number of retained terms with *c-value* > *eps* was ∼ 2 times bigger in the UPM Extractor case; (iv) the values of *thd* and *thdr* were significantly lower (∼ 10 000 times) for TerMine.

---

[11] The values measured in all the reported experiments, though sometimes mentioned in the text, are not presented in the paper for saving space. All these experimental data and results are presented in full detail in the supporting technical report [27] which is publicly available online.

Overall, TerMine results showed a slightly quicker convergence to saturation, compared to UPM Extractor results. From the other hand: (i) the number of retained terms from the saturated sub-collection; and (ii) the cut-off point at the individual term significance threshold were higher in the UPM Extractor results. Based on observing these differences, we can conclude that, linguistically, TerMine was ~ 3 times more selective regarding extracting term candidates. So, the pre-processing in TerMine is more sophisticated. From the other hand, the cut-offs in UPM Extractor outputs happened for approximately two times more significant terms. Hence, the statistical processing part in UPM Extractor circumscribes more compact, yet significant sets of terms. This points out that, due to the statistical processing phase, UPM Extractor is a more selective instrument.

It was further checked if both tools extracted statistically similar sets of terms from the 1DOC collection. The measurements are visualized in Fig. 5. The figure shows that both tools extracted statistically identical bags of terms despite the fact that the numbers of retained terms differed significantly in the individual cases (reported above). The terminological difference became statistically negligible at the second measurement point, where the *thd* value (2.291409) went significantly below *eps* (9.509775). This situation was stable, since the *thd* values oscillated around 2.1 and the *eps* values steadily went up to 95.

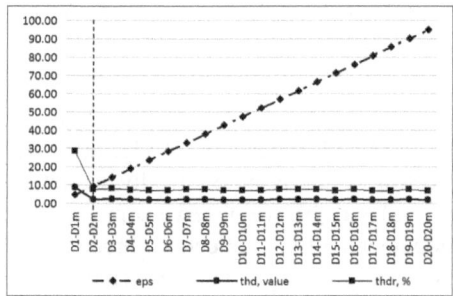

Fig. 5. Comparison of the retained sets of terms extracted from the 1DOC collection by UPM Extractor and TerMine

For the bags of terms extracted from RAW the results of measuring saturation look as follows.

We first processed the bags of terms extracted by TerMine. The results of measuring individual term significance thresholds (*eps*) and terminological differences (*thd*, *thdr*) are visualized in Fig. 6(a).

We then analyzed B20, extracted by TerMine, going from the top of the list down to the terms having *c-value*s greater than 40. Based on this scan, we extracted the list of ~ 200 stop terms. These stop terms have been removed from the bags of terms B1, ..., B20 and saturation analysis has been repeated. The results of measuring individual term significance thresholds (*eps*) and terminological differences (*thd*, *thdr*) for so denoised bags of terms are visualized in Fig. 6(b).

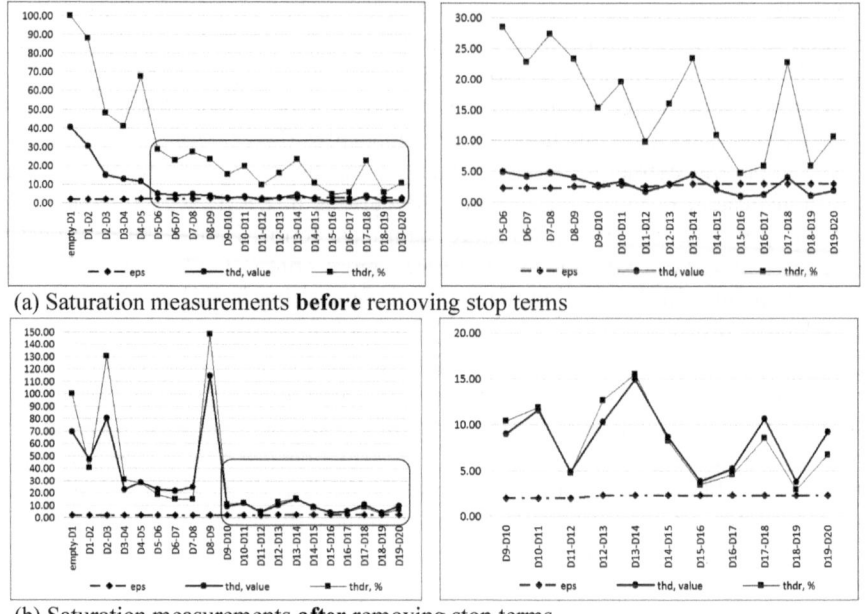

(a) Saturation measurements **before** removing stop terms

(b) Saturation measurements **after** removing stop terms

Fig. 6. Visualization of saturation measurements on the RAW bags of terms extracted by TerMine. The diagram to the right represents a more granular look into the rounded rectangle in the diagram to the left

When looking at Fig. 6(a) and, especially, at Fig. 6(b), we observe that, as it was expected, the RAW collection is not terminologically saturated. Further, looking at the differences between Fig. 6(a) and (b), we observe some nice indicators of the presence of noise in the textual documents of the collection. Indeed, the *thdr* values in Fig. 6(a) are much higher than the corresponding *thd* values. Though the *thd* values hint that the bags of terms might be close to saturation, the values of *thdr* are far beyond *eps*. Very interestingly, the values of *thd* measured after removing stop terms become similar to that of *thdr*. At the same time the *thd* and *thdr* curves in Fig. 6(b) very much resemble the *thdr* curve in Fig. 6(a). So, substantial differences between *thd* and *thdr* values signal about a possible need to clean the bags of terms, or the source texts, by removing the stop terms which have no relevance to the domain of the collection.

The same experiment has been then repeated for the bags of terms extracted by the UPM Term Extractor. The results of measuring saturation look as follows.

The values of individual term significance thresholds (*eps*) and terminological differences (*thd, thdr*) are visualized in Fig. 7(a). We then analyzed B20, extracted by UPM Extractor, going from the top of the list down to the terms having *c-value*s greater than 40. Based on this scan, we extracted the list of ∼220 stop terms. These stop terms have been removed from the bags of terms B1, …, B20 and saturation analysis has been repeated. The values of individual term significance thresholds (*eps*) and terminological differences (*thd, thdr*) for so denoised bags of terms are pictured in Fig. 7(b).

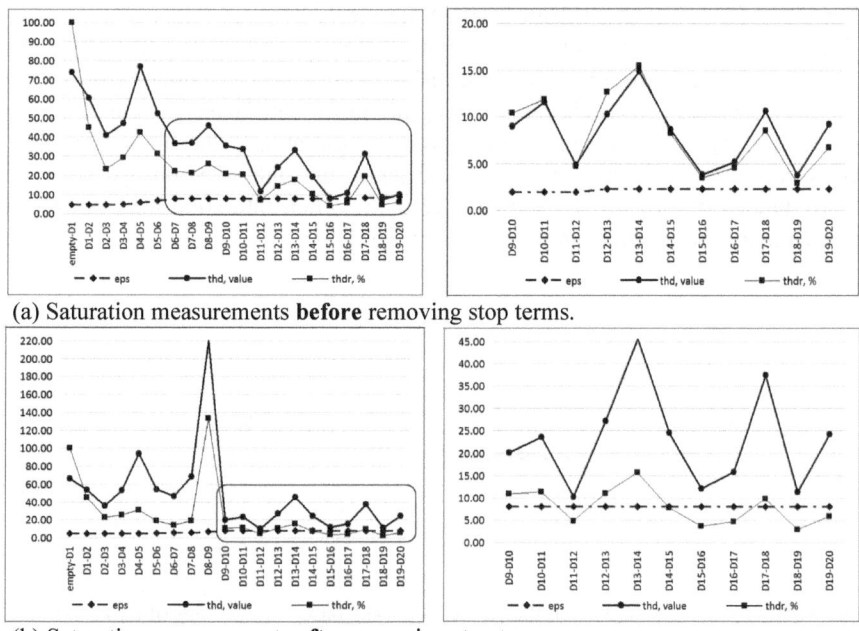

(a) Saturation measurements **before** removing stop terms.

(b) Saturation measurements **after** removing stop terms.

Fig. 7. Visualization of saturation measurements on the RAW bags of terms extracted by UPM Extractor.

Compared to the saturation measurements for the bags of terms extracted by Ter-Mine, the values of *thd* for the bags of terms extracted by UPM Extractor form a clearer picture of the absence of saturation. In fact, the *thd* values measured on UPM Extractor results before removing the stop terms are 2.5–3 times higher than those measured on TerMine results after removing the stop terms. So, the results by UPM Extractor are more highly contrast compared to those of TerMine in terms of detecting the absence of saturation. From the other hand, the values of *thdr* measured on TerMine results are a clearer indicator of the need to denoise the bags of terms. The *thdr* values measured on the UPM Extractor results do not differ from the corresponding *thd* values. If UPM Extractor is used to detect the absence of saturation, there is no real need however to analyze if *thdr* values indicate the presence of noise. So, the use of UPM Extractor is preferred in this case as it is a sharper instrument.

For this collection, it has not been measured if both tools extract statistically similar bags of terms. This measurement would have had no value in the absence of saturation.

6.2   Terminological Saturation in Real Collections

Our results in measuring terminological saturation in the real document collections are presented and analyzed in this subsection.

For the datasets extracted from DMKD the results look as follows.

The bags of terms extracted by TerMine were first processed. The results of measuring individual term significance thresholds (*eps*) and terminological differences (*thd, thdr*) are visualized in Fig. 8. The diagram at the left visualizes the whole set of measures. The rounded rectangular circumscribes the area in the diagram at the left, which is presented in finer detail in the diagram at the right. The dashed vertical line points to the bag of terms (extracted from *D*14) in which saturation indicator has been observed for the first time as *thd* went below *eps*.

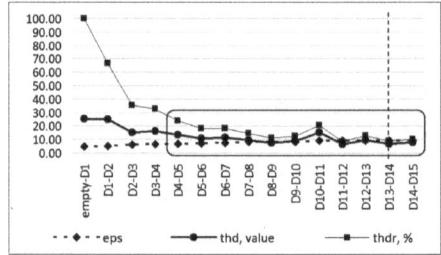
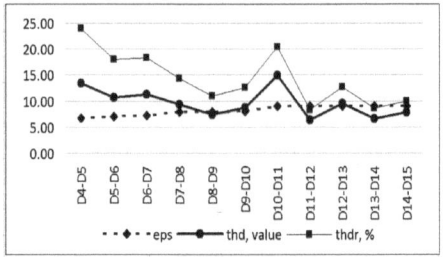

Fig. 8. Saturation measurements on the DMKD datasets based on the bags of terms extracted by TerMine

The analysis of these results points out that there is a trend to reaching terminological saturation, perhaps for bigger datasets. The *eps* values have the tendency to go up and *thd, thdr* values go down with the increase in dataset numbers. The increase in the numbers of retained terms is also going down. There are three terminological peaks in the area of our closer interest at *D*10–*D*11, *D*12–*D*13, and *D*14–*D*15. The contribution of these peaks is not very significant however as the *thd* value increases not very much compared to the vicinity – please see DAC results for much higher peaks. Overall, it is too early to consider DMKD saturated based on the extraction results by TerMine.

The results of measuring saturation based on the bags of terms extracted by UPM Extractor are pictured in Fig. 9. It could be noted that steady saturation is reached at

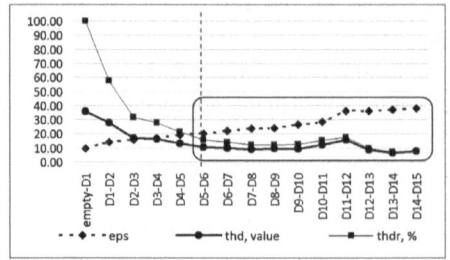
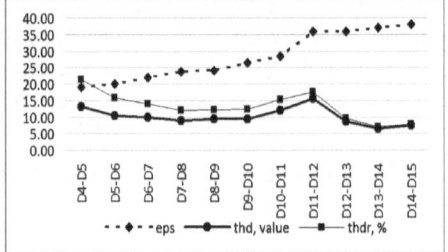

Fig. 9. Saturation measurements on the DMKD datasets based on the bags of terms extracted by UPM Extractor

D5–D6. The number of retained terms (from *B6*) is 4113, which is substantially lower than 5009 at the first potential saturation point in the TerMine case. Interestingly, *thd* and *thdr* values measured on UPM Extractor results behave quite similarly to those measured on TerMine results, also hinting about terminological peaks at the same points. The numbers of retained terms are lower, though not significantly, for UPM Extractor results. Saturation is reached due to much higher values of individual term significance threshold *eps*.

Hence, for this document collection, **UPM Extractor** yields **better circumscribed** and **more compact** sets of **significant terms** and the cut-off happens at much higher values of term significance.

One hypothesis about the reason for better UPM Extractor performance could be that it extracts not all the terms from the documents it takes in, and TerMine reaches a substantially higher recall. To check that, we measured terminological differences between the bags of terms extracted, from the same datasets by UPM Extractor and TerMine. The result is pictured diagrammatically in Fig. 10.

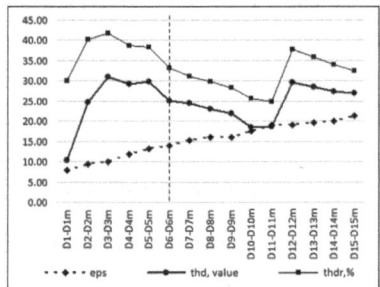

Fig. 10. Comparison of the retained sets of terms extracted from the DMKD collection by UPM Extractor and TerMine

Figure 10 shows that both tools extract somewhat similar bags of terms. This similarity increases with the growth of a dataset. The numbers of retained terms are higher than in Figs. 8 and 9. These also hint that the extracted bags of terms are similar and recall values of individual tools differ not too much, which is acceptable.

Interestingly, terminological difference (*thd*) in Fig. 10 goes below *eps* exactly at the point when TerMine results show the highest terminological peak (c.f. Fig. 8). So, it looks like both tools extract similar bags of terms but TerMine reaches the saturation level a bit later, when it collects the contribution from the increment at the highest terminology peak. Yet interestingly, *thd* values go beyond *eps* after *D11*. We think[12] that the reason for that is the increasing influence of the accumulated noise in the datasets, which is perceived differently by the individual tools.

---

[12] We did not yet check this. So, it is only a hypothesis.

The results of saturation measurements for TIME are pictured in Fig. 11.

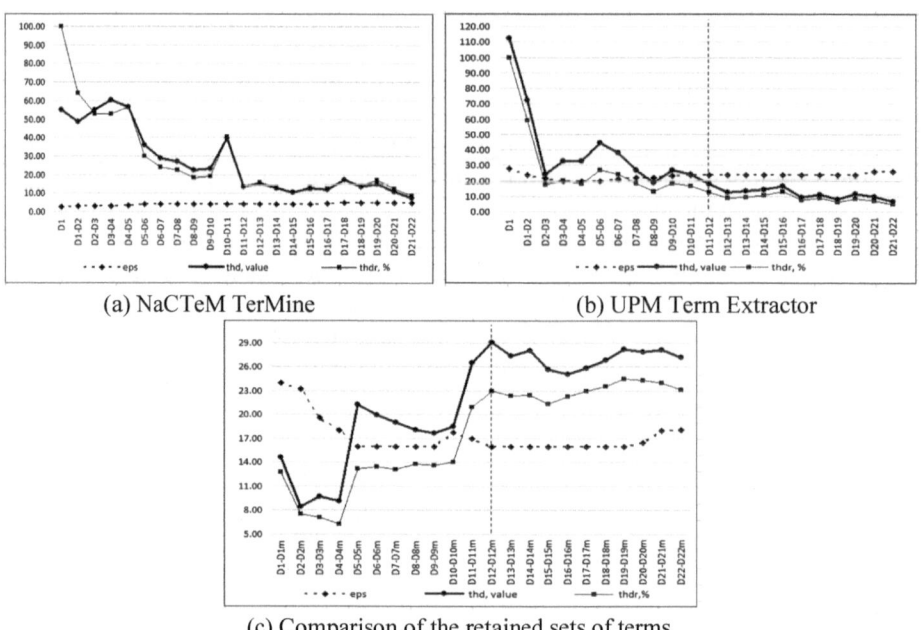

    (a) NaCTeM TerMine   (b) UPM Term Extractor

(c) Comparison of the retained sets of terms

Fig. 11. Saturation measurements for the TIME collection

The saturation measurements based on the bags of terms extracted by TerMine **did not show any saturation** –Fig. 11(a). The *thd* values did not go below *eps*. The tendency is similar to the DMKD experiment – a trend to reaching terminological saturation, perhaps for bigger datasets. The *eps* values go up with the increase in dataset numbers, though significantly slower than in the DMKD case. The maximal observed *eps* value is 5 for TIME versus 9 for DMKD. The *thd* and *thdr* values go down with the increase in dataset numbers, but not quickly enough to go below *eps*. As a consequence, the maximal number of retained terms is significantly higher that in the DMKD case: 8343 versus 5438, though the difference in the extracted numbers of terms is not that significant: $\sim 287K$ versus $\sim 253K$. Interestingly, the terminological peaks in the TIME collection are observed at $D3$–$D4$, $D10$–$D11$, $D17$–$D18$, and $D19$–$D20$. The highest peak is at $D10$–$D11$, which repeats the DMKD case, probably by a coincidence. Similarly to DMKD, the contribution of these peaks is not very substantial as the *thd* value increases not very much compared to the vicinity.

The saturation measurements based on the bags of terms extracted by UPM Extractor **reveal stable saturation** starting from $D11$–$D12$ – as pictured in Fig. 11(b) by the vertical dashed line. The values of *thd* and *thdr* resemble these of the TerMine case, so the saturation curve has terminological peaks nearly at the same points. The height of those peaks is however lower. The values of individual term significance threshold *eps* are however much higher – similarly to the DMKD experiment. Saturation is detected at *eps* equal to 23.774, whereas the values of *eps* in the TerMine case do not increase beyond 5.000. The number of retained terms, from $B12$ is 7110, which is only 2.47% of the total number of extracted terms in $B12$. Therefore, we may draw a similar conclusion for this experiment. Saturation is reached due to much higher values of individual term significance threshold *eps*. For TIME, **UPM Term Extractor** yields **better circumscribed** and **more compact** sets of **significant terms** and the cut-off happens for much higher values of term significance.

We also checked if both tools extract similar bags of terms from the TIME collection. The results have been measured following the same approach as in the case of DMKD and are pictured in Fig. 11(c). It could be seen, that the terminological difference (*thd*) between the bags of retained terms at the saturation point $D12–D12m$[13] equals to ~ 29, while *eps* equals to 16. So, *thd* is 1.81 times higher than *eps*. In the DMKD case the difference between *thd* and *eps* at the saturation point is slightly lower – 1.80 times. Very similarly to the DMKD case, the difference grows after the saturation point, which, as we believe, could be explained by the same reason – the influence of the accumulated noise in the datasets beyond the saturation point. Hence, manual cleaning of the TIME datasets did not really help a lot, as the results very much resemble the DMKD case, for which the datasets were not cleaned.

The results of saturation measurements for DAC are shown in Fig. 12. DAC collection is much noisier than DMKD and TIME. The results also differ – in values but not in the overall picture.

The saturation measurements based on the bags of terms extracted by TerMine revealed the potential saturation point only in the last measurement at $D25–D26$ – as pictured in Fig. 12(a). However, the terminological peak at $D24–D25$, with *thd* equal to 135.49, hints about the further instability. So, speaking about a tendency to reach stable saturation later would be a speculation. More measurements are needed to judge about it.

It is also interesting to compare the saturation behaviour in DAC to that in TIME, as both collections come from the same publisher, so have the same layout, and represent papers of similar size. The difference is that TIME was manually cleaned and DAC was not. Figures 11(a) and 12(a), if compared, show the differences in measurement values for the dataset pairs of roughly similar sizes.

The comparison of the measurements for TIME and DAC, based on the extraction results by TerMine, reveals that: (i) the values of *eps* grow faster for TIME than for DAC; (ii) the numbers of extracted and retained terms for DAC are substantially higher than for TIME; (iii) the numbers of retained terms for TIME grow monotonically and this growth slows down – an indicator of possible saturation in the upcoming measurements; (iv) the number of retained terms for DAC substantially drops below the previous value at $D24–D25$ and the *thd* dramatically picks up from 21.51 to 135.49.

---

[13] $D12$ is the dataset from which $B12$ is extracted by UPM Extractor and $B12m$ by TerMine. $B12m$ is further converted to the UPM Extractor format and the pair ($B12$, $B12m$) is fed into the THD module. The module returns *eps*, *thd*, and *thdr* values for the pair as described in Sect. 3.

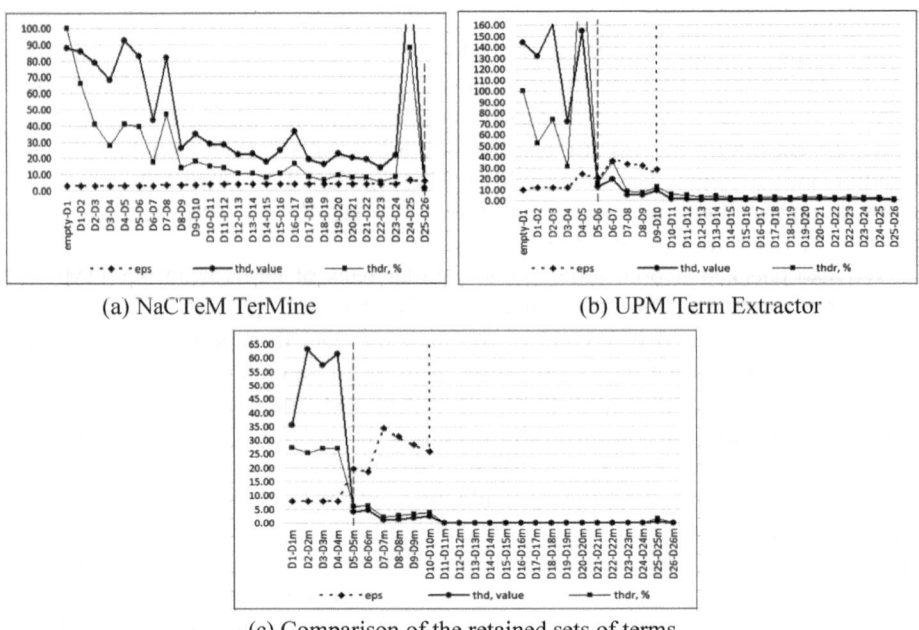

(a) NaCTeM TerMine

(b) UPM Term Extractor

(c) Comparison of the retained sets of terms

Fig. 12. Saturation measurements for the DAC collection

We believe, again, that the reason for the peak at *D24–D25* is the influence of the accumulated noise. However, TerMine signals about the problem quite lately.

The saturation measurements based on the bags of terms extracted by UPM Extractor **reveal steady saturation** starting from *D5–D6* with *eps* at about 20 – as pictured in Fig. 12(b) by the vertical dashed line. However, the values of *eps* peak up to 18 294 at *D10–D11* and the numbers of retained terms go down to 34 which is more than 100 times less than the previous value. A closer examination of the bags of terms revealed that these 34 terms are nothing but the noise which has been accumulated much earlier in the case of UPM Extractor. Therefore, in the case of a noisy document collection, UPM Extractor is much more sensitive in detecting excessive noise, compared to TerMine. So, the situation pictured in Fig. 12(b) could be used as an indicator of the need to denoise the collection datasets before terminology extraction.

Though not very relevant for this collection, we still compared if the bags of terms extracted by both tools were statistically similar. The result is pictured in Fig. 12(c). The comparison showed that, starting from *D5*, where *thd* equals to 3.97 and *eps* to 19.65, both tools successfully extracted the very similar sets of accumulated noise terms.

6.3   Summary of Results and Recommendations

This subsection summarizes our findings after analyzing the results of the experiments on cross-evaluating TerMine and UPM Extractor. The summary is structured along the cases based on our document collections.

Case 1: 1DOC – quick saturation expected. For the bags of terms extracted by both tools very stable saturation has been observed quite quickly – which was expected. The differences in saturation measurements are as follows: (i) UPM Extractor generated bigger bags of terms with *c-value* > 1: 3 019 terms versus 1 208 in the TerMine case; (ii) individual term significance thresholds (*eps*) were about 2.5 times higher for UPM Extractor; (iii) the number of retained terms with *c-value* > *eps* was approximately 2 times bigger in the UPM Extractor case; (iv) the values of *thd* and *thdr* were significantly lower ($\sim 10\,000$ times) for TerMine. Overall, TerMine results showed a slightly quicker convergence to saturation than that by UPM Extractor. From the other hand: (i) the number of retained terms from the saturated sub-collection; and (ii) the cut-off point at the individual term significance threshold were higher in the UPM Extractor results. Both tools extracted statistically similar bags of terms despite the fact that the numbers of retained terms differed significantly. Overall, both tools behaved, in detecting saturation and extracting similar bags of terms, exactly as expected by the design of the case.

Conclusions (case 1): (i) linguistically, TerMine is more selective in extracting term candidates, (ii) the cut-offs in UPM Extractor outputs happen for substantially more significant terms; (iii) UPM Extractor circumscribes more compact, yet more significant sets of terms and is a more sensitive instrument; (iv) these results confirm the adequacy of our saturation metric for the boundary case of quick saturation.

Case 2: RAW – saturation should not be reached. While measuring saturation in the bags of terms extracted by TerMine, we observed that saturation has not been reached. We also noticed that the measurements of *thd* and *thdr* on these bags of terms differed noticeably for the cases before and after removing stop terms. So, these differences between *thd* and *thdr* values signal about a possible need to clean the bags of terms, or the source texts, by removing the stop terms which have no relevance to the domain of the collection. The *thd* values measured on UPM Extractor results before removing the stop terms are 2.5–3 times higher than those measured on TerMine results after removing the stop terms. So, the results by UPM Extractor are more highly contrast compared to those of TerMine in terms of detecting the absence of saturation. Overall, both tools behaved, in failing to detect saturation and extracting similar bags of terms, as expected by the design of the case.

Conclusions (case 2): (i) TerMine is more sensitive in indicating the need to denoise the bags of terms; (ii) UPM Extractor is more sensitive in detecting the absence of saturation; (iii) these results confirm the adequacy of our saturation metric for the boundary case of non-reachable saturation.

Recommendation: The use of UPM Extractor is preferred to detect that saturation is hardly expected.

Case 3: DMKD (automatically pre-processed). Overall, it cannot be reliably judged that the DMKD collection is saturated based on the extraction results by TerMine. In difference to that, the saturation measurements using the bags of terms extracted by UPM Extractor reveal steady saturation quite quickly. It has also been noticed that both tools extracted statistically similar bags of terms.

Case 4: TIME (manually denoised). Saturation measurements using the bags of terms extracted by TerMine failed to detect saturation in the TIME collection. Very similarly to the DMKD case, the saturation measurements using the bags of terms extracted by UPM Extractor reveal steady saturation quite quickly, also with much higher individual term importance thresholds *eps*. These result in significantly more compact sets of retained significant terms.

Conclusion (cases 3, 4): Both cases demonstrated similar advantages of UPM Extractor over TerMine in detecting saturation and retaining significant terms. In both cases UPM Term Extractor yielded better circumscribed and more compact sets of significant terms. Manual cleaning of the TIME collection did not help noticeably to improve the results of saturation measurements, therefore was not really necessary.

Case 5: DAC (very noisy). UPM Extractor demonstrated the capacity to accumulate excessive noise from the datasets to the bags of terms substantially earlier than TerMine. The saturation curve, built for the measurements using UPM Extractor results, signals about this noise quite sharply – with the numbers of retained significant terms dropping down by two orders of magnitude and individual term significance thresholds going up by three orders of magnitude.

Conclusion (case 5): In the case of noisy datasets and due to not being very selective in extracting term candidates, UPM Extractor is much more sensitive in detecting excessive noise, compared to TerMine.

Recommendation (cases 3–5): The use of UPM Extractor is preferred over TerMine to detect terminological saturation or excessive noise; this is not constrained by a subject domain and does not depend on manual denoising of the source data in the collection.

7   Conclusions and Future Work

This paper reported on cross-evaluating the two software ATE tools: NaCTeM TerMine and UPM Term Extractor. The tools were selected for cross-evaluation based on the analysis of the related work in ATE and availability of software as reported in Sect. 2.

The objective of our cross-evaluation experiments was to find the most fitting software for extracting the bags of terms to be the part of our instrumental pipeline for exploring terminological saturation in text document collections in an arbitrary domain of interest. The technique for measuring terminological saturation, based on the use of the THD algorithm, has been outlined in Sect. 3.

The paper presented the set-up of experiments by outlining the generic workflow and instrumental software tools developed to automate the activities in the workflow, such as document collection retrieval, pre-processing, dataset generation, term extraction, terminological difference measurement, bags of terms denoising. It also explained which kinds of measurements and observations were planned to cross-evaluate the fitness of the selected ATE tools for their use in terminological saturation measurement pipeline. Specifically we were interested in: (i) how quickly the bags of terms, extracted, by different tools, from the incrementally growing datasets, saturated terminologically in terms of *thd* versus *eps*; and (ii) if the tools extracted the similar bags of terms from the document collections.

The paper then presented the data collections which were used in the experiments. The experiments were first been planned on the two synthetic collections to find out if the measurements of terminological saturation are adequate in the boundary cases: (i) the 1DOC collection in which saturation should be detected swiftly; and (ii) the RAW collection in which terminology can not be saturated. Secondly, the experiments were planned on the three real document collections, DMKD, TIME, and DAC. These collections represent different domains. The documents in these collections had different layouts and were processed differently, leaving more or less noise in the datasets. The summary of the collection and dataset features was provided in Table 3.

Finally, the results of our experiments on the datasets generated from the five data collections, particularly on the results of the phases of term extraction, saturation measurement, analysis and comparison, were reported and discussed. Based on the analysis of experimental results, conclusions were made in Subsect. 6.3. The conclusions revealed that:

- The metrics we used to measure terminological saturation are adequate as the results in the boundary cases of 1DOC and RAW were as expected
- The use of UPM Extractor is preferred, over TerMine, to detect that saturation is hardly expected, like in the RAW case
- When terminological saturation was reachable, the bags of terms extracted by UPM Extractor converged to saturation quicker than that by TerMine. Their use yielded better circumscribed and more compact sets of significant terms.
- In the cases of noisy datasets and due to not being very selective in extracting term candidates, UPM Extractor was much more sensitive in detecting excessive noise, compared to TerMine.

Based on these conclusions it has been recommended that the use of UPM Term Extractor is more preferable than the use of NaCTeM Termine in our terminological saturation measurement and detection technique.

Our future work will follow the research agenda outlined in Sect. 2 as the list of research questions **Q2–Q5**. Currently[14], the series of experiments aimed at answering **Q2** are finished and the technical report is being written. Our next step will be to configure and perform the experiments for answering **Q3**. The answers to **Q4** and **Q5** are in our mid-term plans for the future work.

Acknowledgements. The first author is funded by a PhD grant from Zaporizhzhia National University and the Ministry of Education and Science of Ukraine. The research leading to this paper has been done in part in cooperation with the Ontology Engineering Group of the Universidad Politécnica de Madrid in frame of FP7 Marie Curie IRSES SemData project (http://www.semdata-project.eu/), grant agreement No. PIRSES-GA-2013-612551. A substantial part of the instrumental software used in the reported experiments has been developed in cooperation with BWT Group. The collection of Springer journal papers dealing with Knowledge Management, including DMKD, has been provided by Springer-Verlag.

---

[14] At the time of writing the final version of this paper, December, 2017.

References

1. Kosa, V., Chugunenko, A., Yuschenko, E., Badenes, C., Ermolayev, V., Birukou, A.: Semantic saturation in retrospective text document collections. In: Mallet, F., Zholtkevych, G. (eds.) Proceedings of ICTERI 2017 PhD Symposium, CEUR-WS, Kyiv, Ukraine, 16–17 May, vol. 1851, pp. 1–8 (2017). Online
2. Tatarintseva, O., Ermolayev, V., Keller, B., Matzke, W.-E.: Quantifying ontology fitness in OntoElect using saturation- and vote-based metrics. In: Ermolayev, V., Mayr, H.C., Nikitchenko, M., Spivakovsky, A., Zholtkevych, G. (eds.) ICTERI 2013. CCIS, vol. 412, pp. 136–162. Springer, Cham (2013). https://doi.org/10.1007/978-3-319-03998-5_8
3. Osborne, F., Motta, E.: Klink-2: integrating multiple web sources to generate semantic topic networks. In: Arenas, M. et al. (eds.) ISWC 2015, Part I. LNCS, vol. 9366, pp. 408–424. Springer, Heidelberg (2015). https://doi.org/10.1007/978-3-319-25007-6_24
4. Astrakhantsev, N.: ATR4S: toolkit with state-of-the-art automatic terms recognition methods in scala. arXiv preprint arXiv:1611.07804 (2016)
5. Zhang, Z., Iria, J., Brewster, C., Ciravegna, F.: A comparative evaluation of term recognition algorithms. In: Proceedings of Sixth International Conference on Language Resources and Evaluation, LREC08, Marrakech, Morocco (2008)
6. Fahmi, I., Bouma, G., van der Plas, L.: Improving statistical method using known terms for automatic term extraction. In: Computational Linguistics in the Netherlands, CLIN 2007, vol. 17 (2007)
7. Wermter, J., Hahn, U.: Finding new terminology in very large corpora. In: Clark, P., Schreiber, G. (eds.) Proceedings of 3rd International Conference on Knowledge Capture, K-CAP 2005, pp. 137–144. ACM, Banff (2005). https://doi.org/10.1145/1088622.1088648
8. Daille, B.: Study and implementation of combined techniques for automatic extraction of terminology. In: Klavans, J., Resnik, P. (eds.) The Balancing Act: Combining Symbolic and Statistical Approaches to Language, pp. 49–66. The MIT Press, Cambridge (1996)
9. Cohen, J.D.: Highlights: Language- and domain-independent automatic indexing terms for abstracting. J. Am. Soc. Inf. Sci. **46**(3), 162–174 (1995). https://doi.org/10.1002/(SICI)1097-4571(199504)46:3<162::AID-ASI2>3.0.CO;2-6
10. Caraballo, S.A., Charniak, E.: Determining the specificity of nouns from text. In: Proceedings of 1999 Joint SIGDAT Conference on Empirical Methods in Natural Language Processing and Very Large Corpora, pp. 63–70 (1999)
11. Medelyan, O., Witten, I.H.: Thesaurus based automatic keyphrase indexing. In: Marchionini, G., Nelson, M.L., Marshall, C.C. (eds.) Proceedings of ACM/IEEE Joint Conference on Digital Libraries, JCDL 2006, pp. 296–297. ACM, Chapel Hill (2006). https://doi.org/10.1145/1141753.1141819
12. Ahmad, K., Gillam, L., Tostevin, L.: University of surrey participation in trec8: Weirdness indexing for logical document extrapolation and retrieval (wilder). In: Proeedings 8th Text REtrieval Conference, TREC-8 (1999)
13. Frantzi, K.T., Ananiadou, S.: The C/NC value domain independent method for multi-word term extraction. J. Nat. Lang. Process. **6**(3), 145–180 (1999). https://doi.org/10.5715/jnlp.6.3_145
14. Sclano, F., Velardi, P.: TermExtractor: a web application to learn the common terminology of interest groups and research communities. In: Proceedings of 9th Conference on Terminology and Artificial Intelligence, TIA 2007, Sophia Antinopolis, France (2007)
15. Kozakov, L., Park, Y., Fin, T., Drissi, Y., Doganata, Y., Cofino, T.: Glossary extraction and utilization in the information search and delivery system for IBM Technical Support. IBM Syst. J. **43**(3), 546–563 (2004). https://doi.org/10.1147/sj.433.0546

16. Astrakhantsev, N.: Methods and software for terminology extraction from domain-specific text collection. Ph.D. thesis, Institute for System Programming of Russian Academy of Sciences (2015)

17. Bordea, G., Buitelaar, P., Polajnar, T.: Domain-independent term extraction through domain modelling. In: Proceedings of 10th International Conference on Terminology and Artificial Intelligence, TIA 2013, Paris, France (2013)

18. Park, Y., Byrd, R.J., Boguraev, B.: Automatic glossary extraction: beyond terminology identification. In: Proceedings of 19th International Conference on Computational linguistics, Taipei, Taiwan, pp. 1–7 (2002). https://doi.org/10.3115/1072228.1072370

19. Nokel, M., Loukachevitch, N.: An experimental study of term extraction for real information-retrieval thesauri. In: Proceedings of 10th International Conference on Terminology and Artificial Intelligence, pp. 69–76 (2013)

20. Zhang, Z., Gao, J., Ciravegna, F.: Jate 2.0: Java automatic term extraction with Apache Solr. In: Proceedings of LREC 2016, Slovenia, pp. 2262–2269 (2016)

21. Justeson, J., Katz, S.M.: Technical terminology: some linguistic properties and an algorithm for identification in text. Nat. Lang. Eng. **1**(1), 9–27 (1995). https://doi.org/10.1017/S1351324900000048

22. Evans, D.A., Lefferts, R.G.: Clarit-trec experiments. Inf. Process. Manag. **31**(3), 385–395 (1995). https://doi.org/10.1016/0306-4573(94)00054-7

23. Church, K.W., Gale, W.A.: Inverse document frequency (IDF): a measure of deviations from Poisson. In: Proceedings of ACL 3rd Workshop on Very Large Corpora, pp. 121–130. Association for Computational Linguistics, Stroudsburg, PA, USA (1995). https://doi.org/10.1007/978-94-017-2390-9_18

24. Oliver, A., V`azquez, M.: TBXTools: a free, fast and flexible tool for automatic terminology extraction. In: Angelova, G., Bontcheva, K., Mitkov, R. (eds.) Proceedings of Recent Advances in Natural Language Processing, pp. 473–479, Hissar, Bulgaria, 7–9 September 2015

25. Corcho, O., Gonzalez, R., Badenes, C., Dong, F.: Repository of indexed ROs. Deliverable No. 5.4. Dr Inventor project (2015)

26. Ermolayev, V., Batsakis, S., Keberle, N., Tatarintseva, O., Antoniou, G.: Ontologies of time: review and trends. Int. J. Comput. Sci. Appl. **11**(3), 57–115 (2014)

27. Kosa, V., Chaves Fraga, D., Naumenko, D., Yuschenko, E., Badenes, C., Ermolayev, V., Birukou, A.: Cross-evaluation of automated term extraction tools. Technical report TS-RTDC-TR-2017-1, 30.09.2017, Department of Computer Science, Zaporizhzhia National University, Ukraine, 60 p. (2017). http://ermolayev.com/TS-RTDS-TR-2017-1.pdf, https://doi.org/10.13140/rg.2.2.31187.07207

Complex Industrial Systems Automation Based on the Internet of Things Implementation

Yuriy Kondratenko[1,2]([✉]) [iD], Oleksiy Kozlov[2] [iD],
Oleksiy Korobko[2] [iD], and Andriy Topalov[2] [iD]

[1] Petro Mohyla Black Sea National University, 10, 68th Desantnykiv Street,
Mykolaiv 54003, Ukraine
yuriy.kondratenko@chmnu.edu.ua
[2] Admiral Makarov National University of Shipbuilding, 9 Heroes of Ukraine
Av., Mykolaiv 54025, Ukraine
{oleksiy.kozlov,oleksii.korobko}@nuos.edu.ua,
topalov_ua@ukr.net

Abstract. This paper presents the analysis of the Internet of Things (IoT) approach and its application for the development of embedded monitoring and automatic control systems (EMACS) for technological objects and processes that are included in complex industrial systems. The functional structure and main components of the generalized embedded monitoring and automatic control system for complex technological objects and processes based on IoT approach are given. The examples of IoT applications in design of specialized EMACS for such complex technical objects as gas turbine engines, floating docks and specialized pyrolysis complexes (SPC) are presented. Considerable attention is given to particular qualities of the functional structures, software and hardware implementation as well as multi-level human-machine interfaces (HMI) of the developed embedded systems for monitoring and automatic control of main process parameters. The developed EMACS based on IoT approach provide: high precision control of operating processes of gas turbine engines, floating docks and SPCs in the real time mode, monitoring and automatic control of their current technological parameters with high quality indicators, that leads to significant increasing of energy and economic efficiency of both given complex technical objects.

Keywords: Complex industrial systems · Automation · SCADA
Internet of things · Embedded monitoring and automatic control systems

1 Introduction

The development of computer aids and modern computer networks has led to the creation of new types of automated control systems of technological processes (ACSTP) [1]. Modern information-measuring technical equipment and data transmission technologies solve many problems associated with collection, conversion, transmission and storage of various information for technological processes control [2].

New ACSTP are characterized by the transition to the creating of complex systems in which information processing is decentralized, and some parts of the ACSTP are

© Springer International Publishing AG, part of Springer Nature 2018
N. Bassiliades et al. (Eds.): ICTERI 2017, CCIS 826, pp. 164–187, 2018.
https://doi.org/10.1007/978-3-319-76168-8_8

often remote from each other. There is a trend towards increasing the use of sensor networks and appropriate hardware and software means of conjugation at all hierarchy levels [1].

In the process of ACSTP creating and using for complex industrial systems, that include objects of oil and gas, energy, machinery and other types of industry the following problems are solved: creation of systems for monitoring and control of both manufactured goods and for certain technological processes, taking into account local and systemic approaches [3, 4]. Providing of an operational monitoring of all parameters with high accuracy and a timely control of actuators of various kinds of technological processes are the complex technical tasks that require limiting attentiveness of staff for a long time. Any "human" errors or outdated equipment can lead to an increase of production time per unit, respectively to the decrease of an economic efficiency of equipment using and possibly to emergencies at the facility.

The rapid development of computer and information technologies contributes to the creation of effective supervisory control and data acquisition (SCADA) systems in the production sphere [2, 5, 6]. The usage of SCADA-systems enables the operator to automate the control parameters of various kinds of industrial systems and processes, enable or disable mechanisms and devices, open or close valves on pipelines, monitor any parameters from a specially equipped console with a centralized or supervisory control. SCADA systems have a number of components [5, 6] that facilitate the development of computerized data acquisition and analysis tools, such as communication protocols for external devices connection, built in signals filtering, supporting of structured query language (SQL) data exchange etc. This and many other features make the SCADA software a perfect tool for implementation of control, data analysis and information processing algorithms in industry, household and science research [5–10].

More actively with modern SCADA-systems the wireless data transmission technology is implemented [11]. The combination of SCADA-systems with wireless technologies and the Internet allows creating the WebSCADA-systems [12]. The term WebSCADA usually refers to the implementation of HMIs of SCADA-systems based on the web-technologies. This allows implementing monitoring and control of SCADA-systems through a standard browser, acting in this case as a thin client. The architecture of these systems includes WebSCADA server and client terminals - personal computers, personal digital assistants or mobile phones with a Web browser [11–14]. Connecting of customers to the WebSCADA servers via Internet/Intranet allows them to interact with applied automation tasks as with simple Web or WAP pages.

Even more novel and promising approach for automation of complex industrial systems as well as for ACSTP creation is the Internet of Things approach [15–18].

Internet of Things is the concept of the computer network of physical objects ("things"), equipped with built-in technologies for communication with each other and with the environment [17]. The organization of such networks is recently considered as a phenomenon that can rebuild the economic and social processes as well as exclude the need for human intervention from the part of actions and operations [15]. This concept formulated in 1999 as a comprehension of prospects of wide application of radio frequency identification (RFID) means for interaction of physical objects between themselves and with the external environment [19]. Filling the IoT concept with multiform technological content and introduction of practical solutions for it implementation considered to be a stable trend in information technology primarily due to the widespread dissemination of wireless networks, appearance of cloud computing, development of machine to machine technology, beginning of active transition to the new Internet protocols and development of software-configurable networks [20–29].

Examples of IoT concept implementing are systems of "Smart house" [30], "Smart farm" [21, 31], "Smart city" [20], "Smart environment" [21, 31], "Smart enterprise" [32], "Smart transport" [17], "Smart wearable" [28, 29] and others.

The main purpose of this work is analysis of the IoT approach and its application for the development of embedded monitoring and automatic control systems for technological objects and processes that are included in complex industrial systems.

Basic features, involved technologies, and main applications of the IoT approach are given in the Sect. 2. The functional structures, software and hardware implementation as well as multi-level HMIs of the developed EMACS for complex technological objects, such as gas turbine engines, floating docks and specialized pyrolysis complexes for municipal polymeric waste (MPW) thermal utilization, based on IoT are presented in the Sect. 3. Section 4, in turn, has conclusions, discussion of the results and further research on the IoT approach application for the complex industrial systems, technological objects and processes automation.

2   Internet of Things Approach and Implementation

Basically the IoT is a network consisting of interrelated physical objects ("things") or devices that have built-in sensors and software that allows you to transfer and exchange data between the physical world and computer systems by using standard communications protocols [15, 33]. In addition to sensors the network can have actuators embedded in physical objects and linked together with wired or wireless networks. These interrelated objects ("things") have the ability of data reading and actuating according to the control signals, the functions of programming and identification, as well as allow excluding the need for human participation by using the intelligent interfaces [16, 34].

The basis of IoT approach is a possibility of connection all kinds of objects ("things") that people can use in everyday life, such as refrigerator, car, bicycle, washing machine, etc. [15, 33–35]. All of these objects ("things") should be equipped with built-in sensors that are able to process information coming from the environment, share it and perform different actions depending on the received information. The ideology of the IoT is aimed at increasing of economic efficiency by processes automation in various fields of activity and elimination the need for human participation in them [15–19, 36].

For the implementation of the IoT approach, the following technologies are used.

2.1   IoT Implementation Technologies

Identification tools. The special equipment for information recording and processing as well as for actuators controlling is involved in any IoT system. Obviously, for the effective functioning of the IoT system it is necessary to ensure a high level of network service and consequently the unique identification of software and hardware elements of the system. The identification problems for connected devices depend on the number of concurrent connections to the Internet, which the given system can support, and on the quality of service, which can be guaranteed [15]. Now the majority of Internet-connected devices use IPv4 protocol from the family of TCP/IP protocols, which is based on 32-bit addressing scheme and is limited to 2^{32} (4 294 967 296) unique addresses [28]. Considering that predicted for the IoT possible number of connected units is 50–100 billion for optimal scalability it is required to move to IPv6 protocol from the family of TCP/IP protocol, which uses 128-bit addressing system capable of supporting up to 2^{128} addresses (3, 4 · 10^{38} units) [19, 23, 28]. Currently several initiatives are implementing to influence the development of IPv6 protocol to support the IoT. One of them is the project IoT6, dedicated to research, design and development of service-oriented architecture with high level of scalability based on IPv6.4.

Also, identification of network elements of the IoT can be achieved with the help of RFID chips that can transmit information to reading devices without their own power source [18, 37]. Each chip has a unique number. As an alternative to this technology for the identification of objects the QR-Codes can be used. Furthermore, to determine the exact location of IoT objects the GPS technology can be used, which effectively operates today in smartphones and navigators.

Measuring instruments. By measurement means of the object measuring trans-ducers are generally understood, that are designed to generate measurement data in a form, suitable for transmission, further transformation, processing and storage [7–10]. The IoT technology uses a wide class of measurement tools, from the elementary sensors (temperature, rotation angle, etc.), consumption metering devices (smart meters) to complex integrated measurement systems [9, 21, 29]. Also, all measuring devices are combined, as a rule, in the wired/wireless intelligent sensor networks, due to what is possible to build M2M interaction systems. In recent years, the wireless sensor networks are used due to miniature components, low power consumption, embedded transceivers, sufficient processing power and relatively low cost [10–13].

Measuring sensors can be fixed permanently, and also have a relative mobility, that is to move freely relative to each other in a certain space, without breaking the logical network connectivity. In the latter case, the sensor network has no permanent fixed topology and its structure changes dynamically over time [10, 13].

Data processing means. For the processing and storage of data, given from the sensors, it is advisable to use embedded software and hardware means in the form of small-sized computers (for example, Raspberry Pi, Intel Edison) with access to the Internet [7–10, 22]. Moreover, the final processing of the data and making an informed decision on the cloud service is performed with the use of Big Data technologies [21]. The main difference between Big Data and "ordinary" data is that it is impossible to process these data with traditional database management systems and business intel-ligence solutions because of their large volume and diverse composition. Another important property of them is the accelerated accumulation of data and their continuous change. Such popular tasks as data reduction, obtained from different sources (Data Cleaning, Data Merging, De-deduplication), require special analysis methods in case of inaccurate data, especially huge data. For the processing of measurement data today are available for free in the test mode such cloud services as: Azure, Freeboard, Grove-streams, Developer.ibm, Thingspeak, Thingworx and other [9, 21].

Data transmission means. The range of possible data transmission technologies covers all possible means of wireless and wired networks. For wireless transmission of data between the software and hardware elements of the IoT networks a particularly important role play such qualities as efficiency in conditions of low speeds, resilience, adaptability, the ability to self-organization [9, 16, 17, 20]. Therefore, the class of wireless personal area networks (WPAN) is actively used. Currently WPAN can be with a short range (up to 10 m) and with increased range (up to 100 m), which allows them to be located on the functional capabilities at the junction with the wireless local area networks (WLAN). WPAN can be created based on different technologies of the IEEE 802.15.4 standard: ZigBee, WirelessHart, MiWi, etc. [15–18].

The remote location of the sensors and their automatic operation increases their vulnerability to third-party intrusions and attacks. It is easy enough to intrude into a wireless connection to intercept packets transmitted by the sensor. For example, the biggest threat is the threat of a denial-of-service attack, the purpose of which is to disrupt the correct functioning of the sensor network. This can be achieved by various methods, for example, by feeding a powerful signal that prevents sensors from exchanging information ("white noise" or "jamming attack"). There are various ways to protect systems from intruders, but for many of them you need high requirements for hardware resources, which is difficult to achieve due to limitations on many sensor requirements. Consequently, sensory wireless networks require new solutions in the field of data protection, providence of identification, creation of complex keys among legitimate users of the networks.

Among wired technologies of software and hardware components interaction the long-established industry network standards are used in the IoT, such as Profibus, Canbus, LON, Modbus, etc. [8–10]. It should be also noted, that for the software and hardware elements connection to the Internet the standard family of protocols TCP/IP is basically used in the IoT. Moreover, today for the networks service development in the IoT according to the standard IEEE 802.15.4 it is especially important to use the open 6LoWPAN protocol, standardized by IETF, that allows combining the intellectual sensors in the Internet with a low data rate [28].

Using the given above technologies the IoT approach can be applied in various fields. The main of them are listed below.

2.2 IoT Main Applications

The possibility of networking of the different types of sensors, actuators, embedded devices with CPU, memory and power resources indicates that IoT approach finds applications in almost all spheres [16]. The systems based on IoT may be involved in collecting information and controlling of objects in different settings, buildings, factories cities, natural ecosystems, etc. [17]. The main areas in which the IoT approach is increasingly applied are as follows.

Home automation. In this field the "Smart house" systems are used, that are the residential extension of building automation and realize the control and automation of lighting, air conditioning, ventilation, heating and security [30]. Such systems include different switches and sensors, washers, dryers, ovens, refrigerators and other home devices, that are connected to a central hub for remote monitoring and control. The user interface can be interacted with a wall-mounted terminal, tablet, laptop, mobile phone software or a web interface via internet cloud services [30]. The most popular communications protocols for such systems are: X10, Ethernet, RS-485, 6LoWPAN, Bluetooth LE (BLE), ZigBee, Z-Wave and others [8–10, 28].

City infrastructure automation. In this field the "Smart city" systems are used, that implement monitoring and controlling operations of urban and rural infrastructures like bridges, railway tracks, on- and offshore- wind-farms etc. [20]. The IoT infrastructure can be used for monitoring and control of any parameters of urban objects that can increase safety and compromise risk. For example, the IoT system for city automation can calculate and predict the energy balance point of the city for a certain period of time, automatically sending the control data to generators, power grids and smart household devices in order to maintain the required energy balance [20]. Municipal companies can save large sums of money, while continuing to maintain the reliability and integrity of the power supply instead of buying new equipment.

Transport automation. The IoT can assist in monitoring, control, and information processing across various transportation systems [17]. IoT systems can help to configure dynamically switching of traffic lights and adjustable exits from highways, thereby reducing congestion and improving traffic flow in real-time, rather than in predictive models. Application of the IoT extends to all aspects of transportation systems: smart parking, smart traffic control, vehicle control, fleet management and logistic, electronic toll collection systems, road assistance, etc. [15–17].

Environmental monitoring automation. IoT applications for environmental monitoring use different sensors to aid in the field of environmental protection [21, 31]. These IoT systems can implement monitoring of air and water quality [21] as well as soil and atmospheric conditions [31]. For example, a young Dutch company "Sparked" implants sensors in the ears of cows, that allows farmers to monitor the health and movement of cattle. This technology can increase the amount and quality of produced meat. Also, the IoT applications for tsunami and earthquake early-warning systems can be used by emergency services to provide more effective aid. IoT devices in this application should be enough mobile because they cover a large geographic area [31].

Industrial automation. The application of the IoT in the manufacturing industry is called the Industrial Internet of Things (IIoT) [27, 32]. The IIoT will revolutionize manufacturing by enabling the acquisition and accessibility of far greater amounts of data, at far greater speeds, and far more efficiently than before. A number of innovative companies have started to implement the IIoT [17, 32]. The company "Inductive automation" developed the only IIoT platform "Ignition" with effective MQTT data transfer protocol and full-featured SCADA functionalities built right in. "Ignition's" cross-platform compatibility and flexible modular configurability make it the world's first truly universal industrial application platform. "Ignition" empowers you to connect IIoT data across your entire enterprise, launch clients to any device equipped with a web browser, rapidly develop automated systems without any limits [32, 38].

The IIoT can greatly improve the efficiency of the industrial renewable resources installations, for example, windmills and solar panels. Business leaders can use IIoT data to get a full and accurate view of how their enterprises are doing, which will help them make better decisions [27, 32].

The IIoT networks, by definition, can not be limited by the perimeter of this or that enterprise. Very important is the interaction with the manufactured product ("thing") during its operation, as well as access to cloud services that can be implemented in data centers, scattered throughout the world [13, 32, 39, 40]. Thus, geographically distributed infrastructure is a key feature of the IIoT.

The main complexity of the IoT approach application in the industry is that "things" in the industrial systems are complex technical objects, such as internal combustion engines, industrial robots, steam turbines, chemical reactors, cargo cranes, lathes, etc., that are involved in the performance of complex technological processes. For the productive carrying out of these technological processes it is necessary to implement monitoring and automatic control of their technical objects main process parameters via the internet with high quality indicators in the real time mode [7–10]. Any technical malfunctions or errors, caused by the incorrect control, slowing down of the performance, loss of the Internet for some time, etc., can lead to a reduction of an economic efficiency or serious industrial accidents sometimes even with human victims.

Thus, the IIoT systems should include highly efficient software and hardware means for the implementation of specialized algorithms of monitoring and automatic control. Also, such systems should have an increased level of reliability, performance and information security [26, 39].

Also, broad implementation of the Internet of things in the industry is hampered by complex technical and organizational problems, in particular, related to standardization. The standardization of the Internet of things is very slow, which makes it difficult to integrate the solutions offered on the market and to a large extent hinders the appearance of new ones. The worst global implementation prevents the vagueness of the concept of the IoT and the large number of regulations.

Factors slowing the development of the Internet of things include the difficulties of the transition of the existing Internet to a new, 6th version of the IP network protocol, primarily the need for large financial costs on the part of telecommunications operators and service providers to upgrade their network equipment.

If technological platforms for the IoT are already practically created, then, for example, it juridical and psychological ones are only in the stage of becoming, as well as the problems of interaction of users, data and devices. One of the problems is data protection in such global networks.

Analyzing all the above requirements, we can conclude that at the current stage of development of the IoT technologies it is advisable to develop and implement the specialized EMACS for complex industrial technological objects and processes automation on the basis of the IoT approach. Such systems should have a modular structure with reliable and highly efficient software and hardware means as well as industrial communication interfaces, located in close proximity to the technical objects, for monitoring and automatic control implementation in safe and uninterrupted mode at the local level. Also, these systems should be easily integrated into existing large-scaled IIoT systems through a wired or wireless Internet connections which cover one or a group of industrial enterprises for monitoring and automatic control at the remote level.

Let us consider the developed by the authors EMACS for complex technological objects and processes based on IoT approach.

3 Embedded Monitoring and Automatic Control Systems for Complex Industrial Objects Based on IoT Implementation

The basic diagram of the generalized EMACS for complex technological objects and processes based on IoT approach [18] is presented in Fig. 1, where the following notations are accepted: PC – personal computer; PLC – programmable logic controller; FPGA – field-programmable gate array; SBC – single-board computer; SDAM – sensors data acquisition module; AOM – analog output module; S – sensor; AM – actuating mechanism; u_1, u_2, u_{n-1}, u_n – control signals of actuating mechanisms; y_1, y_2, y_{n-1}, y_n – output variables values of actuating mechanisms; x_1, x_2, x_{n-1}, x_n – technical object process parameters; $u_{S1}, u_{S2}, u_{Sn-1}, u_{Sn}$ – sensors output signals.

The proposed generalized EMACS for complex technological objects and processes based on IoT approach [18] has two levels of monitoring and automatic control: local level and remote level. Local level, in turn, is divided into three hierarchical levels of monitoring and control:

(1) lower level – the level of the sensors and actuating mechanisms of the technical object, that is involved in the performance of a certain technological process;
(2) average level – the level of the peripheral monitoring and control devices (includes modules for data acquisition and analog output as well as PLC/FPGA/SBC);
(3) upper level – the level of HMI (includes industrial PC).

Lower level of the developed EMACS consists of the automatic control sub-systems (ACSS), which perform automatic regulation of the given values of the technical object major controlled data according to a control program in terms of various disturbances operation [8–10].

Industrial PC of the upper level serves as the operator station. It contains a specialized HMI in the form of a control panel of the technological process with the image of the technical object main components and their technical parameters that are measured by various sensors [9].

Also, the set values of the control parameters, that are inputs of the technical object's ACSS, are established on the industrial PC according to a control program. PLC/FPGA/SBC of the average level processes the information received from the sensors and sends it to the industrial PC. Also, it gets the set values of the technological process control parameters and performs the functions of it automatic control. Data acquisition modules receive signals from sensors and transmit it to the PLC/FPGA/SBC in a convenient form for further processing [8]. Analog output

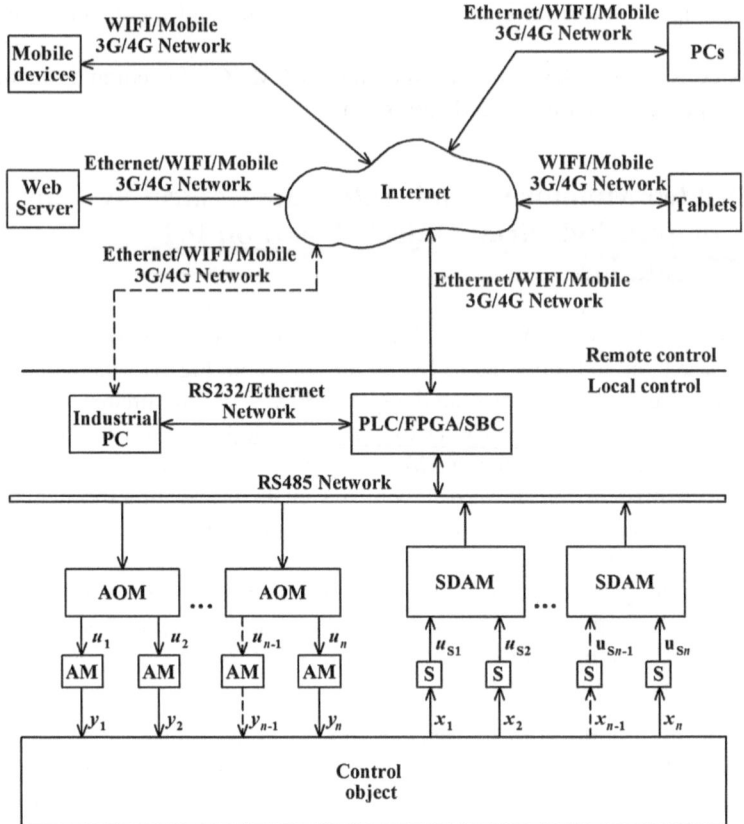

Fig. 1. Basic diagram of the generalized EMACS for complex industrial objects and processes based on IoT approach

modules receive digital control signals from the PLC/FPGA/SBC and produce corresponding analog control signals that go directly to the technical object's actuators.

The monitoring and automatic control operations in the remote level are implemented by means of powerful web servers, remote computers, tablets and different types of mobile devices [10]. In this case PLC/FPGA/SBC or industrial PC with the help of wired (Ethernet) or wireless (WiFi, mobile network 3G, 4G and others) connection technologies and family of protocols TCP/IP exchange data via the Internet with specialized web server that is placed on a powerful computer. Specialized web server, in turn, receives data process parameters and provides Web access to other users (remote computers, tablets, mobile devices). Moreover using the web server the access to the technological process data can be given from any PC of the enterprise IIoT system, that is running under any operating system (Windows, Linux, Mac OS, etc.), and if desired, from any PC in the world connected to the Internet.

In turn, the specialized HMI in the form of a control panel of the technological process is installed on the server and on the all computers of the enterprise IIoT system, where it is necessary, with all available functions of monitoring and control. Also, the specialized server can implement the function of automatic data sending to all the necessary users of the enterprise IIoT system in case of emergency and include the online expert system for data analysis and forming the further control goals [18].

As a concrete examples of the given above approach implementation let us consider the developed by the authors highly effective EMACS based on IoT for such complex technical objects as gas turbine engines, floating docks and SPCs.

3.1 IoT Based Embedded Monitoring and Automatic Control System for Gas Turbine Engines Automation

A new high-performance EMACS for a gas turbine engine is implemented with the modular structure that includes monitoring and automatic control of main technological parameters in the local and remote levels using powerful data storage and analysis tools. This system provides execution of the following functional tasks: monitoring, automatic control and visualization of a gas turbine engine main process parameters in real time mode at the local level and at the remote level via the internet; visual display of information about the state of the engine with clear indication of current states and emergencies; the ability of integration into existing large-scaled IIoT systems of machine-building plants, enterprises or factories; automatic data sending in case of emergency to the all users of the enterprise IIoT system. Also, the developed EMACS for the gas turbine engines has modern and highly integrated programming environment, that is enough flexible and easy to extend, flexible network designs and ability of connection to online expert system for more detailed data analysis.

The functional structure of the proposed by the authors highly effective EMACS for a gas turbine engines is shown in Fig. 2.

As the software facilities of the developed EMACS for a gas turbine engines the TRACE MODE 6 is used, which belongs to the class of integrated systems that provide maximum comfort to designers and users. Basing on the system tasks with the help of TRACE MODE 6 the authors developed the specialized HMI, main screen of which is shown in Fig. 3.

The given HMI is intended to indicate the values of the basic parameters and the position of elements of fuel, oil and air systems, launch systems, and others. Also, the set values of the control parameters, that are inputs of the ACSSs of the gas turbine engine EMACS, are established with the help of HMI on the industrial PC.

PLC, in turn, processes the information received from the sensors and sends it to the industrial PC. Also, it gets the set values of the gas turbine engine control parameters and performs the functions of it automatic control. Data acquisition modules receive signals from sensors and transmit it to the PLC in a convenient form for further processing. Analog output modules receive signals from the PLC and produce corresponding control signals that go directly to the gas turbine engine actuators.

For monitoring of the gas turbine engine controlled process dynamics the EMACS human-machine interface has a specialized trend screen (Fig. 4). Each panel is a unit of information about the process parameters values with the diagram deviations and warning messages. Diagrams deviations have separate horizontal bands for positive and negative values.

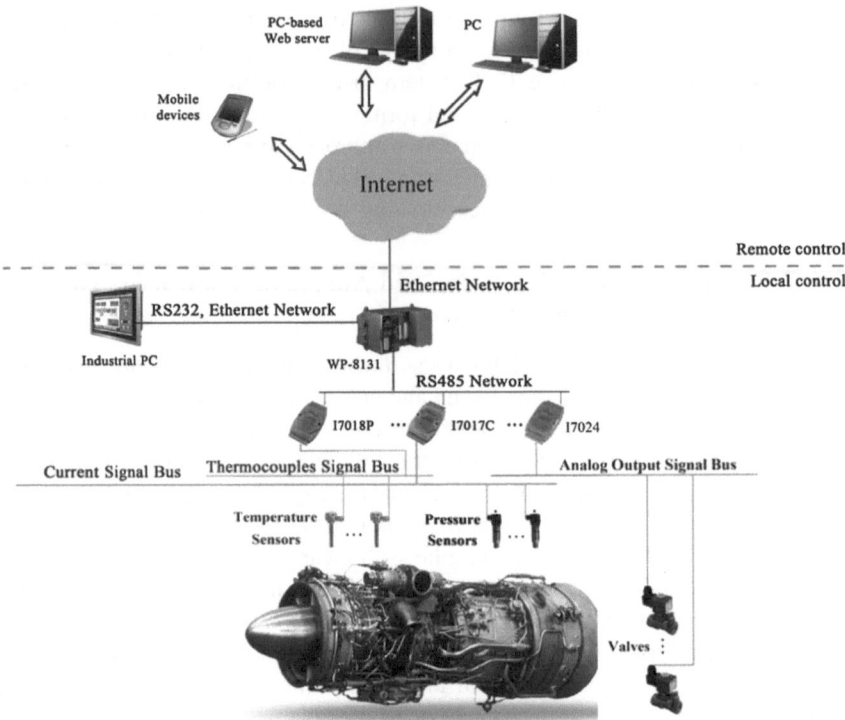

Fig. 2. Functional structure of EMACS for a gas turbine engine automation

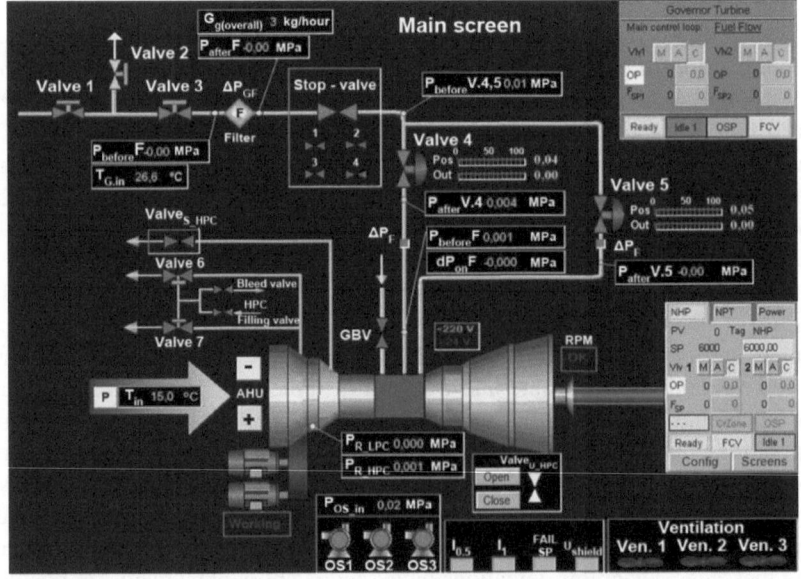

Fig. 3. Human-machine interface of the EMACS for a gas turbine engine

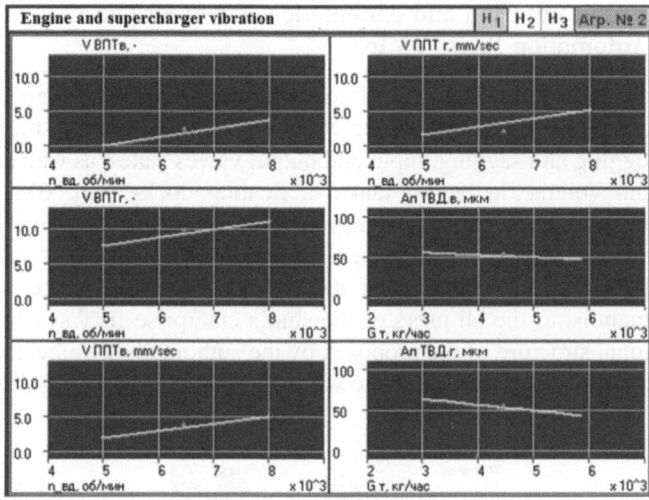

Fig. 4. Trend panel of the EMACS HMI for a gas turbine engine

The hardware facilities for the EMACS for gas turbine engines implementation are data acquisition modules, analog output modules and PLC. As a PLC the WP-8131 of the ICP DAS company is used. To receive signals from sensors of different types in this EMACS 2 types of the ICP DAS company data acquisition modules are used: I-7018P modules with 8 inputs – for data acquisition from thermocouples; I-7017C modules with 8 inputs – for data acquisition from sensors with current output (0...20 mA). To implement the conversion of digital signals from the PLC to analog ones that directly go to the actuators of the complex parameters ACSS the I-7024 modules with 4 outputs of the ICP DAS company are used.

In this EMACS the monitoring and automatic control operations in the remote level are implemented by means of specialized web server, remote computers, tablets and different types of mobile devices. In this case, PLC with the help of Ethernet connection and family of protocols TCP/IP exchange data via the Internet with the enterprise main web server that is placed on a powerful computer. The main server, in turn, receives the gas turbine engines data process parameters and provides Web access to other users (remote computers, tablets, mobile devices).

As a result, the presented IoT based EMACS for a gas turbine engine allows to increase the accuracy of main parameters control as well as to reduce the weight and dimensions of the engaged equipment in comparison with typical systems of monitoring and control. This gives the opportunity to intensify the processes of monitoring and control as well as to ensure the expansion of the measurement range. Moreover, the operations of acquisition, storage and processing of statistical data on the functioning of the gas turbine engine are performed automatically in the remote web server. This allows to free the operator from routine work on registration and analysis of results, which in general increase the efficiency and convenience of the proposed EMACS.

3.2   Embedded Monitoring and Automatic Control System for Floating Docks Automation Based on IoT

The new efficient EMACS for floating docks is designed for implementation of the main docking operations, monitoring and control of current values of the draft, list and trim angles, hogging and sagging, input and output valves states, as well as liquid level, temperature and volume in ballast tanks of floating docks [10]. EMACS modular structure ensures flexibility and scalability of the system, and therefore can be easily embedded into large-scaled IIoT systems of shipbuilding plants, enterprises and shipyards. Also, it provides automatic data sending in case of the floating docks emergency situations to the all users of the ship's enterprise IIoT system.

The functional structure of the proposed by the authors highly efficient EMACS for floating docks docking operations is shown in Fig. 5 [10].

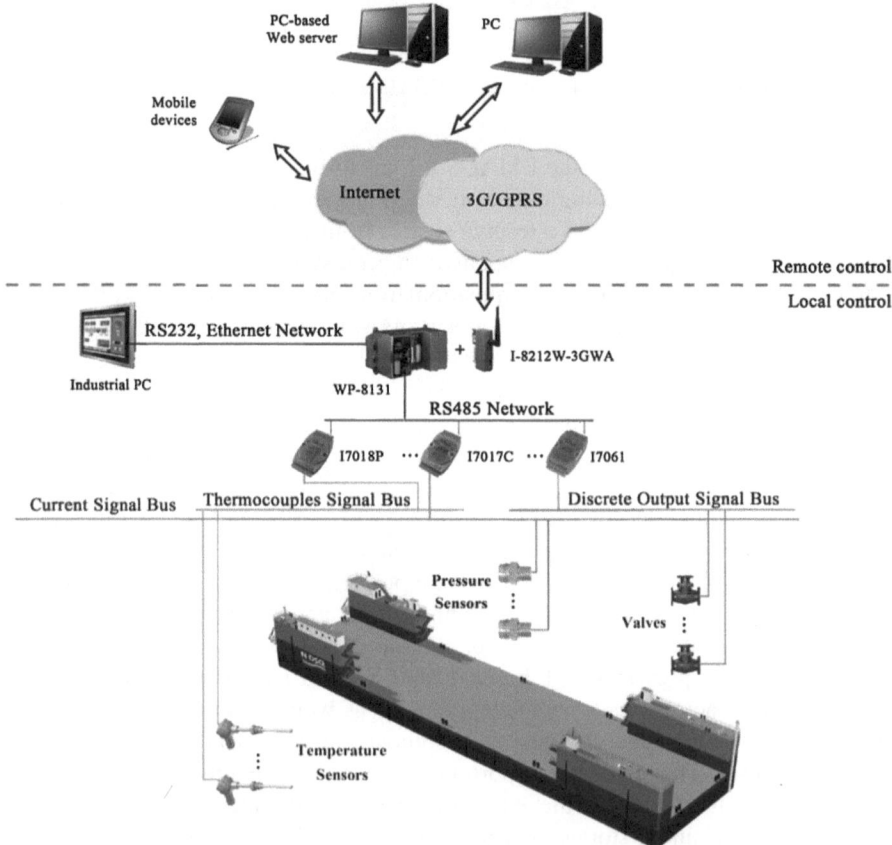

Fig. 5. Functional structure of EMACS for floating docks docking operations

EMACS for floating docks is divided into local and remote control options of floating dock. Local control of parameters is made directly on the floating dock, operator has the ability to monitor all the parameters and control of the dock actuators. Distance control of parameters required for use from shipbuilding plant, enterprise or shipyard land office [10]. It is implemented via the wireless Internet connection.

As the software means of the developed EMACS for floating docks docking operations also the TRACE MODE 6 is used, with the help of which the specialized HMI (Fig. 6) is developed by the authors [10]. The proposed HMI allows displaying the basic parameters recorded by the control system of dock operations for floating docks.

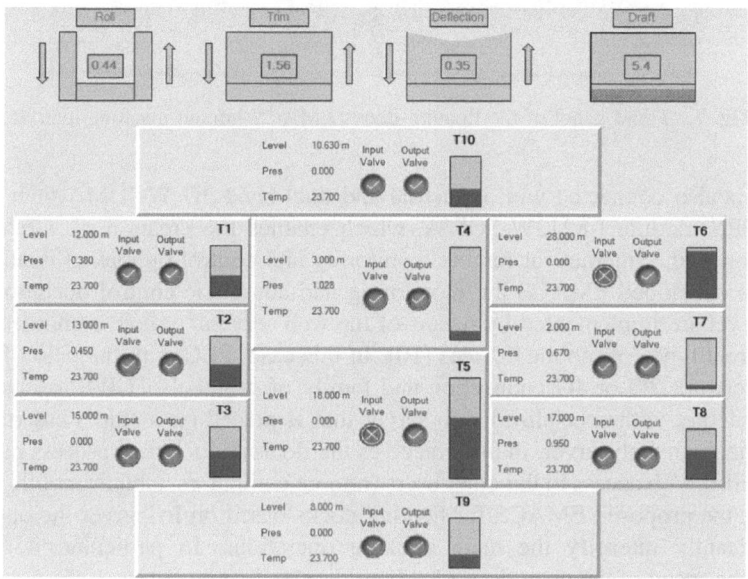

Fig. 6. Human-machine interface of the EMACS for floating docks

For monitoring the dynamics of the floating docks controlled process the HMI has also a trend screen (Fig. 7). This screen displays the graphic form of the information on roll, hogging, sagging and trim angles of floating docks, as well as the draft level.

As a PLC the WP-8131 of the ICP DAS company is used. For the successful launch of the given EMACS the industrial PC and all the computers of the ship's enterprise IIoT system must be equipped with a real-time monitor Trace Mode 6. To receive signals from the floating dock sensors of different types in this EMACS the ICP DAS company I-7018P and I-7017C data acquisition modules are used.

To implement the conversion of digital signals from the PLC to analog ones that directly go to the floating dock parameters ACSS the I-7061 modules for output are used.

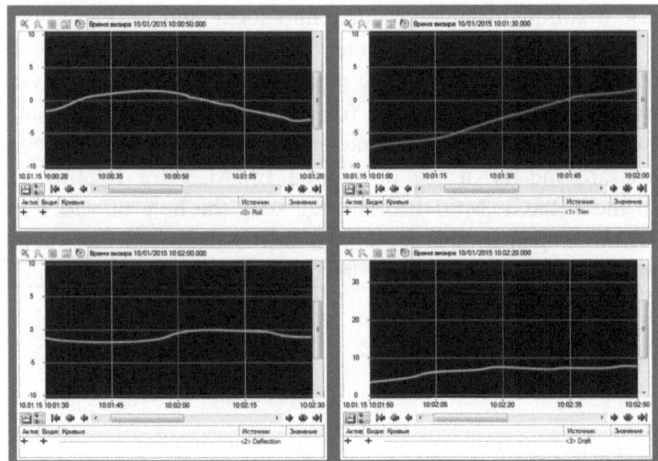

Fig. 7. Trend panel of the floating docks EMACS human-machine interface

PLC is also connected with industrial and dual-band 3G WCDMA with 4 ranges GSM/GPRS module I-8212W-3GWA, which enables the creation of wireless communication to the Internet for remote monitoring and control options of floating dock.

In the developed EMACS the monitoring and automatic control operations in the remote level are implemented by means of the web servers, remote computers, tablets and different types of mobile devices [10]. In this case, PLC with the help of wireless mobile network 3G or 4G connection and family of protocols TCP/IP exchange data via the Internet with specialized web server that is placed on a ship's enterprise land office. The main web server, in turn, receives the floating dock data process parameters and provides Web access to the other users (remote computers, tablets, mobile devices).

Thus, the proposed EMACS for floating docks based on IoT gives the opportunity to significantly intensify the main docking operations. In particular, it allows to increase the speed of the operations of submerging and surfacing by 30%. Accordingly, the bandwidth of the floating docks increases, which in general raises its profitability. In addition, the application of wireless technologies based on IoT allows to implement the operational control of the floating docks parameters in the real time mode from the coast control post. This raises the total efficiency and reliability of the floating docks exploitation and maintenance at the docking operations performing.

3.3   IoT Based Embedded Monitoring and Automatic Control System for Specialized Pyrolysis Complexes Automation

A new highly effective EMACS developed by the authors for the specialized pyrolysis complexes, that are used for municipal polymeric waste thermal utilization, has also modular structure and implement monitoring and automatic control of main technological process parameters in the local and remote levels using efficient data processing, analysis and storage instruments. The given system provides performance of the following tasks: monitoring, visualization and automatic control of the pyrolysis complex main operating parameters at the local level and at the remote level via the internet in real time mode; visual display of information about the state of the SPC main components with clear indication of current states and emergencies; the ability of integration into existing large-scaled IIoT systems of MPW utilization industrial plants, enterprises or factories; automatic data sending to all the operators of the enterprise in emergency cases. Also, the developed by the authors SPC EMACS has flexible and highly integrated programming environment, flexible network designs and ability of connection to online data processing and analysis expert systems.

The functional structure of the proposed by the authors highly effective EMACS for the specialized pyrolysis complex is shown in Fig. 8.

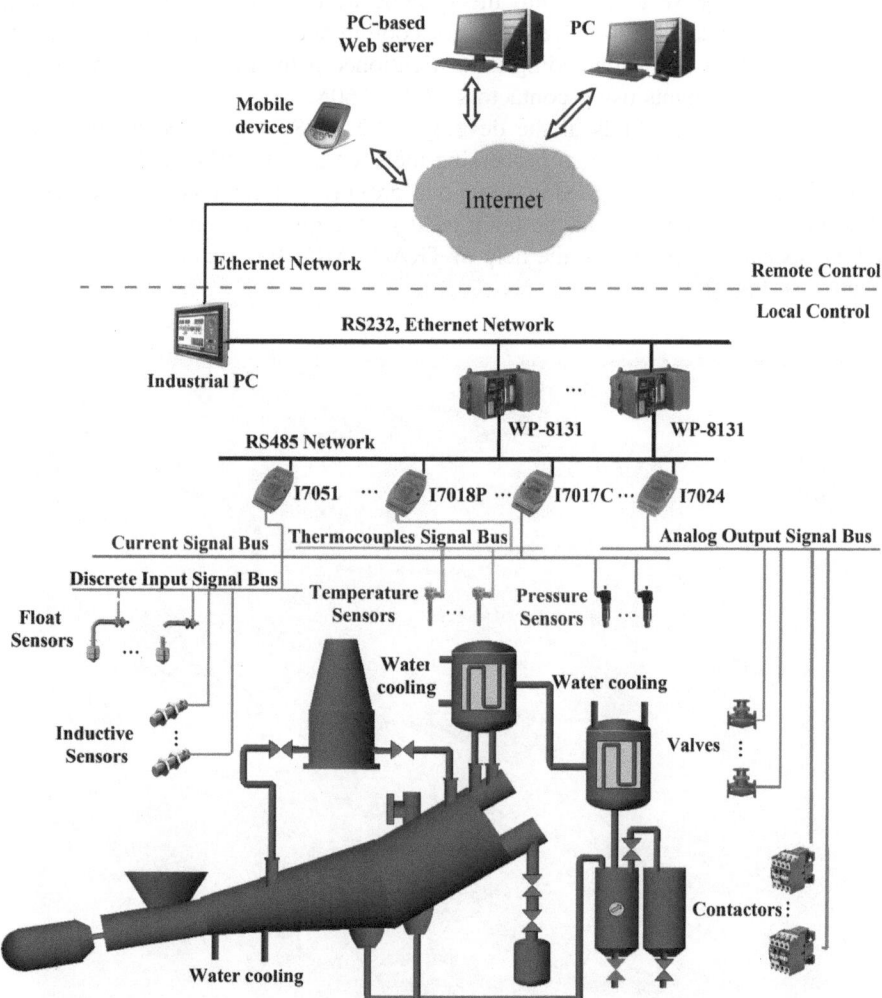

Fig. 8. Functional structure of EMACS for the specialized pyrolysis complex

The proposed structure (Fig. 8) of the EMACS based on IoT is built taking into account the necessity of the simultaneous measurement of various physical quantities, functioning in real-time mode and also the need to build a modular system that has the ability of integration into existing large-scaled IIoT systems. In turn, the designed structure allows to measure and control the main technological parameters of the MPW utilization process, such as: temperature, pressure and load level values in the reactor, fuel liquid fractions level in the fuel tank and a set of temperature values in key points of SPC. Optionally the given EMACS could be additionally equipped with 2 float inductive sensors (upper and lower level values indicating) and 1 radar sensor (intermediate level values determining) for load level value measurement in the SPC reactor, that can increase system dependability and fault tolerance.

According to Fig. 8, main actuating mechanisms of SPC include: the hydraulic drive piston for MPW loading into the reactor, water cooling pumps, fuel pumps, normally closed Jaksa D224 valves, fans for cooling and flue gases blowing, AC gear motors as a part of MPW unloading unit. Mentioned actuating mechanisms are powered from the AC mains using contactors PML 1160M type.

As the software facilities of the developed EMACS of the specialized pyrolysis complexes for the MPW thermal processing the TRACE MODE 6 is also used. which belongs to the class of integrated systems that provide maximum comfort to designers and users. Taking into account the main tasks of the given system the authors developed the specialized HMI with the help of TRACE MODE 6, main screen of which is presented in Fig. 9.

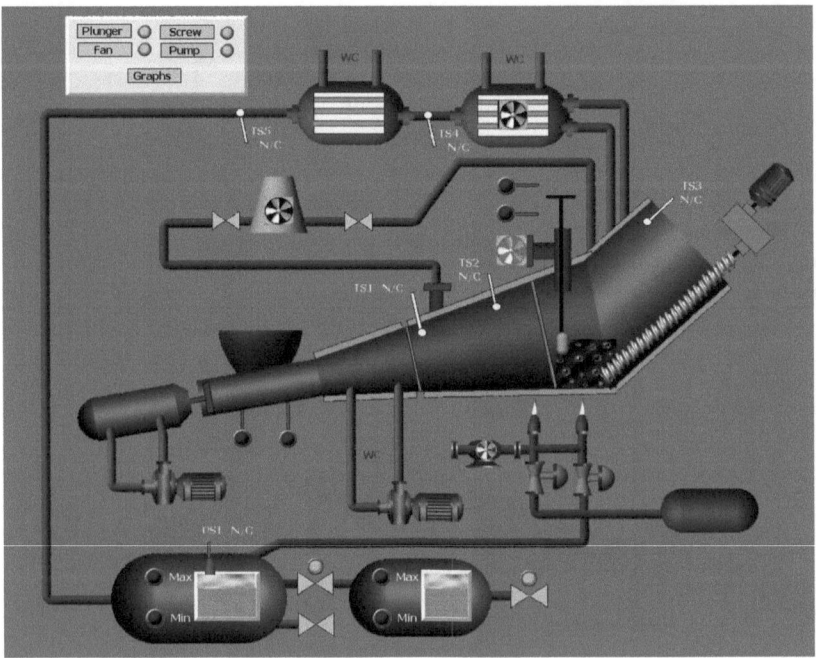

Fig. 9. Human-machine interface of the EMACS for a specialized pyrolysis complex

Designed HMI has a multi-window interface. Main screen (Fig. 9) provides the visualization of the main indicators of the EMACS process parameters on the operator control display and also grants an ability to set needed ranges of the parameters.

The indication of SPC modes is provided by changing the color of the displayed value from red (means manual) to green (means automatic, placed in the upper left corner in Fig. 9). The current state of the discrete sensors is displayed in the same color way (Fig. 9): the green color corresponds to the open state of discrete sensors (there is no liquid fuel at this level or the hydraulic drive piston at this position) and the red color corresponds to the close state (the sensor has been submerged into the liquid or the hydraulic drive piston has achieved this position).

Also the designed software based on TRACE MODE 6 includes the graph screens, which indicates the dynamic of main indicators changes and are called by clicking on the "Graphs" button. For example, the graph screen, presented in Fig. 10, shows the dynamic of the temperature changes of the SPC reactor main control points.

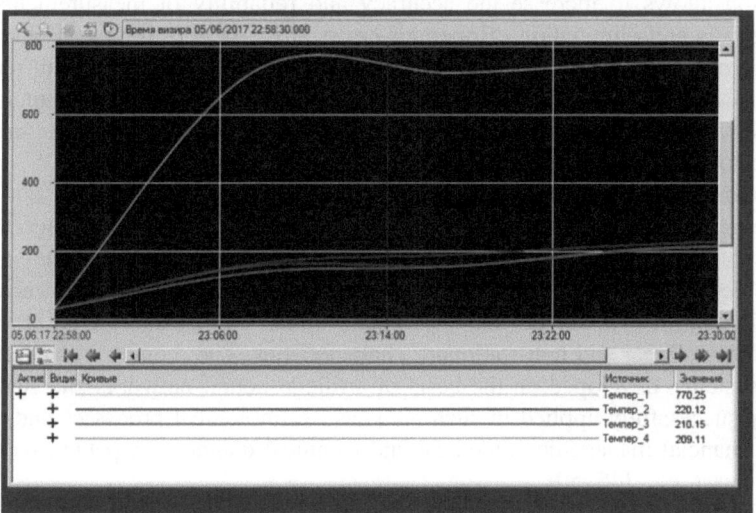

Fig. 10. Graph screen of the temperature changes of the SPC reactor main control points

In turn, the given graphs of the temperature changes (Fig. 10) are obtained at the process of the reactor initial heating.

For hardware implementation of the mentioned above EMACS for the SPC the authors used the next measuring means: pressure sensors PD100 type, thermo-couples of the K- and L-types, inductive sensors of the SN04-N and PIP-8-3 types, discrete float level sensors of the PDU 1.1 type.

ICP DAS I-7018Z modules are used as the data acquisition modules for the thermo-couples and pressure sensors readings. The ICP DAS I7041PD modules for 14 inputs are used as the data acquisition modules for the discrete input signals. In addition, the ICP DAS I-7061D modules with 12 relay power outputs are used for actuating mechanisms automatic control. ICP DAS I7561 modules provide USB to

RS-232/422/485 converting for modules' connection to industrial PC at testing and debugging of all system.

PLCs WP-8131 of the ICP DAS company are used in the current IoT based EMACS as the main execution units. The specifications of the PLC are: CPU PXA270 or Comparable (32-bit, 520 MGz), RW Memory SDRAM 128 Mb, Zeropower SRAM 512 Kb, Flash-memory 128 Mb, also supports storage map of 16 GB microSD. PLC includes VGA, Ethernet, USB 1.1, RS232, RS485 and RS 482 interfaces.

In turn, in the given EMACS the main monitoring and automatic control operations in the remote level are also implemented by means of specialized web server, remote computers, tablets and different types of mobile devices. In this case, PLC with the help of Ethernet connection and family of protocols TCP/IP exchange data via the Internet with the MPW utilization enterprise main web server that is placed on a powerful computer. The main server, in turn, receives the SPC data process parameters and provides Web access to other users (remote computers, tablets, mobile devices).

Thereby, the proposed by the authors EMACS for specialized pyrolysis complexes automation allows to increase the accuracy and reliability of measurements due to self-diagnosis and elimination of operator errors at the system setting up and calibration. This makes possible to increase the SPC productivity by 15% and to reduce the maximum value of its total power consumption by 10.5%. Also, the advantage of this EMACS is the ability to operate with the personnel with low qualification, since all the processes of control and data analysis are automated.

Also, one of the most important particularities of the developed by the authors new highly efficient EMACSs is that they can implement intelligent principles and technologies of automatic control based on the theory of artificial neural networks and fuzzy logic [41–44]. This allows achieving higher quality indicators and accuracy at automatic control of main process parameters of the complex technical objects with essentially nonlinear and non-stationary characteristics. The monitoring and automatic control systems, developed on the basis of artificial neural networks and fuzzy logic, currently successfully applied in such areas as: technological processes and transport control, financial management, medical and technical diagnostics, pattern recognition, stock forecast, etc. [45–50].

At the further development and improvement of the IoT technologies it is reasonable to improve the developed by the authors EMACS in the following way. The main functions and algorithms of monitoring and automatic control of the technical objects main process parameters should be transferred from the software and hardware means of the local level, located in close proximity to the technical objects, to the high performance servers of the remote level, that will be located in the server clusters, data processing centers or clouds. The main benefit of the new structure is that the total number of the monitoring and automatic control systems will be significantly reduced, that simplify the monitoring and control process itself. Moreover, computing resources using effectiveness will increase and will need less means.

This transition can be possible only at a significant quality improving of the network infrastructure, specifically at essential increasing of data transfer performance and connection reliability as well as eliminating of unexpected delays between local level devices and their serving servers. These issues are highly relevant and are still the subject of research for leading scientific and technical teams in different countries.

For IIoT projects, as a new direction for the development of information systems, the most common conceptual and architectural solutions are currently defined. To assess the different IIoT projects in the near future, the standardization is actively rooted in order to form a unified and consistent regulatory normative base for the practical implementation of IIoT. Many international organizations, non-governmental associations, alliances of manufacturers and operators, partner projects are engaged in the issues of standardization and practical implementation of the IIoT. The only standards for IIoT at the stage of development are offered on the market, which makes it difficult to integrate the solutions and to a large extent hinders the appearance of new ones.

The main trends in the development of IIoT technology and their implementation problems are shown in Table 1.

Table 1. Features of IIoT implementation at enterprises

Directions for the development of IIoT technology	Problems of implementation in industry
Development of computerized control systems	The need to adopt common standards
The emergence of powerful and autonomous automation devices	Incompatibility of a number of electronic components
Development of wired and wireless technologies	Construction of complex hybrid networks (complicated topology of networks)
Increasing the number of devices connected to the global network Internet	Slow transition to the protocol IPv6
Development of cryptography and methods of information protection	The problem of data protection and technological process safety
The need to preserve the environment and reduce energy costs	Problems of using alternative energy sources at certain enterprises
Technical solutions for automated production companies	Relatively high cost of implementation

Thus, depending on the degree of reliability, speed of control, ease of use, absolutely different approaches to automation of technological processes based on IIoT can be adopted.

4 Conclusions

The analysis of the IoT approach and its application for the development of embedded monitoring and automatic control systems for technological objects and processes, that are included in complex industrial systems, are presented in this paper.

The IoT information technologies provide unique abilities to the developers of complex data processing, monitoring and control systems. The range of functions that they provide eases the creation of distributed computerized systems.

The examples of IoT applications in design of new effective specialized EMACSs for such complex technical objects as gas turbine engines, floating docks and specialized pyrolysis complexes for municipal polymeric waste thermal utilization, are presented. The functional structures, software and hardware implementation as well as multi-level HMIs of the developed embedded systems for monitoring and automatic control of main process parameters are given. These systems have the modular structures with reliable and highly efficient software and hardware means as well as industrial communication interfaces, located in close proximity to the given technical objects, for monitoring and automatic control implementation in safe and uninterrupted mode at the local level. Also, the given systems implement monitoring and automatic control of the given objects main parameters from the remote servers and clients via the wired and wireless Internet connections and can be easily integrated into existing large-scaled IIoT systems of industrial enterprises.

The main advantages of the proposed EMACSs are considered in detail. As a result, the developed new efficient EMACS based on IoT approach provide: high precision control of operating processes of gas turbine engines, floating docks and SPCs in the real time mode, monitoring and automatic control of their current technological parameters with high quality indicators, that leads to significant increasing of energy and economic efficiency of the given complex technical objects.

Thus, the successful application of the IoT approach for the automation of such diverse and complex technical objects as gas turbine engines, floating docks and specialized pyrolysis complexes on the basis of the developed by the authors EMACSs confirms its versatility, high efficiency and feasibility of application to other complex industrial systems.

Further research should be conducted towards the development of the IoT based systems, which main software and hardware means of monitoring and automatic control functions and algorithms will be transferred from the local level to the high performance servers of the remote level, located in the server clusters, data processing centers and clouds. This transition should be followed by improving of the network infrastructure through increasing of data transfer performance and connection reliability as well as eliminating of unexpected delays between local level devices and their serving servers.

References

1. Merz, H., Hansemann, T., Hübner, C.: Building Automation: Communication Systems with EIB/KNX, LON and BACnet. Springer, Heidelberg (2009). https://doi.org/10.1007/978-3-319-73223-7
2. Mehta, B.R., Reddy, Y.J.: Chapter 7 - SCADA systems. In: Industrial Process Automation Systems, pp. 237–300 (2015)
3. Drozd, J., Drozd, A., Maevsky, D., Shapa, L.: The levels of target resources development in computer systems. In: Proceedings of IEEE East-West Design & Test Symposium (EWDTS 2014), Kiev, Ukraine, pp. 1–5 (2014)

4. Palagin, A.V., Opanasenko, V.N.: Design and application of the PLD-based reconfigurable devices. In: Adamski, M., Barkalov, A., Węgrzyn, M. (eds.) Design of Digital Systems and Devices. LNEE. Springer, Heidelberg, vol. 79, pp. 59–91 (2011). https://doi.org/10.1007/978-3-642-17545-9_3
5. Pidoprigora, D.: TRACE MODE goes to network. J. World Autom. **5**, 22–24 (2007). (In Russian)
6. Trunov, A.N.: An adequacy criterion in evaluating the effectiveness of a model design process. East.-Eur. J. Enterp. Technol. **1**(4(73)), 36–41 (2015)
7. Kondratenko, Y.P., Kozlov, O.V., Topalov, A.M., Gerasin, O.S.: Computerized system for remote level control with discrete self-testing. In: Ermolayev, V. et al. (eds.) Proceedings of the 13th International Conference on Information and Communication Technologies in Education, Research, and Industrial Applications. Integration, Harmonization and Knowledge Transfer, ICTERI'2017, CEUR-WS, Kyiv, Ukraine, vol. 1844, pp. 608–619 (2017)
8. Kondratenko, Y., Korobko, O., Kozlov, O., Gerasin O., Topalov, A.: PLC based system for remote liquids level control with radar sensor. The crossing point of intelligent data acquisition & advanced computing systems and east & west scientists. In: Proceedings of the 2015 IEEE 8th International Conference on Intelligent Data Acquisition and Advanced Computing Systems: Technology and Applications (IDAACS), Warsaw, Poland, pp. 47–52 (2015)
9. Kondratenko, Y., Korobko, O.V., Kozlov, O.V.: PLC-based systems for data acquisition and supervisory control of environment-friendly energy-saving technologies. In: Kharchenko, V., Kondratenko, Y., Kacprzyk, J. (eds.) Green IT Engineering: Concepts, Models, Complex Systems Architectures. SSDC, vol. 74, pp. 247–267. Springer, Cham (2017). https://doi.org/10.1007/978-3-319-44162-7_13
10. Topalov, A., Kozlov, O., Kondratenko, Y.: Control processes of floating docks based on SCADA systems with wireless data transmission. In: Perspective Technologies and Methods in MEMS Design: Proceedings of the International Conference MEMSTECH 2016, Lviv-Poljana, Ukraine, pp. 57–61 (2016)
11. Kim, H.J.: Security and vulnerability of SCADA systems over IP-based wireless sensor networks. Int. J. Distrib. Sens. Netw. **8**(11), 1–10 (2012). https://doi.org/10.1155/2012/268478
12. Aydogmus, Z., Aydogmus, O.: A web-based remote access laboratory using SCADA. IEEE Trans. Educ. **52**(1), 126–132 (2009)
13. Sulthana, S., Thatiparthi, G., Gunturi, R.S.: Cloud and intelligent based SCADA technology. Int. J. Adv. Res. Comput. Sci. Electron. Eng. (IJARCSEE) **2**(3), 293–296 (2013)
14. Kondratenko, Y.P., Kozlov, O.V., Gerasin, O.S., Topalov, A.M., Korobko, O.V.: Automation of control processes in specialized pyrolysis complexes based on web SCADA systems. In: Proceedings of the 9th IEEE International Conference on Intelligent Data Acquisition and Advanced Computing Systems: Technology and Applications (IDAACS), Bucharest, Romania, vol. 1, pp. 107–112 (2017)
15. Weber, R.H., Weber, R.: Internet of Things. Springer, Heidelberg (2010). https://doi.org/10.1007/978-3-642-11710-7
16. Giusto, D., Lera, A., Morabito, G., Atzori, L.: The Internet of Things. Springer, Heidelberg (2010). https://doi.org/10.1007/978-1-4419-1674-7
17. Uckelmann, D., Harrison, M., Michahelles, F.: Architecting the Internet of Things. Springer, Heidelberg (2011). https://doi.org/10.1007/978-3-642-19157-2

18. Kondratenko, Y.P., Kozlov, O.V., Korobko, O.V., Topalov, A.M.: Internet of things approach for automation of the complex industrial systems. In: Ermolayev, V. et al. (eds.) Proceedings of the 13th International Conference on Information and Communication Technologies in Education, Research, and Industrial Applications. Integration, Harmonization and Knowledge Transfer, ICTERI 2017, CEUR-WS, Kyiv, Ukraine, vol. 1844, pp. 3–18 (2017)
19. Sarma, S.E., Weis, S.A., Engels, D.W.: RFID systems and security and privacy implications. In: Kaliski, B.S., Koç, K., Paar, C. (eds.) CHES 2002. LNCS, vol. 2523, pp. 454–469. Springer, Heidelberg (2003). https://doi.org/10.1007/3-540-36400-5_33
20. Ovidiu, V., Friess, P., Guillemin, P., et al.: Internet of things strategic research roadmap. Internet Things-Global Technol. Societal Trends 1, 9–52 (2011)
21. Vermesan, O., Friess, P.: Internet of Things: Global Technological and Societal Trends from Smart Environments and Spaces to Green ICT. River Publishers, Houston (2011)
22. Payam, B., Wang, W., Henson, C., Taylor, K.: Semantics for the internet of things: early progress and back to the future. Int. J. Semant. Web Inf. Syst. (IJSWIS) 8(1), 1–21 (2012)
23. Rellermeyer, J.S., Duller, M., Gilmer, K., Maragkos, D., Papageorgiou, D., Alonso, G.: The software fabric for the internet of things. In: Floerkemeier, C., Langheinrich, M., Fleisch, E., Mattern, F., Sarma, S.E. (eds.) IOT 2008. LNCS, vol. 4952, pp. 87–104. Springer, Heidelberg (2008). https://doi.org/10.1007/978-3-540-78731-0_6
24. Vermesan, O., Friess, P.: Building the Hyperconnected Society: Internet of Things Research and Innovation Value Chains, Ecosystems and Markets. River Publishers, Houston (2015)
25. Bahga, A., Madisetti, V.: Internet of Things: A Hands-On Approach, 1st edn. VPT (2014)
26. Mitton, N., Chaouchi, H., Noel, T., Watteyne, T., Gabillon, A., Capolsini, P. (eds.): InterIoT/SaSeIoT -2016. LNICST, vol. 190. Springer, Cham (2017). https://doi.org/10.1007/978-3-319-52727-7
27. Vermesan, O., Friess, P.: Digitising the Industry - Internet of Things Connecting the Physical, Digital and Virtual Worlds. River Publishers, Houston (2016)
28. Zach, S., Bormann, C.: 6LoWPAN: The Wireless Embedded Internet, vol. 43. Wiley, Hoboken (2011)
29. Mahalle, P., Babar, S., Prasad, N.R., Prasad, R.: Identity management framework towards internet of things (IoT): roadmap and key challenges. In: Meghanathan, N., Boumerdassi, S., Chaki, N., Nagamalai, D. (eds.) CNSA 2010. CCIS, vol. 89, pp. 430–439. Springer, Heidelberg (2010). https://doi.org/10.1007/978-3-642-14478-3_43
30. Li, R.Y.M., Li, H.C.Y., Mak, C.K., Tang, T.B.: Sustainable smart home and home automation: big data analytics approach. Int. J. Smart Home 10(8), 177–198 (2016)
31. Li, S., Wang, H., Xu, T., Zhou, G.: Application study on internet of things in environment protection field. In: Yang, D. (ed.) Informatics in Control, Automation and Robotics. LNEE, Springer, Heidelberg, vol. 133, pp. 99–106 (2011). https://doi.org/10.1007/978-3-642-25992-0_13
32. Lee, J., Bagheri, B., Kao, H.: A cyber-physical systems architecture for industry 4.0-based manufacturing systems. Manufact. Lett. 3, 18–23 (2015)
33. Delgado, E.: The Internet of Things: Emergence, Perspectives, Privacy and Security Issues. Nova Science Publishers, New York (2015). Incorporated
34. Watts, S.: The Internet of Things (IoT): Applications, Technology, and Privacy Issues. Nova Science Publishers, New York (2016). Incorporated
35. Acharjya, D.P., Geetha, M.K.: Internet of Things: Novel Advances and Envisioned Applications. Springer, Heidelberg (2017). https://doi.org/10.1007/978-3-319-53472-5
36. Giaffreda, R., Caganova, D., Li, Y., Riggio, R., Voisard, A. (eds.): Internet of Things. IoT Infrastructures. IoT360 2014. LNICST, vol. 151. Springer, Cham (2015). https://doi.org/10.1007/978-3-319-19743-2

37. Keramidas, G., Voros, N., Hübner, M. (eds.): Components and Services for IoT Platforms: Paving the Way for IoT Standards. Springer, Cham (2017). https://doi.org/10.1007/978-3-319-42304-3

38. Jeschke, S., Brecher, C., Song, H., Rawat, D.B. (eds.): Industrial Internet of Things. SSWT. Springer, Cham (2017). https://doi.org/10.1007/978-3-319-42559-7

39. Goes, J.: Circuits and Systems for the Internet of Things CAS4IoT. River Publishers, Houston (2017)

40. Kalidoss, R., Bhagyaveni, M.A., Shanmugavel, K.S.: Cognitive Radio - An Enabler for Internet of Things. River Publishers, Houston (2017)

41. Zadeh, L.A.: The role of fuzzy logic in modeling, identification and control. Model. Ident. Control **15**(3), 191–203 (1994)

42. Takagi, T., Sugeno, M.: Fuzzy identification of systems and its applications to modeling and control. IEEE Trans. Syst. Man, Cybern. **15**(1), 116–132 (1985). https://doi.org/10.1109/TSMC.1985.6313399

43. Piegat, A.: Fuzzy Modeling and Control. Springer, Heidelberg (2001). https://doi.org/10.1007/978-3-7908-1824-6

44. Jang, J.-S.R., Sun, C.-T., Mizutani, E.: Neuro-Fuzzy and Soft Computing: A Computational Approach to Learning and Machine Intelligence. Prentice Hall, Upper Saddle River (1996)

45. Pomorova, O., Savenko, O., Lysenko, S., Kryshchuk, A.: Multi-agent based approach for botnet detection in a corporate area network using fuzzy logic. In: Kwiecień, A., Gaj, P., Stera, P. (eds.) CN 2013. CCIS, vol. 370, pp. 146–156. Springer, Heidelberg (2013). https://doi.org/10.1007/978-3-642-38865-1_16

46. Wang, L., Kazmierski, T.J.: VHDL-AMS based genetic optimization of fuzzy logic controllers. Int. J. Comput. Math. Electr. Electron. Eng. **26**(2), 447–460 (2007)

47. Kondratenko, Y.P., Kozlov, O.V., Klymenko, L.P., Kondratenko, G.V.: Synthesis and research of neuro-fuzzy model of ecopyrogenesis multi-circuit circulatory system. In: Jamshidi, M., Kreinovich, V., Kacprzyk, J. (eds.) Advance Trends in Soft Computing. SFSC, vol. 312, pp. 1–14. Springer, Cham (2014). https://doi.org/10.1007/978-3-319-03674-8_1

48. Kondratenko, Y.P., Kozlov, O.V., Gerasin, O.S., Zaporozhets, Y.M.: Synthesis and research of neuro-fuzzy observer of clamping force for mobile robot automatic control system. In: Proceedings of the 2016 IEEE First International Conference on Data Stream Mining and Processing (DSMP), Lviv, Ukraine, pp. 90–95 (2016)

49. Kondratenko, Y.P., Zaporozhets, Y.M., Rudolph, J., Gerasin, O.S., Topalov, A.M., Kozlov, O.V.: Features of clamping electromagnets using in wheel mobile robots and modeling of their interaction with ferromagnetic plate. In: Proceedings of the 9th IEEE International Conference on Intelligent Data Acquisition and Advanced Computing Systems: Technology and Applications (IDAACS), Bucharest, Romania, vol. 1, pp. 453–458 (2017)

50. Kondratenko, Y.P., Korobko, O.V., Kozlov, O.V.: Synthesis and optimization of fuzzy controller for thermoacoustic plant. In: Zadeh, L.A., Abbasov, A.M., Yager, R.R., Shahbazova, S.N., Reformat, M.Z. (eds.) Recent Developments and New Direction in Soft-Computing Foundations and Applications. SFSC, vol. 342, pp. 453–467. Springer, Cham (2016). https://doi.org/10.1007/978-3-319-32229-2_31

Software Packages for Econometrics: Financial Time Series Modeling

Olena Liashenko$^{(\boxtimes)}$ (iD), Tetyana Kravets (iD), and Kateryna Krytsun (iD)

Taras Shevchenko National University of Kyiv, Kiev, Ukraine
{lyashenko, tankravets}@univ.kiev.ua,
katyaki2006@ukr.net

Abstract. In the article the comparative analysis of most common among economists software packages R, EViews and Gretl in financial time series modeling is conducted. Advantages and disadvantages of each software are considered. Volatility is often used as a rough approximation to measuring of financial instruments risk. For the modeling of financial time series volatility Polish stock index WIG was chosen. For describing the volatility of financial time series econometric model of family GARCH is built by means of these packages.

Keywords: Software packages · GARCH model · Stock indices
Volatility · Modeling

1 Introduction

The great achievement of mankind is the development of science and technology. Computing operations require much less efforts of researcher thanks to modern computer technology. Today IT sector is developing rapidly. The results of its activities are the funds of multiplying income, reduce the cost of resources, facilitate professional activity.

Information technology facilitates the research process. Analysis of the vast amount of data is possible due to modern software packages. These software products enable to analyze and to model the time series dynamics, to search interdependencies of the time series.

The research of stock indices dynamics and stock prices is an important problem in the investment portfolio management. Stock market indices are the indicators of the global economy, group of countries or national economy, investment climate in the country, tools of analysis of securities market and its forecasting trends. In addition, stock index is also independent financial instrument to hedge the securities market. Typically, absolute index values are not so important for investors as its dynamics, which you can use to determine the direction of the stock market dynamics. Analytical agencies and stock exchanges calculate Stock Indices.

The aim of the article is an analysis of software that is popular among economists and modeling of financial time series volatility using software packages R, Gretl, EViews.

© Springer International Publishing AG, part of Springer Nature 2018
N. Bassiliades et al. (Eds.): ICTERI 2017, CCIS 826, pp. 188–208, 2018.
https://doi.org/10.1007/978-3-319-76168-8_9

Software R is the most popular tool among economists, EViews occupies the second position. The package Gretl is not so widespread and powerful. However Gretl has the ability to use scripts R, Octave, Python, etc. Functions package Gretl is appended by users and it is gaining popularity gradually.

2 Analysis of Recent Research

Modeling and forecasting of time series volatility in financial markets is an urgent problem for investment advisors, economists and other professionals. Therefore, a large number of scientific papers are devoted to this sphere.

The fundamentals of econometric analysis of financial time series are laid in [1–3]. Works [4, 5] are also devoted to this problem. Chiu et al. [6] study the impact of volatility on investor decision.

Subbotin [7] investigates the main approaches to modeling the volatility of shares and exchange rates, and rEViews the cascade of volatility models in multiple horizons.

Leucht et al. [8] suggest the specification test for consistent generalized autoregressive conditional heteroskedasticity model (GARCH (1,1)), based on the Cramer-Mises test statistics in their paper.

Barunik et al. [9] propose an improved approach to the volatility modeling and forecasting using high-frequency data. The model of forecasting based on Realized GARCH with multiple time-frequency data is used.

Research on stock market volatility has used traditional econometric methods like ARCH (Autoregressive Conditional Heteroskedastic) and GARCH (Generalized Autoregressive Conditional Heteroskedastic) models for analysis. However, advanced machine learning techniques like wavelet analysis has also been used as reported in literature. Panda and Deo [10] studied the volatility spillover effect between rupeedollar exchange rate and CNX Nifty returns during the 2008 financial crisis using GARCH and EGARCH (Exponential GARCH) models. Study of Birau et al. [11] observed volatility shocks and clustering in S&P Bombay Stock Exchange BANKEX index over the period January 2002 to June 2014 using standard GARCH model.

Harvey and Lange [12] propose an updated and expanded ARCH in Mean model. EGARCH-M model, which is displayed in the paper, is useful theoretically and practically. This model expansion allows distinguishing long and short effects of return to the volatility.

Lu et al. [13] examined the volatility of Chinese energy market using hybrid ANN and GARCH type models and Exponential GARCH (EGARCH) was found to be the most prominent one among all models. Efimova and Serletis [14] deployed univariate and multivariate GARCH models to study the spillovers and interactions among oil, natural gas and electricity price in USA for the period from 2001 to 2013.

Vejendla and Enke [15] carried out a comparative study of Multilayer Feedforward Neural Network, Recurrent Neural Network and GARCH models for forecasting historic volatility, implied volatility and model based volatility of NASDAQ, DJIA, NYSE and S & P 500.

The global financial crisis of 2008–2009 has raised new questions about the relationship between investment funds and stock market returns. Therefore, Babalos et al.

[16] analyze US monthly data for the period 2000:1–2015:08. Authors estimate VAR-GARCH(1,1)-in-mean model with a BEKK and the switch as a dummy variable, which is necessary to display the global financial crisis. The relationship between the yield of the stock market and direct investment flows fund is investigated. It was found that such relationship is weakened during the crisis.

Kumari and Hiremath [17] investigate idiosyncratic volatility in the Indian stock market. They use conditional EGARCH model to abstract idiosyncratic volatility.

Walther [18] applies GARCH model to account for asymmetry and long memory effects in conditional volatility.

Sharma and Vipul [19] investigate eight Asian markets with 21 stock indices using symmetric and asymmetric GARCH variants.

Vasudevan and Vetrievel [20], AL-Najjar [21], Innocent and Mung'atu [22], Spulbar and Nitoi [23] apply GARCH-model to the stock market volatility investigation.

Renfro [24] describes the history of econometric software from 1950 and gives identification each of the econometric software packages that are used by econometricians worldwide.

Renfro [25] describes all existing packages that are publicly available and used by economists today.

Ooms and Doornik [26] give a short history of econometric software development. They identify the characteristics of econometric software in comparison with mathematical and statistical software.

Liboschik et al. [27] consider the use of R package for analysis of time series.

3 Research Method

One of the characteristics of financial markets is the uncertainty that changes over time. In this regard, there is such a thing as "volatility clustering". It means that the volatility varies periodically, i.e. stock index dynamics changes from slightly changing to more chaotic.

It's worth to note that many financial relationships are nonlinear internally. It dealt with peculiarities of financial data, such as the tendency of financial time series (e.g., income on assets) to have an unusual distribution of critical areas ("tails") and displacements to the average (leptokurtosis). In addition, often financial time series change by clusters or pools (volatility clustering or volatility pooling), while larger deviation of time series prior to high deviation, low deviation of time series - minor deviations (regardless of sign). It is also possible the leverage effect, i.e. the tendency to volatility increasing not of the growth but the fall of certain financial and economic indicators (information asymmetry). Overall volatility modeling and forecasting in the stock market became a priority for both theoretical and applied research in recent years. Volatility, as measured by standard deviation or variance of return (such as securities) is often used as a rough approximation to measuring of overall risk financial instruments (securities).

The measure of volatility is a variance of series. ARIMA model cannot adequately take into account the inherent characteristics for financial time series [28]. Therefore, there is a need to use other tools. One of them is ARCH-processes (Autoregressive Conditional Heteroskedasticity). The first such expansion of regression models was presented by Engle [29], after that numerous modifications of the basic design and examples of the new model for financial and macroeconomic time series were developed. First, ARCH-models studied inflation uncertainty. Later, they were used in the volatility analysis of prices and yields of speculative assets. On the basis of applying ARCH-models it was found that the dynamics of volatility for many financial variables subject to stable laws.

ARCH/GARCH models belong to the class of nonlinear models of conditional variance, which changes over time. This allows, in addition to the average value of the studied parameters, to model the dynamics of its variance simultaneously. Therefore, such model can correctly describe phenomena such as clustering of volatility, asymmetric information, etc.

Examples of financial time series with high frequency are stock prices and indices of commodity exchanges. In practical researches they are often analyzed in the form of geometric income, i.e. the logarithm of the rate of increase in the price of an asset (or rate of stock index growth) y_t:

$$r_t = \log\left(\frac{y_t}{y_{t-1}}\right) = \log(y_t) - \log(y_{t-1}), \tag{1}$$

where r_t – geometric income of the asset.

ARCH-extension model is the GARCH-model volatility, where the current volatility affects both preceding price changes and preceding volatility estimates (so-called "old news"). Memory of ARCH(q)-process is limited by q-periods. We need long lag q and a large number of parameters for using models. Generalized ARCH-process (Generalized ARCH or GARCH), proposed by Bollerslev [30], has infinite memory and allows more economical parameterization.

Overall, ARCH/GARCH methodology can be described as studied parameters dispersion modeling methodology. Since the variance is second-order moment, the dispersion model is nonlinear. Therefore, it cannot be evaluated by the methods developed for linear models, particularly using ARIMA models. Autoregressive conditional heteroskedasticity, i.e. the change of random variables (disturbances) variance in the time, formalized represented as:

$$a_{t+1} = y_{t+1} - \mu_y(y_1, y_2, y_3, \ldots, y_t), \tag{2}$$

where a_{t+1} – perturbations (random variable) at time period (t + 1),

y_{t+1} – value at time period (t + 1),

$\mu_y(y_1, y_2, y_3, \ldots, y_t)$ – mean value estimated on the basis of data that preceded the moment (t + 1).

Dispersion equation in GARCH models unlike ARCH models takes into account variables other than lagged random variables, and more variables lagged conditional variance. Actually overall ARCH/GARCH model can be presented as a series of filters.

Note that the smoothing procedure or seasonal deprivation for time series are optional and executed as needed. Overall, ARCH/GARCH model can be considered as "supplement" for a multi-linear regression and ARIMA models. Evaluation of ACRH/GARCH models can not be implemented by the method of least squares. Special procedures developed for evaluation of these models, including maximum likelihood method.

4   Results

According to the Bloomberg Businessweek, 97% of companies in Fortune 500 have used business analytics and some forms of Big Data analytics to conduct their business. Big Data analytics that processes data into information and particularly knowledge has emerged as a contemporary business trend in industry and academics [31]. Many consultants, scientists, and researchers pay attention to Big Data because it contains meaningful information. Various applications such as healthcare, security, medicine, politics, etc. can use the information to solve data-related problems in society.

One of the most dominant analytics tools in Big Data Analytics is the R Project, or R. R is a general statistical analysis platform that runs on the command line. It is world's most widely used, open-source statistical programming language designed for friendly use (Fig. 1). Other popular packages are EViews and Gretl.

Fig. 1. The popularity of the R software product in the world [32]

Software product R is popular among the countries of North and South America, Canada, Australia, Western and Eastern Europe, Africa. EViews is less popular among the countries mentioned above, but this product is the most-used in Asia. Gretl is not so widespread in America and Europe compared to EViews and R, because it is not as powerful as R. However, today Gretl has the ability to use the scripts R, Octave, Python, etc. Packages of functions are added by Gretl users and are gradually gaining popularity among econometricians.

Here is a comparative description of these software packages (Table 1).

Table 1. Comparative description of data analysis software packages

Features	EViews	Gretl	R
Data extensions	*.wf1	*.gdt, *.gdtb	*.R
User interface	Mostly point-and-click	Scripting/point and click	Programming
Data manipulation	Strong	Strong	Very strong
Data analysis	Powerful	Powerful	Powerful/versatile
Graphics	Good	Good	Excellent
Cost	Expensive, but has free student lite version	Open source	Open source
Output extensions	*.wf1	CSV, gdt, gdtb, GNU R, Octave, Stata, JMulTi, PcGive	*R, *.txt(log files, any word processor can read)

Features in Gretl [33]

1. Easy intuitive interface.
2. A wide variety of estimators: least squares, maximum likelihood, GMM; single-equation and system methods.
3. Time series methods: ARIMA, a wide variety of univariate GARCH-type models, VARs and VECMs (including structural VARs), unit-root and cointegration tests, Kalman filter, etc.
4. Limited dependent variables: logit, probit, tobit, sample selection, interval regression, models for count and duration data, etc.
5. Panel-data estimators, including instrumental variables, probit and GMM-based dynamic panel models.
6. Output models as LaTeX files, in tabular or equation format.
7. Integrated powerful scripting language (known as hansl), with a wide range of programming tools and matrix operations.
8. GUI controller for fine-tuning Gnuplot graphs.
9. An expanding range of contributed function packages, written in hansl.
10. Facilities for easy exchange of data and results with GNU R, GNU Octave, Python, Ox and Stata.

Features in EViews [34]

1. Integrated support for handling dates and time series data.
2. Support for high-frequency (intraday) data, allowing for hours, minutes, and seconds frequencies. In addition, there are a number of less commonly encountered regular frequencies, including Multi-year, Bimonthly, Fortnight, Ten-Day, and Daily with an arbitrary range of days of the week.
3. Long-run variance and covariance calculation: symmetric or one-sided long-run covariances using nonparametric kernel (Newey-West 1987, Andrews 1991), parametric VARHAC (Den Haan and Levin 1997), and prewhitened kernel (Andrews and Monahan 1992) methods. In addition, EViews supports Andrews (1991) and Newey-West (1994) automatic bandwidth selection methods for kernel estimators, and information criteria based lag length selection methods for VARHAC and prewhitening estimation.
4. Linear quantile regression and least absolute deviations (LAD), including both Huber's Sandwich and bootstrapping covariance calculations.
5. Stepwise regression with seven different selection procedures.
6. Threshold regression including TAR and SETAR.
7. Heckman Selection models.
8. Object-oriented command language provides access to menu items.
9. Batch execution of commands in program files.
10. String and string vector objects for string processing. Extensive library of string and string list functions.

Features in R [35]

1. R is free, open-source software distributed and maintained by R-project, R source code is available under the Free Software Foundation's GNU General Public License.
2. R supports most of the data analysis techniques such as virtual data manipulation, statistical model, and charts.
3. R support beautiful and unique data visualizations to present multidimensional data in multi-panel charts, 3-D graphs.
4. A global R community of 2 million users, developers, and contributors support contribute and maintain R language. Revolution Analytics community was acquired by Microsoft.
5. Provides better results faster than legacy statistical software's counterpart does.
6. R has data structures (vectors, matrices, arrays, data frames) that users can operate on through functions for performing statistical analyzes and creating graphs.
7. Object-oriented programming: C, Java, Perl, Python, parallel programming, etc.
8. Applications: Chemometrics, Clinical trial, Econometrics, Medical images, etc.
9. Data Mining and Machine Learning: Arules, Cubist, knnTree, randomFores, etc.
10. Statistical methodology: Bayesian inference, Spatial data, Time Series, etc.

In summary, the paper defined Big Data, compared and contrasted the statistical features of R to its programming features and its relevance. It provided the primary programming features available in R and described how the analytics software tool R was suited for Big Data today [35].

Polish stock index WIG for the modeling of financial time series volatility was chosen. The data obtained from the Google Finance site [36]. The results of volatility modeling for the stock index WIG in software packages R, EViews, Gretl are compared.

First of all we analyze time series data for normality of distribution, define the asymmetry and kurtosis. The package R uses a series of commands and obtain the following numerical characteristics:

```
> skewness(wig$wig_return)
[1] -0.4989079
> kurtosis(wig$wig_return)
[1] 4.254129
```

Asymmetry is −0.4989079, which means that the distribution of data is skewed slightly to the left. We have 4.254129 for excess, that is greater than 4, and therefore, the distribution is leptokurtic. Figure 2 shows the density of index WIG yield (11/21/2003...08/03/2017 daily), which is asymmetric and leptokurtic.

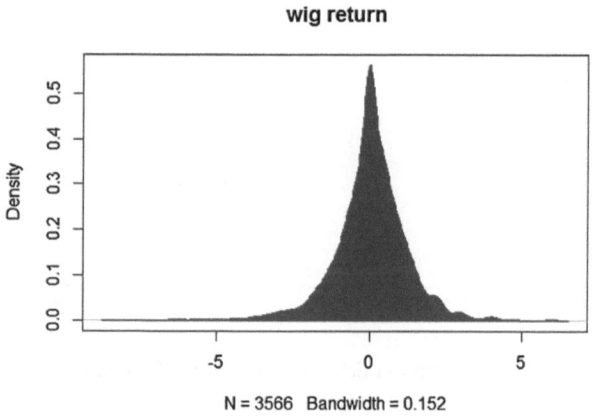

Fig. 2. Distribution density of index WIG yield in R

In EViews software package it is much easier to conduct a preliminary analysis of time series, for pressing a sequence of buttons View-Descriptive Statistics... - Histogram and Stats we obtain simultaneous display table of distribution and numerical characteristics (Fig. 3).

In the software package Gretl we need to make a few clicks to display the graph and numerical characteristics of series or write a script. The results of these actions are presented in Fig. 4. Herewith Skewness = −0.499118, Kurtosis = 7.2582.

In all software package kurtosis and skewness do not differ significantly, but average values are equal.

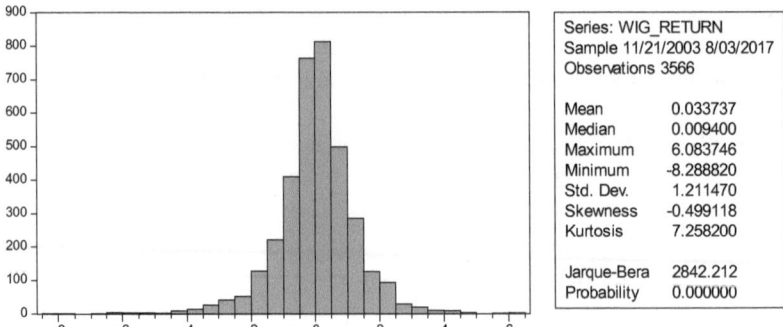

Fig. 3. Distribution density of index WIG yield in EViews

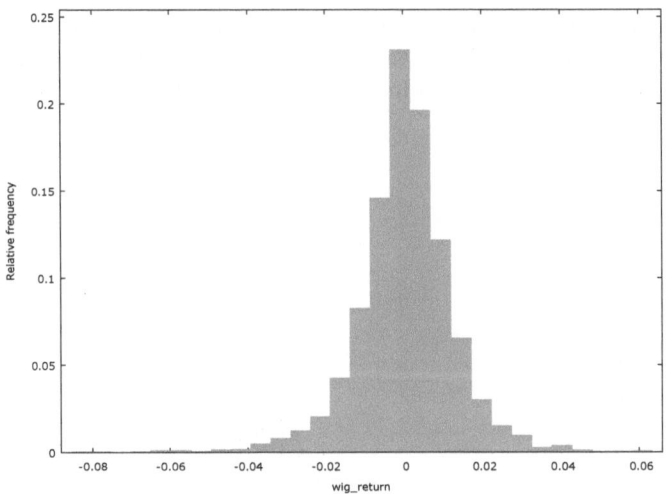

Fig. 4. Distribution density of index WIG yield in Gretl

The next step is to analyze the yield graph to identify the phenomenon of clustering and analysis of autocorrelation and partial autocorrelation for time series. The package R should use the command: tsdisplay(wig$wig_return) to display graphics and return of time series.

Figure 5 shows the results of this command. Graph of yield has signs of clustering. There is also residual autocorrelation. Graphs of autocorrelation function (ACF) and partial autocorrelation residues (PACF) show strong visible emissions for the first order lagged values indicating the feasibility of using GARCH(1,1).

According to the software packages EViews and Gretl we can do this in a few clicks. It is noticeable that received graphic display is identical (Figs. 6 and 7).

However, according to the Fig. 7 it is hard to understand when autocorrelation residues present, and we can be argued that there is autocorrelation residues to 36 order

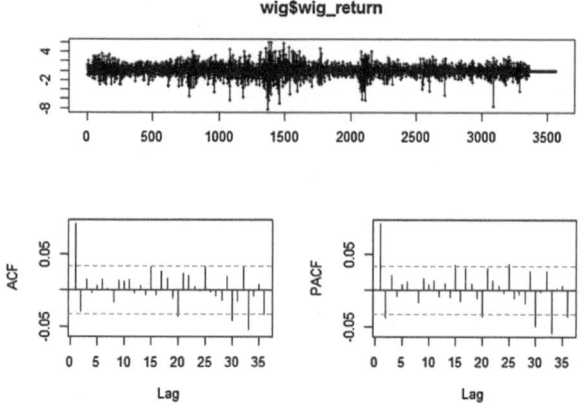

Fig. 5. The graphs of WIG return, autocorrelation function and partial autocorrelation residues function in R

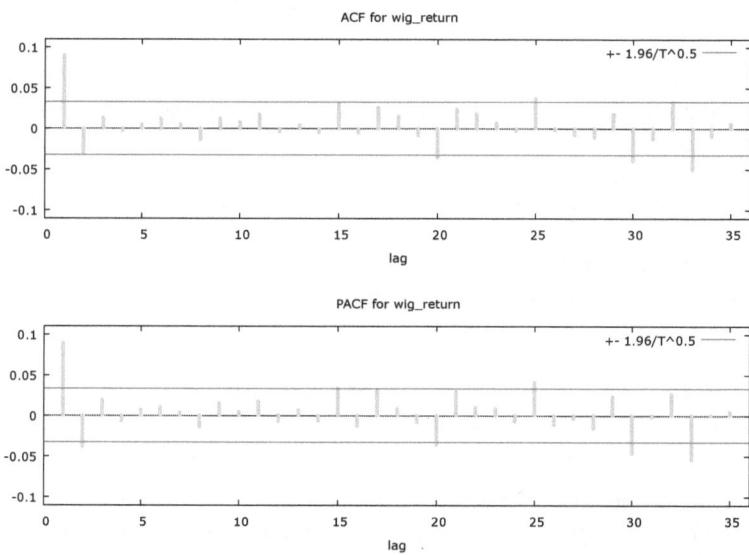

Fig. 6. The graphs of autocorrelation function and partial autocorrelation residues function of WIG returns in Gretl

(lag) given the probability value (Prob.). Therefore, for the analysis of residual auto-correlation and time series clustering the best software packages are R and Gretl.

Traditionally, the GARCH (1.1) is considered to be the most appropriate model for the forecasting of stock indices volatility [37]. The first number defines the length of the lag, and the second number represents the most appropriate AR-model for the mean. GARCH belongs to the class of nonlinear conditional variation models that change over time. This allows to simulate the dynamics of the variation simultaneously

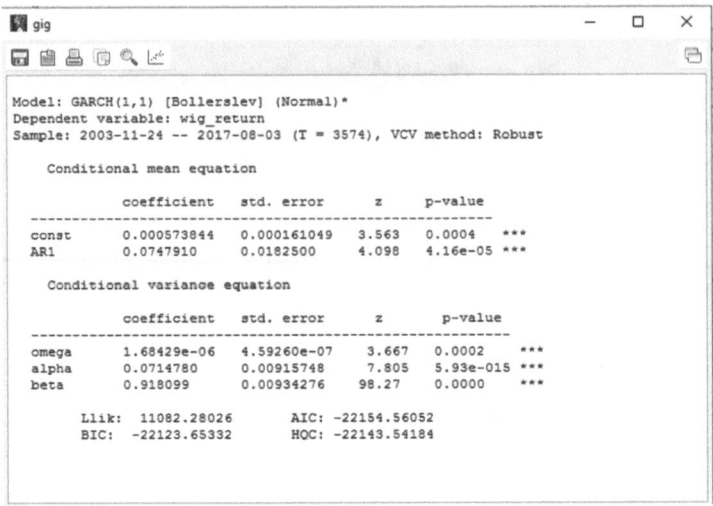

Fig. 7. Model GARCH(1,1) AR(1)

in addition to the average value of the parameters being studied. As a result, such a model can correctly describe the phenomenon of volatility clusterization, asymmetry of information, etc.

We turn to the construction of model and its specification. To select the best models in R, its testing and forecasting should prescribe following code:

```
spec <- ugarchspec()
fit = ugarchfit(data = wr, spec = spec, out.sample =
3000)
show(fit)
forc = ugarchforecast(fit, n.ahead=100, n.roll = 100)
forc plot(forc, which = "all")
```

As a result of the code, we received the best model GARCH(1,1) and model for average ARMA(1,1). Optimal parameters of the model GARCH(1,1) are presented in the Table 2, information criteria of the model are given in the Table 3.

Table 2. GARCH(1,1) optimal parameters

	Estimate	Std. error	t value	Pr(>|t|)
Mu	0.276948	0.095373	2.9038	0.003686
ar1	−0.660731	0.168891	−3.9122	0.000091
ma1	0.787538	0.134935	5.8364	0.000000
omega	0.038012	0.037802	1.0056	0.314628
alpha1	0.085367	0.042689	1.9997	0.045531
beta1	0.892952	0.045171	19.7681	0.000000

Table 3. Information criteria of the model

Akaike	3.2928
Bayes	3.4053
Shibata	3.2903
Hannan-Quinn	3.3384

According to the t-statistics, which probability value indicates the significance of the model parameters, we obtained omega only as insignificant factor. Wherein the information criteria are not high, therefore the model is well constructed.

Then we can make additional calculations in R-studio (Tables 4, 5, 6, 7, 8 and 9).

Table 4. Weighted Ljung-Box test on standardized residuals

	Statistic	p-value
Lag [1]	0.0006166	0.9802
Lag[2 * (p + q) + (p + q) − 1] [5]	1.5580733	0.9968
Lag[4 * (p + q) + (p + q) − 1] [9]	4.3452922	0.6086
d.o.f = 2		
H0		No serial correlation

Table 5. Weighted Ljung-Box test on standardized squared residuals

	Statistic	p-value
Lag [1]	0.7274	0.3937
Lag[2 * (p + q) + (p + q) − 1] [5]	3.6295	0.3040
Lag[4 * (p + q) + (p + q) − 1] [9]	5.2740	0.3903
d.o.f = 2		

Table 6. Weighted ARCH LM tests

	Statistic	Shape	Scale	p-value
ARCH Lag [3]	1.146	0.500	2.000	0.2844
ARCH Lag [5]	1.338	1.440	1.667	0.6358
ARCH Lag [7]	2.414	2.315	1.543	0.6302

According to Ghalanos [38], the Q-statistics and ARCH-LM test have been replaced with the Weighted Ljung-Box and ARCH-LM statistics of Fisher and Gallagher [39] which better account for the distribution of the statistics of the values from the estimated models. The ARCH-LM test is now a weighted portmanteau test for testing the null hypothesis of adequately fitted ARCH process, whilst the Ljung-Box is another portmanteau test with null the adequacy of the ARMA fit (Tables 4, 5 and 6).

Table 7. Nyblom stability test

Joint statistic:	0.7738
Individual statistics:	
mu	0.17569
ar1	0.07127
ma1	0.06159
omega	0.18168
alpha1	0.11692
beta1	0.18718

Table 8. Sign bias test

	t-value	Prob sig
Sign bias	1.4351	0.1532
Negative sign bias	1.2237	0.2229
Positive sign bias	0.3161	0.7523
Joint effect	3.7510	0.2896

Table 9. Adjusted pearson goodness-of-fit test

	Group	Statistic	p-value(g − 1)
1	20	10.63	0.9358
2	30	15.08	0.9843
3	40	30.63	0.8287
4	50	34.00	0.9491

Nyblom test gives information about the stability of the estimated parameters in a model (Table 7). Our statistics results are under 0.47 critical value. Therefore, it confirms that the parameters are stable.

Then we calculate the Sign Bias Test which is displayed in Table 8. It tests the presence of leverage effects in the standardized residuals (to capture possible mis-specification of the GARCH model), by regressing the squared standardized residuals on lagged negative and positive shocks.

The Sign Bias Test points to the presence of the leverage effect, and the effect of negative news is stronger than the appearance of positive news. In aggregate, positive and negative news have a stronger leverage effect to change the trend of yield volatility.

It can be observed from the Table 9 that the hypothesis of the model's correctly specific is accepted.

Pearson's Goodness-of-Fit Test is a very common and useful test for several purposes. It can help determine whether a set of claimed proportions is likely, or whether a pair of categorical variables are independent.

So, we specify GARCH(1,1) in Gretl and EViews similarly. In the package gig.gfn one has the opportunity to evaluate various options of GARCH family models and to add ARMA model for average. In the process of the model constructing, it was found that adding lag for AR automatically added lag for MA, due to the fact that the adding of AR(1) only the model will be not identified. The results are shown in Fig. 7.

All parameters of the model are significant, but the value of information criteria are high compared with those calculated in R. Gig.gfn package does not allow to check ARCH-effects or autocorrelation stability parameters of the model.

The package Gretl doesn't make possible to check the model ARCH-effects or autocorrelation stability parameters. You can build a forecast and graphics in this package.

If you use standard functional (basic), which is immediately available after installing the software package Gretl, it provides an estimate normal GARCH model, which results are shown in Fig. 8.

Model : GARCH, using observations 2003-11-21:2017-08-03 (T = 3575)
Dependent variable: wig_return
Standard errors based on Hessian

	Coefficient	Std. Error	z	p-value	
const	0.000623252	0.000165586	3.7639	0.0002	***
alpha(0)	1.69974e-06	4.05357e-07	4.1932	<0.0001	***
alpha(1)	0.0711515	0.00742614	9.5812	<0.0001	***
beta(1)	0.918371	0.0081786	112.2896	<0.0001	***

Mean dependent var	0.000409	S.D. dependent var	0.012263
Log-likelihood	11076.32	Akaike criterion	−22142.63
Schwarz criterion	−22111.72	Hannan-Quinn	−22131.61

Unconditional error variance = 0.000162233

Fig. 8. GARCH(1,1) in Gretl

Compared with functional package gig.gfn, the basic functional of Gretl allows you to conduct more tests of the results. However, just three tests of the list are available in the tests menu.

Perform forecasting for two GARCH models were built in Gretl. Under the first model, which is shown in Fig. 9, forecast of 100 observations (days) has received. From Fig. 9 it can be seen that the dynamics of the conditional variance will increase. This shows the impact of negative news in the market and the presence of asymmetry, so you should apply the model of GARCH family, which takes into account the asymmetries in the market, namely EGARCH model.

Figure 10 shows the projected range of volatility fluctuation. According to the forecast the WIG return volatility will increase gradually over the forecast period and will increase by almost half.

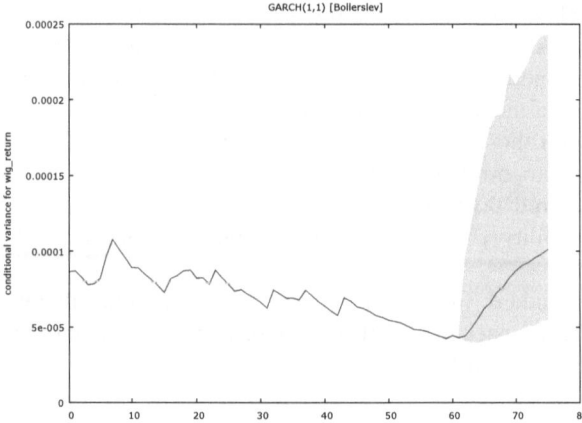

Fig. 9. Forecasting of conditional variance for WIG return volatility in gig.gfn

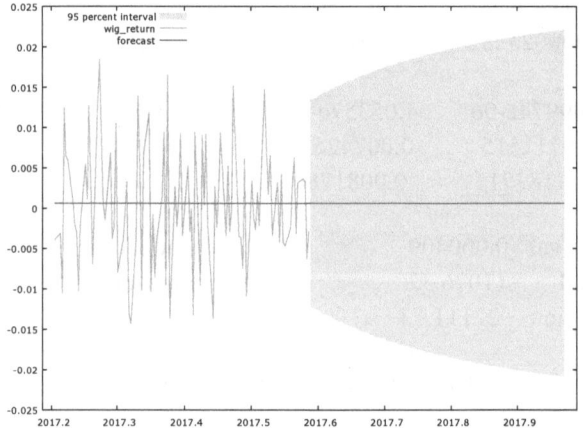

Fig. 10. Forecasting of WIG return volatility (the basic functional of Gretl)

We proceed to the construction of GARCH(1,1), ARMA(1,1) models in the software package EViews 9.5 Student's version Lite. Simulation results are presented in Fig. 11.

The sum of the regression coefficients expresses the impact of variables variance prior period to the current value of the variance. This value is close to 1, which is a sign of the growing inertia effect of shocks on variance of financial assets returns. According to Durbin-Watson statistics the residual autocorrelation is absent, most coefficients of the model are significant. For Inverted ARMA Roots the parameters ARMA(1,1) are stable because they are smaller than 1.

Figure 12 displays the results of checking ARCH-effects. In this model ARCH-effects are absent that is positive for the constructed model. The package allows the testing of the model in squares residual autocorrelation test using Q-statistics. The

Equation: UNTITLED   Workfile: WIG_RETURN_1::Wig_return_1\   _ □ ×

View | Proc | Object | | Print | Name | Freeze | | Estimate | Forecast | Stats | Resids |

Dependent Variable: WIG_RETURN
Method: ML - ARCH (Marquardt) - Normal distribution
Date: 08/05/17 Time: 00:22
Sample (adjusted): 11/24/2003 8/03/2017
Included observations: 3565 after adjustments
Convergence achieved after 21 iterations
MA Backcast: 11/21/2003
Presample variance: backcast (parameter = 0.7)
GARCH = C(4) + C(5)*RESID(-1)^2 + C(6)*GARCH(-1)

Variable	Coefficient	Std. Error	z-Statistic	Prob.
C	0.001269	0.000682	1.860466	0.0628
AR(1)	-0.137894	0.167978	-0.820907	0.4117
MA(1)	0.226163	0.165187	1.369127	0.1710
Variance Equation				
C	-5.90E-07	8.66E-07	-0.681597	0.4955
RESID(-1)^2	0.146619	0.005778	25.37449	0.0000
GARCH(-1)	0.874111	0.003631	240.7621	0.0000

R-squared	0.009013	Mean dependent var	0.033384
Adjusted R-squared	0.008457	S.D. dependent var	1.211457
S.E. of regression	1.206324	Akaike info criterion	2.584567
Sum squared resid	5183.482	Schwarz criterion	2.594966
Log likelihood	-4600.990	Hannan-Quinn criter.	2.588275
Durbin-Watson stat	1.983947		

Inverted AR Roots	-.14
Inverted MA Roots	-.23

Fig. 11. Statistics of GARCH(1,1) model with ARMA(1,1) in EViews

Equation: UNTITLED   Workfile: WIG_RETURN_1::Wig_return_1\   _ □ ×

View | Proc | Object | | Print | Name | Freeze | | Estimate | Forecast | Stats | Resids |

Heteroskedasticity Test: ARCH

F-statistic	2.516604	Prob. F(1,3562)	0.1127
Obs*R-squared	2.516240	Prob. Chi-Square(1)	0.1127

Fig. 12. The test for the presence of ARCH-effects in EViews

lack of residual autocorrelation to 36-th lag allows to include regression for the average as ARMA(1,1).

Note that the GARCH(1,1) model building in EViews and Gretl software packages is complicated process because of the inclusion of ARMA(1,1) model for average. However, the results of obtained model in EViews and its statistics are more visible. The advantage of the software package R is that writing a few lines of code, you can get statistic models, options, and all necessary tests to check for correct specification. The key tests for GARCH models in software packages EViews and Gretl are limited compared with the R. In order to detect, for example, the presence of the effect of leverage you should further evaluate other family of GARCH model and analyze the resulting statistics and conduct tests again.

Let us compare the results of forecasts obtained by Gretl, R and EViews software products. We received the forecast of conditional variance for WIG return volatility, and the forecast of WIG return volatility (Figs. 9 and 10) in gig.gfn additionally installed package and Gretl basic functional.

The package R received several graphic maps expectations. In Fig. 13 we present the results of forecasting time series of absolute dispersion, forecasting real time series data with conventional variance, forecasting unconditional variance and forecasting Rolling Sigma from time series.

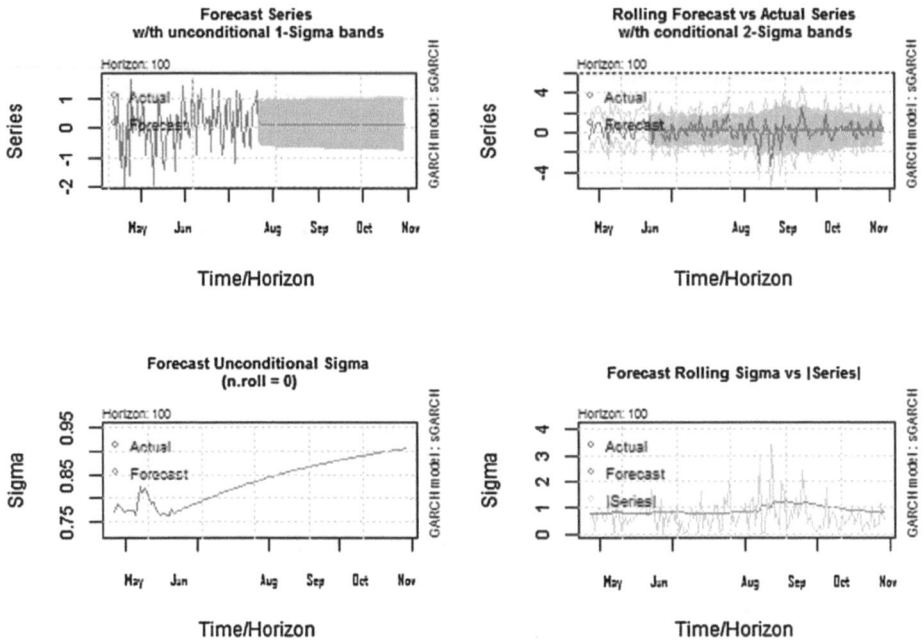

Fig. 13. Forecasting of WIG return volatility in R

Note that the dynamics of unconditional variance has a downward trend. This volatility of the time series will fluctuate at the same level of low growth.

In EViews static and dynamic forecasts of volatility and variance of time series with numerical forecast forward 43 observations (Figs. 14 and 15) can be built.

Note that the forecasts in EViews are difficult to interpret. However, the volatility of dynamic forecast tends to increase. As for static forecast, the volatility of the time series will fluctuate around the same level.

The popular and widely used statistical packages Mathematica, RATS, SageMath, SAS, Stata, which offer a variety of methods for analyzing financial time series must be mentioned. Together with EViews and R, they support models such as ARIMA, GARCH, VAR, Multidimensional GARCH, and provide single rooting and cointegration tests. They also have support for various statistical charts and diagrams.

Stata and R are the most common problem-dependent languages for applied econometricians. In general, it can be mentioned that Stata is more user-friendly than R. One of the disadvantages is that the evaluation of many models of time series in Stata is fairly poor. Therefore, in time series analysis, it is better to use packages such as

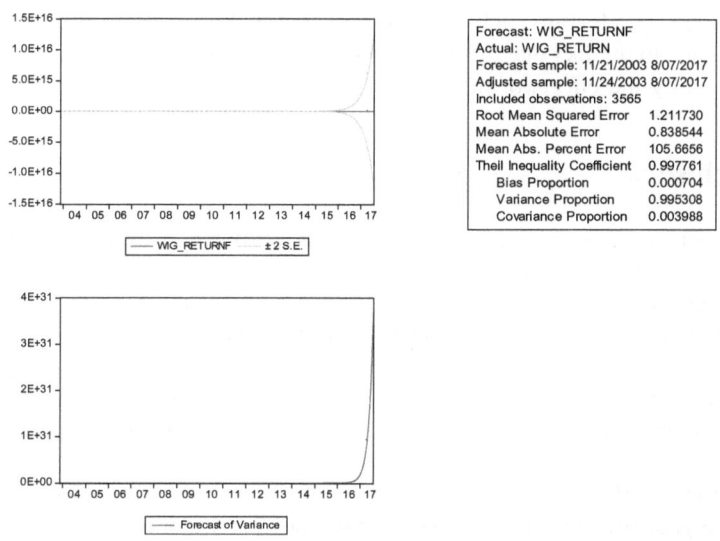

Fig. 14. Dynamic forecasting of WIG return volatility and variance in EViews

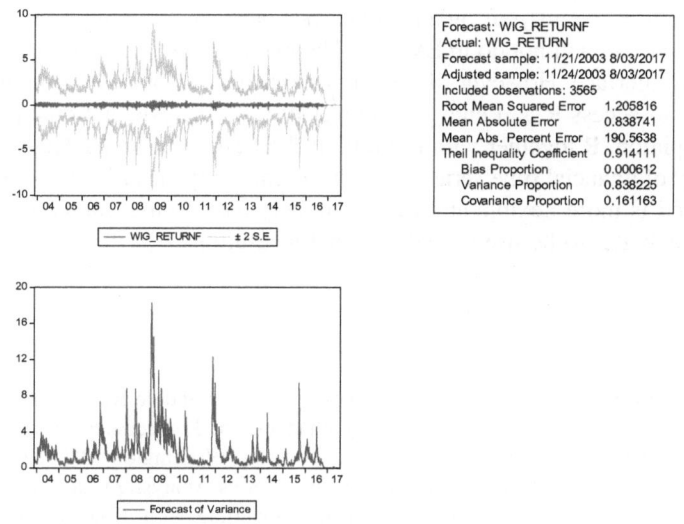

Fig. 15. Static forecasting of WIG return volatility and variance in EViews

EViews or Oxmetrics. R, MATLAB and Python are favorites among econometricians, mainly because they have good support for matrix transformation.

Despite the considerable popularity and advantages of the software package R, it also has a number of disadvantages. Firstly, some time is needed in order to understand how R works and it is not so easy especially for beginners. The documentation is sometimes imperfect, it has gaps and only the person who deals with the statistics can understand it. Some feature packs are not high quality, but if such a feature is useful to many, then due to the fact that this is an open source product, the quality of the package can be raised by the efforts of these users.

5 Conclusions

It can be concluded that Gretl, EViews and R software packages can be used in economic studies for modeling and forecasting the volatility of financial time series, such as stock indexes. The kind of econometric analysis intended to use need to be considered while the choosing an appropriate package. R should be used for more advanced work, for example, to simulate economic models. The Gretl package is powerful enough to apply it professionally at work and in a quick training. Gretl's basic package is completed and covers most applications of time series and panel data applications.

The EViews software is paid, but there is a free Student Lite version in which you cannot save your own results. EViews is a very powerful tool in econometric analysis, it has a nice graphical interface, but its functionality is somewhat limited compared to R and Gretl.

The main advantage of R and Gretl is that they are open sources and free projects. R allows you to program your own data analysis package and run these software tools in Gretl, which you will not do in EViews. The main advantage of Gretl and EViews is a convenient interface. However, if you are experienced enough in programming, you will be easy to access R and enjoy the powerful data analysis and data management.

In our opinion, R together with R-studio is the best software package for modeling the volatility of financial time series. For educational purposes EViews or Gretl should be used. Gretl is more flexible and free, extremely easy to use, unlike other software, therefore it is better to be used in educational institutions.

References

1. Greene, W.: Econometric Analysis. Prentice-Hall, Upper Saddle River (2008)
2. Black, F.: Studies of stock price volatility changes. In: Proceedings of the Business and Economic Statistics. American Statistical Association, Washington, DC (1976)
3. Box, G.E.P., Jenkins, G.M., Reinsel, G.C.: Time Series Analysis. Wiley, Hoboken (2008)
4. Martin, V., Hurn, S., Harris, D.: Econometric Modelling with Time Series, Specification Estimation and Testing. Cambridge University Press, Cambridge (2013)
5. Mills, T.C., Markellos, R.N.: The Econometric Modelling of Financial Time Series. Cambridge University Press, Cambridge (2008)
6. Chiu, C.-W.J., Harris, R., Stoja, E., Chin, M.: Financial market volatility, macroeconomic fundamentals and investor sentiment. Bank of England. Staff Working Paper No. 608 (2016)
7. Subbotin, A.V.: Volatility models: from conditional heteroskedasticity to cascades at multiple horizons. Appl. Econom. **15**(3), 94–138 (2009)
8. Leucht, A., Kreiss, J.-P., Neumann, M.H.: A model specification test for GARCH(1,1) processes. Scand. J. Statist. **42**(4), 1167–1193 (2015)

9. Barunik, J., Krehlik, T., Vacha, L.: Modelling and forecasting exchange rate volatility in time-frequency domain. Eur. J. Oper. Res. **251**(1), 329–340 (2016). https://doi.org/10.1016/j.ejor.2015.12.010

10. Panda, P., Deo, M.: Asymmetric and volatility spillover between stock market and foreign exchange market: Indian experience. IUP J. Appl. Financ. **20**(4), 69–82 (2014)

11. Birau, R., Trivedi, J., Antonescu, M.: Modeling S&P bombay stock eschange BAHKEX index volatility patterns using GARCH model. Procedia Econ. Financ. **32**, 520–525 (2015). https://doi.org/10.1016/S2212-5671(15)01427-6

12. Harvey, A., Lange, R.-J.: Modeling the Interactions Between Volatility and Returns. Cambridge Working Papers in Economics. CWPE 1518. https://doi.org/10.17863/cam.5703

13. Lu, X., Que, D., Cao, G.: Volatility forecast based on hybrid artificial neural network and GARCH-type models. Procedia Comput. Sci. **91**, 1044–1049 (2016). https://doi.org/10.1016/j.procs.2016.07.145

14. Efimova, O., Serletis, A.: Energy markets volatility modelling using GARCH. Energy Econ. **43**, 264–273 (2014)

15. Vejendla, A., Enke, D.: Evaluation of GARCH, RNN and FNN models for forecasting volatility in the financial markets. IUP J. Financ. Risk Manag. **10**(1), 41–49 (2013)

16. Babalos, V., Caporale, G.M., Spagnolo, N.: Equity fund flows and stock market returns in the US before and after the global financial crisis: a VAR-GARCH-in-mean analysis. In: Economics and Finance Working Paper Series, Working Paper No. 16–12. Brunel University London, Department of Economics and Finance, June 2016. https://www.brunel.ac.uk/__data/assets/pdf_file/0009/478314/1612.pdf

17. Kumari, J., Hiremath, G.S.: Determinants of idiosyncratic volatility: evidence from the Indian stock market. Res. Int. Bus. Financ. **41**, 172–184 (2017). https://doi.org/10.1016/j.ribaf.2017.04.022

18. Walther, T.: Expected shortfall in the presence of asymmetry and long memory. an application to vietnamese stock markets. Pac. Acc. Rev. **29**(2), 132–151 (2017). https://doi.org/10.1108/PAR-06-2016-0063

19. Sharma, P., Vipul: Forecasting stock index volatility with GARCH models: international evidence. Stud. Econ. Financ. **32**(4), 445–463 (2015). https://doi.org/10.1108/sef-11-2014-0212

20. Vasudevan, R.D., Vetrivel, S.C.: Forecasting stock market volatility using GARCH models: evidence from the Indian stock market. Asian J. Res. Soc. Sci. Humanit. **6**(8), 1565–1574 (2016). https://doi.org/10.5958/2249-7315.2016.00694.8

21. AL-Najjar, D.: Modelling and estimation of volatility using ARCH/GARCH models in Jordan's stock market. Asian J. Financ. Acc. **8**(1), 152–167 (2016). https://doi.org/10.5296/ajfa.v8i1.9129

22. Innocent, N., Mung'atu, J.K.: Modeling time-varying variance-covariance for exchange rate using multivariate GARCH model. Int. J. Thesis Proj. Diss. **4**(2), 49–65 (2016)

23. Spulbar, C., Nitoi, M.: The impact of political and economic news on the EURO/RON exchange rate: a GARCH approach. Annals of the 'Constantin Brâncuşi' University of Târgu Jiu, Economy Series **4**, 52–58 (2012)

24. Renfro, C.G.: The Practice of Econometric Theory: An Examination of the Characteristics of Econometric Computation. Springer, Heidelberg (2009). https://doi.org/10.1007/978-3-540-75571-5

25. Renfro, C.G.: A compendium of existing econometric software packages. J. Econ. Soc. Meas. **29**, 359–409 (2009)

26. Ooms, M., Doornik, J.A.: Econometric software development: past, present and future. Stat. Neerl. **60**(2), 206–224 (2006). https://doi.org/10.1111/j.1467-9574.2006.00317.x

27. Liboschik, T., Fokianos, K., Fried, R.: tscount: an R package for analysis of count time series following generalized linear models. Vignette of R package tscount version 1.3.0 (2015)
28. Ranganatham, M., Madhumati, R.: Investment Analysis and Portfolio Management. Pearson Education (Singapore) Pte. Ltd., Singapore (2005)
29. Engle, R.: Autoregressive conditional heteroscedasticity with estamates of the variance of United Kingdom inflation. Econometrica **50**(4), 987–1008 (1982)
30. Bollerslev, T.: Generalized autoregressive conditional heteroskedasticity. J. Econom. **31**, 307–327 (1986)
31. Minelli, M., Chambers, M., Dhiraj, A.: Big Data Technology, in Big Data, Big Analytics: Emerging Business Intelligence and Analytic Trends for Today's Businesses. Wiley, Hoboken (2013)
32. Google Trends. https://www.google.com/trends/explore?date=all&q=%2Fm%2F0212jm, EViews,gretl&hl=en-US
33. Gnu Regression Econometrics and Time-Series Library. http://gretl.sourceforge.net/
34. EViews 9.5 Feature List. http://www.EViews.com/EViews9/ev9features.html
35. Le, T.S.: Statistical&Programming Features of R. https://www.linkedin.com/pulse/statistical-programming-features-r-thiensi-le
36. Google Finance. https://www.google.com/finance/historical?q=WSE:WIG&ei=98ZNU6CMMMPJsQfdOQ
37. Matei, M.: Assessing volatility forecasting models: why GARCH models take the lead. Rom. J. Econ. Forecast. **4**, 42–65 (2009)
38. Ghalanos, A.: Introduction to the rugarch package (2015). https://cran.r-project.org/web/packages/rugarch/vignettes/Introduction_to_the_rugarch_package.pdf
39. Fisher, T.J., Gallagher, C.M.: New weighted portmanteau statistics for time series goodness of fit testing. J. Am. Stat. Assoc. **107**(498), 777–787 (2012). https://doi.org/10.1080/01621459.2012.688465

Identification of Persons with Epilepsy from Electroencephalogram Signals Using Fuzzy Decision Tree

Jan Rabcan(✉) and Miroslav Kvassay

Department of Informatics, University of Zilina,
Univerzitna 8215/1, 010 26 Zilina, Slovakia
{jan.rabcan,miroslav.kvassay}@fri.uniza.sk

Abstract. Epilepsy belongs to most common disorders. One of the common methods for its detection is a visual inspection of Electroencephalogram (EEG) signals obtained from electrodes monitoring electrical activity of the brain. This inspection requires a lot of experiences and, therefore, it can be quite complicated for persons that are not trained enough. One of the possible solutions to this issue is the development of algorithms for automatic classification of EEG signal using methods of predictive data mining. The predictive data mining allows finding dependencies between input and output attributes of data. In case of recognizing persons suffering from epilepsy, the input data is EEG signal of a person, and the output data is information whether the person has or does not have epilepsy. This kind of predictive data mining is known as a classification because the output attribute is discrete. One of the most common methods of classification is classification using a decision tree. A decision tree corresponds to a function that returns a value of an output attribute for given values of input attributes. Input attributes can be numerical or categorical. To obtain numerical attributes from EEG signal, preliminary data transformation has to be performed. In this paper, we add one more step to this transformation – fuzzification. After the preliminary data transformation, the data are used in the induction of fuzzy decision tree. In this paper, we compare the influence of two types of fuzzification and two types of fuzzy decision trees on the accuracy of classification of persons suffering from epilepsy based on EEG signal.

Keywords: Electroencephalogram · Fuzzification · Fuzzy decision tree

1 Introduction

According to the World Health Organization approximately 50 million people worldwide suffer from epilepsy and about 2.4 million people are diagnosed with it each year [1]. It is defined as a chronic neurological disorder whose symptoms are recurrent unprovoked seizures [2]. These symptoms are results of the electrical events in the brain, and they can affect any part of the body. The seizures are caused by unexpected electrical disturbance of the brain and excessive neuronal discharge. These disturbances and discharges can be identified in the *Electroencephalogram* (EEG) signal, which describes the electrical activity of the brain [3].

© Springer International Publishing AG, part of Springer Nature 2018
N. Bassiliades et al. (Eds.): ICTERI 2017, CCIS 826, pp. 209–229, 2018.
https://doi.org/10.1007/978-3-319-76168-8_10

EEG signal has been the most commonly used signal for the brain. It is used in medicine to reveal changes in the electrical activity of the brain, to detect disorders that are indicated generally at seizure diseases, loss of consciousness, after a stroke, inflammations, trauma, or concussion [2]. Measuring brain electrical activity by EEG is considered as one of the most important tools in neurology diagnostic [5, 6]. The specifics of this signal have been presented in details in [5].

The communication in the brain cells takes place through electrical impulses. EEG allows measuring these electrical impulses by placing the electrodes on the scalp [1, 2]. Captured signals are amplified and then converted into the graphic form, which has curve shape [4]. The shape and character of the curves depend on the current activity of the brain. The curves of EEG signal can be inspected visually by trained doctors who are able to use them in classification or prediction of the brain state of a patient. However, such an inspection might not provide enough information for doctors or people that are not perfectly trained. This issue can be solved by developing algorithms for automatic analysis and classification of EEG signals. By automatic extraction and analysis of useful information from the captured signal, the brain state of the patient can be predicted or classified.

Development and testing of algorithms for identification of patients with epilepsy based on EEG signal require real data. One of the most commonly used dataset for this task is a collection of 500 samples of EEG signals that were collected and published by Andrzejak in [6]. The samples in this dataset are divided into five disjoint subsets A, B, C, D, and E. Each subset contains 100 samples. A sample represents an EEG signal of a patient with duration of 23.6 s. In subsets A and B, all samples were taken from the surface of heads of five healthy persons. The difference of these subsets is that persons in subset A had eyes open while persons in subset B had eyes closed during EEG recording. Open or closed eyes of patients have an influence on epileptic activity according to [6]. Samples in subset D were recorded from within the epileptogenic zone, and those in subset C were obtained from the hippocampal formation of the opposite hemisphere of the brain. While subsets C and D contain only activity measured during seizure-free intervals, subset E contains only seizure activity. Examples of samples from these subsets are shown in Fig. 1. As one can see, it is not a problem to recognize that signals in A and E are different from those in B, C, and D. However, using just visual inspection, it can be quite complicated to find which of these signals are from healthy persons (A, B) and which are from persons suffering from epilepsy (C, D, E). This is most obvious in case of signals B, C, and D that are very similar to each other and, using visual inspection, we probably state they are from healthy persons. However, this would be incorrect. This illustration shows that development of algorithms for detection of people with epilepsy can be very useful because it allows deciding whether a person has epilepsy without information if they have had an epileptic seizure or have not. Furthermore, development and investigation of such algorithms can permit creating decision support system for early diagnosis of epilepsy [3–5].

The problem of automatic analysis of EEG signals and developing algorithms for finding persons suffering from epilepsy has been considered in several works. Most of these algorithms are based on methods of data mining. For example, neural networks have been used for this purpose in [5]; evolution methods and clustering analysis have

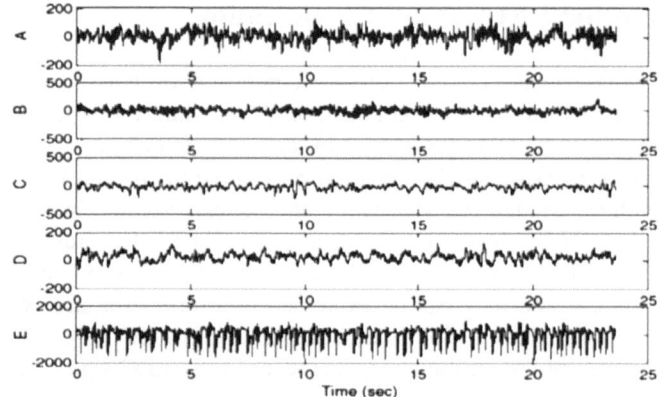

Fig. 1. Randomly chosen raw signals from each subset of dataset [6]

been used in [7] and [8] respectively; K-nearest neighbor classifier in [7]; and, finally, decision trees have been used for EEG signal classification in [9].

Another method for classification of EEG signal and identification of persons with epilepsy has been presented in [10]. This method is based on the transformation of the initial signal into fuzzy data that are then classified using *Ordered Fuzzy Decision Tree* (OFDT). This type of decision trees has been introduced in [11]. An advantage of this tree is a regular structure that contains just one attribute at each level of the tree [11], what allows performing analysis in a parallel way. The OFDT developed in [10] for EEG signal classification was also inducted based on data [6]. The accuracy of the classification was evaluated and compared with algorithms for EEG signal classification mentioned above. The results showed that the classification of EEG signal using *Fuzzy Decision Tree* (FDT) is possible and quite accurate. However, there is a potential for increasing the accuracy. This is discussed in this paper in more details.

EEG signal is a function of time. This means, it cannot be categorized as a categorical or numerical attribute [12, 13] and, therefore, it is not possible to use it in classification. This issue can be solved by preliminary data transformation. This procedure focuses on extracting features from EEG signal. The features are then used as input attributes for classification. In comparison with classification methods of EEG signal mentioned above, the algorithm presented in [10] includes a new step in the preliminary data transformation. This step is fuzzification. In this paper, we study and evaluate this step in more details. More specifically, we compare two methods of fuzzification and evaluate their influence on the accuracy of the results. Data obtained from fuzzification are then used not only in the construction of OFDT considered in [10] but also in the induction of *Unordered Fuzzy Decision Tree* (UFDT), which can contain more than one attribute at a level [11]. These two types of FDTs are inducted based on data obtained from each kind of fuzzification considered in the preliminary data transformation. This investigation allows us to develop a more accurate method for identification of persons suffering from epilepsy based on EEG signal.

2   Algorithm for EEG Signal Classification

Methods for EEG signal classification are composed of two steps – preliminary transformation of EEG signal and classification. Depending on the used classifier, the preliminary transformation can be formed by different procedures.

The method for EEG signal classification considered in [10] has two principal steps too (Fig. 2): preliminary data transformation and the classification with the application of fuzzy classifier. The goal of the first step (preliminary data transformation) is to transform the initial EEG signal into data that can be classified by the fuzzy classifier. These data are fuzzy, and they can be expressed in a form of a table whose columns agree with input and output attributes defining features of EEG signal and rows with EEG signals. Values of the attributes for one record (one EEG signal) are indicated in cells of the table.

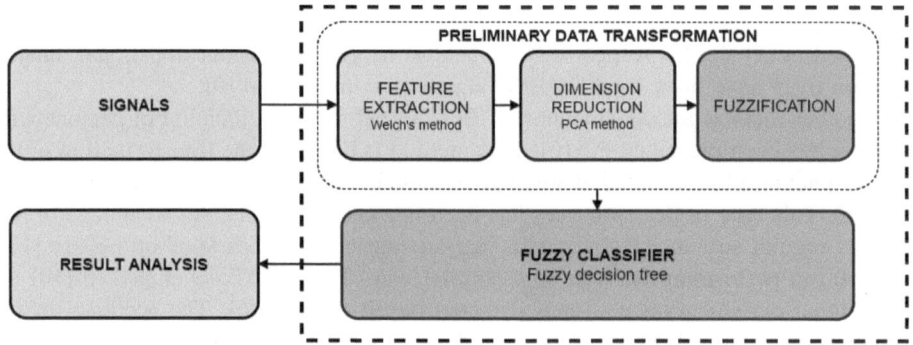

Fig. 2. The principal steps of algorithm for EEG signal classification

The second step of the method developed in [10] is a classification of EEG signal described by fuzzy attributes. The classifier is developed based on FDT. In this paper, two types of FDT are inducted and used for the classification. The first one is OFDT and another one is UFDT.

The first step of the preliminary data transformation includes three procedures (Fig. 2): feature extraction, dimension reduction, and fuzzification. There are numerous methods for extraction of features from a signal. In case of EEG signal, spectral transforms are used typically. In [9, 14], the feature extraction of EEG signal was implemented by the Fourier transform. The wavelet transform used in [15] allows obtaining a better result for EEG signal analysis in comparison with the Fourier transform. In this paper, features were extracted by power spectral density estimation using the *Welch method* that has been considered and used for EEG signal in [10, 16]. The result of this transformation is a matrix of features that indicate specifics of the investigated signal. The matrix, as a rule, has a large dimension and a special procedure has to be used to reduce this dimension. Therefore, the second procedure in the preliminary data transformation is dimension reduction. In [10] and this paper, this procedure is implemented using the *Principal Component Analysis* (PCA) [17], which transforms the matrix of features of EEG signal into a vector. The third procedure, which has been added in [10], is fuzzification of reduced features of EEG signal. Addition of this procedure resulted from the application of classification algorithm based on FDT, which was chosen because it allows taking into account the ambiguity of the transformed and reduced initial EEG signal. This ambiguity is caused by modification of initial EEG signal using spectral transform (the *Welch method*) and PCA [18, 19]. In [20–22], it has been shown that fuzzy data are useful for representation of ambiguous and imprecise data with higher accuracy. This indicates why fuzzification has been introduced in the preliminary transformation of EEG signal in [10] and why we use it in this paper.

The second step of the method is a classification of EEG signal. This can be implemented using different methods, such as neural networks [5], K-nearest neighbor classifier [8], or decision tree [9]. All these classifiers have been developed for EEG signal transformed using preliminary data transformation without application of fuzzification. In particular, the decision tree in [9] has been inducted for numerical data. In [10], OFDT was used for classification of EEG signal and identification of persons suffering from epilepsy. This decision tree is one type of FDTs. However, there are also other types of FDTs. One of them is UFDT [23], which is primarily considered in this paper.

3   Preliminary Data Transformation

The method proposed in [10] was approbated using dataset [6] of EEG signals (Fig. 1). According to the description in [6], all EEG signals were recorded with the same 128-channels amplifier system. After 12 bit analog-to-digital conversion, the data were written continuously onto the disk of data acquisition computer system at a sampling rate of 173.61 Hz. Band-pass filter setting was 0.53–40 Hz. As mentioned above, signals, which were obtained during this procedure, have to be transformed using the preliminary data transformation before classifier can be applied.

The preliminary data transformation includes three steps (Fig. 2). The first of them is the *Welch method* for extraction of features [24]. This transformation provides conversion of the arbitrary signal from its time domain to the frequency domain. The method is based on the concept of periodogram spectrum estimates, where a periodogram represents an estimation of the spectral density of a signal [24]. This transformation divides the time series of a signal into several overlapping segments of equal length (Fig. 3) and then computes the periodgram of each segment. Periodograms are

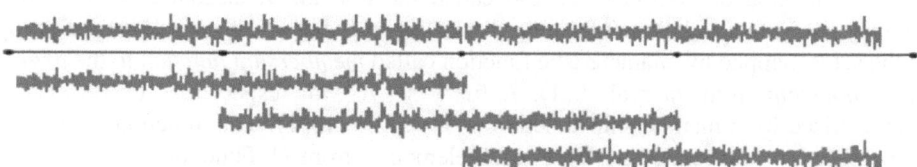

Fig. 3. Illustration of work of Welch's method with periodograms

used to find significant periodic components in the time series. The spectral density of the analyzed signal is calculated as the average of computed periodograms.

The result of the *Welch method* is a matrix of n features. In the case of dataset [6], the resulting matrix contained 128 features. Such number of features is too big for effective classification. Therefore, this number has to be reduced, what means that dimension of the matrix has to be reduced. In case of EEG signal, PCA is often used for this task [14].

PCA is a statistical procedure [25], which converts a set of observations described by n features (attributes) $a_1, a_2, \ldots, a_n$ into linearly uncorrelated latent variables called "principal components". This method is commonly used for the dimension reduction of the features (attributes) space. The resulting number of principal components is less than or equal to the number of attributes that describe original observations. Each principal component is characterized by variance. The bigger variance means larger importance. PCA is designed in such a way that each component has a variance greater than or equal to the variances of the components after them. Therefore, the first component is considered as the most significant and every next component has smaller importance than the preceding components. PCA provides this transformation by landing eigenvectors $V = (v_1 \quad v_2 \quad \cdots \quad v_n)$ of covariance matrix $M = \frac{a^T a}{n-1}$ into feature space, where $a = (a_1, a_2, \ldots, a_n)$. Eigenvector of matrix M is a vector v_i such that $M v_i = \lambda_i v_i$, where λ_i is a corresponding eigenvalue to the vector v_i given by $|M - \lambda I| = 0$ and I is the unit matrix. The resulting number of principal components can be determined by the *Kaiser criterion* [26]. This criterion considers a principal component as significant if its variance is bigger than the average variance of all principal components. The variance of the i-th principal component is equal to λ_i. Hence, the average variance of principal components is $\overline{var(Y)} = \frac{\sum_{i=1}^{p} \lambda_i}{p}$. Accordingly, the component is significant if $\lambda_i \geq \overline{var(Y)}$. Vectors $V = (v_1 \quad v_2 \quad \cdots \quad v_n)$ are sorted by decreasing order of their corresponding eigenvalues, and if eigenvalues are less than $\overline{var(Y)}$, the vector is not used in next transformation. The principal components are computed as $Y = V^T * a^T$. This transformation causes that principal components are orthogonal to each other [17].

3.1 Fuzzification

The fuzzy form of input data for classification is required according to the proposed method. Therefore, the numecal data has to be fuzzified before the classification. This is done by fuzzification, which is the process of transforming precise (crisp) values into degrees of membership for linguistic terms of fuzzy sets [27].

The universe of discourse U, also called the domain of discourse, is a set that contains all instances belonging to the discourse. In fuzzy set theory, the membership to the set is mapped by characteristic function called *membership function* to the *degree of membership* from interval $\langle 0, 1 \rangle$. A fuzzy set A with respect to a universe U is characterized by a membership function $\mu_A(u) : U \rightarrow \langle 0, 1 \rangle$. This function assigns an A-membership degree, i.e., $\mu_A(u)$, to each element u from U. Function $\mu_A(u)$ gives an estimation that u belongs to the fuzzy set A [18, 21, 22]. Based on this, fuzzy set A is defined as an ordered set of pairs $A = \{(u, \mu_A(u)), u \in U\}$, where:

1. $\mu_A(u) = 0$ if and only if x is not the member of set A,
2. $0 < \mu_A(u) < 1$ if and only if x is not the full member of set A,
3. $\mu_A(u) = 1$ if and only if x is the full member of set A.

In this paper, we use a particular case when the sum of membership values of all partitions equals to 1 [28]. This request is caused by application of information characteristic in FDT induction [11].

Nowadays, a lot of methods exist for performing fuzzification. In [10], the fuzzification generating triangular membership functions has been used. This fuzzification was based on the application of *K-means clustering* [29]. It showed good results in classification, but it tends to create a lot of values of fuzzy attribute (size of the domain). This can be considered as a disadvantage because the big count of values leads to decision trees whose internal nodes have a lot of outgoing edges. In such a case, induction of decision tree is usually time-consuming because a lot of training instances are necessary. Hence, another type of fuzzification algorithm for transforming reduced features of EEG signal into fuzzy form is investigated in this paper. This algorithm is based on *fuzzy C-means clustering*. In contrast with traditional clustering algorithms (e.g., *K-means clustering*), fuzzy clustering allows assigning each instance to more than one cluster with some partition degree. Furthermore, *fuzzy C-means clustering* allows creating membership functions with a sigmoidal shape. (The difference between fuzzification by triangular membership functions according to [10] and membership functions with a sigmoidal shape is illustrated in Fig. 4.)

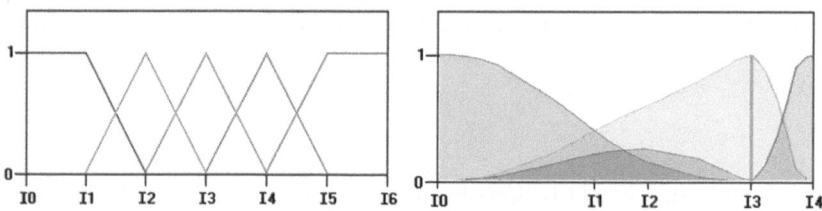

Fig. 4. Illustration of difference between fuzzification methods, where the triangular membership functions are used in the left picture while sigmoidal in the right one

The difference between algorithms for fuzzification from [10] and one used in this paper is how they determine the appropriate number of clusters. Determining the ideal number of clusters is a fundamental problem in clustering. The correct choice of the number of clusters is often ambiguous, and it also depends on analyzed data. The first algorithm based on *K-means clustering* works with the conventional approach, where it is necessary to specify the parameter for the exact number of resulting clusters. This is considered as a disadvantage in many aspects. One of them is a problem to estimate if the number of clusters is ideal or not, especially in case of analysis of large databases and complex instances, such as EEG signals.

In the second algorithm, which is primarily used in this paper, the fuzzification is performed with a modified version of *fuzzy C-means clustering*. The final number of clusters is determined by the conditional entropy between output attribute B and clusters transformed into fuzzy attributes. Transformation of clusters into fuzzy attributes is based on partitions degrees, where membership to one cluster is considered as one value of the fuzzy attribute. This algorithm is iterative and the first iteration starts with two clusters. At the end of iteration, the conditional entropy between the clusters (transformed into fuzzy attribute) and the output attribute is computed. If the entropy at the end of the current iteration is greater than or equal to the entropy in the previous iteration, the algorithm finishes, and the fuzzification is complete. If not, the number of clusters is increased by one, and the algorithm continues to the next iteration.

The fuzzification algorithm used in this paper has the following description. Let A_i is a numerical attribute, which is defined by a vector of k real numbers as $a = (a_1, a_2, \ldots, a_l, \ldots a_k)$. At the beginning, m_i clusters are initialized, where $m_i \geq 2$. The count of clusters agrees with the number of values of resulted fuzzy attribute. Each cluster has center c_j initialized to a random value. Algorithm assigns the partition degree $u_{l,j}$ to each value a_l, such that $0 \leq u_{l,j} \leq 1$. Partition degree $u_{l,j}$ indicates the grade of membership of value a_l to the j-th cluster. *Fuzzy C-means* is aimed to minimize the following objective function:

$$\sum_{j=1}^{m_i} \sum_{l=1}^{k} (u_{l,j})^2 d(a_l, c_j)^2, \tag{1}$$

where $d(a_l, c_j)$ represents an arbitrary kind of distance measurement. The sum of partitions to each cluster for a_l has to be equal to 1, which agrees with a restriction for implemented FDT induction. The mathematical form of this restriction is following:

$$\sum_{j=1}^{m_i} u_{l,j} = 1, \text{for } l = 1, 2, \ldots, k. \tag{2}$$

The minimization of (1) is done by iterative procedure. At the beginning of the iteration, the distances are computed. These distances are used to calculate partition degrees of the l-th instance into the j-th cluster as follows:

$$u_{l,j} = \frac{\frac{1}{d(a_l,c_j)^2}}{\sum_{t=1}^{m_i} \frac{1}{d(a_l,c_t)^2}}. \tag{3}$$

When all values $a_l \in a$ are assigned to the clusters, the centers are recomputed using the following formula:

$$c_j = \frac{\sum_{j=1}^{k} (u_{l,j})^2 a_l}{\sum_{j=1}^{k} (u_{l,j})^2}. \tag{4}$$

The required mapping of continuous numerical values into a fuzzy attribute is provided by (3). The algorithm is proposed in such a way that it tries to determine the best possible size of fuzzy attribute domain (number of clusters). Therefore, there is proposal to reduce the conditional entropy between clusters (transformed into fuzzy attribute) and output attribute B with m_n values. This is also iterative procedure which starts with initialization of cluster count $m_i = 2$ which agrees with the size of domain of resulting fuzzy attribute A_i. Then the clustering is performed. When the clustering is finished, conditional entropy $H(B|A_i)$ is calculated and compared with the entropy of the result from the previous iteration. If the previous result does not exist (only in the first iteration) or if the entropy decreased, then the algorithm continues. Otherwise, the algorithm is finished, and the result of the previous iteration is returned. Conditional entropy $H(B|A_i)$ is defined as follows [30]:

$$
\begin{aligned}
H(B|A_i) &= -\sum_{j=1}^{m_i} p(A_{i,j}) \sum_{s=1}^{m_n} p(B_s|A_{i,j}) * \log_2 p(B_s|A_{i,j}) \\
&= -\sum_{j=1}^{m_i} \sum_{s=1}^{m_n} p(B_s, A_{i,j}) * \log_2 p(B_s|A_{i,j}),
\end{aligned}
\tag{5}
$$

where $p(B_s|A_{i,j})$ is the conditional probability, which is computed using the following formula:

$$
p(B_s|A_{i,j}) = \frac{p(B_s, A_{i,j})}{p(A_{i,j})} = \frac{\frac{M(B_s \times A_{i,j})}{k}}{\frac{M(A_{i,j})}{k}} = \frac{M(B_s \times A_{i,j})}{M(A_{i,j})},
\tag{6}
$$

where $M(.)$ denotes the cardinality of the argument interpreted as a fuzzy set [31].

4   Classification of EEG Signal Using Fuzzy Decision Trees

4.1   Data for Induction of Fuzzy Decision Trees

In this paper, classification algorithms that allow operating with fuzzy data are used. The data for the fuzzy decision trees induction has a form of Table 1. This table is composed of $n+1$ columns associated with n input attributes and 1 output attribute. The i-th column, for $i = 1, 2, \ldots, n+1$, is divided into m_i sub-columns. The j_i-th sub-column, for $j_i = 1, 2, \ldots, m_i$, agrees with the j-th value of the attribute represented by the i-th column. Each row of the repository corresponds to one instance of collected data. The classification algorithm used in this paper works with fuzzy attributes. Each fuzzy attribute A_i is a linguistic attribute, what means that attribute A_i can take fuzzy values $A_{i,j}, j = 1, 2 \ldots, m_i$. Every value $A_{i,j}$ of fuzzy attribute A_i can be considered as a fuzzy set. These sets create the domain of a fuzzy attribute and their count is considered as domain size. For each instance e of the repository, we assume that $\mu_{A_{i,j}}(e) \in \langle 0, 1 \rangle$ and $\sum_{j=1}^{m_i} \mu_{A_{i,j}}(e) = 1$. These assumptions are caused by the strategy for FDT induction.

Table 1. An example of the repository for induction of FDT

Input attributes, A_i								Output attribute, B		
A_1			A_2		$\cdots$	A_n				
A_{1_1}	A_{1_2}	$A_{1_{m1}}$	A_{2_1}	$A_{2_{m2}}$		A_{n_1}	$A_{n_{mn}}$	B_1	$\cdots$	B_{m^b}
0.1	0.5	0.4	0.6	0.4	$\cdots$	0.5	0.5	0.0	$\cdots$	1.0
0.2	0.1	0.7	0.1	0.9	$\cdots$	0.8	0.2	0.3	$\cdots$	0.0
$\cdots$			$\cdots$		$\cdots$	$\cdots$		$\cdots$		
0.3	0.3	0.4	0.0	1.0	$\cdots$	0.4	0.6	0.1	$\cdots$	0.5

4.2 Induction of Unordered Fuzzy Decision Tree for Classification of EEG Signal

Decision trees are one of the most popular data mining techniques used for classification and prediction. The essence of the classification is to divide objects with certain characteristics into individual classes based on a decision model built according to the training set of the data. One of the main advantages of decision trees is their clarity and simple interpretation that allows users to quickly and easily evaluate the obtained results, identify key items, and search for interesting segments of data.

Decision trees are composed of a root, internal nodes, and leaves. The root and each internal node are associated with one of the input attributes, where the values of the attribute are represented by output edges of the node. The leaf nodes have the label of class, which means the decision. A classification of unknown instance starts at the root node of the tree. If a node is associated with an input attribute, then the outcome for the instance is determined, and the classification continues using the appropriate sub-tree. When a leaf is encountered, its label gives the predicted class. In case of fuzzy decision trees, an instance can pass through multiple branches during classification. Hence, it is necessary to take a decision based on a set of leaves. Therefore, it is common that the tree is transformed into a set of classification rules that allow such a classification in an effective way. The usage of classification rules is described in [23].

Nowadays, numerous algorithms for induction of decision tree exist. One of the first was ID3 introduced by Quinlan in [32]. This algorithm is based on information gain measurement. The main problem with this algorithm is that attributes with a larger number of values are preferred. This problem was solved in C4.5 algorithm proposed in [33]. Other decision trees are CHAID [13], CART [13] and fuzzy decision trees inducted using *cumulative mutual information* [11]. In this paper, two types of fuzzy decision trees inducted using *cumulative mutual information* are considered. The first one is OFDT and the second one is UFDT.

In case of OFDT, all attributes at the same level are associated with one attribute. This additional restriction gives the performance benefit during classification because it allows performing classification in a parallel way [9]. The criterion for choosing of association attributes is *cumulative mutual information* [11, 31, 34] $\mathbf{I}(B; A_{i_1}, A_{i_2}, \ldots, A_{i_q})$ where $A_{i_1}, A_{i_2}, \ldots, A_{i_{q-1}}$ is the sequence of attributes from the root to the investigated node, and q denotes the investigated level. The implemented version also takes into account the cost of measuring the value of the attribute. An association attribute is selected by the following criterion:

$$\text{argmax} \left(\frac{\mathbf{I}(B; A_{i_1}, \ldots, A_{i_{q-1}}, A_{i_q})}{H(A_{i_q}) * Cost(A_{i_q})} \right), \tag{7}$$

where function argmax returns the attribute with a maximal value of the *cumulative mutual information* at the q-th level divided by its entropy and cost. The attribute is chosen from a set of attributes that are not associated with the preceding levels.

In case of UFDT, the *cumulative mutual information* has the following form: $\mathbf{I}(B; A_{i_1 j_1}, A_{i_2 j_2}, \ldots, A_{i_q j_q})$ [11, 31, 34] where $A_{i_1 j_1}, A_{i_2 j_2}, \ldots, A_{i_q j_q}$ is the sequence of attribute values from the root to the investigated node and q is the level of the investigated node. The attribute with the greatest value of *cumulative mutual information* is chosen to associate with the investigated node at the q-th level using the following formula:

$$\text{argmax} \left(\frac{\mathbf{I}(B; A_{i_1 j_1}, \ldots, A_{i_{q-1} j_{q-1}}, A_{i_q j_q})}{H(A_{i_q}) * Cost(A_{i_q})} \right), \tag{8}$$

where function argmax returns the attribute with a maximal value of *cumulative mutual information* divided by its entropy and cost. The attribute is chosen from a set of attributes that are not used in the branch that the investigated node belongs to.

The entropy of attribute A_{i_q}, which is present in formulae (7) and (8), is computed using the next formula [31]:

$$H(A_{i_q}) = \sum_{j=1}^{m_i} M(A_{i_q j_q}) * \left(\log_2 k - \log_2 M(A_{i_q j_q}) \right). \tag{9}$$

FDTs considered in this paper use pruning techniques. These techniques are used to remove sub-trees with small classification performance. They improve the robustness of resulting decision trees. The used pruning techniques establish a node as a leaf by stopping the tree expansion during the induction phase according to two input threshold parameters α and β. The threshold α reflects the minimal frequency of occurrences in the given branch. The frequency reflects percentage of instances that belongs to the node. A node is established as a leaf of the tree if the following condition holds [23]:

$$\alpha \geq \frac{M(A_{i_q j_q} \times \ldots \times A_{i_q j_q})}{k}. \tag{10}$$

Every internal node contains confidence levels, where each level reflects the degree of belief to one of the output classes. The node is established as a leaf if the following condition holds for at least one of the values B_j, for $j = 1, 2, \ldots, m_{n+1}$, of output attribute B:

$$\beta \leq 2^{-\mathbf{I}\left(B_j|A_{i_1 j_1}, \ldots, A_{i_z j_z}\right)}, \tag{11}$$

where conditional information $\mathbf{I}\left(B_j|A_{i_1 j_1}, \ldots, A_{i_z j_z}\right)$ can be computed based on the following formula [31]:

$$\mathbf{I}\left(A_{i_1 j_1}|A_{i_2 j_2}\right) = \log_2 M\left(A_{i_1 j_1}\right) - \log_2 M\left(A_{i_2 j_2} \times A_{i_1 j_1}\right). \tag{12}$$

Threshold parameters α and β have a big impact on maximal level of the final tree and the depth of individual branches. Increasing the value of parameter β causes that FDT will contain larger number of nodes. Therefore, the tree depth will be greater. Parameter α also influences the depth of the tree. In this case, greater α causes the smaller depth of branches. The threshold values must be set to satisfied value to perform accurate classification. In case of unpruned decision tree ($\alpha = 0$ and $\beta = 1$), the classification performance is good, but only for training instances. In case of unknown instances, small frequencies of leaf nodes will lead to classification mistakes [32]. The threshold parameters are usually determined by iterative algorithm, i.e., the adjustment of α and β values is performed by repeated induction of FDT with different combination of thresholds. When the iterations are finished, the best combination is chosen. This procedure can be depicted in the form of a flow diagram depicted in Fig. 5. For example, in this paper, several UFDTs were inducted based on dataset [6] according to the restriction in fuzzification process and by modification of threshold parameters α and β. These trees have different structure and classification performance. For example, FDT, whose induction is described, below was inducted assuming that $\alpha = 0.014$, $\beta = 0.75$, and the maximal number of values of each fuzzy attribute is equal to 4. (The classification performance of this tree is shown in Table 2.)

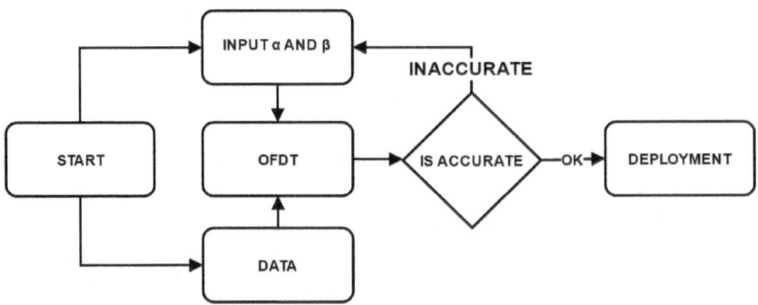

Fig. 5. Process of obtaining good estimation of thresholds α and β

The next example explains the induction of the UFDT. The induction starts with selecting an input attribute, which will be associated with the root of the tree. Therefore, the algorithm for induction has to select attribute with a maximal value of splitting criterion defined in (8). Then, it is necessary to calculate the frequencies and confidence levels according to the formulae introduced in the right-hand sides of inequalities (10) and (11) respectively. The frequency of the root is equal to 1 always. The maximal

Table 2. Table of classification performance for experiments when automatic detection of size of fuzzy attribute domain was performed

Classifier	Maximal number of clusters	Average number of values of attribute	Sensitivity	Specificity	Accuracy
UFDT	2	2.000	93.082	57.092	79.687
UFDT	3	2.833	95.094	67.087	85.298
UFDT	4	3.389	95.708	72.072	87.389
UFDT	5	3.556	94.281	84.843	90.518
UFDT	6	3.667	94.126	84.496	90.301
UFDT	7	3.722	94.352	84.562	90.604
OFDT	2	2.000	93.181	56.821	79.078
OFDT	3	2.833	95.017	67.121	85.080
OFDT	4	3.389	95.708	72.272	87.907
OFDT	5	3.556	94.129	83.185	89.429
OFDT	6	3.667	94.201	82.162	89.212
OFDT	7	3.722	94.184	82.110	89.648

value of splitting criterion has attribute A_1, and the confidence levels are following: *healthy*: 0.6 and *sick*: 0.4. This attribute has 3 values, and each of them corresponds to one of the outgoing branches of the root. The first level of the tree is shown in Fig. 6. Please note that the nodes of the tree contain information about the frequencies and confidence in the second and last line accordingly.

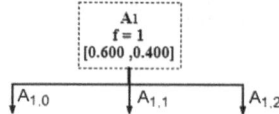

Fig. 6. The first level of UFDT

On the second level, firstly, new nodes are created at the end of the branches. Then the confidence levels and frequencies of the new nodes are calculated. If a node contains the confidence level greater than β or has the frequency less than α, then the node is established as a leaf. Three nodes were created at this level, but two of them are leaf nodes because they contain confidence greater than threshold $\beta = 0.75$. Hence, the tree expansion continues at this level only in one node. In this case, it is also necessary to select attribute, which has the greatest value of criterion (8). In case of internal nodes, the selection considers only attributes that are not used in the branch (from the root to the investigated node). Therefore, attribute A_1 is not included in selection anymore. The tree with the second level is shown in Fig. 7.

The steps are the same as on level before. The new nodes are created at the end of the branches. If some of this node has the confidence level greater than or the frequency

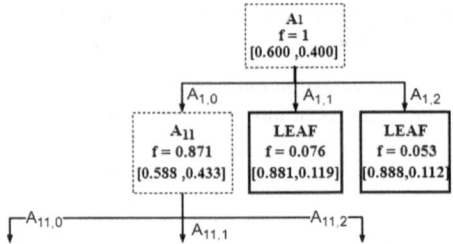

Fig. 7. The second level of UFDT

less than the corresponding threshold parameters, then the node is established as a leaf. If not, then the association attribute is selected, and tree expansion will continue until the set of the unused attributes in a given branch is empty or all new nodes are leaves. By repeating these steps, it is possible to induct the whole decision tree. The final decision tree is presented in Fig. 8.

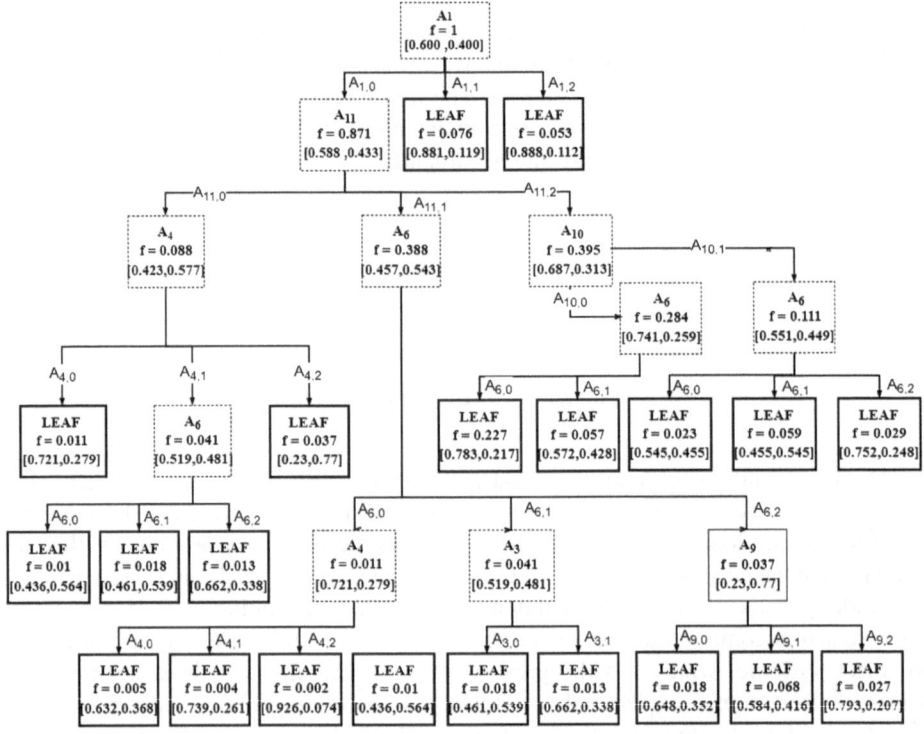

Fig. 8. The final UFDT

5   Evaluation

5.1   Evaluation Procedure

The algorithms were evaluated by three measurements of classification performance, namely by accuracy, sensitivity, and specificity. The important characteristic of the classification is the accuracy. The accuracy is calculated as the proportion of the number of correctly classified instances and the number of all the classified instances. This agrees with the percentage of properly classified instances:

$$\text{accuracy} = \left(\frac{\sum_{i=1}^{k} c(I_i)}{k} \right) * 100, \tag{13}$$

where k is the number of classified instances, I_i is the i-th classified instance from set I, for $i = 1, 2, \ldots, k$, and $c(I_i)$ is defined as follows:

$$c(I_i) = \begin{cases} 1 \text{ if classify}(I_i) = \text{class of } x \\ 0 \text{ otherwise} \end{cases}, \tag{14}$$

where function $\text{classify}(I_i)$ returns the target class of FDT classification for instance I_i from the investigated dataset.

The specificity is a proportion of negative instances which are correctly classified as negatives. In our case, it is the percentage of healthy patients that are properly classified as healthy. In case of epilepsy, the specificity is related to an ability to correctly classify healthy patients. A result with 100% specificity totally excludes epilepsy in healthy samples. So, the specificity is defined as follows [35]:

$$\text{specificity} = \frac{TN}{TN + FP}, \tag{15}$$

where TN denotes number of correctly classified instances as negative (healthy) and FP is the number of incorrectly classified instances as illness.

The sensitivity agrees with a number of positives that are correctly classified as positives. A test with a large sensitivity is reliable if its result is negative because it rarely misdiagnoses those patients who have the disease. For example, in case of epilepsy, if sensitivity is equal to 100%, then the classification recognizes all illness patients as positive and a negative result excludes the presence of epilepsy. So, the sensitivity is calculated in the following way:

$$\text{sensitivity} = \frac{TP}{TP + FN}, \tag{16}$$

where TP is the number of correctly classified instances as positive (epileptics patients) and FN denotes the number of incorrectly classified instances as healthy.

The estimation of classification performance is done in such a way, that the data are divided into two datasets. The first one is used for induction of FDT, and it contains

80% of the instances. Next 20% of the instances are contained in the testing dataset. The mentioned performance evaluation is shown in Fig. 9.

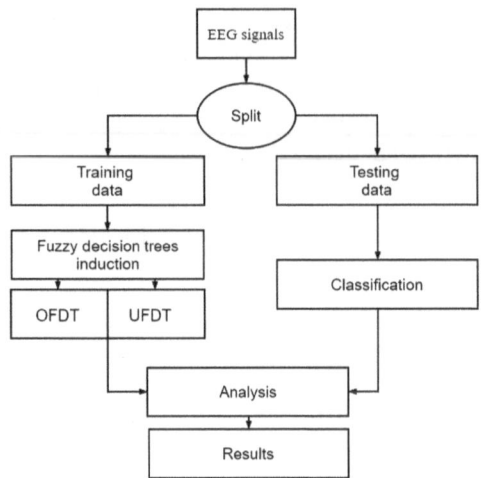

Fig. 9. Flow diagram depicting evaluation of the classification based on FDTs

5.2 Evaluation of Accuracy of Algorithms for Classification of EEG Signal Using Fuzzy Decision Trees

Evaluation of the classification performance was implemented by several experiments. The object of classification was to determine whether a patient suffers from epilepsy or not. Therefore, all classes (A, B, C, D, and E) of the original dataset were merged into two classes – healthy persons and persons suffering from epilepsy.

The whole analysis was done under various conditions of fuzzification of numerical values. Fuzzification is performed by fuzzy clustering. This task is often related to determination of the appropriate number of clusters. One approach in this article uses an algorithm that determines the number of clusters based on the *cumulative mutual information* between the fuzzified input attribute and the output attribute. The maximal number of clusters used in fuzzification of each input attribute is in range from 2 to 7. Further increasing of maximal number of clusters did not lead to any changes because the conditions specified above do not allow rising the *cumulative mutual information* between clusters and the output attribute. Therefore, the algorithm stopped. The classification performance is shown in Table 2 and the accuracy in Fig. 10. Table 2 consists of 6 columns where the first one denotes classifier that was used. The second column carries information about a maximal number of used clusters during fuzzification and the next, third column, informs about an average number of clusters used during fuzzification. This number agrees with an average size of attributes domain. Last three columns are sensitivity, specificity, and accuracy. The big value of the sensitivity means that classifier is able to correctly recognize patients with epilepsy. The big value of the specificity indicates that the classifier correctly excludes epilepsy in healthy patients. As we can see from this table and Fig. 10, the accuracy is settled, when the maximal number of clusters was 5.

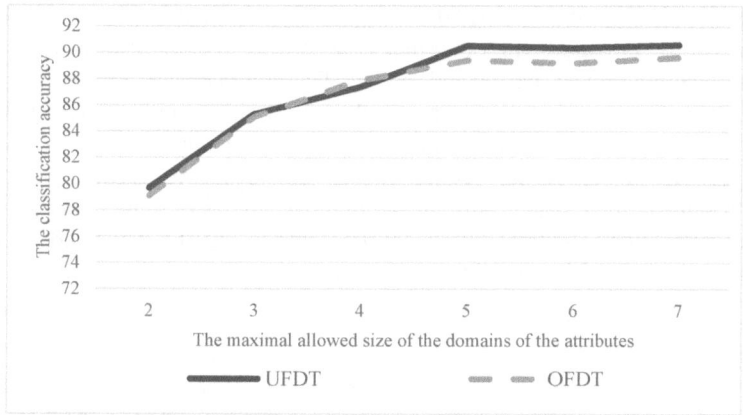

Fig. 10. Dependency of accuracy of the classification using FDTs on the maximal allowed size of the domains of the attributes

In the second approach, the upper limit of the number of clusters was defined to a specific value. It means that the number of values of each input attribute was set to the same value, e.g., each input attribute after the preliminary data transformation had size of domain equal to 2 (the size of the domain of an attribute is equal to the number of its fuzzy values). This approach has computable benefits during fuzzification in comparison with the first approach, but the performance of classification is weaker. In this

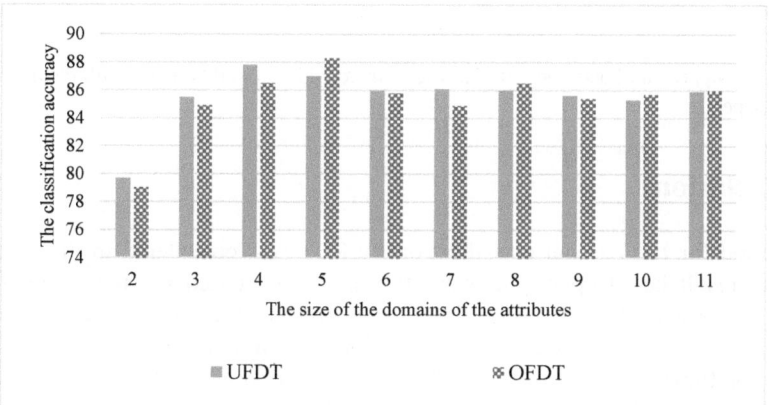

Fig. 11. Dependency of accuracy of the classification using FDTs on the size of the domains of the attributes assuming that all attributes used in the classification have the same size of the domain

approach, the classification was also evaluated according to the accuracy. The results of this evaluation are in Fig. 11. As we can see, the results of classification are worse in comparison with those presented in Fig. 10.

Finally, the results of the experiments performed in this paper were compared with the results from [10]. In that paper, OFDT algorithm was used for classification of EEG signal, and it was compared with other papers according to classification accuracy. Two versions of evaluation were performed in [10]. The first one used the same approach as is in this paper. It means that data were divided into training and testing sets with ratio 80:20. This evaluation was named "*Split*". The second evaluation used the same set of instances for the induction and classification. This test was called "*No split*". To compare results in this paper with those in [10], we also implemented these two versions of evaluation. The final results are presented in Fig. 12. The chart in this figure implies that our method is good in comparison with other existing methods.

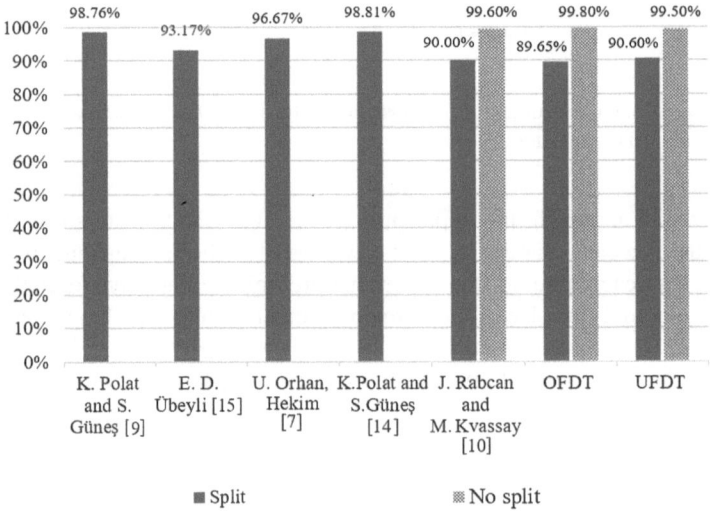

Fig. 12. Comparison of accuracy of classification considered in this paper with results presented in other papers

6   Conclusion

The method for EEG signal classification by FDT was considered in this paper. The presented result has deepened investigation that was started in [10]. In [10], a new method for classification based on OFDT was presented and discussed. The principal characteristic of that method was introduction of a new type of classifier based on analysis of fuzzy data. This type of data was proposed to take into account the ambiguity of data that can arise in step of preliminary transformation of initial EEG signal (the feature extraction and the dimension reduction). The classifier modification resulted in including a new procedure in the preliminary data transformation. This procedure is fuzzification of reduced EEG signal features.

The OFDT as one of types of FDTs were inducted for EEG signal classification in [10]. In this paper, we investigated and analyzed different aspects of fuzzification and classification. In particular, two algorithms for fuzzification of reduced EEG signal features were used. The main difference of these algorithms is the determination of the appropriate number of clusters. The first algorithm is based on the specification of the exact number of resulting clusters. However, use of this algorithm did not allow improving the accuracy in the EEG signal classification. Therefore, the modified version of *fuzzy C-means clustering* was used in the second algorithm. In this case, the number of clusters is determined by the conditional entropy between the output attribute and clusters transformed into fuzzy attributes. This algorithm had the best results in application for EEG signal classification. Therefore, we used it for fuzzification of data for FDT induction.

In this paper, two types of FDTs were also considered and evaluated for classification of EEG signal. In addition to OFDT, which was used in [10], UFDT was also used in this work. Both types of FDTs were inducted based on estimation of the *cumulative mutual information* [11]. Use of the new type of FDT allowed us to slightly improve the accuracy of the EEG signal classification (Fig. 12). Therefore, UFDT can be recommended for future development in EEG classification.

Acknowledgment. This work was partly supported by the grants of VEGA 1/0038/16 and VEGA 1/0354/17.

References

1. World Health Organization. http://www.who.int/mediacentre/factsheets/fs999/en/
2. Engel, J.J., Starkman, S.: Emergency medicine clinics of North America. Emerg. Med. Clin. North Am. **12**, 895–923 (1994)
3. Iasemidis, L.D.: Epileptic seizure prediction and control. Biomed. Eng. IEEE Trans. **50**, 549–558 (2003)
4. Libenson, M.H.: Practical Approach to Electroencephalography (2010)
5. Subasi, A., Erc, E.: Classification of EEG signals using neural network and logistic regression. Comput. Methods Programs Biomed. **78**, 87–99 (2005)
6. Andrzejak, R.G., Lehnertz, K., Mormann, F., Rieke, C., David, P., Elger, C.E.: Indications of nonlinear deterministic and finite-dimensional structures in time series of brain electrical activity: dependence on recording region and brain state. Phys. Rev. E. Stat. Nonlin. Soft Matter Phys. **64**, 61907 (2001)
7. Orhan, U., Hekim, M., Ozer, M.: EEG signals classification using the K-means clustering and a multilayer perceptron neural network model. Expert Syst. Appl. **38**, 13475–13481 (2011)
8. Guo, L., Rivero, D., Dorado, J., Munteanu, C.R., Pazos, A.: Automatic feature extraction using genetic programming: an application to epileptic EEG classification. Expert Syst. Appl. **38**, 10425–10436 (2011)

9. Polat, K., Güneş, S.: A novel data reduction method: distance based data reduction and its application to classification of epileptiform EEG signals. Appl. Math. Comput. **200**, 10–27 (2008)

10. Rabcan, J., Kvassay, M.: Electroencephalogram signals classification by ordered fuzzy decision tree. ICT Educ. Res. Ind. Appl. Integr. Harmon. Knowl. Transf. **1844**, 72–87 (2017)

11. Levashenko, V., Zaitseva, E.: Fuzzy Decision Trees in Medical Decision Making Support System (2012). http://ieeexplore.ieee.org/xpls/abs_all.jsp?arnumber=6354402

12. Jantan, H., Hamdan, A.R., Othman, Z.A.: Data Mining Classification Techniques for Human Talent Forecasting (2011)

13. Maletic, J.I., Marcus, A.: Data Mining and Knowledge Discovery Handbook (2005)

14. Polat, K., Güneş, S.: Artificial immune recognition system with fuzzy resource allocation mechanism classifier, principal component analysis and FFT method based new hybrid automated identification system for classification of EEG signals. Expert Syst. Appl. **34**, 2039–2048 (2008)

15. Übeyli, E.D.: Wavelet/mixture of experts network structure for EEG signals classification. Expert Syst. Appl. **34**, 1954–1962 (2008)

16. Naderi, M.A.: Analysis and classification of EEG signals using spectral analysis and recurrent neural networks. In: Biomedical Engineering, 3–4 November 2010

17. Bro, R., Smilde, A.K.: Principal component analysis. R. Soc. Chem. **6**, 2812–2831 (2014)

18. Witten, I.H., Frank, E., Hall, M.A.: Data Mining: Practical Machine Learning Tools and Techniques. Morgan Kaufmann Series in Data Management Systems xxxiii, 629 p. (2011)

19. Stanton, N.A., Baber, C.: Error by design: methods for predicting device usability. Des. Stud. **23**, 363–384 (2002)

20. Ley, D.: Approximating process knowledge and process thinking: acquiring workflow data by domain experts. In: Conference Proceedings - IEEE International Conference on Systems, Man, and Cybernetics, pp. 3274–3279 (2011)

21. Gueorguieva, N., Georgiev, G.: Fuzzyfication of principle component analysis for data dimensionality reduction. In: 2016 IEEE International Conference on Fuzzy Systems, pp. 1818–1825 (2016)

22. Tsipouras, M.G., Exarchos, T.P., Fotiadis, D.I.: A methodology for automated fuzzy model generation. Fuzzy Sets Syst. **159**, 3201–3220 (2008)

23. Levashenko, V., Zaitseva, E., Puuronen, S.: Fuzzy classifier based on fuzzy decision tree. In: EUROCON 2007 - International Conference on Computer as a Tool, pp. 823–827 (2007)

24. Gupta, H.R., Mehra, R.: Power spectrum estimation using welch method for various window techniques. Int. J. Sci. Res. Eng. Technol. **2**, 389–392 (2013)

25. Dunteman, G.: Principal Components Analysis. Sage Publications, Thousand Oaks (1986)

26. Ferré, L.: Selection of components in principal component analysis: a comparison of methods. Comput. Stat. Data Anal. **19**, 669–682 (1995)

27. Bhattacharyya, S., Dutta, P.: Fuzzy Logic: Concepts, System Design, and Applications to Industrial Informatics. Handbook of Research on Industrial Informatics and Manufacturing Intelligence: Innovations and Solutions (2012)

28. Zaitseva, E., Levashenko, V.: Construction of a reliability structure function based on uncertain data. IEEE Trans. Reliab. **65**, 1710–1723 (2016)

29. Rabcan, J.: Ordered fuzzy decision trees induction based on cumulative information estimates and its application. In: ICETA, 6 p. (2016)

30. Rokach, L., Maimon, O.: Data Mining with Decision Trees. Theory and Applications (2008)

31. Levashenko, V.G., Zaitseva, E.N.: Usage of new information estimations for induction of fuzzy decision trees. In: Yin, H., Allinson, N., Freeman, R., Keane, J., Hubbard, S. (eds.) IDEAL 2002. LNCS, vol. 2412, pp. 493–499. Springer, Heidelberg (2002). https://doi.org/10.1007/3-540-45675-9_74

32. Quinlan, J.R.: Induction of decision trees. Mach. Learn. **1**, 81–106 (1986)
33. Quinlan, J.R.: C4.5: programs for machine learning. Mach. Learn. **240**, 302 (1993)
34. Levashenko, V., Zaitseva, E., Kvassay, M.: Deserno: reliability estimation of healthcare systems using fuzzy decision trees. Ann. Comput. Sci. Inf. Syst. **8**, 331–340 (2016)
35. Sokolova, M., Lapalme, G.: A systematic analysis of performance measures for classification tasks. Inf. Process. Manag. **45**, 427–437 (2009)

Simulation Agent-Based Model
of Heterogeneous Firms Through
Software Module

Vitaliy Kobets$^{(\boxtimes)}$ and Alexander Weissblut

Kherson State University, 27, Universitetska Street, Kherson 73000, Ukraine
vkobets@kse.org.ua, veits@ksu.ks.ua

Abstract. *Research goals and objectives:* study of the simplest agent-based model with heterogeneous firms using a software module.

Object of research: microeconomics system with heterogeneous agents.

Subject of research: agent-based model of microeconomic system with different types, equilibrium and disequilibrium states of the systems with specially developed desktop application.

Research methods: optimization methods, bifurcation analysis, stability analysis, simulation methods, game theory.

Results of the research: a market moves from stability to dynamic chaos with an increase in number of firms provided the firms have heterogeneous types. If no less than two-thirds of firms use naive expectations, the state of dynamic chaos will also appears in the market. The crucial factor which ensures market stability is the adaptive approach of firms' competitive strategy.

Keywords: Agent-based model · Heterogeneous type · Bifurcation
Adaptive expectations

1 Introduction

Implausibility of rational choice theory, the idea that firms are autonomous economic agents, the need for a more dynamic, and less equilibrium-focused economic methodology are weak issues of neoclassical economics which belongs to economic mainstream [1]. Equilibrium behavior (that each player's strategy is a best response to their beliefs about other players' strategies) is one of the fundamental concepts of neoclassical economics. The game theory approach has solved the equilibrium under assumptions of perfect information, full rationality and representative agents. The recent application of behavioral economics allows richer assumptions such as heterogeneity agents, imperfect information and evolutionary survival to be included in agent-based models. Competition among firms reflects the logic of evolutionary selection: free market is a struggle for survival, in which successful firms survive and unsuccessful ones die. This view may support three pillars of neoclassical economics: (1) economic actors are self-interested; (2) self-interest leads to public goods (Adam Smith's "invisible hand"); and (3) that together these lead to market optimization. However application of evolutionary selection to competition among firms leads to the

© Springer International Publishing AG, part of Springer Nature 2018
N. Bassiliades et al. (Eds.): ICTERI 2017, CCIS 826, pp. 230–254, 2018.
https://doi.org/10.1007/978-3-319-76168-8_11

opposite predictions: reciprocity of firms and the suppression of selfishness. This approach reveals that, while firms may generally pursue their own interest, they also have aligned their own interest with wider society interests as well. Stages of social responsibility of firms are revealed as: well-doing business practice, guaranteeing the employment and safety of work, formation and development of local community, preservation of environment, orientation on a consumer and a quality of products, stimulation of innovative activity. A new stage of development of social and production consciousness, when the human is perceived as the valuable resource having the bigger importance, than natural resources or the wealth accumulated, has come into being [2].

A long-standing question in economics is whether economic agents evolve to behave as if they were striving to maximize own goal function during market interaction. In real life no simple and general individual-centered goal function emerges from the analysis. Individuals, as a rule, play a Nash equilibrium of a game with a goal function which combines self-interest (own material payoff) and group interest (group material payoff) [3]. Keynes' mathematical Treatise addresses what some call 'radical uncertainty', which he thought endemic in world affairs. In contrast, economic mainstream has worked as if it were realistic to ignore even the possibility of radical uncertainty [4]. At the same time we need a new approach of decision making under chaos as a type of radical uncertainty.

The agent-based approach allows us to develop an economic mechanism that could explain why the microeconomic system is sometimes stable, and in other cases - not. Simulation models are grounded on the basis of 3 computer paradigms (object-oriented, dynamic and multi-agent system) that are used to predict the development of microeconomic systems [5]. The traditional method of constructing a scientific theory is first to synthesize and investigate the example of the simplest possible mathematical model of microeconomic system. Simplest model means identical linear cost function for all firms and one homogeneous product. Then we can study complex real systems which are grounded on this basis.

Traditional static models of competition (e.g., Cournot, Bertrand and Stackelberg) were converted in dynamics models which were investigated on existence, stability and local bifurcations of the equilibrium points [6]. Numerical simulations demonstrate that the system with varying model parameters may drive to chaos and the loss of stability may be caused by period doubling bifurcations [7]. One of main task for such models is to keep the system from instability and chaos using feedback parameters [8]. Through local analysis we provide conditions for the stability of the market equilibrium and through global analysis we investigate some bifurcations which cause qualitative changes in the market structure [9].

We suppose microeconomic system consists of two types of agents with heterogeneous types, such as selfish and reciprocator firms. Reciprocity implies that the firms are ready to sacrifice some of their own profits for the benefit of consumers without direct compensation for it by the state. Such targets can be stipulated by the firms' desire to get stable profits in the long run rather than maximal short-run profits [7, 10]. Such forward-thinking reciprocator firms are considered in the model of this paper. Their objective function is a weighted average of the profits and consumer surplus of their market segment. In other words, the reason of reciprocator firms' appearance is their desire to obtain stable profit in the long-run period instead of short-run maximal profit.

Modern development of dynamic paradigm in microeconomics is a wide stream of researches which do not form a general theory and have no connection with real markets [11]. The model of simplest competitive market with different types of participants and homogeneous product is synthesized in the paper. This paper is a continuation and a summary of our previous works [7] and [10].

The **purpose** of the paper is a study and simulation of agent-based model of firms with heterogeneous types through specially developed software module to reveal universal properties and effectiveness of different strategies of firms in stable and chaos states.

The paper is organized as follows: part 2 describes related works, part 3 demonstrates agent-based model with heterogeneous firms according to new paradigm; part 4 demonstrates desktop application *Model* for computational experiments; part 5 includes computational investigations of universal properties of agent-based model using this application; the last part concludes.

2 Related Works

2.1 Behavioral Economics as Real Life Approach

Critics of mainstream economics typically vest important weight on the differences between people and the 'agents' that populate economic theory and economic models. Behavioral economics (BE) within the mainstream has encouraged a 'paradigm shift' which includes the rejection of 'rational economic man'. The current leading developers of BE are generally more circumspect, claiming that their approach complements the standard theory. However, they generally join the majority of critics in supposing that microeconomics is restricted to improve its empirical relevance to the extent that it substitutes the study of people for that of abstract economic agents. Another approach promotes standard economic agents as 'rational fools', through the argument that since economic agents lack some essential social properties of human individuals, microeconomics requires fundamental reform to make progress in explaining human behavior [12]. Bounded rationality was essentially derived from Simon's view of the impossibility of full rationality on the part of economic agents. Modern complexity theory uses agent-based modeling for specific behavioral responses to be assigned to agents who interact without full rationality [13].

'Self-regarding agents' are economic actors who make decisions independently of social context and without regard to the behavior of other consumers and firms. We can distinguish two selfish forms of behavior in the market: as rational economic behavior, i.e. the most effective from the gains and losses point of view (in the works of A. Smith) or as selfish from the psychological point of view (this is mostly presented by J. S. Mill's theory). Competitiveness of egoists assumes that somebody has to lose, because someone gains (zero sum game).

Other-regarding behavior, such as altruism, altruistic punishment, reciprocity, cannot be fully captured in the standard economic model. Altruism is a deep and complex phenomenon which has few distinct but related concepts need to be distinguished: (a) psychological altruism, the genuine motivation to improve others' interests and welfare; (b) reproductive altruism, which involves increasing others' chances of survival and reproduction at the agent's expense; (c) behavioral altruism, which involves bearing some cost in the interest of others; and (d) preference altruism, which is a preference for others' interests [14]. Standard economic assumptions about human behavior make pure altruism an irrational "anomaly" that cannot survive the evolutionary selection process. However, recent findings from neuroscience, behavioral economics, and evolutionary game theory have grounded realistic, science-based, and policy-relevant foundation of other-regarding behavior.

2.2   Agent-Based Approach and Types of Economic Agents

Author [15] traces four origins of agent-based computational economics (ACE), namely, the markets origin, the cellular-automata origin, the tournaments origin, and the experiments origin. These origins have motivated different designs of agents in ACE, which starts from the work on simple programmed agents, randomly behaving agents, zero-intelligence agents, human-written programmed agents, autonomous agents, and empirically calibrated agents, and extends to the newly developing cognitive agents, psychological agents, and culturally sensitive agents. These concepts are part of a general attempt to study humans and their behavior. There is deep shift in the conception of the economy, focusing on five areas: mechanism design, zero-intelligence agents, 'market microstructure', engineering economics and artificial intelligence. The shift identified markets as diverse algorithms [16].

These micro-behavioral foundations of agents help us to examine results of agent interaction by complementing analytic modeling and game theory analyses. They help us to investigate the role of social responsibilities in constraining individual strategies and economic behavior more precisely than in orthodox microeconomics. Simulation agent-based model of firms with competing types give us a more dynamic view of the interplay between different types of agents. Attention here has been paid to social norms, social influence and microeconomic dynamics across different disciplines such as behavioral sciences, computer science and experimental microeconomics [17]. Modern markets and economic agents are reproduced by artificial evolutionary systems. Agent-based computational models are used for modeling of institutes in economics [18]. We can experimentally test effectiveness of different strategies by using a multi-agent simulation [19, 20]. Agent-based evolutionary simulation can answer the question how benefits and prediction of economic agents' decision making will co-evolve. Recent findings from human-subject economic experiments on the effects of granularity on decision making will give various learning models used in agent-based computational economics, such as reinforcement learning and evolutionary computation. The structure and method of the model in is similar to a conventional agent-based model except the authors allow to evolve decision rules for each agent rather than supplying those rules ourselves. This allows agents to change their behavior, i.e. to learn and adapt, as their environment changes. Involved agents can interfere in microeconomic system consciously and purposefully. The authors [21] discuss developing and using agent-based models for evaluating effects of economic policy interventions. To ensure that derived policies are suitable to intervene in the real world and not just the stylization of it, we can discuss the adequacy and reliability of agent-based models as well as interpretation of simulation results.

2.3   Implications of Agent-Based Model and Nash Equilibrium

The dynamic non-linear nature of complex microeconomic systems makes mathematical modeling and simulation software crucial. Complexity generates a greater role for mathematical models, especially game theory approach which captures the dynamics of human actions and their interactions [22]. Only strict Nash equilibria of the game are the competitive equilibria of economic agents. This result has two main corollaries: (i) competitive equilibria can be strategically stable even in small microeconomic system; (ii) competitive equilibria have good local stability properties under a large class of evolutionary learning dynamics [23]. Some Nash solutions are not relevant for multiple equilibria microeconomic systems as they are not stable under evolutionary or adaptive learning [24].

An agent-based model is a computer simulation driven by the individual decisions of programmed agents. Such models provide a promising alternative to traditional economic modeling in that they can fully capture the diversity of agents and the institutional detail of the underlying an microeconomic system modeling financial markets [25]. Methodological tools comprised of evolutionary game theory and agent-based modeling is used to study oligopoly competition in different industries, such as oil, motor-car, aircraft industry etc. [26]. Evolutionary stability of Nash equilibrium for supply chain is distinct under different (linear and nonlinear) demand types. The evolutionarily stable strategies of supply chain depend on preference parameters of producer and retailer, such as fairness and altruism concerns. Evolutionary agent-based model can be used to evaluate climate policies that take the heterogeneity of strategies of individual agents into account. Agent-based simulation is used to study firm growth and firm dynamics in a stochastic evolutionary model using econometrical methods [27].

3   Dynamical Microeconomic Model

In general, almost any microeconomic market model is constructed as follows: (1) n firms operate in the market (to simplify the notation suppose $n = 2$); (2) these firms produce homogeneous products in quantities $x_1(t)$ and $x_2(t)$ in time period t; (3) they use adaptive approach, i.e. they try to predict the quantity of their competitor in the next time period; (4) let $x_j^e(t+1)$ is the expected quantity of rival j by a firm i in next period $t+1$ $(i, j = 1, 2)$. Then under planning of their quantity $x_i(t+1)$ in the next period the firms decide the following optimization problem:

$$Max\Pi_1(x_1(t+1); x_2^e(t+1)), \ Max\Pi_2(x_1^e(t+1); x_2(t+1)),$$

where Π_i, $i = 1$, 2 is a profit function of firm i. The assumption about unchangeable quantity of the competitor (i.e. firm i will use $x_j(t)$ instead of $x_j^e(t+1)$ when it solves the optimization problem) is an example of imperfect, bounded rationality in firm's strategies; it is called naive expectations. As a rule these two approaches (adaptive and naive) coexist in the market with a certain probability. Our model is based on this assumption.

First we consider general microeconomic agent-based model of homogeneous product market and then we study partial cases of this model.

3.1   General Dynamic Market Model

We consider a market of homogeneous product, where exogenous parameter $n(t)$ indicates how many firms operate at time t. Each firm produces output $x_i(t)$, where $i = 1, \ldots, n(t)$. Thus the industry output of the firms is $Q(t) = \sum\limits_{i=1}^{n} x(t)$ at time t. Product price P is given by isoelastic demand function $P = P(Q) = b(t)/Q$ ($b(t) > 0$). This demand function leads to a non-linear dynamics. Alternative demand function is linear $P = P(Q) = b(t) - c(t) \cdot Q(t)$ ($b, c > 0$) which is used to test the general model's properties.

Firm maximizes both its own profit $\pi_X = (P - v) \cdot x - fc$ (where v is the firm's cost per unit in the market; fc is fixed cost) and consumer surplus CS (difference between maximum price which consumer can pay and real price) of its market segment (loyal consumers) $CS = \Theta \cdot \left(\int\limits_{\varepsilon}^{Q} P(q) dq - P \cdot Q \right)$, where parameter Θ specifies the segment of the market, which the reciprocator firm believes its own and optimizes; ε is the minimal technologically possible product quantity. Then $CS = \Theta \left(b \cdot \ln(\frac{Q}{\varepsilon}) - \frac{b}{Q} \cdot Q \right) = b\Theta \cdot \left(\ln(\frac{Q}{\varepsilon}) - 1 \right) = b\Theta \cdot \ln\frac{Q}{\hat{\varepsilon}}$, where $\hat{\varepsilon} = \varepsilon \cdot e$ (specific choice of ε does not affect the model dynamics and so we suppose $\varepsilon = 1$). Then general profit function of firm is:

$$\Pi = \alpha \cdot \pi + (1 - \alpha) \cdot CS = \alpha \cdot ((P - v) \cdot x - fc) + (1 - \alpha) \cdot b\Theta \cdot \ln\frac{Q}{\varepsilon}, \quad (1)$$

where α is share of short-run own profit π in the objective function, $1 - \alpha$ is share of stable expected long-run profit CS, fc is a fixed cost. In other words Π is a weighted average short-run profit π and expected stable long-run profit CS.

Two types of agent-based market model

1. In the model we assume that only two types of firms operate in the market with homogeneous product. Among them are k reciprocator firms ($\alpha \equiv \alpha_i < 1$, $i = 1, \ldots, k$) and $n - k$ selfish firms ($\alpha_j = 1$, $j = k + 1, \ldots, n$).
2. All firms of each type are identical. It means that the output of each firm of the same type is equal in equivalent model.

3. In models we consider all actions, expectations and strategies of firms in short-run period, therefore the models parameters are assumed as constants which are independent of time.

Thus we consider a market of homogeneous product, where n firms operate, among them are k identical reciprocator firms with the same output x and $n - k$ identical selfish firms with the same output y. According to Eq. (1) the profit function of selfish firm is $\pi_Y = (P - v) \cdot y$, profit function of reciprocator firm is a $\Pi = \alpha \cdot (P - v) \cdot x + (1 - \alpha) \cdot b\Theta \cdot \ln(Q/\varepsilon)$.

Dynamic of the model is considered for discrete time $t = 1, 2, \ldots$. Then $x_i(t)$, $y_j(t)$ be the outputs at time t of reciprocator and selfish firms respectively. Thus the industry output of the two types of firms is $Q = k \cdot x + (n - k) \cdot y$. Our model is uniquely defined by firms' objective functions and their expectations types. It does not use any additional assumptions or restrictions.

3.2 Quantity Setting Strategy of Firms with Naive Expectations

Each selfish firm j $(j = k + 1, \ldots, n)$ is looking correspondingly for such value of $y_j(t + 1)$ at which it maximizes its profit π_j, suggesting that all other firms leave their quantities $x_i(t)$, $y_{-j}(t)$ unchanged $(x_i^e(t + 1) = x_i(t),\ y_j^e(t + 1) = y_j(t))$:

$$Max\pi_j(x_1^e(t+1),\ldots,x_k^e(t+1); y_1^e(t+1),\ldots,y_{j-1}^e(t+1), y_j(t+1), y_{j+1}^e(t+1)\ldots,y_{n-k}^e(t+1)) =$$
$$Max\pi_j(x_1(t),\ldots,x_k(t); y_1(t),\ldots,y_{j-1}(t), y_j(t+1), y_{j+1}(t),\ldots,y_{n-k}(t)).$$

Here $x_1(t) = \ldots = x_k(t) = x(t)$, and $y_{k+1}(t) = \ldots = y_n(t) = y(t)$, profit maximization quantity of selfish firm is determined from first order condition:

$$\frac{\partial \pi_j}{\partial y_j(t+1)} = \frac{b(y_j(t+1) + kx(t) + (n - k - 1)y(t) - by_j(t+1)}{(y_j(t+1) + kx(t) + (n - k - 1)y(t))^2} - v = 0,$$

where from $v(y_j(t+1) + kx(t) + (n - k - 1)y(t))^2 = b(kx(t) + (n - k - 1)y(t))$. Then we obtain reaction function of selfish firm:

$$y_j(t+1) = \sqrt{\frac{b}{v}(kx(t) + (n - k - 1)y(t))} - (kx(t) + (n - k - 1)y(t)). \qquad (2)$$

Similarly each reciprocator firm i is looking for such value of $x_i(t + 1)$ at which it maximizes its own profit function, suggesting that all other firms leave their quantities $x_{-i}(t)$, $y_j(t)$ unchanged: $x_i^e(t + 1) = x_i(t),\ y_j^e(t + 1) = y_j(t)$:

$$Max\Pi_i(x_1^e(t+1),\ldots,x_{i-1}^e(t+1), x_i(t+1), x_{i+1}^e(t+1),\ldots,x_k^e(t+1); y_1^e(t+1),\ldots,y_{n-k}^e(t+1)) =$$
$$Max\Pi_i(x_1(t),\ldots,x_{i-1}(t), x_i(t+1), x_{i+1}(t),\ldots,x_k(t); y_1(t),\ldots,y_{n-k}(t)).$$

Here profit maximization quantity of reciprocity firm is determined from the following FOC:

$$\frac{\partial \Pi_i}{\partial x_i(t+1)} = \alpha \cdot \left(\frac{b(x_i(t+1) + (k-1)x(t) + (n-k)y(t)) - bx_i(t+1)}{(x_i(t+1) + (k-1)x(t) + (n-k)y(t))^2} x_i(t+1) - v \right)$$

$$+ (1-\alpha) \cdot b\Theta \cdot \frac{1}{x_i(t+1) + (k-1)x(t) + (n-k)y(t)} = 0.$$

Then after equivalent algebraic transformation we get:

$$v(x_i(t+1) + (k-1)x(t) + (n-k)y(t))^2 = b((k-1)x(t) + (n-k)y(t))$$
$$+ \frac{1-\alpha b}{\alpha k}(x_i(t+1) + (k-1)x(t) + (n-k)y(t)).$$

Let $z = x_i(t+1) + (k-1)x(t) + (n-k)y(t)$, then we can rewrite previous equation as follows $z^2 = \frac{b}{v} \cdot ((k-1)x(t) + (n-k)y(t)) + \frac{1-\alpha}{\alpha} \cdot \frac{b}{vk} \cdot z$. Therefore $\left(z - \frac{1}{2}\frac{1-\alpha}{\alpha}\frac{b}{vk} \right)^2 = \frac{b}{v} \cdot ((k-1)x(t) + (n-k)y(t)) + \left(\frac{1}{2} \cdot \frac{1-\alpha}{\alpha} \cdot \frac{b}{vk} \right)^2$, whence $z - \frac{1}{2}\frac{1-\alpha}{\alpha}\frac{b}{vk} = \sqrt{\frac{b}{v} \cdot ((k-1)x(t) + (n-k)y(t)) + \left(\frac{1}{2} \cdot \frac{1-\alpha}{\alpha} \cdot \frac{b}{vk} \right)^2}$.

Hence, in view of (2), we obtain a dynamic system model of firms' reaction functions:

$$\begin{cases} x_i(t+1) = \sqrt{\frac{b}{v}((k-1)x_i(t) + (n-k)y_j(t)) + (\frac{1}{2}\frac{1-\alpha}{\alpha}\frac{b}{vk})^2} - ((k-1)x_i(t) + (n-k)y_j(t)) + \frac{1}{2}\frac{1-\alpha}{\alpha}\frac{b}{vk}, \\ y_j(t+1) = \sqrt{\frac{b}{v}(kx(t) + (n-k-1)y(t))} - (kx(t) + (n-k-1)y(t)). \end{cases} \quad (3)$$

The last equations of this system mean that k reciprocator firms and $n-k$ selfish firms are identical for all discrete time $t = 0, 1, \ldots$. At Nash equilibrium (NE) we have $x(t+1) = x(t) = x$, $y(t+1) = y(t) = y$ for all t. After algebraic transformation equations from system (3) we obtain:

$$\begin{cases} x = \frac{\alpha + (1-\alpha)\frac{n-k}{k}}{2\alpha-1} \cdot y, \\ y = \frac{k(2\alpha-1)}{\alpha k + (1-\alpha)(n-k)} \cdot x. \end{cases}$$

After solving system (4) we have Proposition 1.

Proposition 1. There is a unique Nash equilibrium for the dynamic system (3) with naïve expectations:

$$\begin{cases} x^* = \frac{b}{vn}\left(1 - \frac{2\alpha-1}{\alpha n}\right)\left(1 + \frac{1-\alpha}{\alpha}\frac{n-k}{k}\right), \\ y^* = \frac{b}{vn}\frac{2\alpha-1}{\alpha}\left(1 - \frac{2\alpha-1}{\alpha n}\right). \end{cases} \quad (4)$$

Is this point stable? Consider the following propositions.

Proposition 2. For any given b, $v > 0$ and α $(0 \le \alpha \le 1)$ Jacobian J of system (3) for Nash equilibrium (4) is proportional to value $n - 1$ for sufficiently large n. Its absolute value increases with growth of n, if $\left|\frac{k}{n}\right| > \varepsilon$ and $\left|\frac{k}{n} - \frac{3}{4}\right| > \varepsilon$ for any $\varepsilon > 0$.

Proof of Proposition 2 is presented in paper [10].

Proposition 3. For any given b, $v > 0$ and α $(0 \le \alpha \le 1)$ fixed point (4) of discrete dynamic system (7) is unstable for sufficiently large number of firms n if $\left|\frac{k}{n}\right| > \varepsilon$ and $\left|\frac{k}{n} - \frac{3}{4}\right| > \varepsilon$ for any $\varepsilon > 0$.

Proof. According to Proposition 2 absolute value of Jacobian J is proportional to value $n - 1$ for sufficiently large n. If $|\det J| > 1$ then at least one of its eigenvalues is greater than 1, which means the instability of the fixed point (4).

3.3   Quantity Setting Strategy of Firms with Adaptive Expectations

Since all selfish firms and all reciprocator firms are assumed as identical and they have the same strategies at moment t so it is natural to suggest that their production quantities will be equal at next moment $t + 1$ too. This is a step from naïve expectation to adaptive one which is required by common sense.

In accordance with such expectations each selfish firm j $(j = k+1, \ldots, n)$ believes under quantity setting that $y_j(t+1) = y_1^e(t+1), \ldots, y_{n-k}^e(t+1)$. So this firm solves the following optimization task to define its own output:

$$Max\pi_j(x_1^e(t+1), \ldots, x_k^e(t+1); y_1^e(t+1), \ldots, y_{j-1}^e(t+1), y_j(t+1), y_{j+1}^e(t+1), \ldots, y_{n-k}^e(t+1)) =$$
$$Max\pi_j(x_1(t), \ldots, x_k(t); y_1(t+1), \ldots, y_j(t+1), y_j(t+1), y_j(t+1) \ldots, y_j(t+1)).$$

Here $x_1(t) = \ldots = x_k(t) = x(t)$, $y_{k+1}(t) = \ldots = y_n(t) = y(t)$. Profit maximizing output $y_j(t+1)$ for selfish firm is defined from condition $\frac{\partial \pi_j}{\partial y_j(t+1)} = \frac{b(kx(t) + (n-k)y_j(t+1)) - b(n-k)y_j(t+1)}{(kx(t) + (n-k)y_j(t+1))^2} - v = 0$. From here $(kx(t) + (n - k)y_j(t+1))^2 = \frac{b}{v}kx(t)$, then $(n - k)y_j(t+1) = \sqrt{\frac{b}{v}kx(t)} - kx(t)$.

Similarly under quantity setting each reciprocator firm i $(j = 1, \ldots, k)$ in accordance with common sense assumes that $x_i(t+1) = x_1^e(t+1) = \ldots = x_k^e(t+1)$. Therefore, to determine its quantity in the next period this firm solves the following optimization problem:

$$MaxΠ_i(x_1^e(t+1), \ldots, x_{i-1}^e(t+1), x_i(t+1), x_{i+1}^e(t+1), \ldots, x_k^e(t+1); y_{k+1}^e(t+1), \ldots, y_n^e(t+1)) =$$
$$MaxΠ_i(x_i(t+1), \ldots, x_i(t+1), x_i(t+1), x_i(t+1), \ldots, x_k(t+1); y_{k+1}(t), \ldots, y_n(t)).$$

Profit maximizing output $x_i(t+1)$ for reciprocity firm is determined from the following condition

$$\frac{\partial \pi_i}{\partial y_i(t+1)} = \alpha \cdot \left(\frac{b(kx_i(t+1) + (n-k)y(t)) - bkx_i(t+1)}{(kx_i(t) + (n-k)y(t))^2} - v \right) + (1-\alpha) \cdot b\Theta$$
$$\cdot \frac{k}{kx_i(t+1) + (n-k)y(t)} = 0.$$

From   here $(kx_i(t+1) + (n-k)y(t))^2 = \frac{b}{v}(n-k)y(t) + b\,\Theta \cdot \frac{1-\alpha}{\alpha} \cdot (kx_i(t+1) + (n-k) \cdot y(t))$.   Let $z = kx_i(t+1) + (n-k) \cdot y(t)$,   then $\left(z - \frac{1}{2}\frac{1-\alpha}{\alpha}\frac{by}{v} \right)^2 = \frac{b}{v} \cdot (n-k)y(t) + \left(\frac{1}{2} \cdot \frac{1-\alpha}{\alpha} \cdot \frac{by}{v} \right)^2$.   From this $z - \frac{1}{2}\frac{1-\alpha}{\alpha}\frac{by}{v} = \sqrt{\frac{b}{v} \cdot (n-k)y(t) + \left(\frac{1}{2} \cdot \frac{1-\alpha}{\alpha} \cdot \frac{by}{v} \right)^2}$. Thus we obtain dynamic equation system (5) reaction functions of firms with adaptive expectations:

$$\begin{cases} kx_i(t+1) = \sqrt{\frac{b}{v}(n-k)y(t) + (\frac{1}{2}\frac{1-\alpha}{\alpha}\frac{by}{v})^2} - (n-k)y_j(t) + \frac{1}{2}\frac{1-\alpha}{\alpha}\frac{by}{v}, \\ (n-k)y_j(t+1) = \sqrt{\frac{b}{v}kx(t)} - kx(t). \end{cases} \qquad (5)$$

Conditions $x_1(t) = \ldots = x_k(t) = x(t)$ and $y_{k+1}(t) = \ldots = y_n(t) = y(t)$ imply $x_1(t+1) = \ldots = x_k(t+1) = x(t+1)$ and $y_{k+1}(t+1) = \ldots = y_n(t+1) = y(t+1)$. It means the dynamic system has two dimension phase space.

At Nash equilibrium we have $x(t+1) = x(t) = x$, $y(t+1) = y(t) = y$ for all $t = 0, 1, \ldots$ After algebraic transformation equations from system (5) we get:

$$\begin{cases} x = \frac{n-k}{k} \cdot \frac{\alpha + (1-\alpha)\gamma}{\alpha - (1-\alpha)\gamma} \cdot y, \\ y = \frac{k}{n-k} \cdot \frac{\alpha - (1-\alpha)\gamma}{\alpha + (1-\alpha)\gamma} \cdot x. \end{cases}$$

After solving system (5) we have Proposition 4.

Proposition 4. There is a unique Nash equilibrium for the dynamic system with adaptive expectations (5):

$$\begin{cases} x^* = \frac{b}{vk} \left(\frac{\alpha + (1-\alpha)\gamma}{2\alpha} \right)^2, \\ y^* = \frac{b}{v(n-k)} \frac{\alpha^2 - ((1-\alpha)\gamma)^2}{(2\alpha)^2}. \end{cases} \qquad (6)$$

As above without loss of generality, we can always assume $\gamma = 1$, otherwise we can redefine the share of profit $\tilde{\alpha} = \frac{\alpha}{\alpha + (1-\alpha)\gamma}$. If $\gamma = 1$ then system (6) takes the form

$$\begin{cases} x^* = \frac{b}{vk} \cdot \frac{1}{(2\alpha)^2}, \\ y^* = \frac{b}{v(n-k)} \cdot \frac{2\alpha - 1}{(2\alpha)^2}. \end{cases} \qquad (7)$$

Proposition 5. The equilibrium point (7) is stable for all affordable values of the parameters.

Proof. Dynamic system (5) is stable at the Nash equilibrium point (7) if and only if when Jacobian J of this system in (7) satisfies the following Shur's conditions:

$$\begin{cases} 1 + tr\,J + \det J > 0, \\ 1 - tr\,J + \det J > 0, \\ 1 - \det J > 0. \end{cases}$$

Here for the Jacobian of system (5):

$$J = \begin{pmatrix} J_{xx} & J_{xy} \\ J_{yx} & J_{yy} \end{pmatrix} = \begin{pmatrix} \frac{\partial x(t+1)}{\partial x(t)} & \frac{\partial x(t+1)}{\partial y(t)} \\ \frac{\partial y(t+1)}{\partial x(t)} & \frac{\partial y(t+1)}{\partial y(t)} \end{pmatrix}.$$

It is clear that $J_{xx} = J_{yy} = 0$, whence $trJ = J_{xx} + J_{yy} = 0$. Thus, to verify the Shur's conditions it is sufficient to establish that $\det J < 1$. But at point (6) $y^* = \frac{b}{v(n-k)} \frac{\alpha^2 - ((1-\alpha)\gamma)^2}{(2\alpha)^2}$ and thus

$$kJ_{xy} = \frac{\frac{b}{v}(n-k)}{2\sqrt{\frac{b}{v}(n-k)y^* + d^2}} - (n-k) = \frac{\frac{b}{v}(n-k)}{2\sqrt{\frac{b}{v}(n-k)\frac{b}{v(n-k)}\frac{\alpha^2 - ((1-\alpha)\gamma)^2}{(2\alpha)^2} + (\frac{1}{2}\frac{b}{v}\gamma\frac{1-\alpha}{\alpha})^2}} - (n-k)$$

$$kJ_{xy} = \frac{n-k}{2\sqrt{\frac{\alpha^2}{4\alpha^2}}} - (n-k) = 0$$

Therefore $\det J = J_{xx} \cdot J_{yy} - J_{xy} \cdot J_{yx} = 0$, Q.E.D.

Product price P is given by the isoelastic market demand function $P = P(Q) = \frac{b}{Q}$, industry output is $Q = k \cdot x + (n-k) \cdot y$ and price is no less than 1 cent $P \geq 0.01$. It means that output of reciprocator and selfish firm is $x_0 \leq \frac{100b}{k}$ and $y_0 \leq \frac{100b}{n-k}$ correspondingly.

Corollary. The trajectories of the dynamical system (5) converge to the fixed point (6) for any initial values $x_0 \leq \frac{100b}{k}$ and $y_0 \leq \frac{100b}{n-k}$.

3.4   Quantity Setting Strategy in General Case

In real life both decision making approaches (adaptive and naive) coexist in the market with a certain probability p for adaptive and correspondingly $q = 1 - p$ for naïve expectations. According to such expectations typical (representative) reciprocator firm i suggests that production quantities of its rival j will be equal to $x_j^e(t+1) = p \cdot x_j(t) + q \cdot x_i(t+1)$ $(j = 1, \ldots, k, \; j \neq i)$. Typical reciprocator firm i $(i = 1, \ldots, k)$ resolves following optimization problem:

$$MaxΠ_i(x_1^e(t+1),\ldots,x_i(t+1),\ldots,x_k^e(t+1);y_1^e(t+1),\ldots,y_{n-k}^e(t+1)) =$$
$$MaxΠ_i(px_1(t)+qx_i(t),\ldots,x_i(t+1),\ldots,px_k(t)+qx_i(t+1);y_1(t),\ldots,y_{n-k}(t)).$$

Similarly typical selfish firm j $(j=1,\ldots,n-k)$ solves following optimization problem:

$$Maxπ_j(x_1^e(t+1),\ldots,x_k^e(t+1);y_1^e(t+1),\ldots,y_j(t+1),\ldots,y_{n-k}^e(t+1)) =$$
$$Maxπ_j(x_1(t),\ldots,x_k(t);py_1(t)+qy_j(t+1),\ldots,y_j(t+1),\ldots,py_{n-k}(t)+qy_j(t+1)).$$

This hybrid case leads to following dynamics (when $x_1(t)=\ldots=x_k(t)$, $i=1,\ldots,k$, $y_{k+1}(t)=\ldots=y_n(t), j=k+1,\ldots,n$):

$$
\begin{cases}
(1+p(k-1))x_i(t+1) = \sqrt{\frac{b}{v}w_x+d^2}+d-w_x,\ i=1,\ldots,k,\\
(1+p(n-k-1))y_j(t+1) = \sqrt{\frac{b}{v}w_y}-w_y,\ j=k+1,\ldots,n,
\end{cases}
\tag{8}
$$

where $d=\frac{1}{2}\frac{1-\alpha}{\alpha}\frac{b(1+p(k-1))}{vk}$ and $\begin{cases} w_x = q(k-1)x_i(t)+(n-k)y_j(t),\\ w_y = kx_i(t)+q(n-k-1)y_j(t). \end{cases}$

Reaction curve for system (8) after algebraic transformation will be as follows

$$\frac{x}{y} = G = \frac{p(n-k)+q(\alpha+(1-\alpha)\frac{n-k}{k})}{(2\alpha-1)(1+p(k-1))}. \tag{9}$$

After substitution $\frac{x}{y}$ in equation $((kx+(n-k)y)^2 = \frac{b}{v}(kx+q(n-k-1)y)$ we will have $y^2(kG+(n-k))^2 = \frac{b}{v}y(kG+q(n-k-1))$, hence it yields:

Proposition 6. There is a unique Nash equilibrium for the general dynamic system (8):

$$
\begin{cases}
x^* = Gy = \frac{(b/v)(k+q(1/G)(n-k-1))}{v(k+(1/G)(n-k))^2},\\
y^* = \frac{(b/v)(kG+q(n-k-1))}{(kG+(n-k))^2}.
\end{cases}
\tag{10}
$$

where G is given as reaction function $G(p,q,n,k,\alpha)$.

Proposition 7. For $p=0$ $(q=1)$, the equilibrium point $(x^*;y^*)$ of general dynamic system coincides with Nash equilibrium (4) of the dynamical system (3) with naïve expectations. For $p=1$ $(q=0)$, the equilibrium point $(x^*;y^*)$ coincides with the equilibrium point (6) of the dynamical system (5) with adaptive expectations.

Proof. For $p=0$, $q=1$ reaction curve (9) takes the form $\frac{x}{y} = G = \frac{\alpha+(1-\alpha)\frac{n-k}{k}}{2\alpha-1}$ which corresponds to reaction curve under naïve expectations. For $p=1$, $q=0$ reaction curve (9) has a look $\frac{x}{y} = \frac{n-k}{(2\alpha-1)k}$ which corresponds to reaction curve under adaptive expectations.

For $p=0$, $q=1$ in denominator and numerator of (10) we will have $kG+(n-k) = k\frac{\alpha+(1-\alpha)\frac{n-k}{k}}{(2\alpha-1)}+(n-k) = \frac{\alpha n}{2\alpha-1}$ and $\frac{\alpha n}{2\alpha-1}-1$ accordingly. From here

$y^* = \frac{(b/v)(\alpha n - (2\alpha - 1)(2\alpha - 1))}{(\alpha n)^2} = \frac{b}{vn} \cdot \frac{2\alpha - 1}{\alpha} \cdot \left(1 - \frac{2\alpha - 1}{\alpha}\right)$. This result coincides with NE for naïve expectations (4).

For $p = 1, q = 0$ in numerator and denominator of (10) we will have $kG = \frac{n-k}{2\alpha - 1}$ and $kG + (n - k) = (n - k) \cdot \left(1 + \frac{1}{2\alpha - 1}\right)$ accordingly. After cancellation on $n - k$ we receive $y^* = \frac{b}{v} \frac{\frac{1}{2\alpha - 1}}{(n-k) \cdot \left(1 + \frac{1}{2\alpha - 1}\right)^2} = \frac{b}{v(n-k)} \cdot \frac{2\alpha - 1}{(2\alpha)^2}$ which coincides with NE for adaptive expectations (6). Thus values for y^* coincide for both types of expectations. Since values of y^* unambiguously follow from reaction curve $x^* = Gy^*$ because values for x^* coincide too, Q.E.D.

4 Software Module for Computational Investigations of Dynamic Models

During our research we developed software module as desktop application *Model* to support the research process using computational experiments with dynamic systems on small-dimensional phase spaces: one-, two- and three-dimension. The main purpose of the application is to provide the best service for research cycle: hypothesis → experiment → hypothesis. For full-scale experiments after appearance of a new idea we can check it using application window with the appropriate tools. The results of new experiment give rise to new ideas; which we can check immediately using new windows and so on. The highest possible support for this process is the goal of *Model*.

Model is a C# application created on the basis of the graphical interface of the C# System.Drawing and System.Windows.Forms system libraries. All calculations related to the model are localized in the *Calc* method, which makes it easy to modify the equations of the model or move to other models. The following figure represents the diagram of the *Model* application (Fig. 1). *Model* application additionally uses *Open Maple* to work with differential equations and 3D graphs.

Open Maple is access interface to Maple computational core from various programming languages: C#, Java, Visual Basic etc. In addition to the above standards is also used the System.Runtime.InteropServices namespace, which allow us to make links to the Maple dynamic linking core library - maplec.dll.

The following figure demonstrates the main application window which automatically appears when you open it (Fig. 2).

In the center of the window is located a two-dimensional projection of Lorentz system's attractor. In Fig. 2 above in the left corner are the application menu buttons. From left to right: 1. *Save* button is used to save current model which is displayed on the screen with all the given parameters' values and settings under the chosen user name. 2. *Edit* button is used to modify the current model. 3. *Open* button demonstrates a list of saved models' names with the date of their last modification, which allows you to select and open a window of any of them. 4. *Add* button is served to define new models. 5. *Delete* button gives possibility to delete the current model (depicted on the screen) from the list.

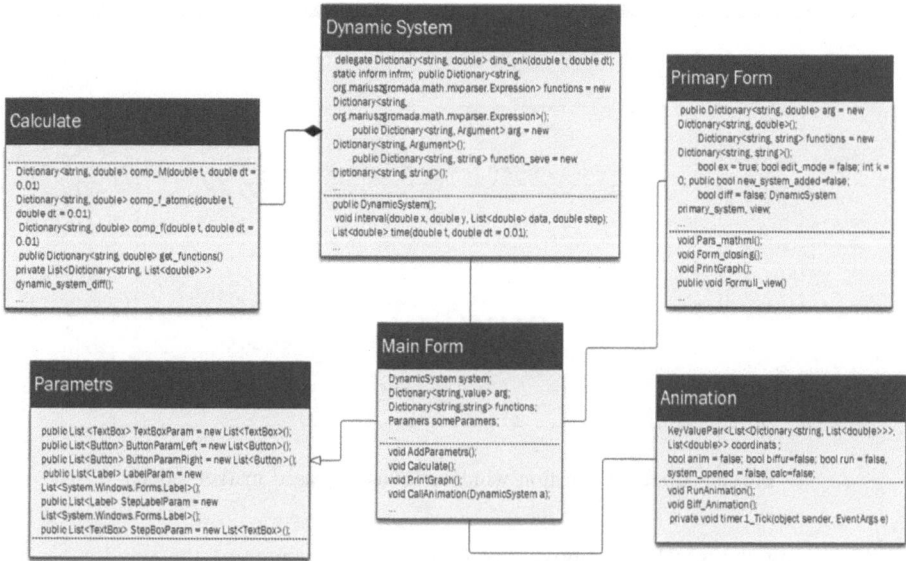

Fig. 1. Diagram of the *Model* application

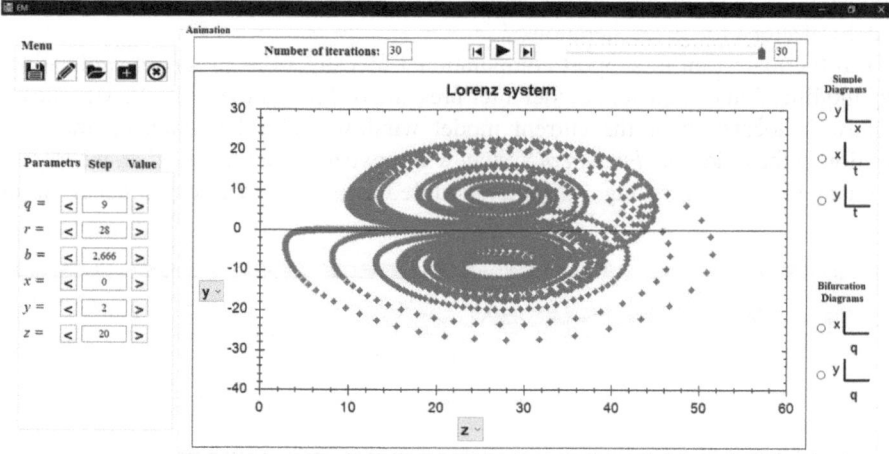

Fig. 2. Main window of the *Model* application

The following Fig. 3 shows the application window for our model.

On the right are 5 types of graphs, which are used most often; their examples are pointed out later in the paper. We can set model parameters and the initial values of the model trajectory using counters on the left. After these settings the graph of given model automatically appears in the center of the window. The number of iterations we

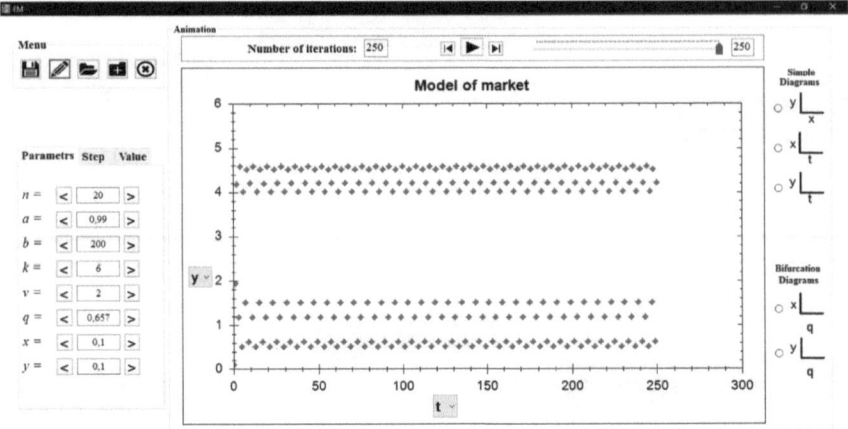

Fig. 3. *Model* application window for agent-based market model

can be set on the scroll bar above the graph. In the center of the window is also displayed the animation of the selected path when the button (near the scroll bar) is pressed.

When you click *Step* button on the left, you can set step of changing for a list of parameters. When you click *Value* button, you can obtain the table with coordinates of model trajectory for given iterations.

But the main tool to support computational investigations in *Model* application is easy modification of a current model after pressing of *Edit* button (Fig. 4). Modification window is located over the current model window. After left click on the model equation in the field *The dynamical system* will move to the field *Equation*, where it can be changed. After pressing *Add* the modified equation will return back. Similar

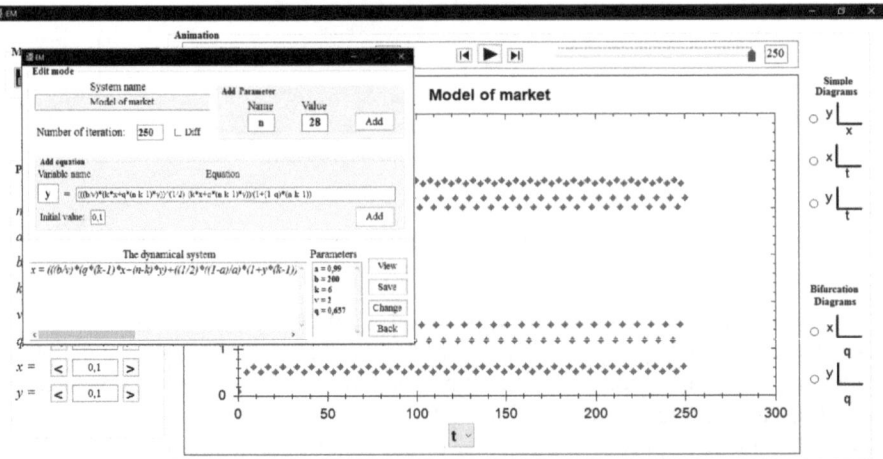

Fig. 4. *Model* application window for modifying the current model

procedure can be done with parameters. We can also add new equations and parameters and delete the previous ones. In the field *System name* we can specify the name of the new model modification. After clicking *Save* button, new model falls into the saved list. If you click *Change*, the new modification will be saved under the name of the current model, which is deleted. When you click *Back*, the modification is temporarily suspended and we return to the current window. *View* button displays information about the model (equations, parameters and settings).

5 Computational Investigation of Agent-Based Model Using Software Module

5.1 From Stability to Chaos with Increasing of Number of Firms in the Market

Apparently the main assumption of the traditional neoclassical microeconomics is the idea of automatic stabilization and market order due to increasing the number of independent firms and achievement of perfect competition. This is realization of Adam Smith's 'invisible hand'. Let us compare it with the behavior of our model after increasing number of firms n in the market.

Let $n = 26$; the number of reciprocator firms $k = 25$; $b = 200$; marginal cost $v = 2$; the share of profit in the objective function of reciprocator is $\alpha = 0.9$; probability of naive expectations is $q = 0.61$. The trajectory of dynamical system (8) with such initial parameters and initial output $x_0 = 0.1$, $y_0 = 0.1$ is shown in following Fig. 5.

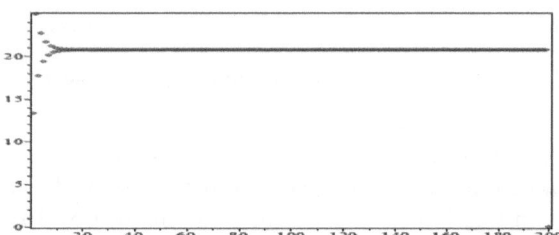

Fig. 5. Quantity trajectory of selfish firm under initial conditions ($n = 26$, $k = 25$, $b = 200$, $v = 2$, $q = 0.61$, $x_0 = 0.1$, $y_0 = 0.1$)

Here along horizontal axis are given iterations of system (3) from $t = 1$ to $t = 200$, along ordinate axis are given corresponding quantities of selfish firm $y(t) = y_j(t)$, $j = k+1, \ldots, n$. As you can see from the graph, the path quickly converges to the equilibrium quantity $y^* = y_j^* \approx 21$. The graph for quantity path of reciprocator firm $x(t) = x_i(t)$, $i = 1, \ldots, k$ looks like this one ($x^* = x_i^* \approx 2$) under the same conditions.

Let us consider the graph of the trajectory for the same parameters except n. Now let $n = 29$ (Fig. 6).

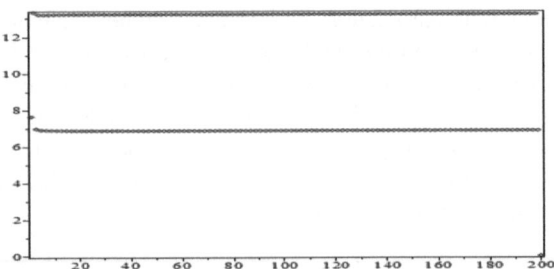

Fig. 6. Quantity trajectory of selfish firm in bifurcation point ($n = 29$)

In Fig. 6 instead of equilibrium point there appeared bifurcation and a stable cycle where $y(t)$ approximates to point $y^* \approx 13$ for even t and to point $y^* \approx 7$ for odd t. After doubling the lag between iterations is either even or odd iteration. Thus either quantity $y^* \approx 13$ or $y^* \approx 7$ respectively will be equilibrium output.

Stable cycle has already four points for $n = 36$ (Fig. 7). There was a new flip bifurcation.

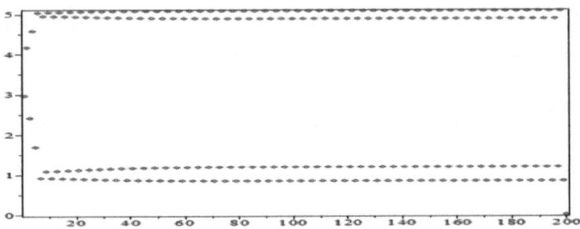

Fig. 7. Quantity trajectory of selfish firm for cycle of order 4 ($n = 36$)

Our research confirms the more firms number n the more series of doubling bifurcation cycle according to Shvarkovskii's order. State of dynamic chaos already exists for $n = 100$ (in Fig. 8 the ordinate values are divided by 10).

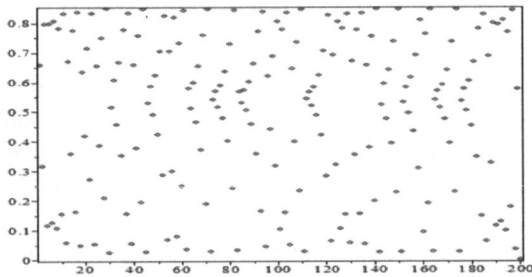

Fig. 8. The state of dynamic chaos for selfish firms' output ($n = 100$)

The reason for strengthening of market instability due to increasing the number of firms is disclosed in Proposition 2. To analyze this effect, which contradicts traditional microeconomics, let us consider how the change in the number of selfish firms affects the dynamics of the model for fixed total number of firms n. Let $n - k = 1$, $n = 100$, other parameters are the same as above. Figure 9 shows the graph of corresponding trajectory $y(t)$ which converges to Nash equilibrium.

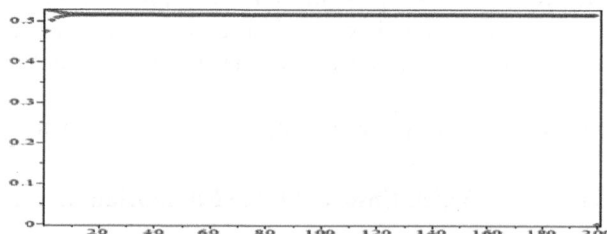

Fig. 9. Selfish firm's quantity trajectory for fixed $n = 100$ ($n - k = 1$)

Now let $n - k = 3$. There occurs a flip bifurcation (Fig. 10).

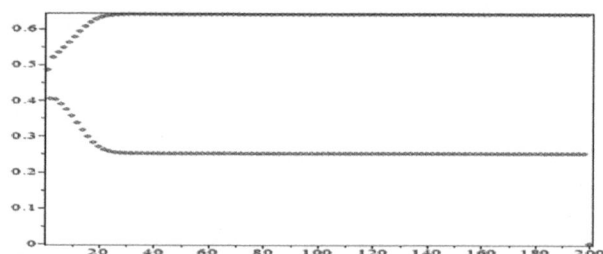

Fig. 10. Selfish firm's quantity trajectory for fixed $n = 100$ ($n - k = 3$)

Assume further that $k = 10$. We have one more flip bifurcation (Fig. 11).

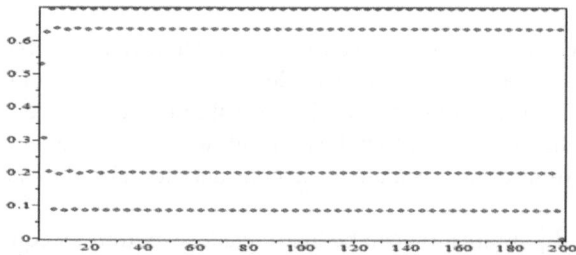

Fig. 11. Quantity trajectory of selfish firm for fixed $n = 100$ ($n - k = 10$)

If $k = 25$ or $k = 100 - 25 = 75$ we will get the same chaos as in Fig. 8. For $k = 100 - 10 = 90$, $k = 100 - 3 = 97$, $k = 100 - 1 = 99$ we obtain the same dynamics as in Figs. 11, 10 and 9 correspondingly.

Thus, if only identical firms act in the market, then a stable equilibrium exists. But if there is even an insignificant difference (segregation) between firms, it leads to complex dynamics and the transition to chaos due to increasing of firms number. The destabilizing role of number of firms for evolutionary games in oligopoly is well known [14]. But our model describes a simplest market where firms have only one difference in their type when some firms (egoists) are focused exclusively on short-run profits, while others (reciprocators) take into account long-run factors. And this difference is inevitable for any real life market.

How can we generally achieve the stability of a real market with such effects?

5.2   The Crucial Factor Which Ensures Stable Equilibrium in the Market

We found that adaptive behavior is the main tool that ensures the stability of markets. Due to growth of adaptive expectations (i.e. with increase in p) predictability and stability of market becomes stronger. At the same time due to growth of naive expectations ($q = 1 - p$), the market loses stability and chaos grows. The process of loss of stability and transition to chaos of dynamic system (8) with increasing of q is the most visual in the bifurcation diagram. Let $n = 20$, $k = 6$, $b = 200$, $v = 2$, $\alpha = 0.9$ (Fig. 12).

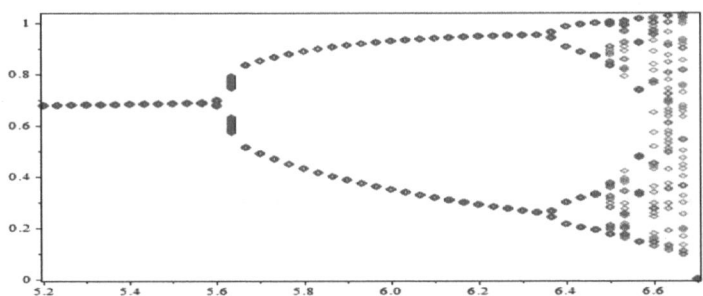

Fig. 12. The bifurcation diagram of dependence of quantity dynamics (3) on the probability of naive expectations (q)

Here along horizontal axis are given values of parameter q, along ordinate axis are given values of reciprocator firms on a stable cycle. If two-thirds of firms choose their output with naive expectations ($q \approx 0.67$), then the market will be in dynamic chaos state. The possibilities of *Model* application allow us to make sure that in all conceivable cases two-thirds here is a universal constant, not related to the choice of model parameters.

As the above flip bifurcation can be interpreted as splitting of equilibrium state into several directions and each firm prefers more profitable direction. *Model* tools allow us to demonstrate the dependence between reciprocator firm's profit π and probability of naïve expectations $q \approx 0.67$ (Fig. 13) for the same parameter values of bifurcation diagram.

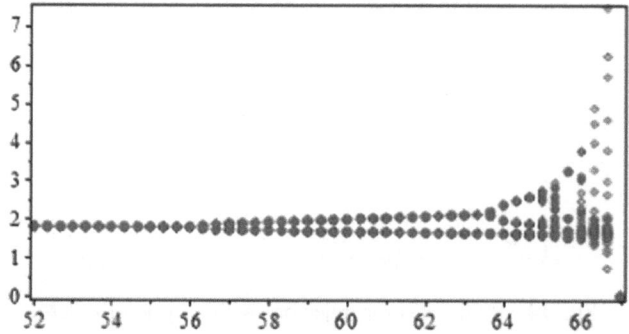

Fig. 13. The bifurcation diagram of dependence of profit π on the probability of naive expectations q

Real choice of bifurcation's direction here depends on quantity output. The smaller quantity output the bigger the firm's profit. Moreover, the profit for bigger output direction varies around zero and often converts into a loss. But quite unexpected is the effect in Fig. 13, when firm's profit in chaos state is on average greater than in stable state: $\sum_{t=m}^{T} \bar{\pi}(x_i^t) > \sum_{t=1}^{h} \bar{\pi}(x_i^t)$, $m > h$, where stable period exists during discrete time interval $t \in [1; h]$, whereas chaotic period continues during $t \in [m; T]$.

5.3 Competition Between Different Types of Firms

This part reveals the factor that ensures the stability of the market in a complex and even chaotic dynamics. If any type of firms increases their profit more quickly than their rivals then these firms will survive and expand their type between all firms. In our model, the profit ratio of reciprocator firm in time t $\pi_X(t) = (P - v) \cdot x(t)$ to profit of selfish firm $\pi_Y(t) = (P - v) \cdot y(t)$ in the same period will equal:

$$\lambda_{xy}(t) = \frac{\pi_x(t)}{\pi_y(t)} = \frac{(P(t) - v)x(t)}{(P(t) - v)y(t)} = \frac{x(t)}{y(t)}.$$

One more unexpected finding of our research during computational experiment is that in this model $\lambda_{xy}(t)$ is adiabatic invariant of a dynamical system, i.e. is almost independent for all acceptable values of parameters (for $t > 3$). As example, consider the phase curves for certain sets of parameter values used in Sect. 5.1, when increasing in the number of firms causes chaos in the market. The ration between the outputs of reciprocator and selfish firms remains unchanged both for steady state and dynamics chaos. For example, profit ratio for trajectory in Fig. 7 with a cycle of order 4 is presented in Fig. 14. Profit ratio for dynamic chaos trajectory (Fig. 8) is demonstrated in Fig. 15.

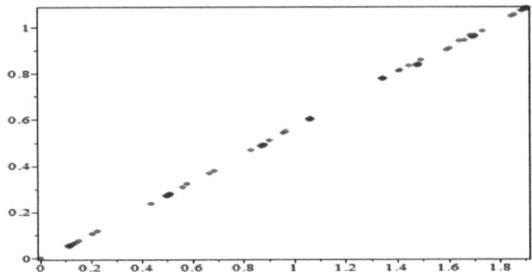

Fig. 14. Profit ratio for trajectory with a cycle of order 4

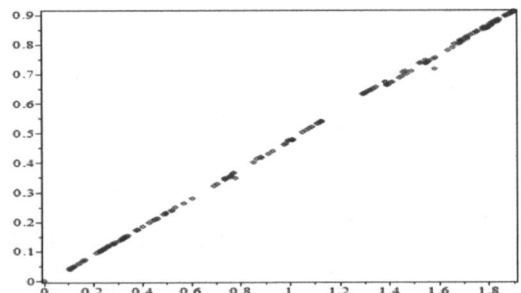

Fig. 15. Profit ratio for trajectory with dynamic chaos

The more chaotic dynamics, the more densely populated points of phase curve which almost coincide with line segment, whose slope is equal to $y(t)/x(t) = 1/\lambda_{xy}(t)$. It means that ratio between outputs of firms with heterogeneous type remains almost unchanged. Every conceivable example can be easily viewed through the application *Model* and gives the same result. This unexpected stability of the profits ratio and quantity outputs of heterogeneous firms under chaotic dynamics is an important stability factor of many real markets for which such dynamics are usual.

5.4 Universality of Model's Properties

Each market consists of heterogeneous firms which differ only in their types (selfish or reciprocator firms). But any national or global markets includes local markets, where different type of firms operate. Thus we can suppose that Sects. 5.1–5.3 are universal for real markets in new dynamic paradigm. It is a mistake to assume, however, that any property of market is automatically universal. Let consider the following example.

Proposition 8. The total quantity of reciprocator firms exceeds the total quantity of selfish firms in model (5) for sufficiently large t ($t > 3$) for all values of parameters.

Proof. In accordance with Proposition 5 the trajectories of system (5) converge to a Nash equilibrium (6) for any acceptable initial values. Since value $\lambda_{xy} = \frac{x(t)}{y(t)}$ is constant for $t > 3$, then it is sufficient to check proposition only at Nash equilibrium (6). But at (5):

$$k \cdot x^* - (n - k) \cdot y^* = \frac{b}{v(2\alpha)^2}\{(\alpha + (1 - \alpha)\gamma)^2 - (\alpha^2 - ((1 - \alpha)\gamma)^2)\}$$
$$= \frac{b}{v(2\alpha)^2}(\alpha + (1 - \alpha)\gamma)\{(\alpha + (1 - \alpha)\gamma) - (\alpha - (1 - \alpha)\gamma)\}$$
$$= \frac{b}{v(2\alpha)^2}(\alpha + (1 - \alpha)\gamma)2(1 - \alpha)\gamma > 0, \quad Q.E.D.$$

Is this fact the model's universal property which does not depend on the choice of demand function? No. We show this through considering a similar result for a model using linear demand $P = b - c \cdot Q$ function instead of non-linear one $P = \frac{b}{Q}$.

Proposition 9.

(1) There is unique Nash equilibrium for dynamic microeconomic system which consists of heterogeneous firms with adaptive expectation and linear demand function $P = b - c \cdot Q$:

$$\begin{cases} x^* = \frac{[1 - \alpha \cdot (n - k + 3)] \cdot M}{k \cdot (1 - \alpha) - \alpha \cdot (n + 1)}, \\ y^* = \frac{\alpha \cdot (k - 1) \cdot M}{k \cdot (1 - \alpha) - \alpha \cdot (n + 1)}. \end{cases} \tag{11}$$

where $M = \frac{b - v}{c}$, $x^* = x_1^* = \ldots = x_k^*$, $y^* = y_{k+1}^* = \ldots = y_n^*$.
(2) The trajectories of this system converge to a fixed point (11) for any acceptable initial values.

Proof. Without loss of generality we assume that $\alpha_1 = \ldots = \alpha_k = \alpha$ and simplify the system:

$$\begin{cases} x + (k - 1) \cdot \frac{2\alpha - 1}{3\alpha - 1} \cdot x + (n - k) \cdot \frac{2\alpha - 1}{3\alpha - 1} \cdot y = M, \\ \frac{1}{2}k \cdot x + y + \frac{1}{2}(n - k - 1) \cdot y = \frac{M}{2}. \end{cases} \tag{12}$$

where $x_1 = \ldots = x_k$ are quantities of reciprocity firms; $y_1 = \ldots = y_{n-k}$ - quantities of selfish firms. The solutions of system (12) are the equilibrium quantities in Proposition 9, Q.E.D.

Proposition 10. Reciprocator firm (for $k \geq 2$):

(a) produces more product in the market than selfish one $x^* > y^*$ if and only if the share of its private interest is within the interval: $\alpha \in (0; \alpha_1) \cup (\alpha_2; 1)$;
(b) produces less product in the market than selfish firm $x^* < y^*$ if the share of its private interest is within the interval: $\alpha \in (\alpha_1; \alpha_2)$, where $\alpha_1 = 1/(n + 2)$, $\alpha_2 = k/(n + k + 1)$.

Proof. According to (6) inequality $x^* > y^*$ is equivalent to inequality:

$$(n+2) \cdot (n+k+1) \cdot \alpha^2 - (n \cdot (k+1) + 3k + 1) \cdot \alpha + k > 0.$$

The solutions of corresponding equation are $\alpha_1 = 1/(n+2)$, $\alpha_2 = k/(n+k+1)$, Q. E.D.

So in compliance with Proposition 8 $\lambda_{xy} = x(t)/y(t) > (n-k)/k = 1$ if $k = n-k$ for all α. However according to Proposition 10 $\lambda_{xy} = x^*/y^* < 1$ if $\alpha \in (\alpha_1; \alpha_2)$ where $\alpha_1 < \alpha_2$ for $k = n-k$, $k > 1$. Thus the result of Proposition 8 is not universal for linear demand functions.

The following Fig. 16 shows the graphs of dependence of Nash equilibrium point (11) $(x^*; y^*)$ on number of firms n according to Proposition 9 at fixed parameters $k = 4$, $\alpha = 0.04$ and $M = 50$.

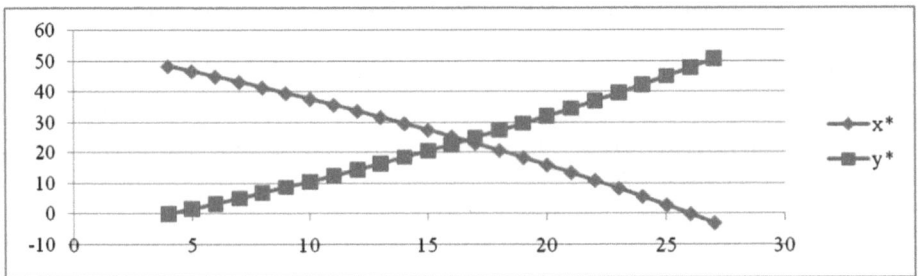

Fig. 16. Dependence of Nash equilibrium (11) on number of firms n

These graphs are set at $5 \leq n \leq 26$. Out of this interval linear demand model is not defined, and coordinates x^* or $y^* = 0$ have invalid negative values. For $n = 5$, $y^* = 0$ there are no selfish firms in the market; for $n = 26$, $x^* = 0$ reciprocator firms have been pushed out. As we see the ratio of profit λ_{xy} can vary from zero to infinity, depending on market conditions, in particular on number of firms.

6   Conclusion

Thus we have developed the heterogeneous agent-based model of competitive market according to new microeconomic paradigm as intersection of dynamic system theory, evolutionary game theory, and theory of optimal control. Any national or global market includes local markets, where firms with different types operate. Thus we can expand the universal properties of our model to real markets.

For our investigation we developed a desktop application *Model* to support the research process using computational experiments. As a result of simulation experiments through *Model* application we have found that flip bifurcations occur with an increase of number of firms in the market (on conditions that the types of firms are heterogeneous). We disclosed that any type of firm unambiguously chooses the output direction which gives more profit with smaller output. Surprisingly in this case the average profit of firm does not decrease or even increase in comparison with the stable state.

The crucial factor which ensures the market stability is the adaptive approach during preparation of competitive strategy. In the market with only adaptive expectations there is unique Nash equilibrium which is stable for all possible values of parameters. If no less than two-thirds of firms use naive expectations, then the state of dynamic chaos will also appears in the market. On this basis we plan to study complex real economic systems, which, in our opinion, involve the construction of a neural network which simulates the real market decision making.

References

1. Schulz, A.W.: Beyond the hype: the value of evolutionary theorizing in economics. Philos. Soc. Sci. **43**(1), 46–72 (2013)
2. Andreeva, E.L., Myslyakova, Y.G., Karkh, D.A.: Evolution of social responsibility of economic entities. In: 3rd International Multidisciplinary Scientific Conference on Social Sciences and Arts, pp. 237–244. SGEM, Albena (2016)
3. Lehmann, L., Alger, I., Weibull, J.: Does evolution lead to maximizing behavior? Evolution **69**(7), 1858–1873 (2015)
4. Marsay, D.: Decision-making under radical uncertainty: an interpretation of Keynes' treatise. Econ.-Open Access Open-Assess. e-J. **10**, 219–326 (2016)
5. Baiardi, L.C., Lamantia, F.G., Radi, D.: Evolutionary competition between boundedly rational behavioral rules in oligopoly games. Chaos Solitons Fractals **79**, 204–225 (2015)
6. Peng, Y., Lua, Q., Xiaoa, Y.: A dynamic Stackelberg duopoly model with different strategies. Chaos Solitons Fractals **85**, 128–134 (2016)
7. Kobets, V., Weissblut, A.: Nonlinear dynamic model of a microeconomic system with different reciprocity and expectations types of firms: stability and bifurcations. In: CEUR Workshop Proceedings, vol. 1614, pp. 502–517 (Indexed by: Sci Verse Scopus, DBLP, Google Scholar) (2016). http://ceur-ws.org/Vol-1614/paper_90.pdf
8. Wu, W., Chen, Z., Ip, W.H.: Complex nonlinear dynamics and controlling chaos in a Cournot duopoly economic model. Nonlinear Anal.: Real World Appl. **11**, 4363–4377 (2010)
9. Agliaria, A., Naimzada, A.K., Pecora, N.: Nonlinear dynamics of a Cournot duopoly game with differentiated products. Appl. Math. Comput. **281**, 1–15 (2016)
10. Kobets, V., Weissblut, A.: Mathematical model of microeconomic system with different social responsibilities in software module. In: CEUR Workshop Proceedings, vol. 1844, pp. 502–517 (Indexed by: Sci Verse Scopus, DBLP, Google Scholar) (2017). http://ceur-ws.org/Vol-1844/10000139.pdf
11. Federici, D., Gandolfo, G.: Chaos in economics. J. Econ. Dev. Stud. **2**(1), 51–79 (2014)
12. Ross, D.L.: The economic agent: not human, but important. In: Handbook of the Philosophy of Science. Technishe Universiteit Eindhoven, Eindhoven (2012)
13. Rosser, J.B., Rosser, M.V.: Simonian bounded rationality and complex behavioral economics. In: Matsumoto, A., Szidarovszky, F., Asada, T. (eds.) Essays in Economic Dynamics, pp. 3–22. Springer, Singapore (2016). https://doi.org/10.1007/978-981-10-1521-2_1

14. Clavien, C., Chapuisat, M.: Altruism across disciplines: one word, multiple meanings. Biol. Philos. **28**(1), 125–140 (2013)
15. Chen, S.-H.: Varieties of agents in agent-based computational economics: a historical and an interdisciplinary perspective. J. Econ. Dyn. Control **36**(1), 1–25 (2012)
16. Mirowski, P.: Markets come to bits: evolution, computation and markomata in economic science. J. Econ. Behav. Organ. **63**(2), 209–242 (2007)
17. Bianchi, F., Squazzoni, F.: Agent-based models in sociology. Wiley Interdiscipl. Rev.-Comput. Stat. **7**(4), 284–306 (2015)
18. Graebner, C.: Agent-based computational models - a formal heuristic for institutionalist pattern modelling? J. Inst. Econ. **12**(1), 241–261 (2016)
19. Kobets, V., Yatsenko, V.: Adjusting business processes by the means of an autoregressive model using BPMN 2.0. In: CEUR Workshop Proceedings, vol. 1614, pp. 518–533 (Indexed by: Sci Verse Scopus, DBLP, Google Scholar) (2016). http://ceur-ws.org/Vol-1614/paper_97.pdf
20. Kobets, V. Yatsenko, V., Poltoratskiy, M.: Dynamic model of double electronic Vickrey auction. In: Ermolayev, V., et al. (eds.) Proceedings of 11-th International Conference on ICTERI 2015, Kherson, Lviv, 14–16 May 2015, vol. 1356, pp. 236–251. CEUR-WS.org (2015). CEUR-WS.org/Vol-1356/ICTERI-2015-CEUR-WS-Volume.pdf, ISSN 1613-0073
21. Vermeulen, B., Pyka, A.: Agent-based modeling for decision making in economics under uncertainty. Econ.-Open Access Open-Assess. e-J. **10**, 43–54 (2016)
22. Greenwood-Lee, J., Hawe, P., Nettel-Aguirre, A.: Complex intervention modelling should capture the dynamics of adaptation. BMC Med. Res. Methodol. **16**, 52–64 (2016)
23. Mandel, A., Gintis, H.: Decentralized Pricing and the equivalence between Nash and Walrasian equilibrium. J. Math. Econ. **63**, 84–92 (2016)
24. Guse, E.A.: Heterogeneous expectations, adaptive learning, and evolutionary dynamics. J. Econ. Behav. Org. **74**(1-2). 42–57 (2010)
25. Todd, A., Beling, P., Scherer, W., Yang, S.Y.: Agent-based financial markets: a review of the methodology and domain. In: 2016 IEEE Symposium Series on Computational Intelligence (SSCI) (2016)
26. Wood, A.D., Mason, C.F., Finnoff, D.: OPEC, the Seven Sisters, and oil market dominance: an evolutionary game theory and agent-based modeling approach. J. Econ. Behav. Organ. **132**, 66–78 (2016)
27. Luis Santos, J., Mancha Navarro, T., Pablo-Marti, F.: An evolutionary simulation model of the effect of innovation and firm dynamics on market power. Int. J. Appl. Behav. Econ. **5**(3), 31–49 (2016)

Author Index